The Points of the Horse

THE

POINTS OF THE HORSE.

BY THE SAME AUTHOR.

RIDING: ON THE FLAT AND ACROSS COUNTRY. A Guide to Practical Horsemanship. Third Edition. Illustrated by J. H. OSWALD BROWN and STURGESS. Square 8vo. 10*s.* 6*d.*

The Standard.—"A master of his subject."

ILLUSTRATED HORSE-BREAKING. A description of the Art of giving Horses Good Manners and Snaffle Bridle Mouths. With 51 Original Illustrations by J. H. OSWALD BROWN. Imp. 16mo. 21*s.*

The Field.—"A work which is entitled to high praise as being far and away the best reasoned out one on breaking under a new system we have seen."

VETERINARY NOTES FOR HORSE OWNERS. A Popular Manual of Veterinary Surgery and Medicine. Fourth Edition. Illustrated. Crown 8vo. 12*s.* 6*d.*

The Field.—"Of the many popular veterinary books which have come under our notice, this is certainly one of the most scientific and reliable."

TRAINING AND HORSE MANAGEMENT IN INDIA. Fifth Edition. Crown 8vo. 9*s.*

The Veterinary Journal.—"No better guide could be placed in the hands of either amateur horseman or veterinary surgeon."

SOUNDNESS AND AGE OF HORSES. Over 100 Illustrations. Crown 8vo. 8*s.* 6*d.*

The Field.—"Is evidently the result of much careful research, and the horseman, as well as the veterinarian, will find in it much that is interesting and instructive."

INDIAN RACING REMINISCENCES. Illustrated by I. KNOX FERGUSSON. Crown 8vo. 8*s.* 6*d.*

The Field.—"The last page comes all too soon."

THE HORSEWOMAN. A Practical Guide to Side-Saddle Riding. By Mrs. HAYES. Edited by Captain HAYES. Illustrated by J. H. OSWALD BROWN. Square 8vo. 10*s.* 6*d.*

Saturday Review.—"With a very strong recommendation of this book as far and away the best guide to side-saddle riding that we have seen."

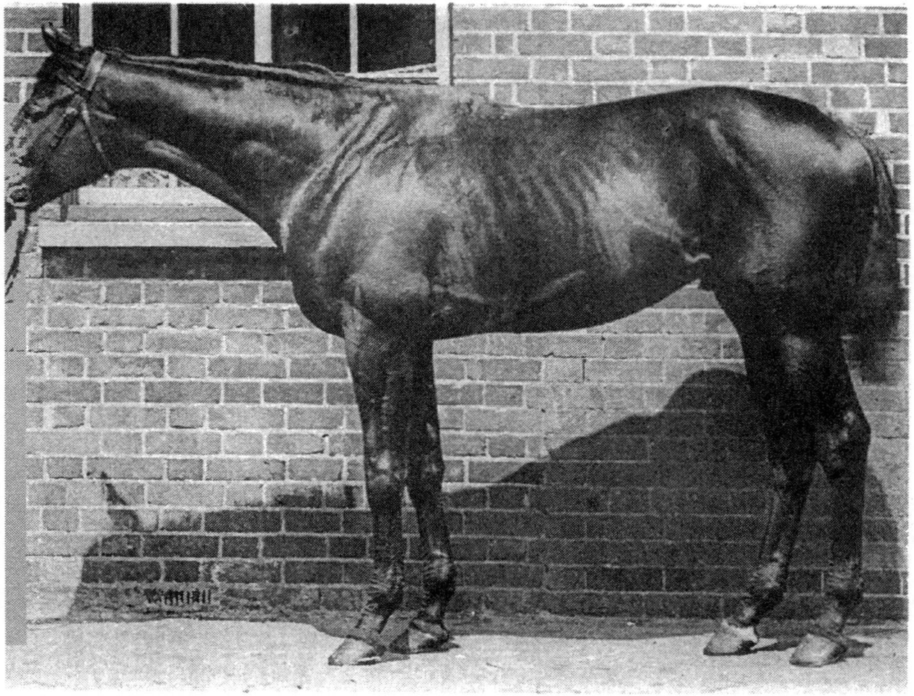

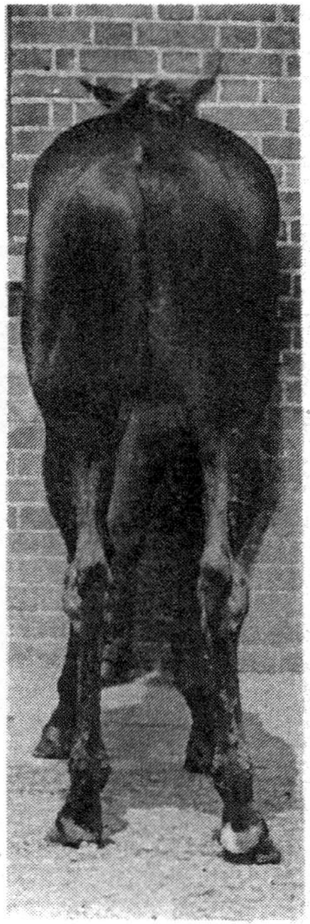

TO. BY DIXON AND SONS

FRONTISPIECE

THE DUKE OF WESTMINSTER'S ORMONDE. SIDE AND BACK VIEWS

THE

POINTS OF THE HORSE

A FAMILIAR TREATISE ON EQUINE CONFORMATION.

BY

M. HORACE HAYES, F.R.C.V.S.,

Late Captain "The Buffs,"

AUTHOR OF "VETERINARY NOTES FOR HORSE OWNERS,"
"RIDING: ON THE FLAT AND ACROSS COUNTRY,"
"ILLUSTRATED HORSE-BREAKING," ETC.

ILLUSTRATED BY

77 REPRODUCTIONS OF PHOTOGRAPHS, AND 205 DRAWINGS

CHIEFLY BY J. H. OSWALD BROWN.

LONDON:

W. THACKER AND CO., 87, NEWGATE STREET.

CALCUTTA: THACKER, SPINK AND CO.

BOMBAY: THACKER AND CO., LIMITED.

1893.

LONDON:
PRINTED BY WILLIAM CLOWES AND SONS, Limited,
STAMFORD STREET AND CHARING CROSS.

To

GEORGE FLEMING, C.B., LL.D., F.R.C.V.S.,

AS A MARK OF RESPECT

FOR THE BRILLIANT AND USEFUL WORK HE HAS DONE
IN MANY FIELDS OF HORSE KNOWLEDGE.

PREFACE.

MUCH as Englishmen pride themselves on being good "judges" of a horse, the fact remains that exact ideas on the important subject of Conformation are current neither in the traditions of our "horsey" people, nor in our literature. The few English authors who have written on it, have done so in a fragmentary manner, and have contented themselves for the most part with laying down rule-of-thumb maxims for the blind acceptance of their readers. The French, on the contrary, have written on *l'extérieur*, several elaborate books upon which they have expended an amount of scientific knowledge that does them infinite credit. It must be admitted that although they have proved themselves, in this respect, much superior in scientific research to our countrymen; their works seem to show that their experience has been gained more in the study and dissecting room, than in the stable and in the field. Both classes of authors, I venture to submit, have erred in trying to make general rules suitable to all kinds of horses, instead of pointing out that the standard of shape should, to a great extent, vary according to the work demanded. I may mention that illustrations of horses or of special "points" of these animals drawn without the aid of photography, having a bias difficult to be repressed, render the ideas of the artist more accurately than they portray the realities of nature.

In the attempt to conform to the requirements of truth, I have, as far as practicable, relied on photography for illustration. This art not alone gives exact representations with marvellous minuteness of detail, but has completed the solution (begun by Professor Marey) of the once vexed question of the action of the horse's limbs during the various forms of movement, and has accordingly afforded us, in our present study, *data* which are as instructive as they are reliable. As I have written this book for non-scientific readers, as well as for those who desire to thoroughly master the subject; I have placed in small print the few chapters which I have devoted to the anatomical and mechanical details which were necessary to render the work complete. A perusal of the large print chapters will give a good general view of the practical side of the subject, and, in most cases, the reasons for the opinions advanced. The information contained in the small print ones is, however, indispensable for the full comprehension of all the principles discussed, and as it is of a very elementary character, I trust it will not be neglected. We must here remember that the horse is a living machine, the capabilities of which cannot be accurately gauged, without a knowledge of its construction, and of the principles of its working. Having treated on *Soundness and Age of Horses* in another book, I have omitted these subjects entirely from the present one. I must, however, state that as they are directly connected with the question of a horse "standing" work, it is impossible to judge his capabilities with a near approach to correctness, without a knowledge of veterinary science.

Besides the new features in this book to which I have already drawn notice, I may mention that I have tried to arrive at a knowledge of the respective "points" of speed and strength in the horse, by examining the conformation of other animals that are distinguished by the possession of one or other of these "gifts" in a high state of perfection. Also, I have made a more exhaustive inquiry into the nature of the paces and of the leap of the horse than has previously been attempted; my object being to obtain from it exact deductions as to the best kind of conformation for various forms of work.

At the suggestion of my friend, Veterinary Colonel Anderson, I began, about fifteen years ago, to write a book on the Points of the Horse, which subject I resolved to treat according to the time-honoured methods of my literary predecessors. I worked at it while studying to become a veterinary surgeon, and after that at Newmarket, where I went to reside in order to increase my knowledge of English thoroughbreds. For this, every facility was given me by my kind friends, Mr. John Hammond, Edwin Martin, Jarvis, Tom. Jennings, Junr., Alf. Sadler, R. Sherwood, and others, who were always glad to show me their horses, and discuss their various points. When the book was completed in 1883, I despatched the manuscript to my publishers by the hand of a friend, who, by an extraordinary piece of good luck, lost it so effectually that I have not seen it since. While suffering from the shock caused by the loss of the results of seven years' toil, I happened to read Professor Marey's *Machine Animale* (Animal Mechanics), and before I got half through it, I grasped the fact that I had been working in an entirely wrong groove, and that my careless friend had, most fortunately, saved me from publishing a book which would not have satisfied my more matured judgment. In 1884 I gave in London a short course of private lectures on the conformation of the horse, to some of the best known English artists. While endeavouring to convey instruction, I found great help from the use of a few photographs I had by me as illustrations, and accordingly determined to learn photography, and to utilise it in the preparation of the new book on the "shape and make" of horses which I had already begun, though on different "lines" to those on which the lost volume had been completed. On the following year I went abroad on a horse-breaking tour, and have spent the eight years which have elapsed since then, in hard practical work (breaking, training for racing and chasing, and horse dealing) among horses in India, Burma, Ceylon, China, Japan, Egypt, South Africa, England and elsewhere. The facilities afforded by such an active and public life have enabled me to procure for this book a number of illustrations which it would have been impossible for me to have obtained under less favourable circumstances. No one who has not made the attempt oneself, can form an idea of the difficulty there often is in getting horses which have the required "points" (bad or good). For instance, I once examined 600 horses belonging to a dealer, and only obtained one specimen for my camera. Another time, a search through the troopers of two cavalry regiments was fruitless of results. For the photographs in this book, I have "run my eye" over certainly more than 10,000 horses! From this statement my readers will be able to form some idea of the extreme kindness and forbearance with which I have been treated by my horse-owning friends. Having obtained an animal with a required "point," the next thing to do was to photograph him, which frequently involved the expenditure of much time and trouble on account of the special character of the work.

Among the gentlemen to whom I am indebted for having granted me permission to have their horses photographed, I have the honour to number: His Grace the Duke of Westminster, Colonel Anderson, Captain Woolmer, Captain Mowbray of the Black Watch, Mr. W. H. Walker, Mr. A. A. Apcar, Mr. Tom. Jennings, junr., Mr. Spooner Hart, Messrs. Milton and Co., Messrs. Ralli and Co. of Sydney and Calcutta, Messrs. Cook and Co., Mr. Oscar Dignam, Mr E. Gregory, Mr. Vansittart, Mr. Steve Margarett of Melbourne, Mr. John Stevens of New Zealand, and Colonel Simpson. I am greatly obliged to Mr. Frank Haes, Major Nott, and Mr. Dixon, 112 Albany Street, N.W., for the negatives they have lent me; to Sir William Flower for allowing me to take photographs of Figs. 187, 188 and 189, in the South Kensington Museum; to Professor C. Stewart for similar permission with respect to Figs. 185, 190, 197 and 201, in the Museum of the R.C.S.; and to the Zoological Society for the loan of Figs. 181, 182 and 183. The action shown in the figures of the paces and of the leap has been adopted from the admirable photographs done by Mr. E Muybridge, and published in his *Animal Locomotion*; although the artistic "treatment" of the horses is original. This matchless American work is solely a collection of photographs, and does not contain any analysis of the movements of the horse. I may also mention that the photographs of Anschutz, on the same subject, are excellent.

In order to facilitate comparison, I have tried, as far as I have been able, to get the portraits of the horses, asses and zebras which are in this book, done to a uniform scale, namely, 1 to 20. I have added an index, which I have tried to make as easy of reference and as exhaustive as possible.

While strictly confining myself to the limits which bound the subject of Equine Conformation, I have had, while writing this book, the fortunate opportunity of throwing light on many points of horse knowledge which I have been, hitherto, unable to discuss in print. I therefore hope that the appearance of this work will help to complete what I have already written, in my books, on veterinary science, riding, breaking, training and stable management; and that they and it will now form a useful horseman's library.

Without the skilful aid and kindly sympathy of the late Mr. J. H. Oswald Brown, I would not have been able to have finished this book, even in its present imperfect form. Since the year 1884 we laboured together on this subject. The pleasure in knowing that the work, after innumerable corrections and revisions, is at last done, has lost more than half its charm, from the fact that I cannot share it with him. He had finished the most of the illustrations before his sad and untimely death last autumn. The sketches which he left were completed by Mr. Frank Hobden, to whom I tender my best thanks.

Junior Army and Navy Club,
St. James's Street, S.W.
24th May, 1893.

INTRODUCTION.

THE subject of Conformation has been so little studied from an exact point of view, that in default of sound reasons based on a knowledge of anatomy and mechanics, and tested by practical experience, a number of horsey maxims and expressions have been adopted by many people, as unquestionable authority for the soundness of the opinions they advance. Take, for instance, the descriptive terms, "long and low," and "good to follow," which we frequently hear applied in indiscriminate approval to draught animals and race-horses, and which, if suitable for one class, must necessarily be incorrect for the other. Some men who have had experience with horses, but who recognise the fact of their own ignorance, get out of the difficulty of appearing less learned than their fellows by boldly declaring, with reference to racers, that "horses run in all shapes"—a remark which has passed almost into an adage. Throughout the animal kingdom, we may see that the possession of speed or strength is associated with certain peculiarities of shape which can be readily recognised by an instructed observer. In this respect, the horse is no exception. He, like other animals that have the power of moving from one place to another, is a locomotive machine, which is constructed according to principles that may be studied with a fair amount of accuracy and with much profit. The value of our investigations in this direction is, however, limited by two restrictions. First: we cannot, except to a small extent, examine the interior of our machine—a fact which is not of much moment if we be afforded an opportunity of testing its working powers. Second: we can, from inspection, tell little or nothing of the agency which directs its movements, and which is known as its nervous system. Thus, a race-horse may be of the most fashionable blood, be sound in wind and limb, "fit as hands can make him," be possessed of every galloping and staying "point"; and, yet, if we be rash enough to predict his success on the turf, he may falsify our too hastily expressed judgment by "refusing to try a yard," the moment the starter's flag falls. Our carefully selected hunter may persist in running out at the smallest obstacle, and our chosen cart-horse may jib on meeting the first incline which requires him to throw his weight into the collar. I may, therefore, state that the study of Conformation will not enable us to predict absolutely that a certain horse will perform, with credit to himself, the work for which he is intended. It can only permit us to say that an animal possessing the necessary "points" will, in the majority of cases, fulfil the expectation formed of him. It does, however, provide us with an unerring guide in deciding that certain horses are *not* suitable for certain kinds of work.

In the study of Conformation, particular points should be rarely taken separately; for a defect in one is frequently compensated by special excellence in another.

Also, on the principle that the strength of a chain is equal only to that of its weakest link, we must remember that uncompensated inability in any one particular respect may render a horse altogether unfit for the purpose for which he was intended. We may, therefore, see that to make and combine the investigations necessary for forming a sound judgment respecting a horse's capabilities, requires no small amount of special knowledge and reasoning power. Although we cannot claim that Conformation is an exact science ; we may be assured that it offers practical advantages which will well repay the time and trouble necessary for its acquisition.

CONTENTS.

CHAPTER I.

FIRST PRINCIPLES OF CONFORMATION.

CHAPTER II.

STRUCTURES OF THE BODY.

CHAPTER III.

NAMES OF EXTERNAL PARTS AND DEFINITIONS.

CHAPTER IV.

SKETCH OF THE ANATOMY OF THE HORSE.

CHAPTER V.

CHAPTER VI.

DISTRIBUTION OF WEIGHT IN THE HORSE'S BODY.

CHAPTER VII.

LEVERS.

CHAPTER VIII.

MECHANISM OF EQUINE LOCOMOTION.

CHAPTER IX.

CHAPTER X.

ATTITUDES OF THE HORSE.

CHAPTER XI.

STATIONARY MOVEMENTS OF THE HORSE.

CHAPTER XII.

PACES OF THE HORSE.

CHAPTER XIII.

LEAPING.

CHAPTER XIV.

CHAPTER XV.

COMPARATIVE SHAPE OF HORSES.

CHAPTER XVI.

HEAD AND NECK.

CHAPTER XVII.

THE TRUNK.

CHAPTER XVIII.

THE FORE LIMB.

CHAPTER XIX.

THE HIND LIMB.

CHAPTER XX.

SKIN, COLOUR, AND HAIR.

CHAPTER XXI.

CHAPTER XXII.

CHAPTER XXIII.

CHAPTER XXIV.

CHAPTER XXV.

SPECIAL POINTS OF VARIOUS CLASSES OF HORSES.

CHAPTER XXVI.

REMARKS ON VARIOUS BREEDS OF HORSES.

CHAPTER XXVII.

EXAMINATION OF OUR PHOTOGRAPHS OF HORSES.

CHAPTER XXVIII.

WILD HORSES.

CHAPTER XXIX.

ASSES.

CHAPTER XXX.

EVOLUTION OF THE HORSE.

CHAPTER XXXI.

CHAPTER XXXII.

CHAPTER XXXIII.

LIST OF ILLUSTRATIONS.

REPRODUCTIONS OF PHOTOGRAPHS.

LINE DRAWINGS, ETC.

THE
POINTS OF THE HORSE.

CHAPTER I.

FIRST PRINCIPLES OF CONFORMATION.

Animals of Speed and Animals of Strength—Comparative Conformation—Marey's Law.

Animals of Speed and Animals of Strength.—When we speak of the conformation of a horse, we refer to the adaptability of his body for general or special work. We all know, without the aid of science to tell us, that a light-boned thoroughbred would be as unsuitable to carry a fifteen-stone man, as a thick-set cob would be to win a five-furlong race. The "weed" would not fail, necessarily, from deficiency in weight of bone and muscle; for there are many ponies of thirteen hands or under, which would weigh no more than the slender T. Y. C. performer, and yet could bear the welter burden through a long day's journey, with ease to themselves and comfort to their rider. The failure to carry weight in the one case, and the inability to display a high degree of speed in the other, would obviously be due (in the absence of any particular defect) to the fact of the conformation of the animal not being suitable to the kind of work to which he was put. In our study of the "make and shape" of horses, we may profitably begin by taking a comparative view of animals of great speed and those of immense strength, so as to arrive at a knowledge of the principles by which their special characteristics are developed to a high degree of excellence. As the conformation best adapted for the one is different from that for the other, we cannot find both united in the same animal. I need hardly say that the manner in which the proportions of speed and strength are varied in each particular horse, is the measure of the suitability of the animal to the kind of work it is called upon to perform. Thus, a dray-horse which can trot a mile in eight minutes with 3,000 lbs. behind it, may be quite as useful, in its own way, as a match-trotter which, with a sulky and driver weighing together 200 lbs., can do a mile in two minutes twenty seconds.

Comparative Conformation.—In this proposed research, we shall find that the two classes (those of speed and those of strength) to which I have just alluded, differ essentially in shape from each other, and that individuals of each respective class have a similar kind of conformation. As an example of the gallopers, let us take the Indian black buck (*see* Pl. 1), which, for half a mile, could give five hands and a beating to the fastest horse that ever looked through a bridle. Then there is the cheetah (*see* Pl. 2), which can give the antelope 100 yards start and catch him in a furlong. It is true that the spotted cat effects his purpose a good deal by surprise · but it is equally certain that for a

PHOTO. BY DIXON & SONS PL. 1—BLACK BUCK.

[illegible]

TO FACE PAGE 2

PLATE 2. CHEETAH.

couple of hundred yards he can travel with the velocity of an express train. Also, there is the greyhound, with whose speed we are all familiar. In comparison with these fleet of foot animals, let us note the "make and shape" of the buffalo (*see* Pl. 3) and rhinoceros (*see* Pl. 4), both of which are endowed with vast muscular power. And as the opposite of the "long-tailed dog," let us take the bulldog or dachshund. On examining these animals we shall observe that the limbs (especially the hind ones, from which is derived the greater part of the forward propulsion) of the gallopers are much longer in proportion to the animal's height than those of the representatives of strength. We see this fact best illustrated when we compare individuals of the same species, like the greyhound and bulldog. We also obtain good examples among horned cattle, in the Indian trotting bullock (*see* Pl. 5), and the Indian heavy draught bull (*see* Pl. 6), whose sex is indicated by the large size of his hump. Special length of hind limb is well shown in the hare and in the lynx (*see* Pl. 17), both of which are animals of great speed. As it is not the custom to breed men with reference to their physical development, we do not find the difference in question so well marked in them as in the lower animals. Yet, for all that, we may note among "sprinters" and wrestlers the working of this principle. I may explain that the muscles of the limbs of the horse, ox, buffalo and antelope do not, practically, extend below the knees and hocks (being continued by tendons from these joints); but in the dog and cat tribe, they go down to the foot.

From the examples cited of animals of great strength and those of high speed, we may conclude that the former are distinguished by a long body and short legs; and the latter, by a short trunk and long extremities. I am here assuming that the length of the body is taken comparatively with that of the legs, and without reference to the proportions of the body itself.

We may also observe from the photographs before us, that the limbs of speedy quadrupeds are proportionately as slender as they are long, and that those exhibiting strength are as thick as they are short.

I may explain that muscles are the active and essential part of the machinery used by animals in locomotion, bones being merely passive agents. In fact, there are myriads of the lower animals which move about with considerable speed by means of their muscles, but which have no bones of any kind.

Marey's Law.—The foregoing observations will prepare us for the law cited by Professor Marey in *La Machine Animale,'* which states that muscles of speed are long and slender, and those of strength are short and thick. This distinguished Frenchman gives as instances the long breast-bones of birds—such as the snipe and partridge—which can move their wings with great rapidity, and the short ones of hovering birds—such as the eagle and albatross—which can overcome the immense resistance of the air upon which the large area of their pinions presses, only with slow, but very powerful strokes. The expanse of the outspread wings of birds of quick stroke—such as wild pigeon and partridge—is of far less comparative size than is that of those of hovering birds. The relative speed with which these birds can cleave the air does not, of course, affect the question of the form and action of their muscles.

PHOTO. BY M. H. HAYES

TO FACE PAGE 4

PLATE 3—THE INDIAN BUFFALO.

I may remark that the foregoing principles govern the ɔnformation of horses as closely as they do that of other ıimals. I shall, however, defer their application to horses ll further on, when we shall have acquired a certain amount exact knowledge of the physical conditions of the horse, hich will greatly aid us in drawing accurate conclusions as his "shape and make."

CHAPTER II.

STRUCTURES OF THE BODY.

Bones—Cartilage—Muscles and Tendons—Ligaments—Connective Tissue —The Nervous System.

THE frame-work of the body consists of the skeleton (*see* Fig. 3), which is composed of a large number of connected bones that are moved by muscles. In considering the general conformation of the horse with respect to the purpose for which he may be suitable, we should, generally, regard difference of length in his various parts, as those of muscles, rather than of bones; for the former are the producers of all movements of progression, the latter aiding only in the application of the force exerted.

Bones.—*The chief duties of bones in the act of progression* are—(1) to bear weight; (2) to resist the effects of concussion; and (3) to act as levers. Capability for performing (1) and (2) is dependent on conditions of texture ("quality"), size ("substance"), and arrangement.

Quality and substance of bone.—Whether the animal be intended to carry heavy burdens, or to gallop over hard ground, it is always a matter of the greatest importance that his bones, especially those below his knees and hocks,

PHOTO. BY FRANK HAES

TO FACE PAGE 6

PLATE 4—RHINOCEROS.

should be of strong and compact texture. It has been customary to state, in a vague way, that the bones of Arab horses and English thoroughbreds are denser than those of other breeds. It would, however, be more exact to say that the drier the soil on which a horse has been bred and brought up, and the "harder" the food upon which he has been fed, the better will be the quality of his bone; for we find that in dry, hot climates in the East, native ponies, which can have little or no admixture of Arab blood, have legs as clean and hard as any that are to be met with in the Desert. We need not test our theories on this subject by the microscope, or by determining the specific gravity of various sections of bone taken from different animals; for we can obtain a far more reliable and practical proof from the fact that, other things being equal, the more porous are bones, the more liable are they to bony deposits, such as splints, spavins, and ringbones. I here purposely omit to add "sore shins;" for this disease is almost peculiar to immature thoroughbreds that are put into training at an age much earlier than that at which ordinary horses are broken. The nature of a horse's hoofs, which can always be determined by inspection, or by using the "drawing knife," will generally afford us a safe guide by which to judge of the quality of his bone. Thus we find that animals which have been reared amid damp surroundings and on soft food, will, as a rule, be prone to bony enlargements, and will have flat feet of soft horn. We cannot fail to notice this if we compare the horses of the English fen counties with those bred on high, dry land. In Australia we see the same difference between the horses of the damp Swan River Settlement, and those of the comparatively dry climate of New South Wales; in India, between the stock raised in the arid plains of the Punjab and Deccan, and those of swampy Lower Bengal. Hence, if, when judging an animal about the history of which we know nothing, and which does not appear to have undergone enough work to test the soundness of his legs, we find that he has weak, flat hoofs, we shall not err, in the large majority of cases, by concluding that his bone is of inferior quality. I may add, as regards climate, that although dryness is always a favourable condition for horses, the effect of excessive heat apparently is to diminish the size of the bone of the indigenous animals: a circumstance which may, to a great extent, account for the fact that horses bred in tropical climates, however hardy and wiry they may be, are very rarely of a weight-carrying type, like those met with in temperate countries.

What is popularly called "want of bone" seriously detracts from the usefulness of an animal, whatever its work may be, as it implies deficiency of muscular development; for muscles, I may say, cannot act properly unless they have a sufficient surface of bone on which to attach themselves. It would, however, be more correct to state that we cannot have large bones without large muscles; for the size and development of a bone is directly dependent on the condition and state of activity of the muscles connected with it. This follows from the fact that a bone, like all other parts of the animal system, in order to be strong, requires a plentiful supply of blood for its nourishment, the circulation being quickened by exercise, which can alone be obtained by muscular action. As pointed out by Professor Marey, in cases of paralysis of a limb, the bones of the part become wasted on account of the loss of function of the muscles. In

PHOTO. BY M. H. HAYES

TO FACE PAGE 8

PLATE 5—THE INDIAN TROTTING BULLOCK.

making practical observations on horses, we may often be greatly assisted in our investigations by judging of the muscles by the bones, and *vice versâ.* Thus, if we see an animal in poor condition which has been brought on by hardship or want of food, we may, by the appearance of his "bone," form a good idea of what his muscles will be when he "fills out." Even when a horse is "fit and well," a display of large, well-shaped bone (of the body as well as of the limbs) should dispose us to consider that his muscles are more powerful than they appear at first glance. I was much struck with this fact on the first occasion I had an opportunity of closely inspecting the celebrated St. Gatien, whom Mr. John Hammond very kindly showed me in his box, some time before he ran his dead heat with Harvester for the Derby of 1884; for I was greatly "taken" with the sight of the large, symmetrically formed bones of his legs, his long back ribs, and his well-developed pelvis, the inner angle of which was so prominent as to make a distinct "rise" in the outline of his croup; not to mention his long, sloping shoulders, and immense gaskins. On the other hand, if we observe that an animal which is in "dealer's condition" is light of bone, we may, as a rule, conclude that there is not very much muscle in the load of flesh which he carries. Among sound, good horses, "Mr. Morton's" well-known handicap winner, Dalmeny, was one of the lightest below the knee I have ever seen; but no exception could have been taken to him on that account, for his shape was particularly true and level, and his muscles were of the long slender type which is generally characteristic of the possession of speed. I need hardly say that the bones and muscles of the limbs are not always in keeping with those of the body;

for we daily see instances of animals that are too heavily "topped" for their legs, like the one in Pl. 30.

Men of experience know that a horse should have plenty of bone in order to be able to carry weight with ease to himself for long distances and at comparatively fast paces—as, for example, when hunting. If we take two horses that can perform about equally well in a long run with a similar welter weight up, one having the "pull" in speed, the other in bone and muscle, we shall usually find that the latter will not feel the effects of the work so much as the former. I may explain this on the reasonable supposition that the weight-bearing muscles of the lighter-built horse, not being so strong as those of the "heavier" animal, will naturally become more fatigued. The objection sometimes advanced against thoroughbreds for hunting, that they cannot "come out again" as quickly as half-bred animals, is valid only when the former are lighter built than the latter; for, if blood horses of equal bone and muscle were obtained, the difference would be all the other way.

Large muscles, as we have seen, require large bones. It also goes without saying that the more are bones exposed to the effects of concussion, the denser and stronger should they be. Consequently, we may conclude that the lighter an animal's body is, in comparison to the strength of its component parts and the amount of its muscular force, the greater will be its powers of rapid progression. Hence we find that the race-horse, like all quadrupeds of which speed is the chief characteristic, has comparatively slender bones of extremely dense texture, and that his muscles make up in strength what they lack in substance. Owing to the law of compensation, which governs the conditions of animal life, it

PHOTO. BY M. H. HAYES

TO FACE PAGE 10

PLATE 6—HEAVY DRAUGHT INDIAN BULL.

is almost impossible to obtain bone of great volume, and, at the same time, of the finest quality. On this account, as size is indispensable with the cart-horse, we endeavour, with him, to obtain large bone of sufficient strength to meet his requirements. In the intermediate classes of horses, the relations between volume and quality should be judged according to the nature of the work in view.

Arrangement of bones.—The relative position which bones occupy with respect to each other affect their leverage, weight-carrying, and concussion-resisting powers—conditions which will be treated in detail when we consider the various points which they affect.

Cartilage.—Cartilage or gristle is a strong, flexible, bluish-white substance which is found in connection with bone, and of which there are various kinds. *Articular cartilage* covers the ends of bones that form moveable joints. *Temporary cartilage* is bone in a transition form. The ribs are connected to the breastbone by cartilages which form elastic prolongations. Cartilages also are interposed between the bones of various joints in order to connect or protect them. The *cartilage of prolongation* forms an elastic continuation of the top of the shoulder-blade.

Muscles and Tendons.—The animal's moving power is derived from *muscles*, which form the lean of meat, and which, as a rule, are attached to bones. Muscles act by virtue of the property they possess of being able to shorten themselves on being stimulated by the nervous system. Thus, if we wish to raise, say, our right hand to the shoulder, our brain telegraphs, so to speak, the order, by means of the nerves, to the *biceps* muscle, which is attached at one end to the shoulder-blade, close to the shoulder-joint, and, at the other, to the bones of the fore-arm, a little below the elbow. Hence this muscle, on contracting, draws the hand up in the required direction.

As muscles are built up of contractile fibres, their strength, other things being equal, is proportionate to their thickness.

In order to economise space, muscles are generally attached to bones by means of *tendons* (sinews), which are hard, fibrous cords of great toughness. The tendon at one extremity is firmly united to the end of the muscle, and, at the other, to the bone.

We find from experiment that a muscle can contract to about two-thirds of its ordinary length, which is, therefore, proportionate to the extent of movement it is capable of producing. If the muscles which move the limbs be comparatively short, the stride will also be short, and the horse will be slower than he would otherwise be, no matter how thick and powerful are his muscles. We may, therefore, conclude that speed is associated with length of muscle, as has been stated on page 4.

As length of muscle is necessarily accompanied by length of bone, we may judge of the former by the latter, which can usually be readily estimated.

The "give and take" principle, which applies more or less to all created things, holds good with muscles. Hence, in the race-horse, for which the possession of speed is the chief essential of success, we should seek the greatest possible length of muscle, with just sufficient strength to meet his requirements for carrying weight and for sustaining the exertion he may be called upon to undergo. In the cart-horse, on the contrary, thickness of muscle is the great desideratum, always supposing that he has sufficient activity to walk well and on occasion to trot at a moderately brisk rate. As a thin muscle will contract at least as quickly as a thick one of the same length, it follows that an increase in the thickness of muscles is useful only in making the work more easy, and that it does not otherwise add to the speed. Massive muscles, compared to slight ones, have two disadvantages, namely—they add to the weight to be carried, both in muscle and bone; and they necessitate the possession of large joints, which, from increased friction, are not so easily bent and extended as smaller ones; besides this, it has been proved that they do not respond as quickly to nervous stimulus. Although it is impossible to lay down any exact rules on this subject, we may say, speaking generally, that the thickness of muscle which would be commendable in a weight-carrying hunter, would be quite out of place in a race-horse. We may often observe that horses which were very smart as two-year-olds, lose their "form" after that age without any assignable reason, except that as they "thickened," they got slow. I may remark that those speedy animals, the cheetah, greyhound, and antelope, like the race-horse, are comparatively narrow behind, and that the hind-quarters of the cart-horse are very wide. As the great tendency among English thoroughbreds is to undue lightness of bone and muscle, we generally find that our best race-horses are comparatively strong animals; although the muscles of their legs are always long, and they have little or no approach to coarseness of limb. Ormonde, St. Gatien, Bendigo, Isonomy, Barcaldine, and Carbine (the New Zealand son of Musket), for example, were all muscular horses. St. Simon (Pl. 7) was a notable example of a horse of the highest class, being of remarkably light build. He had, however, marvellously good shoulders and loins.

We know from experiment that muscles of the same thickness are stronger in animals of one species than they are in those of another kind; and we may reasonably infer that even among individual horses the same rule holds good. In fact, we may take for granted that the "quality" of muscle, tendon and ligament, as well as of bone, is better in some horses than in others; the great factors in producing strong tissue appearing to be: heredity; residence in a dry, warm climate; "hard food"; exercise; and Eastern blood.

Ligaments.—The ends of the bones that form joints are held together by white *ligaments*, which are similar in structure to tendons; but, unlike them, they serve to connect bones with bones, and, in a few cases, bones with tendons. They have no direct connection with muscles. There are, also, yellow ligaments, which, being elastic, aid in supporting weight without fatigue to the animal.

Connective Tissue.—The skin, which covers and protects the body, is largely composed of a strong, fibrous structure called *connective tissue*, which, proceeding inwards from the skin in the form of, more or less, thick layers and bands, furnishes a supporting network for the component parts of the other tissues. Thus, if we compare a slice from the under-cut of a sirloin of beef with one from a round of beef, we shall see that the relative coarseness of grain of the latter is due to the thickness of the layers of connective tissue which run through it. As connective tissue has only the passive action of support, I need hardly say, that the coarser in grain a muscle is, the less powerful will it be ; although it will be better able to resist the effects of external violence than one of finer grain. The protective duty of connective tissue, as regards muscles, may be readily inferred from the fact that the less exposed muscles are to injury from without, by reason of their position, the less connective tissue do they contain. This tissue, also, forms ligaments and tendons, and ensheathes bones, cartilages, nerves, etc. There is always a large amount of it immediately underneath the skin, in the form of loose fibrous sheets, as we may see in the dead animal. The presence of a great quantity of it in this position will, naturally, cause the underlying parts to be ill-defined, a fact which will be especially noticeable about the tendons and ligaments below the knees and hocks, owing to the absence of muscle about these parts. We may, therefore, draw the following deductions : (1) That, as the thickness of the skin is a measure of the amount of connective tissue it contains ; the thicker the hide, other things being equal, the more connective tissue will there be in and about the muscles. (2) That, as its action is only passive, the more of it a muscle contains, the slower will be the movements of the muscle. Hence, we may reasonably conclude that the fact of a horse having a thick skin, and ill-defined suspensory ligaments, owing to natural "fleshiness," would warrant us in supposing that he was deficient in speed. I may remark that, with age, the amount of connective tissue in the body greatly increases. As M. Guérin states : "In the old man, the tendon seems to invade the muscle, so that the portion of the calf of the leg which remains, is placed very high, and is much reduced in length. The muscles of the loins and back present the same character. In old age they are poorer in red fibre, but richer in tendon."

I may here mention that the component parts of the body which, respectively, have the same structure, are called *tissues*. Thus we have bony tissue, consisting of bone; muscular tissue, of muscle; nervous tissue, of nerve substance; connective tissue, of white fibrous material; and so on.

The Nervous System.—While considering the form of the horse from a mechanical point of view, we must not lose sight of the marked differences which exist in the nervous system of various animals, and which greatly heighten, or may altogether nullify, advantages obtained from good conformation. We are aware, speaking within reasonable limits, that the amount of contraction—*i.e.* force—exhibited by a muscle is proportional to the degree of stimulation given by its nerves. As the nervous system of some animals acts far more energetically than that of others, it follows that the former, other things being equal, will be stronger than the latter; although no difference in conformation, or in development of muscle, may be perceptible. Not alone does the amount of nervous force differ much among animals of the same kind, but, also, some have the faculty of stimulating their muscles by means of their nerves quicker than their fellows can do. We see this well exemplified in adepts at fencing, cricket, boxing, and other kindred sports; at which, so-called quickness of eye is all-essential. I may mention that the brilliant bat, or accomplished *maître d'armes*, apart from the possession of the necessary amount of knowledge, judgment, and physique, excels because he has the gift of moving his muscles, in response to the stimulus received by the nerves of his eyes, quicker, as well as in more accurately regulated style, than ordinary men. This assertion is in no way based on mere theory; for we find that among men whose duty it is to record (as in observatories) the exact moment at which they see certain phenomena occur, it is necessary, in order to avoid error, to allow for the difference in time these men, respectively, take; although it may only be a fraction of a second. To do this, it is requisite to obtain, for each man, his "personal equation," as it is termed. We can, therefore, conclude that speed and strength are as dependent on the nature and quality of the nervous system as they are on conformation and muscular development. It also goes without saying that a horse may possess every physical excellence, and yet be worthless on account of having a "soft heart," or bad temper.

CHAPTER III.

NAMES OF EXTERNAL PARTS AND DEFINITIONS.

Head—Neck—Breast and Chest—Shoulders—Withers—Elbow—Fore-arm—Knee—Cannon—Fetlock—Pastern—Hoof—Back—Loins—Ribs—Flank—Belly—Brisket—Croup—Thigh—Gaskin—Hock—Dock—Height of a Horse—Length of the Body of a Horse—Depth of Chest at Withers—Depth of Body—Height at Croup.

As the external parts and regions of the body do not, in many cases, admit of very accurate definition, I crave the indulgence of my readers in this attempt to mark out their positions and boundaries. I have omitted mention of some parts which, being known to every one, require no explanation. The figures and letters employed in the following list have reference to those on Fig. 1.

Head (1).—Looking at the horse in profile, we may regard the head as being divided from the neck by a line proceeding from the back of the ear, along the rear edge of the lower jaw to its angle.

The *forehead* (*a*) forms the upper part of the face. It extends down to a line joining the inner angle (*canthus*) of each eye, and reaches as high as the fore-lock and the base of the ears.

The *fore-lock* is a tuft of hair which lies between the ears, and is a continuation of the mane.

The *temples* are those portions of the head, on each side of the forehead, which lie between the ear and eye.

The *nose* (*b*) is a continuation of the forehead, and ends opposite the nostrils at the angle (*c*) formed by the line of the face and the line of the muzzle.

The *muzzle* is the lower end of the head, and includes

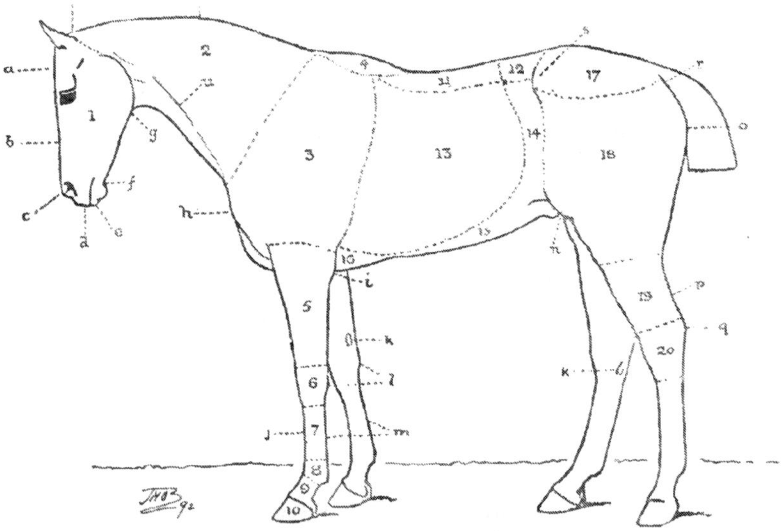

FIG. 1.—EXTERNAL PARTS OF HORSE.

the nostrils, upper (*d*) and lower lip (*e*), and the bones and teeth covered by them.

The *bars of the mouth* are the bare portions of the gums of the lower jaw which lie on each side, between the back teeth and the tushes, or the place usually occupied by the tushes.

The *chin-groove* (*f*) is just under the bars of the mouth.

It is the smooth and rounded under-part of the lower jaw, in which the curb chain should rest when a curb bit is used.

The *angles of the lower jaw* (*g*) are the bony angles between which the upper end of the wind-pipe lies

The *branches of the lower jaw* run from the chin-groove to the angles of the lower jaw.

The *occipital crest* is the bony prominence which constitutes the top of the head, and which more or less rises between the ears. It is particularly high in the head shown in Pl. 26.

Neck (2).—The neck is separated from the shoulders by a line which goes from the dip that is just in front of the withers, to the depression which is made by the union of the neck and breast.

The *poll* (*v*) is the part which is on the top of the neck and is immediately behind the ears.

The *crest* (*t*) is the upper part of the neck, extending from the withers to the ears.

The *jugular groove* (*u*) is the groove which is on each side of the neck, just above the wind-pipe. It is well shown in Pls. 20 and 35.

Breast and Chest.—Among horsemen who are unacquainted with anatomy, the latter of these two terms is frequently used to express the former. At the risk of employing a word contrary to colloquial custom, I would suggest that the term "chest" be applied exclusively to the cavity which occupies nearly the front third of the trunk, and in which the lungs and heart are situated. It is divided from the belly (abdomen) by the diaphragm. (*See* Fig. 4.)

Shoulders (3).—The line of union between the shoulders and the neck is well shown in the majority of harness and draught horses; there being, in such cases, a distinct depression immediately in front of the shoulder. In well-shaped saddle horses, this dip between shoulder and neck will be more or less difficult to find. The withers form the upper boundary of the shoulder. The rear border of the shoulder may be taken from behind the "swell" of the muscle which is just below the withers, to the elbow.

The *point of the shoulder* (*h*) is the prominent bony angle, on each side of the chest, a little below the junction of the neck and shoulder.

The Withers (4) are the bony ridge which is the forward continuation of the back. Its posterior limit is, as a rule, ill-defined; for the curve made by the withers usually runs into that of the back in a gradual manner. Its anterior termination can generally be easily felt by the fingers; as this bony ridge ends abruptly in the crest.

The Elbow, which is a portion of the fore-arm, is the large bony projection at the upper and posterior part of the fore-arm. The *point of the elbow* (*i*) is the top of this bony projection

The Fore-Arm (5) is placed between the shoulder and knee. Its upper boundary may be taken as a horizontal line drawn across the fore limb, just below the lump of muscle which is at the bottom of the shoulder.

The *castors*, or *chesnuts* (*k*) are the horny growths that are above the knees, and just below the hocks, on the inside of the legs.

Knee (6).—The upper boundary of the knee may be regarded as a line drawn at right angles to the direction of the leg, above the knee joint, and just clear of the bony prominence that is on the side of the knee. The lower boundary of the knee may be taken as a line joining the point where the line of the cannon-bone meets that of the knee, with that where the line of the back tendons is terminated by the bone (the trapezium, *l*) which is at the back of the knee.

The Cannon (7).—A suitable designation for the part of the leg which is situated between the knee and fetlock is much required. The term "cannon" is apt to give one the impression that only the cannon-bone is meant: it would be more convenient if the back tendons and suspensory ligament were also included. The line dividing the cannon from the fetlock is one drawn across the leg immediately above the prominence caused by the fetlock joint.

The *back tendons* (*m*) or *back sinews* are the fibrous cord which runs down the back of the leg between the knee and the fetlock. This cord consists of two tendons which lie closely together.

The *suspensory ligament* is a fibrous cord which lies between the cannon-bone and the back tendons, and which can be seen in a well-formed leg that is not unduly covered with hair (*vide* Pl. 42).

The *cannon-bone* (*j*) is the bone which lies between the knee and the fetlock. It has two small bones (outside and inside *splint bone*) at its back.

Fetlock (8).—The *fetlock joint* is the joint which the cannon-bone makes with the pastern. The term *fetlock* signifies the tuft of hair that usually grows behind this joint, and also the joint itself and the enlargement made by the bones which form it.

Pastern (9).—This is the short column of bones which is placed between the fetlock and the hoof.

The *hollow of the pastern* is the hollow at the back and lower part of the pastern.

The *coronet* is the comparatively soft lower portion of the pastern which is immediately above the hoof.

The Hoof (10) is the horny box which encloses the lower part of the limb. The front part of the hoof, near the ground surface, is called the *toe;* the side portions, the *quarters;* and the rear parts, on the ground surface, the *heels.* The outer portion of the hoof is termed the *wall,* which is divided into a hard, fibrous outer covering called the *crust,* and a soft inner layer of non-fibrous horn. The designations "wall" and "crust" are often used indiscriminately.

The *frog* is the triangular buffer which is in the centre of the ground surface of the hoof.

The *cleft of the frog* is the division in the middle line of the frog. In healthy feet, it consists of only a slight depression.

The *bars of the hoof* are the portions of the wall of the hoof which are turned inwards at the heels, and run more or less parallel to the sides of the frog. The *sole* is that portion of the ground surface of the foot which is included between the wall, bars, and frog.

Back (11).—Anatomically speaking, the back consists of

that portion of the spinal column to which ribs are attached, and it consequently includes the withers; but not the loins The term "back" is, in common parlance, an ill-defined region. Some regard it as consisting of the whole of the upper line of the body, from the front of the withers to the root of the tail. Others would exclude from this the croup. Probably, the majority of horsemen would say the back of a horse is included between the highest point of the croup and the commencement of the withers. For convenience sake I shall adopt the anatomical definition, with the omission of the withers, which have separate functions, and which I shall consider by themselves. I may, therefore, state that the back is bounded in front by the withers; behind, by the loins; and on each side, by the ribs.

Loins (12).—The loins are placed between the back and croup, at front and rear, with the flanks at each side. We may regard the loins as that portion of the spinal column which is devoid of ribs, and which is in front of the highest point (*posterior iliac spine*, see Fig. 3) of the pelvis.

Ribs (13).—The ribs are bounded by the shoulders in front, by the flanks behind, by the back above, and by the belly and brisket (*sternum*) below.

Flank (14).—The flank is that part of the side of the horse which is free from bone and which thinly covers the intestines. It is placed between the loins above, the ribs to the front, the thigh and point of the hip to the rear, and the belly below.

The *hollow of the flank* is the upper portion of the flank, which is bounded above by the loins, and below by a line joining the end of the last rib with the lower edge of the point of the hip.

Belly (15).—The belly or abdomen is the large cavity (*see* Fig. 4) which contains the stomach, liver, spleen, intestines, kidneys, bladder, etc. The term "belly" is applied, in common phraseology, to the underneath portion of the body which is not covered by bone.

The Brisket (16) is the lower part of the horse's chest.

The *girth place* is the rear portion of the sternum (breast-bone) which is just behind the fore legs, and underneath which the girths pass when the horse is saddled.

Croup (17).—The croup is that portion of the upper part of the body which is situated between the loins in front and the tail behind. Roughly speaking, it may be said to extend down, on each side, to a line drawn from the lower edge of the point of the hip, to the point of the buttock.

The *point of the hip* (*s*) is the bony surface, more or less prominent, which is a little to the rear of the last rib. It is the anterior point of the pelvis.

The *point of the buttock* (*o*) is the bony prominence which is the rearmost point of the pelvis. It is a few inches below the root of the tail.

Thigh (18).—The thigh is bordered by the stifle, flank, croup, buttock, and gaskin, from which it is separated by a horizontal line drawn from the upper end of the straight line made by the *hamstring* or *tendo Achillis* (*p*), which proceeds towards the thigh from the point of the hock (*q*). I am aware that this definition is far from being anatomically correct, but it is one which fairly represents the acceptation of the term among horsemen.

The Stifle (*n*) is the joint of the hind leg which is at the lower part of the flank.

The Gaskin (19) is situated between the thigh and the hock, from which it is divided by a line drawn from the point of the hock, clear of the bony prominences of the joint.

The Hock (20) is placed between the gaskin and the hind cannon-bone, from which we may separate it by a line drawn across this bone at the point at which its head begins to enlarge in order to form a joint with the lower bones of the hock.

The *point of the hock* (*q*) is the bony projection at the back and top of the hock.

The parts of the hind leg below the hock are similarly named to those of the fore leg below the knee.

The Dock (*r*) is the solid part of the tail.

N.B.—The following definitions have reference to Fig. 2 :—

The Height of a Horse (*a b*) is the vertical distance of the highest point of his withers from the ground, when he is standing with his fore legs nearly vertical and with the points of his hocks in a vertical line with the points of his buttocks. I have qualified "vertical" with "nearly" when referring to the fore legs; for when the hind legs are placed as in Fig. 2, the weight of the head and neck, which are in front of the fore legs, would cause the animal to stand somewhat "over." I may mention that this figure was drawn from a photograph of a well-shaped

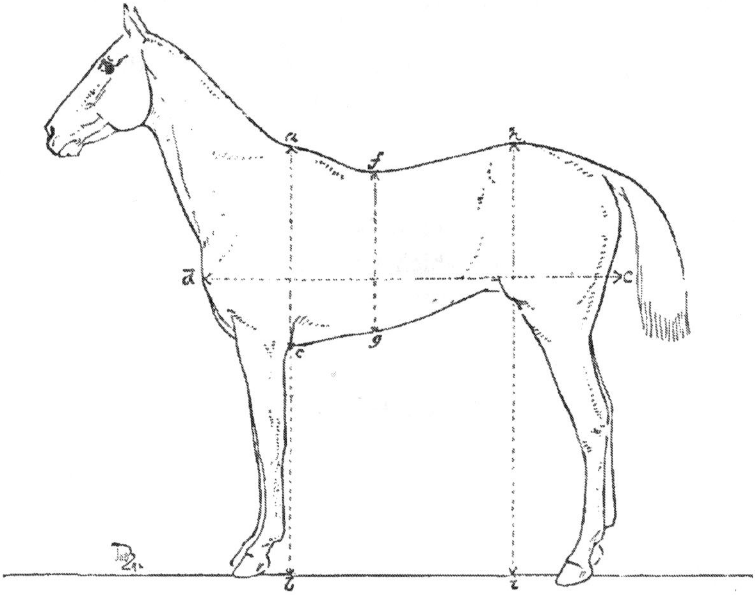

FIG 2.—MEASUREMENTS OF HORSE.

race-horse, Tristan, who was standing, if I may use the expression, "at attention." When a pony is being measured for racing, his legs should be placed in the position I have described.

The Length of the Body of a Horse (*d e*) is the horizontal distance from the front of the chest to a line dropped vertically from the point of the buttock. I must explain that this measurement is a somewhat arbitrary one; but it is, as far as I can see, the best for the purpose.

Colonel Duhousset, in his book, *Le Cheval,* takes the length of a horse as the distance from the point of the shoulder to the point of the buttock. As this is not a horizontal measurement; I prefer to it the one I have just given.

The Depth of the Chest at the Withers (*a c*) is the vertical distance from the top of the withers to the bottom of the chest This measurement, being taken for convenience sake, is an arbitrary one; for the chest is lower between the fore legs than behind the elbow, which is the spot I have selected. Besides this, the actual height of the withers above the roof of the chest has no fixed relation to the depth of the chest.

Depth of the Body (*f g*).—The best and most uniform point to take this is, I think, the lowest point of the back.

Height at the Croup (*h i*) is measured from the highest point of the hind quarters.

CHAPTER IV.

SKETCH OF THE ANATOMY OF THE HORSE.

Definitions—Bones—Joints and Ligaments—Muscles—Heart and Lungs—Nervous System of the Horse.

Definitions.—When one bone unites with another bone, or with a piece of cartilage, to form a joint, it is said to *articulate* with it. The term *articulation* is used as a synonym for *joint.*

A *ball and socket joint* is formed by the head of one bone resting in a cavity of another bone. The more shallow the cavity, the more extensive will be the power of movement. The horse's shoulder joint and hip joint are good examples of this kind of articulation. A *hinge joint* is one which works only by extension and flexion, like the horse's knee.

"A limb," as Professor Huxley states, "is *flexed* when it is bent; *extended,* when it is straightened out." We may adopt this definition, with the exception that the fetlock joint becomes bent when it is extended, and straightened out when it is partly flexed.

The word *dorsal* is used with reference to things of, or belonging to, the back, which, anatomically, is limited to that portion of the spine which is connected with the ribs.

If a muscle is attached, by one end, to a bone which it can move, and, by the other end, to one which is fixed, the former is called the *insertion* of the muscle; the latter, the *origin.* Thus, the origin of the biceps in man (*see* p. 12) is near the shoulder joint; and its insertion is on the bone of the forearm. When a muscle, on contracting, can move the bones at both its ends, the points of connection are called *attachments*, an expression which is also applied collectively to the origin and insertion. I may mention that muscles are not invariably attached to bones, but may, on the contrary, be connected to cartilages, ligaments, to the fibrous covering of muscles, or even to the skin.

Bones.—The skeleton is composed of the limbs and spinal column, which consists of the head, vertebræ, ribs, and breast-bone (*see* Fig. 3). A *vertebra* is one of the short bones which, when united, form the column of bones that extends from the head to the end of the tail. There are seven vertebræ of the neck, eighteen of the back, six of the loins, five of the croup (or *sacrum*) and from thirteen to twenty of the tail. All the vertebræ, except

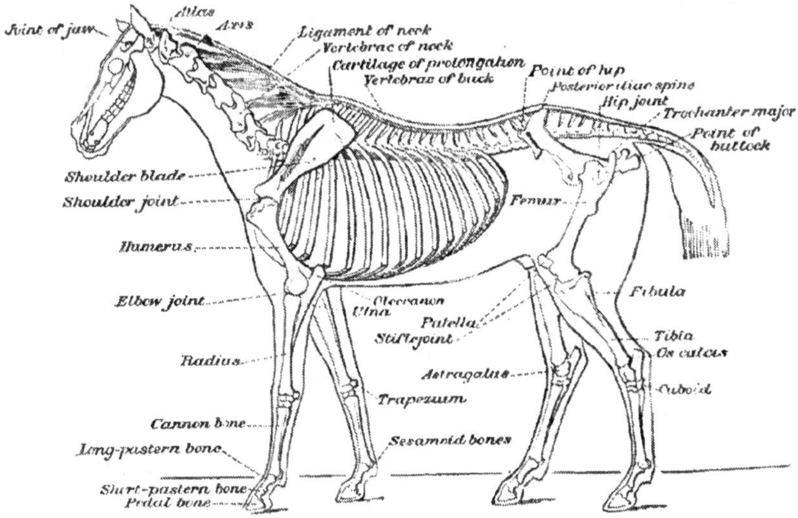

FIG. 3.—SKELETON OF HORSE.

those of the tail, have a canal in which the spinal cord lies. They are united one to another with more or less power of movement, except those of the croup, which, in the grown-up horse, form one solid bony mass. The head may be said to be composed of vertebræ in a peculiarly altered shape.

The *withers* are the long spines of the seven or eight dorsal vertebræ which come after the first. Generally speaking, the better bred a horse is, the further to the rear do the withers extend. The spine of the fifth dorsal vertebra forms the summit of the withers.

There are eighteen *ribs*—eight true and ten false—attached to the dorsal vertebræ. Both kinds have pieces of cartilage attached to their lower ends. The true ribs are connected by their respective cartilages with the breast bone; but the false ones are only indirectly connected to it, the cartilage of the first false rib resting on that of the last true one, that of the second false rib on the first false one, and so on.

The *fore limb* consists of the shoulder blade, humerus, bones of the fore-arm, bones of the knee, cannon-bone, splint bones, long pastern bone, short pastern bone, pedal (or coffin) bone, two small bones at the back of the fetlock, and the navicular bone, which lies at the back of the joint formed by the small pastern bone and the pedal bone.

The *shoulder blade* (or *scapula*) is a broad, thin bone, which is flat on its inside surface and has a narrow ridge of bone (the spine of the scapula) on its outer surface. This spine serves as a partition to divide the muscles which extend the shoulder joint from those that flex it.

There are two bones of the forearm, namely, the radius, which makes a joint with the humerus and with the bones of the knee; and the ulna, which is united to the back and upper part of the radius, above which it projects The free part of the ulna is called the *olecranon*, the top of which is termed the *point of the elbow.*

There are two rows of bones of the *knee*, at the back of which a bone (the *trapezium*) is placed. It is curved inwards so as to form a groove for the passage of the back tendons of the fore leg.

The two *splint bones* are placed at the back of the *cannon-bone*, one on the outside, the other on the inside. They form a groove in which lies the upper portion of the *suspensory ligament.*

There is a joint between the cannon-bone and the *long pastern bone*, between the two pastern bones, and between the *short pastern bone* and the *pedal* (or *coffin*) *bone.* The *navicular bone* articulates with both the short pastern bone and the pedal bone. It and the two bones behind the fetlock (the *sesamoid bones*) serve as pulleys for one of the back tendons.

The pedal bone is surrounded by a membrane, which secretes the horn of the wall of the hoof, sole and frog, in somewhat the same manner as the skin which covers the bones of the head, secretes the hair of that part.

The *pelvis*, which rests on, and is firmly attached to, the sacrum, appears as a single bone in the adult animal, although it really consists of two halves, which we may regard as the respective shoulder blades of the hind quarters. Each half furnishes a socket for the head of its respective thigh bone. The *point of the hip*, on either side, is the front and outer corner of the pelvis. The two inner corners of the pelvis are firmly connected with the sacrum, upon which they rest. They form the highest point of the bony framework of the croup. In the absence of a recognised popular term, we may call the rearmost points of the pelvis the *points of the buttock.*

The head of the thigh bone makes a ball and socket joint with the pelvis, while its lower end articulates with the tibia to form the stifle joint, in front of which the *patella* (knee cap) is placed. The patella serves for the attachment of muscles which extend the stifle joint. It is kept in position by strong ligaments. A portion of the thigh bone projects, from the outside, above the hip joint. The *tibia* articulates, at one end, with the thigh bone; and, at the other, with the *astragalus,* which is one of the bones of the hock. The part of the astragalus which makes a joint with the tibia, is formed like a pulley, the grooves of which have an outward and forward direction. The *os calcis* is placed behind the astragalus, and projects above it; its summit being called the *point of the hock. The small bones of the hock* are interposed between the astragalus and os calcis, and the cannon-bone and the two splint bones. The *fibula* is a rudimentary bone, which is attached to the tibia, and which corresponds to the ulna. According to Chauveau, the patella has no analogue in the fore extremity. The bones below the hock are similar to those below the knee.

Analogies between the bones of man and the horse.—The horse possesses no collar bone, consequently there is no bony connection between his fore extremity and trunk. The humerus, elbow and forearm are the same in both, except that the ulna is, comparatively, far more developed in man than in the horse. The knee of the latter corresponds to the wrist of the former. The five bones between the wrist and the first row of knuckles are represented by the cannon and splint bones; two of these bones having disappeared in the evolution of the horse (*see* Chap. XXX.). The fetlock is analogous to the first row of knuckles of our hand. The long pastern bone corresponds to the first row of bones of the fingers; the short one, to the second row, the coffin bone, to the third row; and the hoof, to our nails. The navicular bone is a detached bone which has no counterpart in our frame. In the hind limb, the stifle represents our knee; the tibia, the shin; the hock, the ankle; the point of the hock, the heel; and so on. In man, the fibula is a fully developed bone. We may thus see that the horse is an animal which moves on the tips of his fingers and toes (unguligrade); and that he has only one toe (or finger) to each leg

Joints and Ligaments.—Joints may be divided into those which admit of more or less motion, and those which are immovable. The ends of the bones which form them are, in both cases, held together by strong inelastic ligaments, of which there are various kinds. *Capsular ligaments*, for instance, loosely encircle their joints in order to protect the apparatus which lubricates the ends of the bones. *Lateral ligaments* are placed on each side of the joint, and, being attached both above and below it, keep the bones together, while admitting often of considerable play. *Annular ligaments* form protecting sheaths for the passage of tendons; and *interosseous ligaments* bind bones closely together. Besides these, we have *suspensory* and *check ligaments*, which, as far as we are at present concerned, are respectively represented by the structures, bearing these names, which are found in the legs, below the knees and hocks.

The ligaments to which I have referred are, like tendons, composed of white fibrous tissue (a variety of connective tissue, *see* p. 14), which is hard, strong and inelastic. *Yellow ligaments* are, without going into minute differences, to be distinguished by the fact of their yellow colour, and by the possession of considerable elasticity, which enables them to passively bear weights which would otherwise fall on the muscles. A familiar instance of the manner in which elastic ligaments mechanically save the expenditure of muscular force, is afforded by the arrangement which keeps the claws of a cat retracted without entailing exertion on the animal; for each claw is kept back by a small elastic ligament, which becomes stretched when the digits of the paw are extended by their muscles. As soon as these muscles cease to act, the ligaments, by their power of contraction, regain their natural length and retract the claws. An enormously powerful elastic ligament is attached to the withers, and goes straight from them, in the form of a cord, to the top of the head (the bony prominence between the ears), to which it is inserted. At about a third of the distance from the head to the withers, a broad sheet of elastic tissue is given off from the corded portion, and is united to all the spines of the neck vertebræ, except the first. This sheet accordingly acts as a partition between the muscles on the respective sides of the upper part of the neck. The entire ligament, therefore, by its strength and elasticity greatly aids the muscles in supporting the weight of the head and neck. The amount of stretching which it can undergo in ordinary circumstances may be approximately estimated by comparing the length of the neck, when the head is held up in its usual position, to that when it is lowered to allow the animal to feed off the ground. In the first case, with a horse 15.3 high, it will probably not exceed 28 inches in length; but in the latter it must be over a yard long, supposing that the animal does not unduly bend his knees. Any depression or elevation beyond the position occupied by the head when the horse is asleep standing, has to be obtained by muscular force. This ligament is popularly called the *packwax*. Without being pedantic, we might, I think, more appropriately term it the *suspensory ligament of the head and neck.* I may add that it is continuous with the strong, white fibrous ligament which commences on the spine of the sacrum and runs along the top of the spines of the vertebræ of the loins and back, binding them together, until it nearly reaches the summit of the withers, where its fibres assume the character of yellow elastic tissue. On the top of this large ligament there is a layer of fat, which in entires (especially if they be coarsely bred) often increases to a great size, and consequently gives them a high and thick crest (*see* Pl. 30). The intestines of the horse are supported by the *abdominal tunic*, which covers the muscles of the lower part of the belly, and consists of a broad, strong sheet of yellow elastic tissue. It acts like an elastic abdominal belt.

There is considerable power of movement between the *head* and the first vertebra of the neck (the *altas*), and between the different *neck vertebræ* themselves, but there is hardly any play between the *dorsal vertebræ.* The *loin vertebræ* can be flexed and extended to a limited degree on each other; but are capable of only very slight motion from side to side. The *sacrum*, as before mentioned, forms a single bone, on which the pelvis rests, and with which it is connected by powerful ligaments that greatly restrict its movements on the spine. We have also seen that the thigh bones articulate with the pelvis. The bones of the *tail* possess considerable mobility. The solid connection thus afforded to the hind limbs, with the trunk, enables the former to transmit to the latter the forward impetus given during progression with the least possible loss of power. The capability of the loins to be flexed and extended is necessary in order to facilitate the action of the loin muscles, which are important agents in locomotion (*see* p. 64). The mobility of the head, neck, and, to a much lesser degree, of the tail, acting as they do as balancing poles, is extremely useful in enabling the animal to perform with ease and precision many of the varied and difficult movements demanded of him. We may see that any power of lateral motion which the trunk (not counting the head, neck and tail) may possess, however much it may make the horse quick and "handy" at turning, will militate against his speed in a forward direction.

The respective ends of the first eight *ribs* form movable joints with the spine and breast bone; the first articulating with the last neck vertebra and first dorsal vertebra; the second with the first and second dorsal vertebræ, and so on. They are rigidly connected to their cartilages, of which those of the first eight, or true, ribs form movable joints with the breast bone. Commencing from the spine, "the ribs pass outwards and backwards, and then in an arched direction downwards, their cartilages inclining inwards and forwards" (*Strangeways*). Owing to the peculiar manner in which the ribs are curved, and to the fact that the ends of the true ribs can pivot round in the joints which they form with the spine and breast bone, while the false ribs also form movable joints with the spine; the capacity of the chest is capable of becoming much enlarged when the middle portion of the ribs are pulled forward by muscles that are attached to them. The mobility of the ribs, which is all but absent in the first one, gradually increases as they go backwards. They also increase in rotundity in the same manner, the first one being the flattest. The first rib is the shortest, and each succeeding one is longer than the one next in front of it, till the eighth or ninth rib, the ribs behind which gradually decrease in length up to the last one, which is nearly as short as the first rib. Owing to the direct connection which the first eight ribs have with the breast bone; their power of movement and, consequently, their action in increasing the capacity of the chest is less than that of the false ribs. Hence, when seeking for signs of good breathing power in a horse, we should attach far more importance to rotundity of the rear portion of the chest than of the front part. As a practical guide I might say that the former region might, in the saddled horse, be regarded roughly as the portion of the ribs behind the saddle flaps, and the latter as that covered by them. "It can be proved by observation, that the middle false ribs are those which have the greatest power of being drawn forwards and outwards. The ribs behind them successively lose more and more their power of displacement up to the last one, the lower end of which can be raised and lowered a little, without appreciably altering its distance from the point of the hip" (*Colin*).

The *fore limb* is connected to the trunk by muscles, to which I shall allude on page 37.

The *shoulder joint* is a ball and socket articulation, which possesses considerable power of motion.

The *elbow* is a hinge joint, which can be bent and extended.

In the *knee* we have three hinge joints, of which that between the radius and first row of bones is capable of a large amount of motion; that between the two rows of much less; while that between the second row and cannon-bones possesses hardly any power of movement.

The bones at the back of the knee are united together by an extremely strong ligament, one of the bands of which closes up the gap left between the point of the trapezium and the inside of the knee, so as to form a channel for the "back tendons" to pass through.

The *sesamoid* bones are fixed immovably to the back of the fetlock joint.

The *fetlock*, *pastern*, and *coffin* joints are hinge joints, which possess more or less play.

The *hind limb is connected to the trunk*, as we have already seen, by the pelvis.

The *hip joint*, formed by the head of the thigh bone and cavity in the pelvis, is a ball and socket joint.

In the *stifle* we find two articulations—one with the thigh bone and tibia, the other with the thigh bone and patella, which is firmly attached to the tibia by ligaments in order to enable it to resist the action of those muscles of the thigh which are inserted on it.

The *true hock joint* is formed by the tibia and astragalus. It is a hinge joint, which, owing to the oblique manner in which its grooves are placed, causes the foot to be turned slightly outward when the joint is either flexed or extended. The other joints of the hock possess hardly any power of movement.

The *astragalus*, *os calcis*, *small bones of the hock*, *hind cannon*, and *splint bones* are firmly connected together by ligaments.

The *joints below the hock* are similar to those below the knee.

Muscles.—I shall now consider, in the briefest possible manner, the principal muscles which are used in locomotion.

A broad sheet of muscle (the *panniculus*) lies immediately underneath the skin that covers the neck, sides of the chest, and abdomen. In thin horses, its rear border is usually defined by an irregular line (*see* pp. 256 and 257) which runs along the side downwards and backwards towards the groin. This muscle is attached, round its borders, to the skin and superficial muscles by sheets of fibrous tissue. By quickly contracting and relaxing alternately, it causes the skin to twitch, and thus gets rid of flies, etc., that may have alighted on the surface underneath which a portion of this muscle lies. It is principally found on those parts which the horse has difficulty in reaching with his lips, tail, or mane. As the process of training for racing purposes appears to largely develop this muscle, I cannot help thinking that it aids in forced expiration—expelling the air from the lungs—during the quickened breathing entailed by fast work; although anatomists do not ascribe such action to it.

The *neck, back, and loins are flexed* by muscles which lie immediately underneath the spine. The *head is bent* by muscles that proceed—one on each side—from the breast bone to the lower jaw, and by others which connect the neck and head together. The *head is extended* by muscles that are attached to the poll and bones of the neck and by others that proceed from the poll to the withers. The *neck is extended* by the last mentioned muscles, and by those which connect the spine of one vertebra with the body of the one in front of it. The *back and loins are extended* by muscles which are similar in action to the ones just alluded to, and by the *longissimus dorsi*, which is the most powerful muscle of the body, and is the chief extensor of the spine. It forms the principal portion of the fleshy mass which lies over the loins and back. It is attached to the pelvis, sacrum, all the loin and dorsal vertebræ, the last four bones of the neck, and to the ribs. As the spines of the vertebræ (including the withers) form a part of its attachments, it follows that the more they are developed, the more powerful will be the extension of the loins and back.

Muscles which connect the fore limb to the body.—The shoulder blade is connected to the trunk principally by a very strong, fan-shaped muscle, which is attached at its middle to the inside of the shoulder blade. Its front end is connected to the last five bones of the neck; and its other end to the first eight ribs. When the front portion contracts, the shoulder blade is drawn forward; when the rear portion contracts, this bone is pulled back. This muscle, from the manner of its attachment, acts as a sling for the fore limb. *The upper part of the shoulder blade is connected to the trunk*, from its inner extremity by a muscle which has one end attached to the suspensory ligament of the head and neck, and the other to the withers. Hence, on contracting, it draws the shoulder blade forwards and upwards. *The outside of the shoulder blade is connected* to the trunk, at about its upper third, by a muscle which has one branch going to the withers, and the other to the suspensory ligament of the head and neck. It can thus raise the shoulder blade, or work it backwards or forwards. *The fore limb is drawn forward* chiefly, however, by the action of a muscle which is attached, at one end, to the top of the head and first four neck vertebræ, and by the other to the middle of the humerus. We may see from the foregoing remarks, that length of neck and height of withers are favourable conditions for the firm attachment of the shoulder blade to the trunk and for the free action of the shoulder.

The fore limb is connected to the breast bone by a muscle which is attached to the breast bone and humerus.

The fore limb is drawn back, principally, by two muscles, one of which is attached, at one end, to the abdominal tunic (*see* p. 34) and breast bone, and at the other, to the humerus and shoulder blade, close to the shoulder joint. The other muscle (the *latissimus dorsi*) has its origin on the vertebræ of the loins and back, and is inserted on the humerus, which it consequently draws backwards and upwards when it contracts. The first mentioned muscle tends to draw it backwards and downwards.

Muscles of the fore limb.—When the fore leg is advanced, the shoulder joint is extended and the elbow joint flexed. When it is drawn back, the opposite to this takes place. Agreeably to these actions, we find a powerful muscle attached, by one end, to the front part of the shoulder blade, just above the joint; and by the other end to the front of the radius immediately below the elbow joint, so that, when it contracts, it *extends the shoulder and flexes the elbow*. Another muscle, being attached to the rearmost corner of the shoulder blade and to the point of the elbow, *flexes the shoulder and extends the elbow*. Besides these muscles, there are various others which respectively aid in the flexion and extension of these joints. The chief muscle that *extends the knee*, has its origin on the front part of the humerus, just above the elbow joint, and running down the forearm, is joined to its tendon, which passes over the knee, and which is inserted on the head of the cannon-bone. The three muscles which *bend the knee* take their origin on the back part of the humerus, just above the elbow joint, and are inserted on the trapezium and splint bones. The two muscles which *extend the fetlock, pastern, and coffin joints*, run down the front of the forearm. One of them has its origin at the head of the radius, and is inserted on the front part of the long pastern bone. The other commences on the humerus, just above the elbow joint, and ends on the front and upper part of the coffin bone. *The muscles which flex the fetlock, pastern, and coffin joints* (*the flexor muscles of the foot*), and aid in bending the knee, take their origin on the back part of the humerus, just above the elbow joint, and proceed down the back of the forearm. A little above the knee they are joined to their tendons (*the back tendons*), which pass through the sheath formed by the trapezium and the annular ligament at the back of the knee. From thence they run down the back of the cannon-bone. The front one, which lies next the suspensory ligament, goes over the sesamoid bones, which form a pulley for it; down the back of the pastern; over the navicular bone, which also acts as a pulley; and is finally inserted on the base of the coffin-bone. The rearmost tendon, which lies between the front one and the skin, forms a sheath for its fellow at the back of the fetlock, and, dividing in two, is inserted on the short pastern bone. There are two small muscles which assist the front one of these two muscles, but which I need not further allude to. As the action of the suspensory and check ligament is closely connected with that of the flexor muscles of the foot, I may appropriately describe them here. The *suspensory ligament* lies at the back of the cannon-bone and between the two splint bones. It has its origin at the head of the cannon-bone and lower row of the small bones of the knee. At about two-thirds of the distance from the knee to the fetlock, it divides into two branches, which are respectively inserted on the summits of the sesamoid bones. They then extend downwards and forwards, and unite together, at the front and about the middle of the pastern, with the tendon of the muscle which extends the foot. The suspensory ligament is composed of white fibrous tissue, with a few muscular fibres in it, and acts in supporting the fetlock. It is generally considered to be inelastic, although MM. Goubaux and Barrier entertain the opposite opinion. They remark that "its obscurely muscular structure, and the manner in which its fibres inter-cross, render it a true, elastic brace, which counteracts the effects of weight, as long as they do not overcome the resistance and strength of the tissues." In omnivorous and carnivorous animals this ligament is replaced by a muscle which has similar functions. The *check ligament* has nearly the same origin as the suspensory ligament and joins the front back tendon, at a point about half-way down the cannon-bone. Its office is to aid in supporting the fetlock and to relieve the muscles of the tendon, with which it is connected, of weight.

Muscles of the hind limb.—The hip is extended by the great croup muscle, and also by some of the muscles which lie at the back of the thigh bone. One end of the great croup muscle is attached to the upper surface of the front portion of the pelvis, and, proceeding along the side of the sacrum, reaches as far as the last rib. The other end is inserted to the summit of the portion of the thigh bone which projects above the hip joint. The muscles at the back of the thigh bone have their origin, chiefly, on the under surface of the pelvis, from behind the hip joint to the point of the buttock; and are inserted principally to the lower part of the thigh bone or to the upper portion of the tibia.

The *hip is flexed* by muscles that have their origin on the under surface of the loin vertebræ, and are inserted on the thigh bone; and also by muscles which are attached to the under surface of the pelvis in front of the hip joint, and to the thigh bone, patella, or tibia.

The *stifle is extended* by one muscle which has its origin on the under surface of the pelvis, just in front of the hip joint, and is inserted on the patella, and by two others which are attached to the upper part of the thigh bone and to the patella. The first mentioned muscle flexes the hip at the same time that it extends the stifle.

The *stifle is flexed* chiefly by a muscle which is attached to the portion of the pelvis behind the hip joint, and to the tibia.

The *hock is extended*, for the most part, by muscles which form the rearmost portion of the gaskin ("second thigh"). They have their origin on the lower end of the thigh bone, and are inserted to the point of the hock by their tendons, which lie one over the other, and constitute the tendo Achillis. The underneath tendon terminates at the point of the hock, but the other is continued down the back of the leg as the rearmost one of the two back tendons, and is inserted on the short pastern bone, as in the fore limb. Owing to the double insertion of this tendon, the hock cannot be extended without the fetlock being flexed at the same time; hence the success of the expedient, for the prevention of kicking, of securely fixing in the hollow of the pastern some hard object of suitable shape, so as to prevent the joint between the two pastern bones from becoming flexed.

The *joints below the hock are extended* by muscles which take their origin near the stifle joint, run down the front of the hind leg, are continued as tendons down the front of the cannon-bone, and are inserted on the bones of the pastern, and to the front and highest point of the coffin bone.

The *joints below the hock are flexed* by a muscle of the gaskin, which muscle originates at the back of the upper portion of the tibia, behind which it runs down to a little above the hock joint, when it is continued as a tendon that passes over the groove formed on the *os calcis*. It then proceeds down the back of the cannon-bone, as the front one of the two back tendons, and terminates in the same manner as in the fore limb. The muscle of the rear back tendon, as we have already seen, also aids in flexing the fetlock and pastern joints.

Heart and Lungs.—The heart is a hollow muscle which acts as a force pump in sending the blood through the *arteries* to the various parts of the body. The arteries commence on the left side of the heart, by one large trunk which splits up, as it goes on, into an innumerable number of small branches, that, as a rule, terminate in a microscopic network of minute canals called *capillaries*. These canals, which probably do not exceed a fortieth of an inch in length, gradually enlarge on the side away from the arteries, and open out into small *veins*, which, uniting with each other as they approach the heart, enter its right side by two large branches and a few small ones. The heart now forces this venous blood through the pulmonary artery to the lungs, which return it by a system of capillaries and veins to the heart. We must remember that the network of *capillaries* runs through every tissue which contains blood. Thus, for instance, the blood which goes to the foot of the horse, and that which proceeds to the substance of the heart itself, flow to their respective parts through certain arteries, pass through a very short network of capillaries, and return to the heart by the veins; a long circuit being made in the first case; a short one, in the second.

The necessary amount of nutritive matter and water is taken up from the food and drink contained in the stomach and intestines by small vessels which carry it into the veins, and is thus finally brought into the capillaries, the walls of which are so thin that it exudes through them, and in this manner nourishes the various tissues. I may mention that, before food can be taken up by the system, it is necessary that it should be thoroughly dissolved. As the tissues are being constantly broken up as well as repaired, the capillaries also serve to take up the waste matters and carry them into the veins. When this impure or venous blood is pumped by the right side of the heart into the lungs, it is acted upon, there, by the oxygen of the air that is taken into the chest at each breath, and is returned from the lungs to the left side of the heart in a comparatively high state of purity. When the blood leaves the lungs, it carries with it a certain amount of oxygen, which, uniting with the broken-up material in the various tissues, converts it into products which can be readily removed. I need not dwell longer on this subject, for it is fully explained in every elementary book on physiology, as, for instance, that by Professor Huxley.

In order that a muscle may work—*i.e.*, contract on being stimulated by its nerves—it is necessary that it should be supplied with oxygen. Also, the severer the labour, the more oxygen is used up in the muscles and the larger is the supply required. As the blood has a shorter distance to travel in order to make a complete circuit in the blood vessels of a small animal, than in that of a large one of the same kind; we might infer that the blood of the former passes more frequently during a given space of time through the lungs, than that of the latter. The truth of this supposition is fully borne out in practice; for we may observe, on an average, that the pulse of a heavy cart-horse beats about thirty-five times a minute; that of a small pony, about forty-five times. Hence we find that, speaking generally, small horses can "stay" better than large ones; for the power of "staying" is dependent on the capability, possessed by muscles, of retaining for a long time their contractile power. Also, they recover quicker than big horses from the effects of severe work, owing to the fact that repair of worn out tissue and removal of waste matters from the system is carried on at a faster rate. In fact, they possess more "vitality." Again, the larger the lungs—other things being equal—the greater will be the amount of oxygen taken into the blood, and of impurities given off from the blood into the air.

Nervous System of the Horse.—The nervous system of the horse is the power which stimulates and directs the action of his muscles in locomotion, and is the source of his mental capacity. We may regard it as divided into *nerve centres* and *conducting nerves*. To employ a well-worn simile, we may look upon a nerve centre as a telegraph station to which and from which messages are sent and despatched. The nerves (the *sensory nerves*) by which the horse sees, feels, hears, smells, and tastes, conduct the impressions they receive to some nerve centre, which may do one of three things. (1) It may, in response to the message received, send, on its own authority, by another line of nerves (the *motor nerves*), an order (or stimulus) to certain muscles to move. Such a movement will be by *reflex action*—that is, the impulse will be immediately reflected back. (2) Instead of acting on its own account, it may merely transmit the message on to another and more important nerve centre to decide what answer will be given. (3) It may use a portion of its transmitting power in reflex action, and a part of it in reporting the matter to head-quarters.

Besides the power which nerve centres have of exciting the muscles to move in response to a stimulus received from the sensory nerves, they can, by their own initiative, make their motor nerves stimulate to movement the muscles which are supplied with these particular motor nerves.

The chief nerve centres that are connected with the muscles of locomotion, are grouped together in a long column which fills the brain cavity and spinal canal, and may be divided into the *brain* and *spinal cord*.

The *spinal cord*, though it is formed of a number of nerve centres, is the chief conducting medium by which impressions received by the senses are conveyed to the brain, and is the means by which orders from the brain are transmitted to the muscles of the limbs.

We may divide the brain into the medulla oblongata, the cerebellum, and the cerebrum.

The *medulla oblongata* connects the other two portions of the brain with the spinal cord. It is the nervous centre of the function of breathing. Animals, for purposes of experiment, have had their spinal cord, and the whole of their brain, except the medulla, removed, and yet they have continued to breathe and live. But were the medulla injured, death from inability to breathe would at once ensue.

The *cerebellum* appears to be the organ of *muscular sense* and of combined muscular effort. By its muscular sense the animal can tell, from experience, the amount of muscular force required in performing its various voluntary movements. We cannot, by an effort of will, move any one particular muscle of our body; but we can cause our limbs to perform definite movements which will require the combined action of various muscles, and which are under the control of the cerebellum

The *cerebrum* is the organ of intellect, thought, and will. "Removal of the cerebrum in the lower animals appears to reduce them to a condition of a mechanism without spontaneity. A pigeon from which the cerebrum has been removed will remain motionless and apparently unconscious unless disturbed. When disturbed in any way, it soon recovers its former position. When thrown into the air it flies" (*Kirke's Physiology*). The cerebrum appears to be the organ in which a conclusion or thought is formed from a message or number of messages proceeding from the senses. If, for instance, a man standing near a horse's hind quarters touches him with a stick, and if the animal kicks the stick, he will perform, more or less, a reflex action. If, however, the horse recognises who the real offending party is, and kicks the man; he will have drawn a conclusion from the message received from his sense of feeling and of sight, and will have acted on such conclusion, which would certainly be an effort of reason.

Among the intellectual faculties, of which the cerebrum is the special organ, we have, prominently, *reason* and *memory*. Although the horse is greatly deficient in the former, which is by far the higher faculty of the two, he possesses the latter in special excellence.

The cerebrum is placed immediately underneath the forehead, at the centre of which it is covered by only a thin plate of bone. The cerebellum, which, in the horse, is a great deal smaller than the cerebrum, lies below the (occipital crest) top of the head, when the face is held at an angle of about 45° with the ground.

The proportion which the weight of the brain bears to that of the spinal cord, is regarded by many as a fair guide to the intellectual capacity of an animal. The following is a list of a few examples of the average number of times the brain is heavier than the spinal cord in certain animals :—

In man	33
„ dog	5·14
„ cat	3·75
„ ass	2·40
„ pig	2·30
„ horse	2·27
„ ox	2·18.

The order of intellectual capacity given in the above table, agrees with the conclusions I have drawn from my own experience with these animals.

CHAPTER V.

MECHANISM OF BREATHING.

THE body of the horse (*see* Fig. 4), viewed apart from his head, neck, limbs, and tail, may be divided into chest and

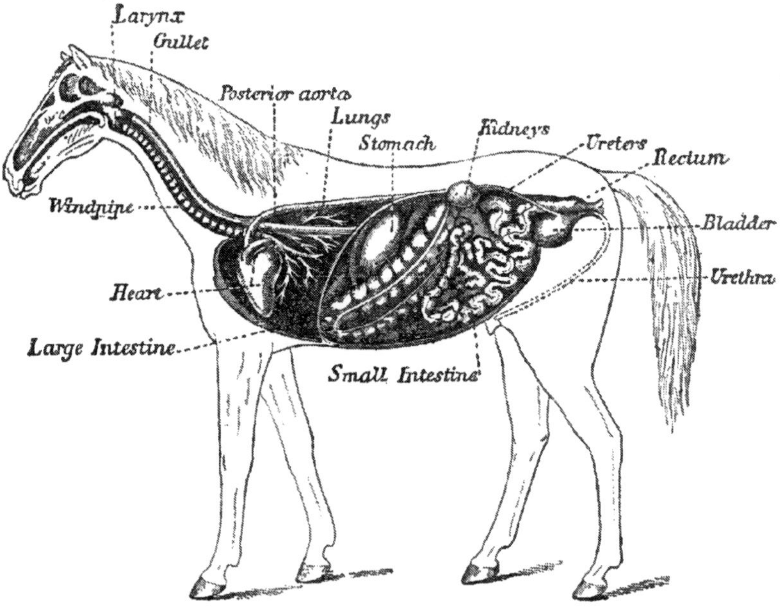

FIG. 4.—INTERNAL ORGANS OF HORSE.

abdomen (belly), the former containing the lungs and heart; the latter, the stomach, intestines, liver, bladder, and other vital organs. This division is effected by a broad and somewhat bell-shaped muscle, the diaphragm or midriff, which is attached, round its margin, to the ends of the last twelve ribs, to the rearmost extremity of the breast-bone, and to the spine under the loins; while its apex or centre projects forwards. When it contracts, it tends to become flat, and thus enlarges the capacity of the chest by pushing back the contents of the abdomen. Its action, especially during forced breathing, is aided by that of another muscle, which is attached by one end to the last four neck vertebræ, and by the other to the first rib, which it pulls forward on contracting, and in this manner helps to increase the size of the chest

Air is taken into, and expelled from, the lungs by means of the alternate increase and diminution of the capacity of the chest. When the former act occurs, the air contained in the lungs becomes rarefied, and consequently the external air rushes in through the animal's nostrils to restore the balance of pressure. When the latter takes place, a portion of the air which is already in the lungs is forced out. It is evident, therefore, that the power of taking a large volume of air into the lungs at each breath, is more dependent on the difference between the respective capacities of the chest when expanded, and contracted, than on the actual size of the chest itself.

The act of breathing is called *respiration;* that of expelling air from the lungs, *expiration;* and that of drawing it in, *inspiration.*

The chest is enlarged by the diaphragm, as we have seen; and also by muscles which pull the middle pieces of the ribs forward, so as to make the cavity wider from side to side, and consequently to increase its size. The ribs are drawn forward by muscles which cover them, and by others which are situated between the successive pairs of ribs. The lower ends of some of the ribs are also drawn up during the act of inspiration. On page 35, I have remarked on the power the ribs have of pivotting on their ends. I may point out that when the air which is within the chest becomes rarefied at the commencement of the act of inspiration, the lungs themselves passively dilate, and thus allow the incoming air to gain ready access to the bronchial tubes and air-cells.

When the animal is at rest, the elastic recoil of the ribs and lungs is sufficient to expel the *tidal air*, as the amount changed at each breath is called. The volume of air which remains in the lungs after expiration greatly exceeds—perhaps five or six times—that of the tidal air.

In forced breathing, as during active movement, several muscles which are not employed for tranquil respiration, are called into play, particularly those used in forced expiration, as we may see by the heaving flanks of an animal which is "blown." The muscles that cover the ribs and belly, aid in forced expiration by compressing these parts, and thereby causing the walls of the chest to "fall in," and the contents of the abdomen to project forward into that cavity. Quick work naturally develops the muscles of forced respiration.

I may point out that the muscles of the flank (known to anatomists as the great and small oblique, and the transverse) aid in respiration. Consequently, when they are well developed, the flank is not so hollow as it would be if they were weak.

I may mention that no hard and fast line can be drawn between tranquil and forced breathing; although the broad differences between them are clearly marked.

In order that the horse may have his breathing power fully developed, it is necessary that the capacity of the chest at the end of an act of expiration, should differ as much as possible from what it will be at the termination of the act of inspiration. For this reason the chest should be deep, the ribs well arched, and, at the same time, they should have a good inclination to the rear. The back ribs should be long, so as to augment the size of the chest; and the muscles which move the ribs, as well as the muscles of the belly, should be largely developed. I shall further allude, in Chapter XVII., to the shape of the chest and ribs.

CHAPTER VI.

DISTRIBUTION OF WEIGHT IN THE HORSE'S BODY.

Comparative Weight borne by the Fore and Hind Limbs—Centre of Gravity.

Comparative Weight borne by the Fore and Hind Limbs.—General Morris, of the French Army, appears to have been the first to make experiments as to the distribution of weight between the fore and hind limbs of the horse. He found that, taking one animal with another, it is as five is to four; and that the fact of the neck being long, as in the thoroughbred, causes more weight to be thrown on the forehand, than when that part is short and massive, as in the heavy cart-horse. The proportion which he obtained from an average of eleven horses that had light heads and necks—the latter being presumably long—was as four is to three. M. Colin puts the average at fully three to two. MM. Goubaux and Barrier have proved by a number of careful trials, that the lower the withers are, as compared to the croup, the greater is the proportion of weight supported by the fore limbs, and *vice versâ*. This is agreeable to what we might have inferred from the manner in which the horse raises his croup to kick, or his withers to rear. As the hind half of the trunk is, in all classes, heavier than the fore half, it follows that the extra weight in front is mainly due to the fact of the head and neck being in advance of the fore legs. The longer the body, and the heavier the belly, the more will this distribution of weight be equalised.

Centre of Gravity.—The centre of gravity of a body is an imaginary point in that body, so placed that if the body be supported immediately underneath the centre of gravity, it will be in equilibrium (or rest). Consequently, if a body be balanced at a point on its surface, a perpendicular line drawn from that point will pass through the centre of gravity; and the intersection of two or more such lines will determine the position of the centre of gravity. If the body be of uniform density, the position of the centre of gravity will be the same as that of the centre of the figure; but if it be heavier at one side than at the other, the centre of gravity will be nearer the former than the latter. For instance, in ships, with the view of obtaining increased security from an upset, the centre of gravity is placed below the centre of the hull. If, for example, we want to ascertain the position of the centre of gravity of a loaded club, we may take one line through its axis, and another across it, at the point where it balances, when placed horizontally. The lower the centre of gravity of a body, the more

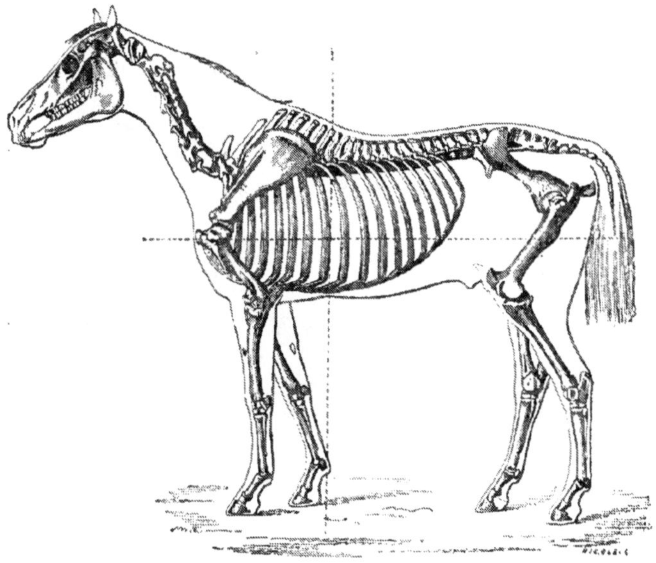

FIG. 5.—POSITION OF CENTRE OF GRAVITY.

stable will be its equilibrium, as we may see by experimenting with a loaded stick of uniform thickness; firstly, balanced on its light end, and, secondly, on its heavy extremity.

In the living animal, the position of the centre of gravity is constantly changing, on account of the manner in which the respective positions of the various parts alter, especially during movements of the head and neck.

Professor Colin, the well-known author of *Physiologie Comparée des Animaux Domestiques*, remarks that "the centre of gravity, the exact position of which has never been determined, nearly corresponds, in the horse, to the intersection of two lines—one, vertical, falling behind the xiphoid appendage [cartilage at rearmost point of the breast bone] of the sternum; the other, horizontal, dividing the middle third from the lower third of the body." Fig. 5, which I have taken from MM. Goubaux and Barrier's work, is drawn in conformity with M. Colin's remarks. The point of intersection of the two dotted lines in this figure, shows the position of the supposed centre of gravity.

We may readily see that the less deep is a horse's body, compared to his length of leg—in other words, the more "daylight" he has under him—the higher and more unstable will be his centre of gravity; and *vice versâ.* Taking the foregoing remarks with those on the effect which instability of equilibrium has on speed (*see* p. 67), we may conclude that the faster the horse, other things being equal, the greater will be the proportion of weight on his forehand.

CHAPTER VII.

LEVERS.

Definition—First Order—Second Order—Third Order—Relations between the Power and Weight in Levers—Comparisons between Power and Weight in Muscular Levers—Directions in which the Power and Weight respectively Act.

THE movements of the limbs are due to the working of various levers, formed by the bones and acted upon by the muscles.

Definition.—A lever is a rigid bar which has a fulcrum, or fixed point, so arranged that movement can be communicated to a *weight* at another point on it, by a *power* acting on a third point on the bar. Agreeably to the relative positions of the fulcrum (F), weight (W), and power (P), we have the three following orders of levers.

First Order.—P.F.W. (*see* Fig. 6), as when two persons make a see-saw by sitting on the opposite ends of a plank which rests on some convenient fulcrum. We have this order of lever in the bones from the

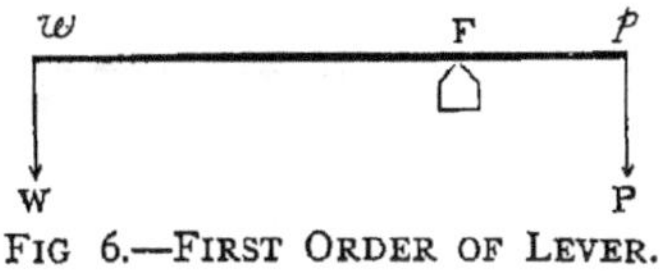

FIG 6.—FIRST ORDER OF LEVER.

point of the hock to the foot, when a horse kicks out with a hind leg (*see* Fig. 30).

Second Order.—P.W.F (*see* Fig. 7). A wheel-barrow, when lifted in the usual manner, furnishes us with an instance of this lever; the ground on which the wheel rests being the fulcrum; the barrow, the weight; and the arms of the person who lifts the handles, the force. We have another example in an oar employed to row a boat; the water being the unstable fulcrum, and the rowlock being the point through which the weight (the boat) is pushed forward. The bones and muscles which I have taken to illustrate

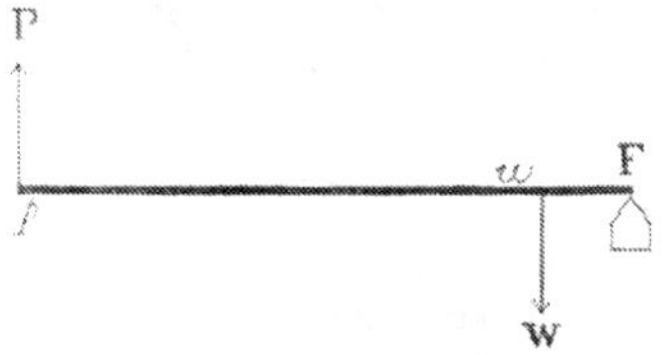

FIG. 7.—SECOND ORDER OF LEVER.

the first order of lever will serve our turn here, if we imagine the power to be exerted in propelling the body to the front, through the *tibia* (the bone that is situated between the hock and stifle), while the toe rests on the fulcrum formed by the ground (*see* Fig. 31).

Third Order.—W.P.F. (*see* Fig. 8). This form of lever occurs in a fishing rod, with which a man tries to lift a heavy trout out of the water. The weight is at the point of the rod; the fulcrum, at the butt, is formed by one hand; and the power is supplied by the other hand, a little above the butt. We have this lever in the bones below the hock, when the horse bends that

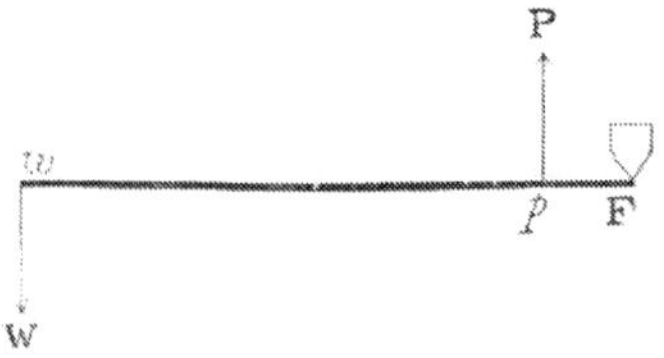

FIG. 8.—THIRD ORDER OF LEVER.

joint by lifting his feet off the ground (*see* Fig. 32). Here, the power is derived from the muscle which is placed in front of the tibia; the weight is that of the limb below the hock; and the fulcrum is formed by the *tibia*. I may remark in passing that the *os calcis* does not come into this lever, except in counterbalancing, to some slight extent, the weight of the leg below the hock.

Relations between the Power and Weight in Levers.—The farther the power is from the fulcrum, the greater will be the mechanical advantage at which it will act; and *vice versâ*. Thus, if one arm of a see-saw is longer than the other, a comparatively light weight at the end of the former will counterbalance a heavy one at the extremity of the latter. Also, the longer an oar is "in-board," as in an outrigger, the greater will be the power which a rower will have. If we apply this principle to the horse, we shall see that the longer is the *os calcis* (*see* Figs. 30 and 31), the greater will be the mechanical advantage at which the muscles of the gaskin will act in kicking or propelling the body forward. As length of *os calcis* gives increased leverage in the hind limb, so does length of *trapezium* afford it in the fore leg.

If we wish to express these relations mathematically, we have the following proportions for the three orders of levers.

$$P : W :: wF : pF, \text{ or } \frac{P}{W} = \frac{wF}{pF}.$$

Here, wF is the distance of the point of application of the weight from the fulcrum; and pF, the distance of the power from the fulcrum.

Comparisons between Power and Weight in Muscular Levers.—We may observe that the power always acts at a mechanical disadvantage in levers of the third order. As the majority of the levers which are used in animal locomotion, act at a mechanical disadvantage; I shall now investigate the cause of this apparent anomaly. I may first remark that the measure of work done by a force is found by multiplying the weight by the distance through which it has been moved. Thus, suppose two men are engaged in raising weights, one having a single block pulley to lift a weight of 25 lbs., while the other, to raise 100 lbs., uses a multiplying block which increases the power fourfold; the former will raise his 25 lbs. 4 ft. off the ground in the same time and with the same expenditure of force as the latter will lift his 100 lbs. to a height of 1 ft. In fact, what is gained in power is lost in distance. This law holds equally good with levers, as we may see from the fact, for instance, that a small amount of contraction of the muscle which bends the hock, causes the hind foot to move through a considerable space. Were the hock bent, for example, by a muscle that had its two points of attachment at the stifle and fetlock (instead, as is actually the case, at the stifle and a little below the hock), such muscle would act at far greater mechanical advantage than the present flexor of the hock; but it could not bend that joint to anything like the same extent, because muscles cannot contract to more than about two-thirds of their normal length. Besides, such an arrangement would be extremely inconvenient for everyday work, and would increase the liability of the limb to injury. Although there is, therefore, a very large expenditure of muscular force in the action of the levers of the limbs; there is an equally large gain in flexion and extension, and consequently in speed. This arrangement, also, enables the body to be made of a compact form, and to be suited to its surroundings.

Directions in which the Power and Weight respectively Act.—In the theoretical levers which I have given (*see* Figs. 6, 7, and 8), I have assumed that the power and weight acted at right angles to the lever, and that they were consequently parallel to each other. In the actual levers (those of the hock) which I have taken into consideration, we may see that this is not the case. I may mention that the nearer a force is to being at right angles with its lever, the greater is the mechanical advantage at which it will work. If, in a lever of the first order, for instance, we have the power and weight, as in Fig. 9, acting in directions which are not parallel to each other,

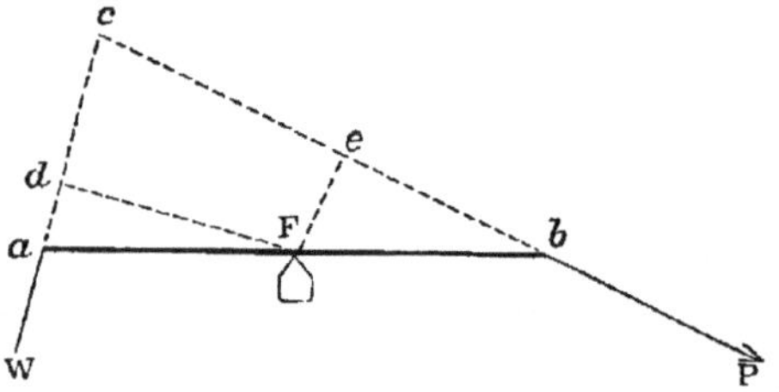

FIG. 9.—LEVER OF FIRST ORDER WITH DIRECTIONS OF POWER AND WEIGHT OBLIQUE TO EACH OTHER.

such forces (if the lever be in equilibrium) will then be inversely proportionate to the length of the perpendiculars drawn to their respective directions. Thus in Fig. 9 we have P : W :: F*d* : F*e*. We therefore see that W, which is nearly at right angles to *a b*, acts much more advantageously than P, which is in a much more oblique direction to it. This would be equally true in the other two kinds of levers. I need not stop to prove the foregoing well-known mechanical law, as its solution can be found in any book on elementary statics.

Acting on the principle just enunciated, the cart-horse, with the view of obtaining all the mechanical advantage he can when trying to draw a heavy load, will naturally endeavour to move the levers of his limbs (when straightening them out) with the power, as nearly as possible, at right angles to each respective lever. Hence he will obtain his results by only slight bending of the joints, and consequently his steps will be short. We may see this action of the levers of the hind limbs well shown by the manner in which he will crouch down behind when he makes a strong effort with his hind legs while exerting the fore legs but little, as may occur when the roadway is slippery. The galloper, on the contrary, will require the power of straightening out his limbs to their utmost extent (*see* p. 63), and will thus obtain speed at a lavish expenditure of muscular effort. This is especially well shown in the action of the fetlock joint (*see* Fig. 29); for if the pastern be long and sloping, the mechanical disadvantage will be great, but the gain in speed will be equally large. If the pastern be upright, the fetlock will work advantageously as far as the weight to be moved is concerned; but it will contribute little to the attainment of speed.

CHAPTER VIII.

MECHANISM OF EQUINE LOCOMOTION.

Displacement of the Centre of Gravity—Manner in which Propulsion is effected by the Limbs—Direction of Propulsion, and Distance through which the Centre of Gravity of the Body is moved—Comparative Speed in the Action of the Limbs—Action of the Muscles which extend the Vertebræ—Width between each respective Pair of Legs as affecting Speed—Effect of Insecurity of Equilibrium on Speed—Fatigue from the various Paces—Action of the Head and Neck in Locomotion—Mechanism of the Fetlock Joint—Mechanism of the Hock Joint.

THE remarks made under this heading should be taken in connection with those in the following five chapters. Some which are here given are necessary for the proper comprehension of the movements of the horse in his various paces, but others, in order that they may be understood, have been kept back, until the paces and draught have been discussed.

Displacement of the Centre of Gravity.—The actions which give rise to locomotion in the horse may be summed up as follows :—Advancement of a limb in order to bring a new base of support under the centre of gravity. Let us suppose that the man represented in Fig. 10 is standing with one foot advanced more than the other. His base of support (*a b*) will then be the area bounded by his feet and the lines joining them at each side. As long as the perpendicular (*p*) dropped from the centre of gravity falls within the base of support, the equilibrium of the body will be maintained. If the man, in this example, brings the centre of gravity of his body forward by straightening his left ankle joint, so that the perpendicular from the centre of gravity shall fall beyond the base of support (*see* Fig. 11); it will be evident that in order to prevent the body from falling, he will have to bring the rear leg (which in this case is the left one) beyond the perpendicular dropped from the centre of gravity (*see* Fig. 12). Precisely the same actions take place when the horse starts from the halt into the walk; for. by the straightening of one or both hind legs, he brings the centre of gravity of his body beyond the toe of the most advanced fore foot, with the result that the other fore leg has to be carried forward in order to restore the equilibrium. In doing this, the first foot to quit the ground will usually be a fore one. I may remark that a succession of these displacements and

FIG. 10.

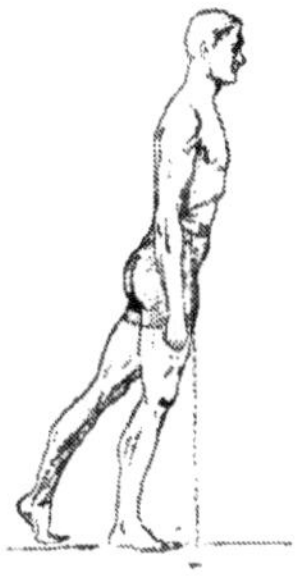

FIG. 11.

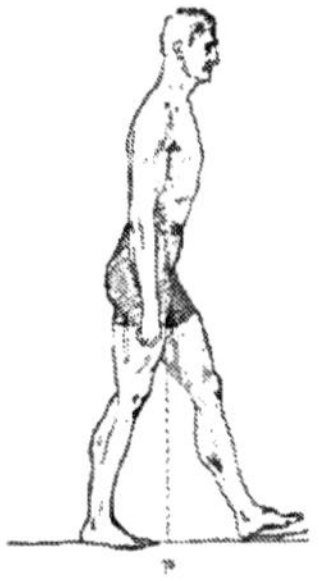

FIG. 12.

DISPLACEMENT OF CENTRE OF GRAVITY BY MAN WHEN WALKING.

recoveries will constitute the walk, run, or other pace. The same movements occur in leaping, except when the spring is made vertically upwards from a state of rest, in which case the centre of gravity is not displaced beyond the base of support.

Manner in which Propulsion is Effected by the Limbs.— The displacement of the centre of gravity, in the propulsion of the body, is accomplished by the straightening out of the limb or limbs, as the case may be. We can readily see how this gives the required impetus, if we consider the manner in which the shove-off is done by an expert swimmer in a bath, when he comes to the end of it, and wishes to touch, turn, and strike off without loss of time. He, as we all know, will, as much as possible, draw up the leg with which he is going to give the shove-off, and having applied it to the side of the bath (*see* Fig. 13), will suddenly straighten it out, with the result that his body will be shot forward (*see* Fig. 14). Here, the drawn-up leg, which acts as a spring, is placed between two objects: one (the body) movable, the other (the side of the bath) immovable. When the leg is extended, the movable object is naturally the one to be displaced. Identically the same action occurs in the various progressive movements of the horse. We may see it, also, in the run of the pedestrian, which is depicted

Fig. 13.

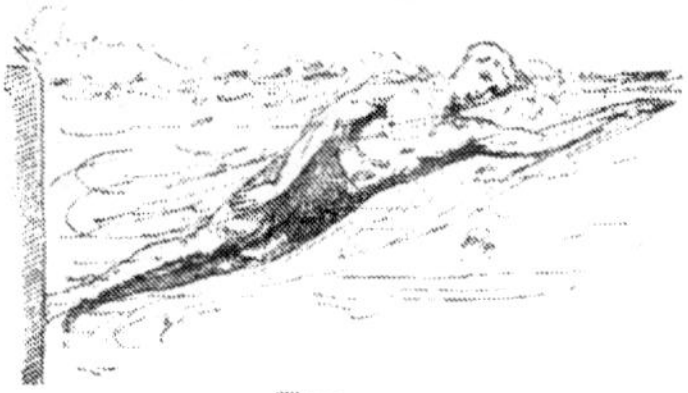

Fig. 14.

Shove-off from Side of Swimming-Bath.

Fig. 15.

Fig. 16.

Fig. 17.

Forward Propulsion of Man when Running.

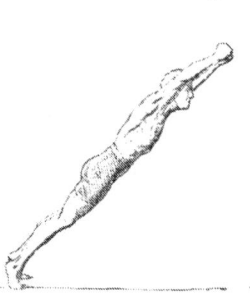

Fig. 18.

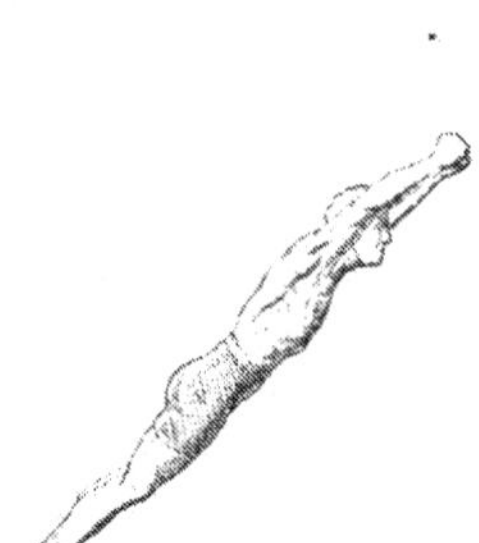

Fig. 19.

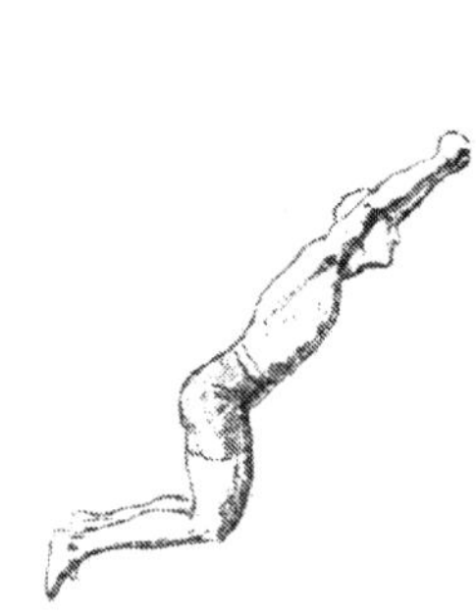

Fig. 20.

Fig. 21.

Forward Propulsion of Man in Standing Leap.

in Figs. 15, 16 and 17; for the right leg, which is a good deal bent in Fig. 15, is nearly straight in Fig. 16. The straightening of the limb or limbs, in effecting the forward propulsion of the body, is even better shown in Figs. 18, 19, 20 and 21, which depict the standing leap.

I may mention that the propulsion of the hind limb of the horse takes place through the hip joint and pelvis. The impetus from the fore leg at the various paces may be regarded as through the elbow joint and *humerus*.

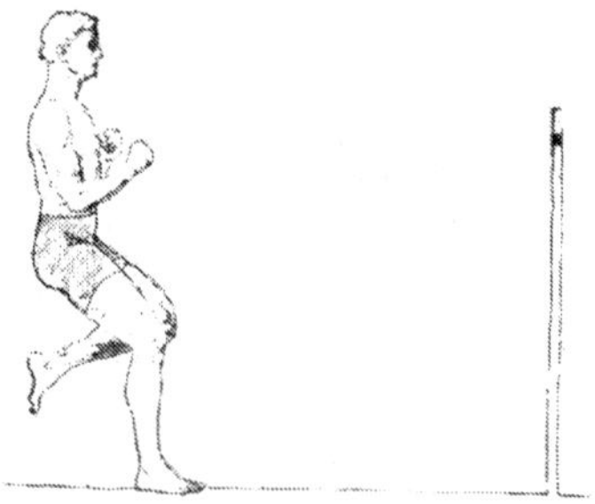

FIG. 22.

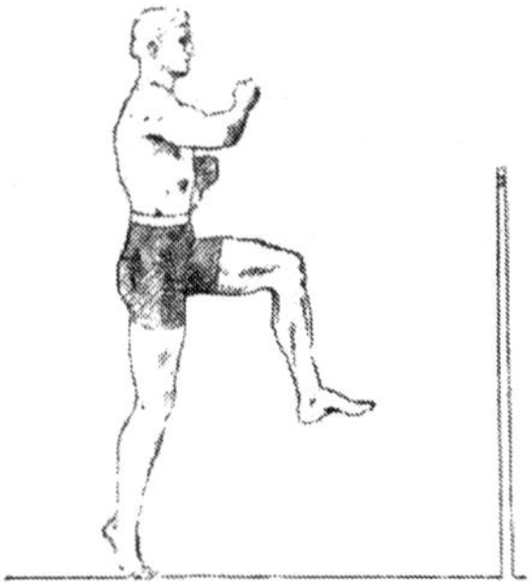

FIG. 23.

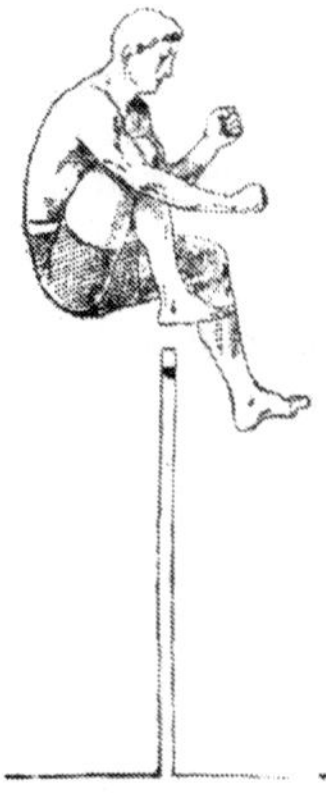

FIG. 24.

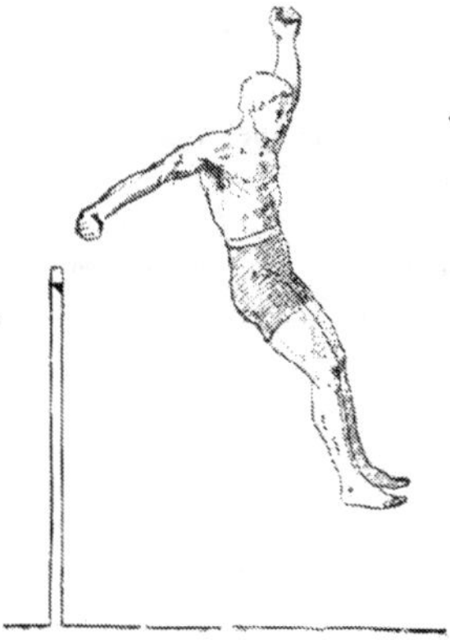

FIG. 25.

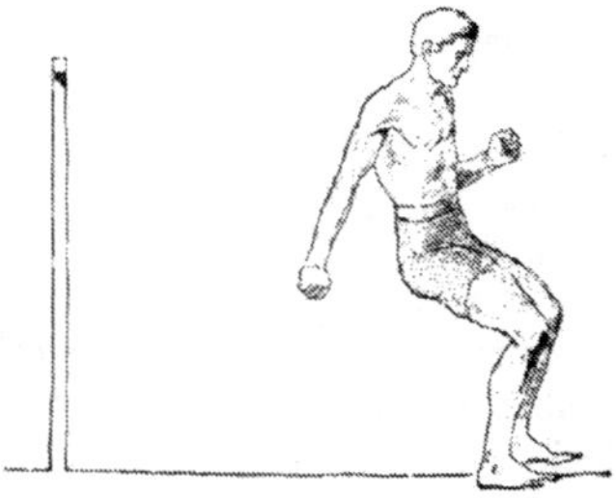

FIG. 26.

RUNNING HIGH LEAP OF MAN.

Direction of Propulsion and Distance through which the Centre of Gravity of the Body is Moved.—The direction of the propulsion given by a limb is necessarily through its column of bones. If we examine all the illustrations of the progressive movements of the horse, from Fig. 39 to Fig. 151, we shall see that in every case, just before a limb leaves the ground, it is directed backward and downward, as, for instance, the near hind in Fig. 54, and the off fore in Fig. 101. Hence the direction of propulsion in these cases must be forward and upward. The speed at which the body is moving will greatly influence the direction of the propulsion. Thus in Fig. 23, which is one of the series (Fig. 22 to Fig. 26) that shows the running high leap of a man, the impetus from the right leg is given vertically; yet the centre of gravity is projected forward at about an angle of 45° to the ground. The reason for this is, that in this case there are two forces of projection, namely, that derived from the

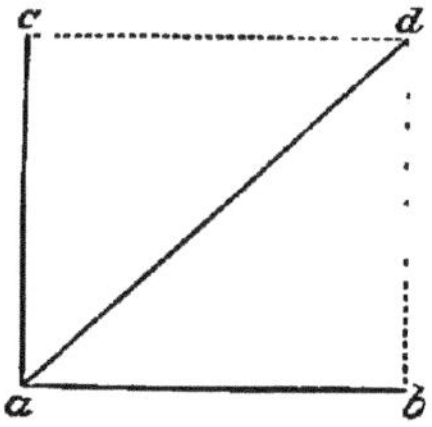

FIG. 27.—ANGLE OF PROJECTION OF CENTRE OF GRAVITY.

extension of the right leg, and that due to the speed at which the pedestrian ran up to the jump before he "took off." We have here the operation of "the parallelogram of forces." Thus, if the line *a b* in Fig. 27 represents the horizontal force (derived from the speed) and *a c* the vertical one (obtained from the right leg), and if we draw *c d* parallel to *a b*, and *b d* parallel to *a c*, we shall have the resultant force represented by the line *a d*, and the angle of elevation, equal to the angle *d a b*.

The upward motion given by the limb to the body is necessary to keep up the centre of gravity, which, if we wish the labour to be accomplished with a minimum amount of muscular effort, should be maintained as nearly as possible at one uniform height from the ground; for the distance through which the centre of gravity is moved, will be a measure of the work done. Let us suppose at each step of a yard long by a horse, that the centre of gravity falls 4 inches, and that the animal has to go a distance of 1000 yards on a horizontal plane. It is evident that, in this case, the muscles of the horse's limbs would not alone have to carry the weight of the body 1000 yards, but would also have to raise it $333\frac{1}{3}$ feet ($1000 \times \frac{1}{3}$), which would be approximately equivalent to going over a hill that was $333\frac{1}{3}$ feet high and whose base was 1000 yards broad. I need hardly say that the less the fall and rise at each step, the lower this supposititious hill would be, and, consequently, the easier it would be to walk over.

Although the duty of forward propulsion is chiefly performed by the hind limbs; the greater part of the work of adjusting the position of the centre of gravity during ordinary locomotion, falls on the fore limbs. When a horse, for instance, performs the high-school feat of cantering to the rear, the respective roles would obviously be reversed. The question of the adjustment of the centre of gravity of the body, so that the muscles of locomotion may act to the best possible advantage, will be considered further on.

Comparative Speed in the Action of the Limbs.—The speed with which the body is projected forward, is directly proportionate to the speed with which the limb or limbs are straightened out, and has nothing to do with the strength of the muscles that move the parts. Hence, any excess of muscular development beyond that required for the due working of the limbs, will tend to diminish the speed by unnecessarily adding to the weight to be carried. For this reason, we never see great race-horses of the weight-carrying hunter build. Some of the best (St. Simon and Tim Whiffler, for instance) have been slight horses. In fact, the son of Galopin and St. Angela (*see* Pls. 7 and 18) had singularly light hind quarters. Even Ormonde, who was very muscular for a race-horse, was anything but broad when viewed from behind (*see* Frontispiece).

The question of the speed of muscular contraction is an abstruse one which still remains unsettled. We know that if a muscle be stimulated by a shock of electricity, it will contract throughout its entire length at (practically) the same moment. Hence, under this condition, a long muscle would contract very nearly in the same time as a short one. When, however, a muscle is stimulated by the nerves which act in obedience to the will, the contraction of its various parts does not take place simultaneously, though at such a brief interval that we may regard the delay as unappreciable. Hence, in two limbs which resemble each other in every particular, except that one is short and the other long, the respective extension of both will be accomplished in very nearly the same time, and consequently, the speed of

TO FACE PAGE 62

PLATE 7—THE DUKE OF PORTLAND'S ST. SIMON.

the propulsion derived from the long leg will exceed that from the short one in nearly the proportion which their lengths bear to each other. This conclusion is in accordance with M. Marey's statement (*see* p. 4), that muscles of speed are long muscles. Besides this, physiology teaches us that the thicker muscles are, the slower, other things being equal, do they contract on becoming stimulated? We should content ourselves with taking a broad view of this subject, for conditions vary so much in individual cases, that it is not safe to dogmatise on it.

I need hardly say to those of my readers who have followed me so far, that the greater the ability to straighten the leg, the higher will be the speed of propulsion, and *vice versâ*. Hence, if a horse is, for instance, unable from peculiarity of conformation to straighten his hocks (a condition called "sickle-hocks," *see* Pl. 49), he will not be so fast as he would have been, had he greater freedom in these joints. We may test the truth of this principle in our own selves; for if, when swimming in a bath (*see* p. 58), we wanted to touch and turn, but were unable to straighten our knee on account of an injury or from some other cause, we would be capable of giving only a comparatively poor kick-off. The great beauty of a "straight dropped hind leg" (*see* Pl. 51), in the horse, as a conformation favourable to speed, will again be alluded to on p. 236.

The action of the fore limb in raising the forehand, which is essential for the regulation of the position of the centre of gravity in locomotion, is also dependent on its difference of length when bent and when straightened out. It is manifest that this difference is mainly due to the action of the shoulder joint and of the fetlock. Hence, oblique shoulders and sloping pasterns are "points" of speed and of leaping power. If the shoulder-blade and pastern be already upright, the limb will be capable of but slight extension.

In heavy draught, full straightening out of the limbs is not desirable; for the last part of this action is accomplished at a great mechanical disadvantage, to which I have alluded on page 56. At present it is sufficient to compare the action of the limbs to that of the oars of a boat, in which the practically useful work is finished after the oars have passed the line at right angles to the length of the boat, the remainder of the propulsive effect being obtained by a wasteful expenditure of force. Consequently, an increase of speed is procured by an amount of work that is greatly out of proportion to the result. Thus, to double the speed during a certain period of time, it may be necessary for the horse to do five or six times the amount of muscular exertion. For instance, it may be more fatiguing for a horse to go twenty miles in one hour, than fifty miles in five hours. The cart-horse, when in heavy draught, moves his load with his hind limbs in a more or less bent condition (*see* Fig. 72), which will give his hind quarters the crouching appearance which must be familiar to us all. Sloping pasterns from a load-pulling point of view are objectionable in the cart-horse; for the more oblique they are, the greater is the mechanical disadvantage at which they work (*see* p. 69). Sloping shoulders, also, from the same point of view, are undesirable.

Action of the Muscles which extend the Vertebræ.—When a horse prepares to kick, he, as a general rule, lowers his head and arches his loins ("puts his back up"), by doing which he relieves his hind quarters of weight and puts it on his forehand. When, on the contrary, he prepares to rear, he raises his head and neck and more or less hollows his loins, so as to lighten his forehand and put more weight on his hind quarters. If we examine Figs. 81 and 82 of the canter, Figs. 90 to 94 of the gallop, and Figs. 140 to 144 of the leap, we shall see that the muscles which enable a horse to rear, greatly aid the forward reach of the fore legs in the canter and gallop. Also, the heavier the forehand, the greater difficulty will they have to raise it. In the leap, they assist the leading fore leg in raising the forehand. If the horse carries a rider, these muscles will have an increased amount of work to do on account of extra weight being put in front, and will tire in a proportionately rapid rate. On examining the drawings of horses in Chapter XII. at the various paces, we shall see that the faster the movement, the more will these muscles be taxed, on account of the greater distance of the centre of gravity from the hind feet, while one or both of which support and propel forward the weight of the body. Hence we find that to gallop fast or to jump "big," a horse must have good "rearing muscles," which consist principally of those which straighten the hock, draw back the thigh, and extend the vertebræ of the loins. These muscles also help to "lighten" the forehand in the flying trot and fast "pacing," in both of which there is a period of suspension, which will vary in length according to the weight that is on the forehand. From these considerations I may lay down the law that the faster the speed required, the stronger should the "rearing muscles" be. The pair of them (one on each side) that is most readily noticed, is the loin muscles, which in the ox constitute the upper cut of a sirloin, and which, in the horse, we may see just behind the cantle of the saddle. I need hardly say that the heavier the shoulder, the sooner will these muscles become tired, the shorter will be the stride; and the slower will be the pace. Consequently, horses for fast work ought to have light shoulders. Carrying out the same train of reasoning, we may see that the longer a horse's body, the greater will be the mechanical disadvantage at which these muscles will work; hence, a short body is a desirable point in the race-horse and jumper.

The combined working of oblique shoulders, well-sloped pasterns and strong rearing muscles, by preventing the forehand going down at each stride, aids in obtaining the much admired "level" action in the race-horse. An animal which has a long body, heavy shoulders, upright pasterns, and weak loins (showing deficiency in the points just advocated), will, if he be put to a gallop, go in an up-and-down style; because his rearing muscles will be over-taxed by the weight of the forehand at the end of the long lever made by his body, and because his fetlock joints will have deficient "play."

I may remark that, although the loin muscles appear to be almost quiescent during easy walking and gentle trotting, they may be observed to act energetically in flexing and extending the loins when the animal is leaping, galloping, and when his powers are taxed in drawing a heavy load. Any one who has ridden races or gallops on speedy thoroughbreds, will know from experience the immense power behind the saddle possessed by animals of this class; for the rider cannot fail to feel the vigorous "lift" given by the loins at each stride.

It is a popular fallacy to imagine that the muscles over the loins are propellers. They have no propelling power at all; for they are not connected either with the thigh bone, or with any of the bones of the limb below it; their office in locomotion being merely to regulate the weight on the forehand. I may mention that the muscles (those which constitute the under-cut in a saddle of mutton, or in sirloin of beef) under the loins draw the thigh forward.

Width between each respective Pair of Legs as affecting Speed.—Let us suppose that the rectangle *a b e d* (*see* Fig. 28) diagrammatically represents the body of the horse, that the fore limbs are placed at the angles *a* and *b*; that the hind limbs are at *d* and *e*; and that the centre of gravity is at *c*. Were both fore legs and both hind legs to act respectively at the same moment, we would have the centre of gravity moved in a straight line, and in the direction in which the animal's body was placed. In the amble (*see* p. 101), the propulsion is given through *a* and *d*, and through *b* and *e* alternately, with the result, in the former case, that the centre of gravity is displaced to the right, and in the latter to the left. In the trot (*see* p. 97), the alternate strokes are through *a* and *e*, and *b* and *d*. If these respective propulsions, in the trot, were equal to each other, and if the centre of gravity were midway between the fore and hind legs, there would be no displacement of it from side to side. As however the impetus derived from the hind limb is greater than that from the fore leg, and as the centre of gravity is nearer the latter than the former, there is a certain tendency to lateral displacement, which has to be corrected by muscular effort. This tendency to a rocking movement from side to side is naturally greater in the amble than it is in the trot. In the gallop there is a strong tendency to lateral displacement; for at this pace each leg gives its own separate stroke (*see* p 112). When either of the near ones act, the centre of gravity is canted to the right; when the off ones make their respective effort, it is thrown to the left. The retention of the centre of gravity in a more or less straight line, entails a certain expenditure of muscular work, and consequent fatigue.

It is evident that the nearer (*see* Fig. 28) *a* is to *b*, and *d* to *e*, the less

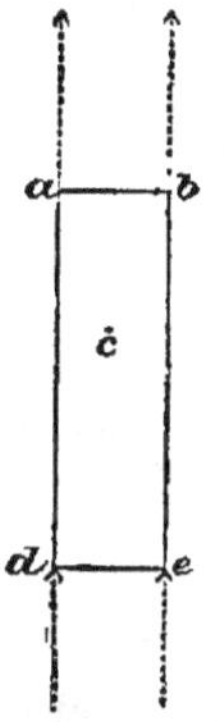

FIG. 28.—LATERAL DISPLACEMENT OF BODY.

will be the lateral displacement of the centre of gravity, and the smaller the loss of speed from this cause. Hence we find that in animals of great speed, like the cheetah, antelope, greyhound, and race-horse, both the fore and hind legs are respectively placed much closer together than in animals of comparatively greater strength, but of slower movement. The faster the pace (*see* p. 124), the more do the footprints of the horse tend to come into the line of the direction in which movement is taking place. This principle is well exemplified in man; for all fast walkers, runners, and skaters try to place the feet, at each step, as nearly as possible, in one straight line.

As I have already said, this tendency to lateral displacement of weight is corrected to a certain extent, in his various paces, by the horse, who has, however, to do it by a muscular effort, which is a lost force as regards propulsion.

Effect of Instability of Equilibrium on Speed.—The more unstable the equilibrium is, during each step of the horse at any particular pace, the greater will be the speed which can be developed at that pace, whatever it may be. This follows from the fact that the more insecure is the equilibrium, the quicker, when it is displaced, will the new base of support have to be formed. Thus, in the walk of the horse (*see* p. 102) there are never less than two feet on the ground; three as often as two; and sometimes even four. In the canter (*see* p. 109), we have respectively in three steps, a support of one foot, of two (or of three) feet, and of one foot. In the trot and amble, there are two feet on the ground during each step. From this we may conclude that the canter is a faster pace, naturally, than the trot or amble. I am aware that this is not the case with many horses which have been specially trained for match-trotting and match-pacing; but that fact does not bear on the subject in question Of all paces, the gallop is the one in which the equilibrium is most unstable; for during each stride of it, the centre of gravity is carried farther beyond the base of support (*see* Fig. 101) than at any other pace. Besides, at each step in it, there are fewer feet together on the ground than at any other pace.

As it is imperative that the body of an animal intended for speed should be as light as possible, provided he has sufficient bone and muscle to meet his requirements; the preponderance of weight on the forehand should be obtained by conformation, and not by any approach to "heaviness" in that part.

Fatigue from the various Paces.—In comparing the fatigue undergone during certain paces, we must be guided by the consideration of the respective distances through which the centre of gravity of the body has to be moved. Let us first of all consider its vertical, and afterwards its horizontal, displacement out of the straight line of the direction in which it has to travel. In the walk and at all other paces in which there is no period of suspension (*see* p. 96), it is carried nearly parallel to the ground, with only a slight fall when each fore leg is taken up At paces in which there is a period of suspension, the centre of gravity will have to be raised just as much as it will fall during that time. This fact is best marked in jumping; for in making even a long leap, the centre of gravity will have to be raised a considerable height. Thus, when Howard of Bradford, the famous jumper and sprinter, leaped over a full-sized billiard-table lengthwise, he was computed to have cleared a height of five feet four inches. Hence, animals like the antelope, and cheetah, which adopt, when going at full speed, a leaping style of gallop (*see* p. 128), can keep it up only for a short time. This fact is particularly well marked in the case of the kangaroo. For the same reason, a horse can go a distance with more ease to himself at a slow trot (which has no period of suspension), than at the flying trot (*see* p. 98) or gallop (*see* p. 112), in both of which there is a period of suspension. Not alone does the consideration of the comparative rise and fall of the centre of gravity give us an idea of the relative fatigue undergone during the various paces; but it also furnishes us with a guide to judge of the comparative ease with which different horses move at the same pace. Consequently, we may conclude that the more "level" a horse goes, whether at the fast trot, gallop, or other pace, the less will he fatigue himself: a fact which proves how thoroughly reasonable is the admiration every good judge has for a "level" style of movement—that is, one in which there is the least possible rise and fall of the forehand at each stride. I have purposely used the word "forehand" here. When noting whether the action of a horse is level or not, we are usually guided by the presence or absence of up-and-down motion in the forehand; for the special prominence of the head and neck will more or less rivet the attention of the eyes. Besides this, the centre of gravity of the horse's body is nearer his fore legs than his hind ones.

I may mention that as soon as fast antelopes, like the Indian Black Buck and South African Springbok, get tired in their bounding kind of gallop, they "settle down" to one resembling that of the horse (*see* Figs. 90 to 105). When the cheetah—who, as far as I can make out, gallops like the cat (*see* Figs. 126 to 131), in a succession of leaps—becomes tired of that pace, he drops into a walk or trot.

On page 66 I have alluded to the effects of the lateral displacement of the centre of gravity in causing fatigue.

The pace which is the speediest, is also the most fatiguing; for, as in fast paces, the centre of gravity will be carried further beyond its base of support than at slow ones, a greater muscular effort will be required in them to form a new base of support. We may see this if we compare, one with another, Figs. 42, 45, 55, 79, and 101.

Action of the Head and Neck in Locomotion.—During movement, the head and neck act as a balancing pole in changing the position of the centre of gravity from one side to the other, and in raising or depressing it. Certain muscles of the neck draw the fore limb forward and upward; other muscles of the neck straighten out the head and neck, and a third group bend them.

Mechanism of the Fetlock Joint.—As Lecoq explains, "the weight of the body, transmitted by the cannon-bone upon the upper articulating surface of the long pastern bone, is the resistance to be overcome. The fulcrum is the ground at the toe of the foot, and the power acts upon the sesamoid bones, which are at the back of the pastern; the shortening of the flexor muscles being the cause of the straightening of the angle formed by their tendons." The diagram given in Fig. 29 will show how this lever (one of the second order) acts. In it we see that the distance between the power and weight remains constant; but that their respective distances from the fulcrum vary according to the slope of the pastern and hoof, and according to the length from the fetlock to the toe. Hence (*see* pp. 52 and 54), the shorter

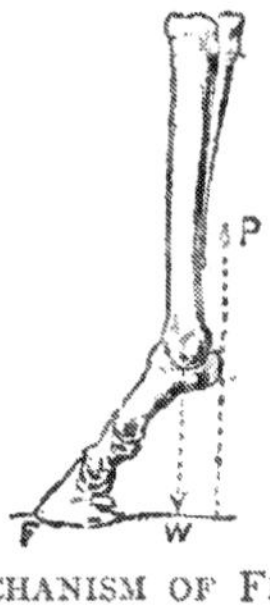

FIG. 29.—MECHANISM OF FETLOCK JOINT.

is this line, the greater will be the mechanical advantage at which the back tendons will act; and *vice versâ.* On the other hand, we may see that the more is the mechanical gain, the worse will the fetlock act as a spring, which function is all-important in saving the limb (especially the fore one) from the injurious effects of concussion. It is evident that the distance of the weight (or power) from the fulcrum (F) is influenced by the length and slope of the pastern; it being greatest when the pastern is long and oblique, and least when that part is short and upright. I may point out that increased growth of hoof, either at the toe or heel, will affect the slope in question, and that the thickness of horn at the toe will, of course, influence the length from the fetlock to the toe. As a practical point I may remark that the toe (except in the treatment of some forms of disease) should always be kept "short," and that shoes should be no thicker at the toes than what would be sufficient to enable them to stand "wear." I need not allude further to this subject, as I have considered it in my *Veterinary Notes for Horse Owners*.

Mechanism of the Hock Joint.- Figs. 30, 31, and 32, show the three actions of this joint as a lever.

Besides flexion and extension, this joint has an outward motion, due to the outward and forward direction of the pulley formed by the astragalus.

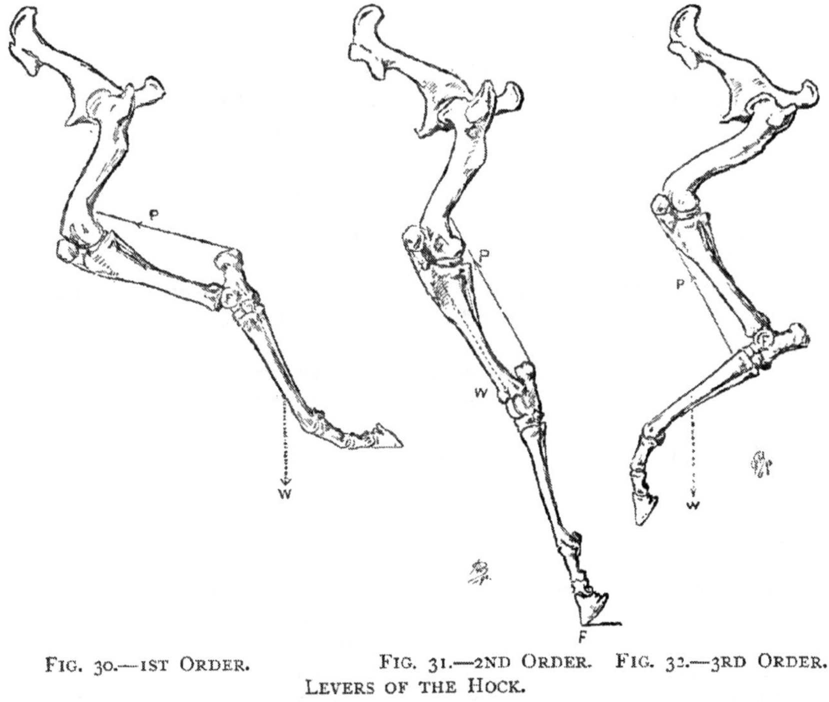

FIG. 30.—1ST ORDER. FIG. 31.—2ND ORDER. FIG. 32.—3RD ORDER.
LEVERS OF THE HOCK.

We find, contrary to what we might have expected from an inspection of this bone, that this oblique play of the hock joint does not affect the direction in which the hind foot is carried; its object being, as explained by M. H. Bouley, to allow the stifle to clear the belly, when the hind limb is brought forward.

CHAPTER IX.

MECHANISM OF DRAUGHT.

DRAUGHT in the collar or breast-harness is, as explained by M. Colin, an act of pushing, and not one of *pulling*. The only kind of draught I have ever heard of, which could be put under the latter heading, is that of making a horse draw by attaching the weight to his tail, like what farmers in some countries used to do long ago, when they wanted to plough!

Propulsion in draught, like in other forms of locomotion, is effected by placing a series of levers, bent on one another, between a fixed point and a movable one. In locomotion of the body itself, the series of levers are those only of the limbs. The movable point, in the hind limb, is the portion of the pelvis against which the head of the thigh bone rests; and in the fore extremity, the lower end of the humerus. In harness, on the contrary, the series of levers is that between the spot against which the foot rests and the centre of pressure on the inner surface of the collar, which, in this case, is the movable point.

In Fig. 33, the line A B represents the direction of the propelling force given by the hind leg which is on the ground; and E B, that by the fore limb; B being the assumed centre of pressure. The resultant of these two forces must pass somewhere between the points A and E, and through the point B. But it is impossible to fix its exact direction; as we cannot determine the respective amounts of these two forces, and as the proportion they bear to each other continually varies. If two hind feet, as in Fig. 70, were engaged in pushing against the collar at the same time, the direction of their resultant would naturally pass between them and between the two points occupied by the respective centres of pressure on each side of the collar. From a practical point of view, we may assume that this centre of pressure, on each side, is on a level with that portion of the harness to which each respective trace is attached. This would place it somewhere between the middle and lower third of the bearing surface of the collar.

The force applied to the collar by the animal is obtained in two different ways, first, by the weight of the animal, and second, by the force of propulsion to which I have just alluded.

The weight of the animal acts on the collar by reason of the centre of gravity being placed in front of the base of support (*see* p. 57), the anterior limit of which is marked by the position of the toe of the fore foot which is on the ground. It is evident that the further a perpendicular dropped from the centre of gravity falls in front of the base of support, the more effectively

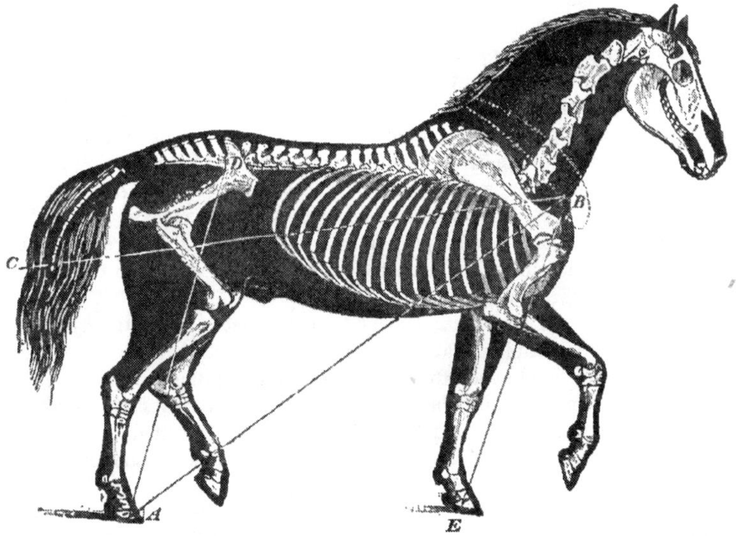

FIG. 33.—MECHANISM OF DRAUGHT. (From Colin's *Physiologie Comparée.*)

will the weight of the body act in propulsion. This forward translation of the centre of gravity with reference to the position of the base of support, is influenced, first, by the degree of slope which the fore leg makes with the ground immediately before it quits it, and before the other fore leg is brought down; and, second, by the lowering of the head and neck. I need hardly say that horses with toe-pieces to their fore shoes can bring the centre of gravity farther beyond the base of support, by the slope of the fore leg which rests on the ground, than they could do with flat shoes; supposing, of course, that the surface of the ground was not abnormally smooth and hard, like wood or asphalte. From the foregoing considerations we may draw, with respect to cart-horses that are required to exert their strength to the utmost, the following deductions, which are fairly self-evident to practical men.

1. Bodily weight, especially in the forehand, is an advantage in draught; for the greater it is, the more effective will be the push against the collar caused by the centre of gravity falling beyond the base of support. Agreeably to this fact, the experienced driver of a heavily-laden two-wheeled cart will endeavour to place a fair share of the burden on the animal's back, so that the horse may pull to the best advantage. The experiment of a man succeeding in pulling along a stronger man than himself, by trying to do so, while carrying a heavy weight on his back, is another familiar instance of this principle. The gain in power from increased weight on the forehand is, also, well illustrated by the practice, which is not very uncommon among drivers of one-horse carts, of the driver mounting his animal and getting well forward on its back, when he finds that it is unable to pull its load up a hill.

2. The cart-horse ought to have a heavy neck as well as massive shoulders. As a natural corollary to this proposition, which infers the lowering of the head and neck, we must condemn the use of bearing reins with the class of horse which we are now considering.

3. The shoes of the horse should have toe-pieces when the ground is favourable to their employment.

On the other hand, when the horse, on account of the slippery nature of the ground, is unable to use his fore legs, except to a very slight degree, as propellers, the forehand should be light and the head carried high. Thus, the weight has to be kept almost entirely off the shafts of London hansom cab-horses, which would be rendered very liable to fall down on the greasy wood pavement and glass-like asphalte, if a fair proportion of the load were to be put on their backs. Not alone is weight kept off their backs, but as a rule it is so distributed as to cause the backband to exert on the "girth-place" an upward pressure, which, naturally, will more or less aid in "lightening" the forehand.

The force of propulsion given by the hind limb is dependent on a series of levers which extends from the toe of the hind foot, along the bones of the hind leg, pelvis, spinal column, up to the centre of pressure on the inner side of the collar. It is manifest that the flatter this irregular line of levers is, with reference to the line of propulsion from the toe of the hind foot to the collar, the greater will be the mechanical advantage at which the hind limb will act. Consequently, we may infer that the cart-horse should be long in the body, as compared to his height, that he should be lower over the croup than he is at the withers; and that he should not have a horizontal croup. We should not, however, desire his hind quarters to be so drooping as to cause him to be actually "goose-rumped" (*see* p. 233).

The amount of forward propulsion given by the fore limb varies according to the position of the humerus; for the more horizontal is this bone, the more effective will be the push. As its degree of slope with the ground is directly affected by that of the shoulder blade, it follows that the shoulders of the cart-horse which has to fully exert the powers of his fore legs in propulsion, should be more upright than sloping.

It is a well-known mathematical fact that the most advantageous direction for the pull in draught to be, is one which makes an angle with the ground equal to the *angle of friction*. I may explain that if, for instance, 10° was the greatest slope of ground upon which a body could rest without sliding down, its angle of friction would be equal to 10°. The best direction then of the traces would be at an angle to the ground equal to the angle of friction. In many cases the pull of the traces is not at a sufficient angle to the ground, and the work is consequently performed at a mechanical disadvantage, which might be remedied by the employment of a taller horse than the one used, by having smaller wheels, or by a change in the harnessing arrangement. For instance, in such a case, instead of attaching the traces to the hooks on the shafts of a dog-cart, they might be connected, as is sometimes done, to the axletree. In the Indian *ecka* (*see* Pl. 8), the slope of the shafts, which act as traces, appears to have been made with due regard to the angle of friction of this cart with the ground.

PHOTO BY M. H. HAYES

TO FACE PAGE 74

PLATE 8 AN INDIAN "ECKA" AND PONY.

CHAPTER X.

ATTITUDES OF THE HORSE.

Standing at Attention—Standing Collectedly—Standing at Ease—Carriage of the Head and Neck.

Standing at Attention.—When a well-shaped and sound horse *stands at attention*, if I may use the term, he has his head and neck raised, ears pricked forward, the profile of the face at an angle of about 45° to the ground, and at about a right angle to the upper line of the neck (the crest); the weight proportionately distributed on all four limbs; and, as a rule, the fore foot of one side not so far advanced as its fellow, and its hind foot more to the front than the other hind foot (*see* Pl. 35). If the hind feet be equally advanced, a perpendicular line dropped from the point of the buttock will, on the respective sides, about touch the point of the hock. If one hind foot be placed in front of the other hind foot, the vertical line will, more or less, divide the interval between the points of the two hocks. As the weight of the horse's head and neck is beyond the base of support formed on the ground by his feet, he would "stand over" on his fore legs—that is, their direction would be downward and backward—if they were equally advanced, and if each of the limbs was bearing its due share of weight. Hence, when one fore leg is advanced more than its fellow, and when it is vertical, the animal will be somewhat over on the other fore leg (*see* Pl. 15).

French writers consider that when a horse stands with the weight properly distributed on all his limbs, a line dropped from each point of his buttock will coincide with the posterior edge of his hind leg, from the point of the hock to the fetlock; and that the direction of the front legs will be vertical, as in Fig. 34, which I have taken from MM. Goubaux

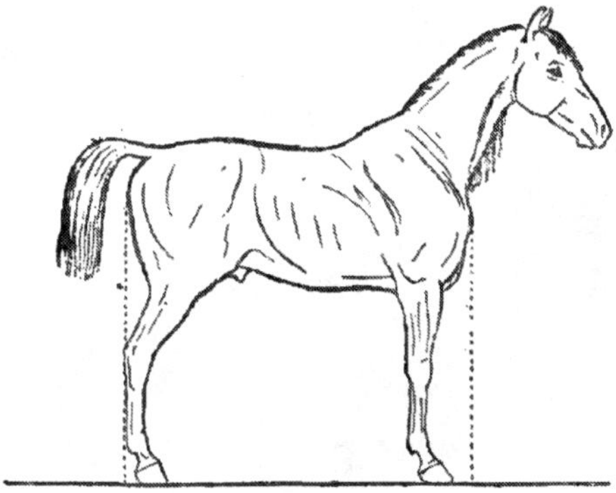

FIG. 34.—LE PLACER.

and Barrier's *L'Extérieur du Cheval.* It may be possible to make a horse assume this attitude (Fr. *le placer*); but I must say I have never seen a horse adopt it. Fig. 35 is the nearest approach in a well-bred horse to this position that I have been able to get in a photograph, of which this illustration is an exact copy.

In the *front view of the horse*—when he is standing in an unconstrained position, with his feet equally advanced and a little distance apart—the forearms will slightly converge, and

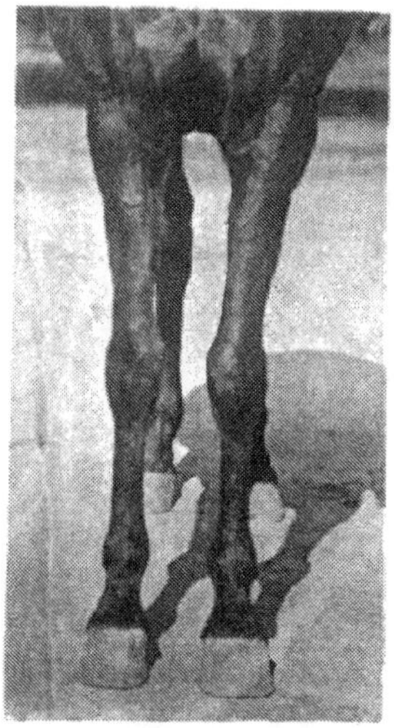

PL. 9—WELL-SHAPED FORE LEGS.

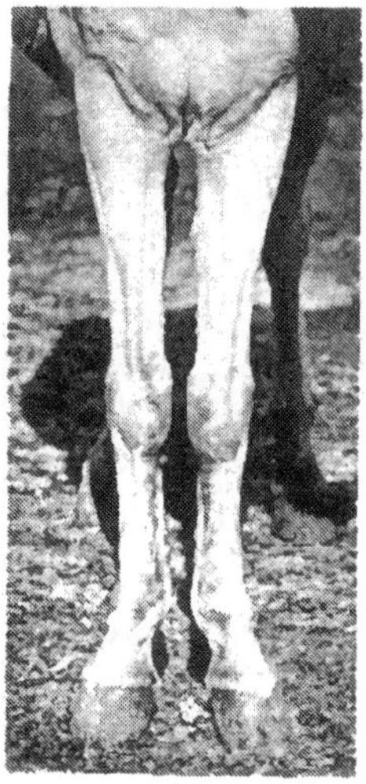

PL. 10—TURNED-OUT TOES.

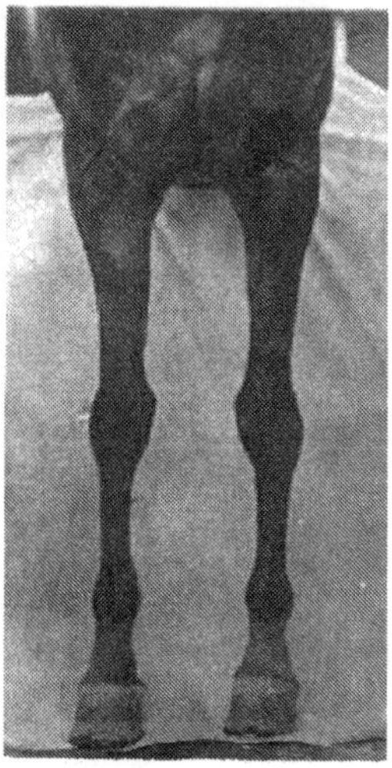

PL. 11—TURNED-IN TOES.

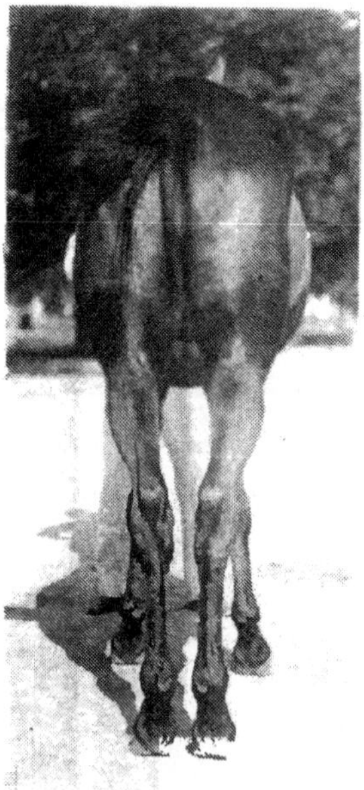

PHOTO. BY M. H. [illegible]

PL. 12—WELL-SHAPED HIND LEGS

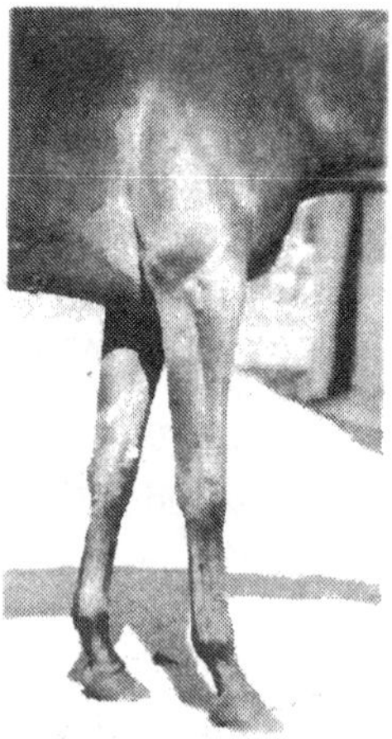

PL. 13—UPRIGHT PASTERNS.

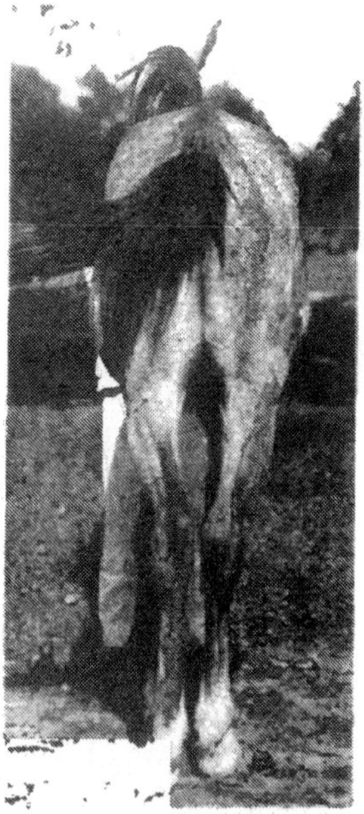

TO FACE PAGE 76

PL. 14—TURNED-IN HOCKS.

the cannon-bones will be about parallel to each other (*see* Pl. 9). A vertical and longitudinal plane passing through the centre of the knee and fetlock of each leg will cut the centre of the toe. In Pl. 10 the toes are turned out, and in Pl. 11 they are turned in.

The rear view of the horse is shown in Pl. 12, in which we can see that the hocks are slightly turned in and the toes

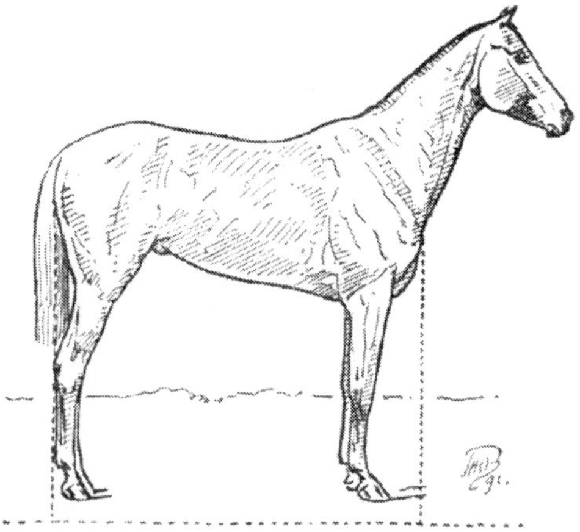

Fig. 35.—Standing at Attention.

a trifle turned out. The hind legs here depicted were symmetrically shaped. Although I have devoted much careful study to this subject, I can apply no geometrical rules to determine, as some have done, the correct shape of the legs from this point of view. It can, in my opinion, be judged only by the trained eye of the observer—I mean in deciding whether the hocks are correctly placed, turned in, or turned out. In Pl. 14 the hocks are, to a marked extent, turned in.

Standing "Collectedly."—This is the position (*see* Fig. 36) a horse assumes when he makes ready to move quickly away from the place in which he is standing. His hind feet will be well in front of a perpendicular line dropped from the points of the buttocks, his fore feet will be brought back more than usual, and he will stand more or less over on them. His head and neck will be raised, and he will be looking to his front, with his ears pricked forward, if he be one of the quick, observant class.

FIG. 36.—STANDING COLLECTEDLY.

Many persons who hold decided views on horse conformation, maintain that a true shaped horse will, when he stands, have his hind legs "well under him," as in Fig. 36; such a position being regarded by them as a point of conformation, and not as an attitude. To prove the fallacy of this idea, I may mention that the same mare, photographed on the same day, is shown in Fig. 36 and Pl. 15. In the former, her hind legs are well under her, in the latter they are a little

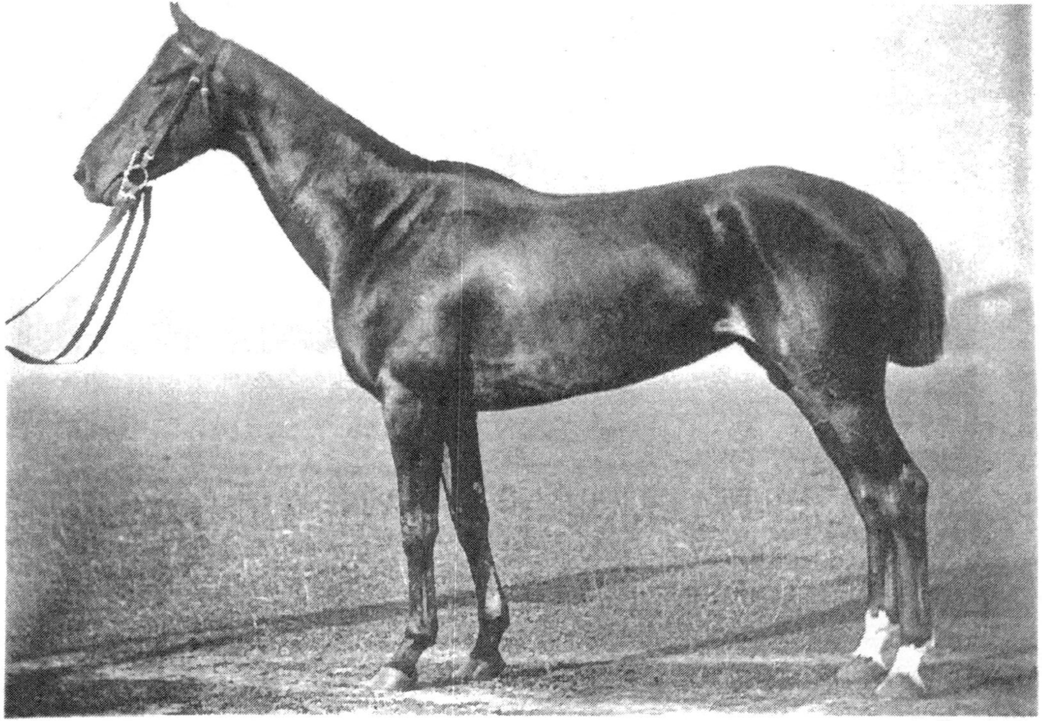

PHOTO. BY M. H. HAYES

TO FACE PAGE 78

PLATE 15—MR. GREGORY'S IRISH HUNTER, STEPASIDE.

behind her; the difference being merely one of position or attitude. With reference to this subject, I need hardly say that a horse may assume many attitudes, but he has only one kind of conformation. On the other hand, however, we must not ignore the fact that if a horse is unable to bend the joints (the hocks, fetlocks and pastern joints are the ones which are usually affected) of his hind limbs properly, he will naturally refrain from bringing his hind feet forward, when standing or moving to the front, as freely as he would do were his hind limbs in good working order. In judging of this, we should form our opinion more from the action of the animal during movement, than from the position he takes up when standing; although both should of course be considered.

Standing at Ease.—The sound horse will, almost always, when standing at ease, have both fore feet equally advanced, and with his weight chiefly on them; for he can obtain this support in front, without muscular effort on his part (to which fact I shall presently again refer), and consequently without fatigue. His head will be lowered, and will be supported by the suspensory ligament of the neck, the action of which is also accomplished without fatigue (*see* p. 33). As the hind limbs are unprovided with an apparatus by which they can bear weight without fatigue, their muscles have to obey the law which requires, for the health of muscular tissue, alternate periods of rest and work. Hence, one hind limb is rested by its joints being bent and its heel raised, while its fellow supports the weight of the hind quarters. When the working limb becomes tired, the other one takes its turn of work; and so on.

The fore limbs of the horse are furnished with special

fibrous bands (ligaments) which, during rest, take the weight off the muscles that straighten the various joints. I may here remind my readers that these ligaments are composed of hard, inelastic, fibrous tissue, and act simply as strong cords in connecting the parts together The work they do being entirely of a passive nature; they do not get tired, like muscles, the work of which is of an active form, and cannot be continued without suitable intervals of rest. As an instance of this "bracing" function of ligaments, I may mention that the fetlock is passively supported during rest (taken in a standing position) by an inelastic fibrous cord, which goes behind the fetlock point, and is attached by one end to the head of the cannon-bone, and by the other to the base of the pedal bone. Not alone are the fore legs provided with these special ligaments, to prevent the limbs from "doubling up"; but most of the muscles which straighten these limbs during work are composed of a large amount of ligamentous fibres. Such muscles, therefore, during their periods of rest, can assume to some extent the functions of ligaments. In fact, one powerful muscle in the fore leg of the dog is represented in the horse by a ligament. Besides this, the muscles which straighten the fore limb are not single, but multiple muscles, one of which can take its turn at work, while its fellows rest.

This mechanism enables the horse to sleep standing without extraneous support. It is clearly and exhaustively described in Colin's *Physiologie Comparée.*

Carriage of the Head and Neck.—The attitude which the head and neck assume is determined by the following considerations: (1) *For the horse to be able to see in the required direction.* If we regard a horse that is standing at attention (*see* p. 75), and is looking straight in front of him, we shall, as a rule, note that his neck is held in an easy position, being neither stretched out nor drawn back, and his head is placed so that the line of his face will make an angle of about 45° to the ground. We may, therefore, consider that the axis of each eye is at about that angle to the line of the face. In man, the angle is about 90°, the difference between the two being chiefly one of brain capacity. In the horse, the occipital crest, which is the highest point of the horse's head, may be regarded as a continuation of his forehead. In man, owing to the bulging-out condition of the brain, it is placed at the back of the head. When a horse wishes to take a good view of the ground in front of him, he will, by the adjustment of his neck, adopt a lofty carriage of the head, while keeping the line of the face at an angle of about 45° to the ground. If he requires his line of vision to be at about that angle to the ground in order to see, for instance, an object six or seven feet in front of his feet, he will bring the line of his face perpendicular, or nearly so, to the ground. Of course, the axes of the eyes can be altered, more or less, without the head being moved; but the horse possesses such mobility of head and neck that, when he is free, he will adjust his line of vision principally by the movement of these parts.

It is therefore evident that if we want a horse, when riding or driving him, to have a good look at the ground over which he is about to go, we should allow him, or endeavour to induce him, to carry his head at an angle of about 45° to it. A more perpendicular carriage of the head would be permissible only for school work, or for evolutions in which freedom of movement has, to some extent, to be sacrificed for obtaining thorough power of control. If the angle which the face makes with the ground be much less than 45°, the animal will not be able to see where he is going.

(2) *To permit of free movement of the fore limbs.*—My readers will remember that the shoulder-blade of the horse, on each side, is connected to the body by muscles which allow it to work backward and forward on the chest. The shoulder-blade and *humerus* (*see* Fig. 3) being drawn forward and upward by muscles of the neck; it follows that the direction of this pull will be regulated, to a great extent, by the direction in which the horse carries his head. Hence, if we require "lofty" shoulder action, we must get him to carry it comparatively high. If he carries it low down, only a slight upward lift can be given to the shoulders. In such a case, to make up for want of shoulder action, the horse will probably increase his knee action, which is obtained by muscles that have no power to move the shoulders. Thus, we may see a horse who has free shoulder action and gallops with a straight knee when he carries his head fairly high, go in a "round" and cramped style, if he be permitted or induced to carry his head low down. I may here explain (as we may see by reference to the figures in Chapter XII.) that in all paces, and especially in fast ones, in order to obtain good forward reach, it is requisite that the fore limb should be drawn upwards as well as forwards. The defect, as regards want of safety, in the fore feet not being lifted sufficiently off the ground by the play of the shoulder, may be compensated for by increased knee action, which, however, will have no effect in lengthening the stride; but will, in causing loss of time in putting down the fore feet, tend to diminish the speed. As practical points directly connected

with this subject, I may mention that the use of the curb bit has been found to injuriously affect the action of race-horses by, as a rule, making them carry their heads low down, and consequently to gallop "round." Trainers of match-trotters employ an "over-draw check-rein" (bearing rein) with horses which do not carry their heads high enough, and which, on that account, have too low action. The bearing rein is also, in many cases, necessary for the attainment of that "extravagant" action which is greatly sought for among fashionable carriage horses : a fact which accounts for its retention in the stables of the rich, despite the adverse criticism that is being constantly directed against its use. As a rough guide to the direction of the neck (supposing it to be straight or only slightly bent) when the line of the face is at an angle of about 45° to the ground, I may say that, at ordinary paces, the upper part of the nostril should not be lower, or only slightly so, than the top of the withers. In the fast gallop, the horse will carry his head lower down than this, so as to bring his weight forward, and thus to increase his speed (*see* p. 67). This difference in the carriage of the head will be evident, if we compare Figs. 81 to 89 with Figs. 90 to 105 A fairly high carriage of the head, with the face at the angle just mentioned, is a most desirable point in the cross-country horse, who requires to obtain a good view of the ground or obstacles in front of him, and to have free shoulder action; in other words, to be "light in front," which implies that his hind legs are well "under him." If, on the contrary, we want a horse to rein back (*see* p. 119), we should make him lower his head and bring it perpendicular, or nearly so, to the ground, in order to put weight on his fore legs and lighten his hind ones.

Those of my readers who have studied high school riding, will remember that, according to the teaching of Baucher, who introduced many valuable improvements in military equitation, the normal position of the head of the school horse was perpendicular to the ground; and that the head was carried comparatively low. That admirable exponent of the modern *haute école*, M. Fillis (see his *Principes de Dressage*), having wisely rejected, even in the most elaborate *airs de manege*, this artificial style, teaches that the school horse should carry his head high and the muzzle well advanced out of the perpendicular. If the head be carried too high; forward reach will be proportionately sacrificed to upward shoulder action, with consequent loss of speed. Hence, jumpers, animals that require to be clever over bad ground, such as pig-stickers and Colonial stock horses, and those in which showy action is sought, such as chargers, school horses, and park hacks, should carry their heads higher than animals in which speed is the chief consideration. The more the lift to the fore legs is obtained by the play of the shoulders, and not by the mere raising of the knees; the safer, more brilliant, less fatiguing, and faster will the action be in every class of horse.

The chief muscle which draws the fore limb (of each side) forward and upward, is attached by one end to the humerus and by the other to the top of the head. Other muscles that draw the shoulder-blade forward and upward, are attached to it and to the ligament of the neck, which stretches from the withers to the top of the head. As muscles act best when their points of attachment are wide apart; the horse, during rapid movement, regulates, under normal conditions, the amount of the extension of his neck, according to the speed at which he is going. In this case, the head and neck are the fixed point; the fore limb, the movable one. As long, therefore, as the speed of any particular pace remains uniform, the length of the neck (measured roughly from withers to top of head) should continue unchanged. Consequently, when riding or driving, if we desire the horse to maintain a uniform rate of speed, we should keep a uniform tension on the reins (note, for instance, the fixed position of the hands of a capable lad from a racing stable when he is riding a steady training gallop), and should not "give and take" with them. If the speed be increased, the hands, supposing their hold on the reins remains unaltered, should be advanced, as may be required; if it be decreased, they should be drawn back. Thus, any alteration by the rider, of tension on the reins which might impede the legitimate movements of the neck, is avoided. As the joint which the head makes with the *atlas* (first vertebra of the neck) is situated some distance below the top of the head, it follows that if the muzzle be unduly stretched out, the occipital crest (top of the head) will be brought back, and the tension of the ligament of the neck lessened, with consequent decrease of power to the muscles which are attached to this ligament. The muscle which is attached to the humerus and top of the head, also would work to disadvantage if the muzzle were stretched out to a greater extent than would bring the line of the face to a right angle with the direction of this muscle, which forms the upper border of the jugular groove. Even in the fast gallop (*vide* Figs. 90 to 105), the horse rarely carries his head at a less angle than 45° to the ground.

(3) *To regulate the position of the Centre of Gravity.*— The more the head is advanced to the front, the more unstable will be the equilibrium, and the greater will be the

speed during progression (*see* p. 67). Hence, the race-horse, when galloping at full speed, will bring his head forward as much as the other conditions which affect its carriage will allow him to do. As I have before remarked, the angle which his face makes with the ground will seldom be less, even at the highest speed, than 45°. The cart-horse, if he has good foot-hold, will also, when pulling a heavy load, lower his head and stretch it out, so as to bring the centre of gravity forward as much as possible. Here I assume that the ground is soft enough to allow him to "dig his toes" into it, or, if it be rough, that he is provided with toe-pieces on his front shoes. If, on the contrary, the roadway is slippery, like the London streets which are covered with asphalte or wood, the cart-horse in heavy draught, being afraid of falling down if he throws his weight into the collar, will try to keep the centre of gravity back by holding his head high, while trusting almost entirely to his hind legs to push the body forward. When a horse rears, halts suddenly, or reins back in heavy draught (*see* p. 119), he will raise his head and neck so as to bring the centre of gravity back. Any one who has ridden much "over a country," will know the great use a horse makes of his head and neck for regulating the position of his centre of gravity when jumping, and especially when he makes a "mistake." When a horse turns, or "circles," he ought to have his head and neck bent in the direction he is going, in order to see where he is proceeding, and to increase his stability by shifting the centre of gravity towards the side to which the turn is being made.

(4) *To enable the Mouth-piece of the Snaffle to act efficiently on the "bars" of the Mouth.*—I may explain that

the "bars" of the mouth are those parts of the gums of the lower jaw which are bare of teeth, and which are situated between the back teeth and the tushes of the horse or gelding, or the spots which they would occupy, were these canine teeth developed in the mare. As the "bars" are much more sensitive to pressure than the corners of the mouth; we should, when using the snaffle, endeavour to make the horse carry his head so that he will not shift the mouth-piece off the former and on to the latter. The mouth-piece will, naturally, act best when the head is carried perpendicularly to the ground; but it can also act efficiently if the line of the face is not at a less angle to the ground than about 40°. The apparent anomaly of the mouth-piece of the snaffle not slipping off the "bars" and on to the corners of the mouth in this case, may be explained by the fact that the well-broken horse, when being ridden or driven, keeps the joints of his lower jaw in a more or less relaxed condition, so that the "bars," as a rule, will make a greater angle with the ground than the line of the face will do. When a horse which is ridden in a snaffle, is made to carry his head in a more or less perpendicular manner, he may, as a "defence," relax his jaw, with the object of letting the mouth-piece slip down in his mouth as much as possible, in order that a certain amount of the pull of the reins may be transferred from it to his poll, over which the crown-piece of the bridle passes. Any "defence" which a horse makes by opening his mouth, may be counteracted by the use of a properly applied nose-band.

CHAPTER XI.

STATIONARY MOVEMENTS OF THE HORSE.

Lying Down and Getting Up—Rearing—Kicking—The Piaffer.

Lying Down and Getting Up.—When a horse prepares to lie down, he will bring all his feet well under his body, while resting his weight chiefly on his hind feet. After making a few tentative movements with his fore limbs, he will gently lower his forehand until his knees lightly touch the ground. He will then give his body a twist, and will roll over, and rest, partly on his side and partly on his breast bone. M. Colin describes as follows the position of the horse when lying down. If, for instance, he is on his right side, the right fore leg will be under the chest, with its foot facing the inside of the left elbow. The other fore, equally bent, but clear of the body, will have its foot close to its own elbow, and there will be a space of about twelve inches between the two knees. The hind limbs will be bent up under the body, with the feet carried to the front. The near hind, far removed from the side, will have its hock on a line with the hip joint, and the hoof with the point of the hock. The neck will be raised and the head will be inclined to the left side. Sometimes the animal rests his lower jaw on the ground. He may even, at certain moments, support his head on the flank or hock, which is a favourite position with cattle, buffalo and deer, when they have stopped ruminating, and appear to want to go to sleep. They cannot, however, long maintain this position.

As the suspensory ligament of the neck can support the weight of the head and neck without giving rise to the sensation of fatigue; a horse can sleep comfortably on his side and breast bone and with his head turned to the opposite side. When a horse is very tired, or even when he feels secure from disturbance, he may sleep entirely on his side, with his cheek resting on the ground. On rare occasions, a horse will repose lying down on his breast bone, with his knees advanced and his heels more or less close to the points of his elbows. This position is considered apt to give rise to "capped elbow," on account of the pressure of the heel of the doubled-up fore leg on the point of the elbow. This is not an easy position for the horse; for the sharp keel of his breast bone will be liable to be hurt by contact with the ground. It is, however, the natural sleeping position of horned cattle, which can rest at ease in this manner; as the keel of their breast bone is flat.

In getting up, the horse straightens his fore legs out to the front, and with a strong effort places his fore feet on the ground and raises his forehand, so as to sit up like a dog. With another effort he raises his hind quarters and stands on all four feet.

Rearing.—When a horse prepares to rear, he will get his hind feet well under him and will raise his head, so as to "lighten" his forehand, which he will lift off the ground by the straightening out of one or both fore legs, and by the action of his "rearing muscles" (*see* p. 64). He will then keep his fore legs bent at the knees and his head high (*see* Fig. 37). In guarding against the rear, the rider should, therefore, lean well forward. If he wishes, by inflicting punishment, to stop the horse from rearing, he may hit the animal on one of the

FIG. 37.—REARING.

hind legs, so as to prevent him from fixing them on the ground, in order to "get up;" but he should on no account strike him on the shoulders; for doing so would tend to make him raise his forehand. We may break a horse of rearing by teaching him to rein back in a "collected" manner (*see* p. 119, *et seq.*). By doing this, we "lighten" the hind quarters and accustom him to lift them and move them freely. In the rear, the horse usually keeps one hind foot advanced more than the other, and his hind feet more or less apart, so as to widen the base of support.

The rear is a particularly insecure and fatiguing attitude for the horse to maintain; as the column of bones formed by the body and the hind legs has to be kept in position, at its joints (or angles), by the exercise of muscular force. In a biped, like man, this column of bones can be brought into a nearly vertical position, so that its component parts can rest on each other, with but little muscular exertion to maintain them in that position. Owing to the large amount and continued nature of this muscular effort, there will be a very appreciable backward and forward sway (caused by the alternate contraction and relaxation of the opposing muscles) at the various joints. This, added to the narrowness of the base of support (formed by the hind feet and the respective lines which join their toes and heels), will render the rearing position so insecure that, to support it, the horse will have to keep frequently changing it. The danger of falling backwards which the animal incurs, if he gets too erect, will naturally help to deter him from trying to assume a comparatively vertical position. Hence, he will have to keep the joints of his hind limbs more bent than if he was not exposed to this risk of falling backwards.

The hocks are particularly liable to injury from rearing, owing to the great strain thrown on them when the animal assumes an upright position. "Curbs" and other enlargements are of frequent occurrence among circus horses which are trained to walk on their hind legs.

Kicking.—The term "kick" is usually restricted to a blow given by one or both hind legs (*see* Fig. 38). A horse is said to "strike out" with one or both fore legs. We may regard both these movements as kicks.

A horse can kick in three ways: (1) To the rear with one or both hind legs; (2) to the front with a hind leg; and (3) to the front with one or both fore legs. Unlike horned

FIG. 38.—KICKING.

cattle, a horse is unable, without moving the body, to kick to one side, except to a slight extent, owing to the presence of a ligament which connects the thigh bone to the pelvis, and which greatly restricts the side action of the limb. If a horse, therefore, wants to kick a man who is standing a little away from its side, it will have to turn round to do so. For this reason, if a person wishes to stand in safety by the side of a horse's hind quarters, as for instance when examining its hocks, he should get an assistant to stand on the same side, and to draw the head round to it a little, so that the animal will not be able to turn round to kick if so inclined. If the horse be a vicious kicker, the advisability of getting the fore leg of the side at which one is standing, held or tied up, will be self-suggestive to any one who has had experience with horses. The forward kick with a hind leg (called a *cow kick*) has a good deal of range; as a horse can, in this manner, hit a man who is standing at its shoulder

When striking out in front, the horse will generally do so with one foot; for the blow can be delivered with greater speed when the other fore foot is on the ground, than if both were off it. If he strikes out with both fore feet, he will do so with a quick, short effort, with the object of giving a blow; or he will make a greater or less attempt at rearing, so as to bring his feet or legs on the top of the offending person or animal with the view of knocking it down. The governing idea, more or less developed, of thus overthrowing his enemy is, evidently, to kneel on him and to bite him. This mode of attack is seldom seen in its complete form, except in the case of entires, which are more prone to bite and strike out with both fore feet than are mares and geldings. Mules usually kick out behind with greater freedom than horses, but are not so much inclined to bite or to strike out in front. Mares, from sexual causes, are more inclined to kick with their hind legs than are the other two. Horses sometimes kick with a hind foot in a good-tempered way, not with the purpose of inflicting pain, but merely to push the object of the attention out of the way, as we may occasionally see a dam do to her foal. Horses often kick in play without any vicious intention. I am convinced that many apparently vicious kicks which miss their marks, are delivered, not with the desire of sending the blow home, but to warn the intruder against nearer approach.

When a horse kicks out behind, he will put extra weight on his forehand, and, as a rule, will lower his head. When he cow-kicks or strikes out in front, he will raise his head and bring his weight back.

In almost all cases, just before a horse kicks, he will draw back his ears, and more or less show "the white of his eye." If the suspicious object be behind him, he will bring his head slightly round so as to see it, and will prepare for his attack by bending the fetlock and raising off the ground the heel of the hind leg of that side. I may mention that a horse cannot kick with the hind leg upon which he is resting his weight; for he has to transfer the weight to its fellow before he brings it into play. My readers will observe that I have used the word "slightly" with reference to the extent the animal turns his head when he gets ready to "lash out;" for if he brought it round a good deal, he would be obliged to throw more weight on the hind leg of the side to which he is looking than on its fellow, and would consequently have a difficulty in using it.

The Piaffer.—This is an *air de manège*, which is simply a *passage* (*see* p. 117) without gaining ground. The most brilliant kind of *piaffer* is when the movement is slow, lofty, in true cadence, and with a well-marked pause when each leg is raised to its highest point.

CHAPTER XII.

PACES OF THE HORSE

Definitions—The Trot—The Amble—The Walk—The Canter—The Gallop—The Passage—The Spanish Walk and Spanish Trot—The Rein Back—Foot-prints of the Horse during various Paces.

I MAY remark that there is no such thing as absolute uniformity in the paces of the horse.

Definitions.—To simplify explanation, we may, when speaking of the limbs, call the near (left) fore and near hind, the *left pair;* the off (right) fore and off hind, the *right pair;* the off fore and near hind, the *right diagonals;* and the near fore and off hind, the *left diagonals.* The meaning of *both fore* and *both hind* is evident.

We may use the word *support* to signify the fact that the weight of the body is borne by one or more limbs, as, for instance, *left support*, when only the left pair are on the ground; and *right diagonal support*, when the right diagonals alone prevent the horse from falling.

A *stride* is the distance from the foot-print of any one leg to the foot-print of the same leg, when it next comes to the ground; or it is the action of the limbs while that distance is being covered.

A *step* is the forward or backward movement of one foot;

or it is the distance one foot is removed from its fore or hind fellow.

The term, *period of suspension*, will serve to designate the time during which the animal is completely off the ground at any particular pace, or when jumping.

Natural paces are those which the horse adopts of his own accord, without any teaching from man; *artificial paces*, those which he performs only after special training.

Time (as applied to the rhythm of a pace) is the number of separate steps in each stride of that pace. Thus, the amble, in which the right pair and left pair move alternately, is a pace of two time; and the walk, in which each limb moves separately, is a pace of four time.

To prevent any chance of confusion, I shall limit, in this chapter, the meaning of the word *pace* to particular and distinct methods of progression, and shall not use it as a synonym for the word *speed*.

The Trot.—We may select the trot to begin with, as it is the simplest of all ordinary paces. Although it is essentially a natural pace, some horses which have been trained to amble, require a good deal of teaching to give up the amble and to trot in true style. It consists of the alternate action, in progression, of the two diagonals, in each one of which the fore and hind leg move in the same manner. Thus, in Figs. 39 and 41, we have the left diagonal support and right diagonal support shown, as the diagonal pairs of feet come alternately to the ground. Figs. 40 and 42 depict the position the limbs occupy, just before the feet quit the ground. I need hardly say that it is a pace of two time.

We may divide the trot into three kinds: (1) The *short* or *slow trot*, in which the prints of each respective hind foot do not reach as far forward as those of the fore foot of the same side; and there is no period of suspension. (2) The *ordinary trot* (*see* Figs. 39, 40, 41, and 42), in which the hind feet more or less cover the fore feet, or even go slightly beyond them, in which case there will be a brief period of suspension. (3) The *flying* or *fast trot*, in which

FIG. 39.—BEGINNING OF LEFT DIAGONAL.

FIG. 40.—END OF LEFT DIAGONAL.

FIG. 41.—BEGINNING OF RIGHT DIAGONAL.

FIG. 42.—END OF RIGHT DIAGONAL.

ORDINARY TROT.

there is a well-marked period of suspension between each stroke of the diagonals (*see* Figs. 43 to 47); the movements represented being those of *alighting*, *support*, *quitting*, *suspension*, and alighting on the opposite diagonals.

The trot is the least fatiguing pace to the horse, by which he can go a long distance continuously at a fair rate of speed; because both fore and hind limbs, respectively, have the same

Fig. 43.—Commencement of Right Diagonal.

Fig. 44.—Right Diagonal.

Fig. 45.—Right Diagonal.

Fig. 46.—Suspension.

Fig. 47.—Left Diagonal.

Fast or Flying Trot.

amount of work to do ; the body can be maintained in a state of equilibrium by a diagonal support, which would not be the case with a side support, as in the amble ; there is but little loss of power in keeping the centre of gravity (*see* p. 49) level ; and because the pace is a tolerably fast one. It is more suitable for draught, than for saddle. First of all, it is very fatiguing to the rider, especially if he bumps up and down *à la militaire.* Consequently, we find that men who are accustomed to go long distances on horseback, as in the Colonies, almost always combine the canter and walk instead of adopting the trot. Although rising in the stirrups will make this pace much more easy for the rider, it will not benefit the animal to the extent one might imagine ; for, strange to say, almost every horseman, when rising at the trot, invariably comes down on one particular pair of diagonals. Thus, some will put their weight only on the right diagonals ; others, only on the left. I may mention that, when rising in the stirrups, the rider's weight is borne by only one pair of diagonals. As each pair has to do its own allotted work, it is nearly as well to have both tired, as one fresh and the other fatigued. The chief advantage which rising in the stirrups has to the horse, is that the man who adopts it, conforms better to the movements of the animal than one who bumps up and down. Men who ride, might with advantage learn how to change their time of rising in the trot, so that, after having made one pair of diagonals bear their weight for a time, they might be able to change it on to the other pair. Ladies whose stirrup is on the near side, and who rise in the trot almost always do so during the left diagonal support, and come down during the right diagonal support. As the weight at the trot is distributed between one hind and one fore leg, it (or, possibly, the amble) should be used, when practicable, for going over hard ground, in preference to the canter, and still more so to the gallop.

The Amble.—A few horses naturally adopt this pace in preference to the trot; but it is an artificial one with the majority of amblers. MM. Goubaux and Barrier tell us that some foals begin at the amble, and that they do not learn to trot until later, when they have acquired age and strength. These eminent French authorities also point out that it sometimes happens that horses which were formerly good trotters, take to ambling at the decline of their life, on account of their legs becoming worn out.

The amble is a pace of two time, and consists of the alternate movement, in progression, of the right and left (or left and right) pair of legs. In Figs. 48 to 52, which depict what we might call the flying amble, there is a period of suspension between each stroke. This fast amble is known in America as "pacing." There is little or no period of suspension in the ordinary amble. The amble is a very easy pace for the rider, but is unpopular (why, I cannot tell) in England. The slow amble (the "tripple") is the favourite pace among the Dutch farmers in South Africa. Baron de Curnieu (*Leçons d'Hygiène Hippique Générale*) tells us that Napoleon I. was accustomed to ride amblers during his campaigns, when he had to go long distances at a fast pace. If a horse takes readily to the amble, his rider will find it a comfortable method of travelling. The remarks I have made on page 97 *et seq.* with reference to the merits of trotting, apply equally well to ambling, with the exception that the equilibrium of

FIG. 48.—BEGINNING OF RIGHT SUPPORT.

FIG. 49.—MIDDLE OF RIGHT SUPPORT.

FIG. 50.—END OF RIGHT SUPPORT.

FIG. 51.—SUSPENSION.

FIG. 52.—LEFT SUPPORT.

FAST OR FLYING AMBLE.

the animal's body is not maintained as easily in it as in the trot, which, consequently, is the less fatiguing pace to the horse. The amble is a natural pace of the camel.

The amble is, probably, a slightly faster pace than the trot; the apparent cause being that the equilibrium is more insecure (*see* p. 67) in the former than in the latter.

The Walk.—This is a movement of four time, and is a pace in which all the limbs move, respectively, one after the other. If, for instance, the off fore leads, the sequence is: 1. off fore (*see* Fig. 54), 2. near hind (*see* Fig 55), 3. near fore (*see* Fig. 58), 4. off hind (*see* Fig. 60). If the near hind begins, it will be: 1. near hind, 2. near fore, 3. off hind, 4. off fore. Each foot comes after the one which precedes it, at an interval of about half the time occupied in taking one step. The result of this is that we have the following order of supports: 1. left pair (*see* Fig. 53), 2. left diagonals (*see* Fig. 55), 3. right pair (*see* Fig. 57), 4. right diagonals (*see* Fig. 60). As a rule, a horse begins the walk with a fore leg.

We may divide this pace into: (1) *The short stepping walk*, in which the prints of the hind feet do not come as far forward as those of the fore feet of their respective sides. (2) *The ordinary walk*, in which they more or less cover them. (3) *The long striding walk*, in which they go clear in front of them. (4) *The high stepping walk*, which is generally an artificial pace, and in which the feet are raised off the ground higher than usual. (5) *The walk in heavy draught*, which is a short stepping walk, and which has peculiarities that I shall presently consider.

Figs. 53 to 60 give an example of the ordinary walk; for the hind feet cover, as nearly as possible, the prints of the

FIG. 53.—LEFT SUPPORT.

FIG. 54.—END OF LEFT SUPPORT.

FIG. 55.—LEFT DIAGONAL.

FIG. 56.—END OF LEFT DIAGONAL.

FIG. 57.—RIGHT SUPPORT.

FIG. 58.—END OF RIGHT SUPPORT.

ORDINARY WALK.

FIG. 59.

FIG. 60.—RIGHT DIAGONAL.

ORDINARY WALK (*continued*).

fore feet of their respective sides, and there is no exaggerated knee action.

The long striding walk is shown in Figs. 61 to 66. As an example of the high stepping walk, we may take the action of Napoleon's horse in Meissonier's great picture "1814" (*see* Fig. 209).

In the various forms of the walk—except in heavy draught on the level or up an ascent, or when going up an incline without having to pull a heavy weight—the healthy horse brings the heel of the foot first on the ground, or the flat of the foot. When the heel precedes the toe in touching the ground, the interval is so short that it is all but imperceptible. In cases suffering from certain diseases, especially laminitis (fever of the feet), this interval is so well marked as to be characteristic of the ailment. In heavy draught which taxes the pulling powers of the horse (we have in Figs. 67 to 73 a representation of this pace), and particularly when going up a steep hill, the toe will be first brought down, as in Fig. 68. In Fig. 67, the right diagonals bear the weight of the horse. In Fig. 68 the near fore comes to their aid. There is a brief left support (*see* Fig. 69). As the off fore is quitting the ground, the off hind comes down,

FIG. 61.

FIG. 62.

FIG. 63.

FIG. 64.

FIG. 65.

FIG. 66.

LONG STRIDING WALK.

FIG. 67.

FIG. 68.

FIG. 69.

FIG. 70.

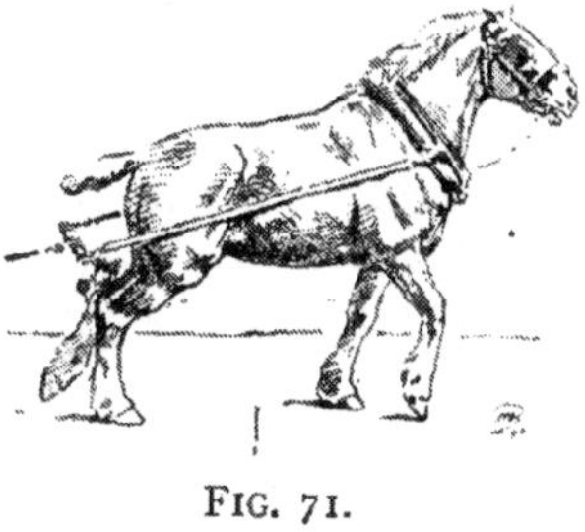

FIG. 71.

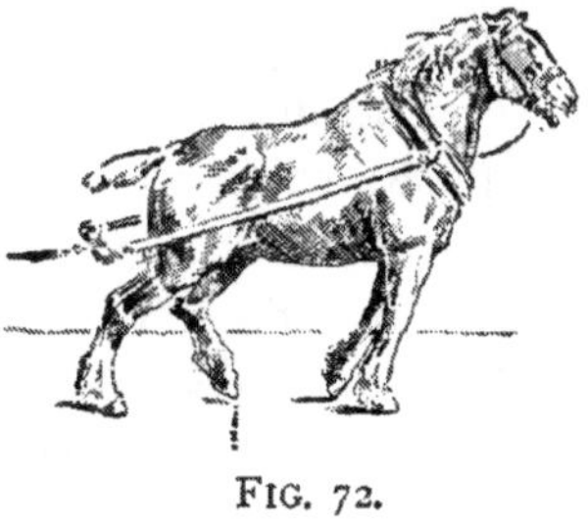

FIG. 72.

SHORT STEPPING WALK IN DRAUGHT.

FIG. 73.
SHORT STEPPING WALK IN DRAUGHT (*continued*).

and continues its assistance while the weight becomes shifted on to the left diagonals (*see* Fig. 71). After that, the weight falls on the right pair of limbs (*see* Fig. 72), and again on the right diagonals (*see* Fig. 73). In heavy draught, we may see that during the side supports there are never less than three feet on the ground, and sometimes even four. In the diagonal support, however, the two limbs may be alone on the ground for a brief period, or only very slightly assisted by the other legs. From this we may conclude that a fore and a hind limb work better together when they are diagonals, than when they are on the same side. This would support the assumption that the horse would work at the trot, other things being equal, with more mechanical advantage than at the amble.

In the representations of the walk, as shown in Figs. 67 to 73, and in Figs. 61 to 66, dotted lines are used to mark the positions of the toe of one of the fore feet, so as to compare it with that taken up by the toe of the hind foot of the same side. We see from this, that in the long striding walk, as depicted, the hind foot oversteps the print of the fore one, nearly as much as it fails to reach it in the walk during heavy draught.

FIG. 74. SUPPORT ON OFF HIND (1ST TIME). FIG. 75.

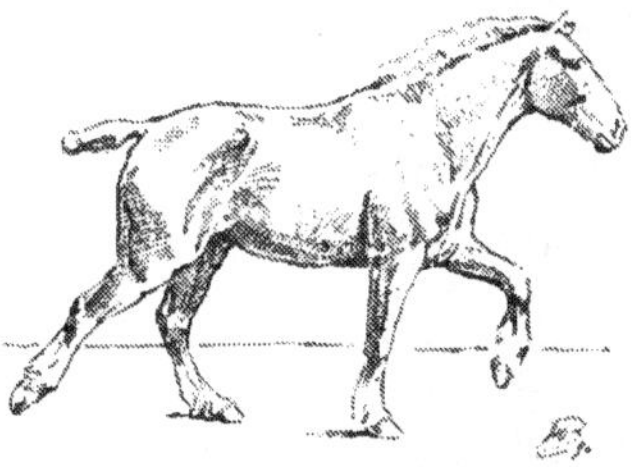

FIG. 76. RIGHT DIAGONAL (2ND TIME). FIG. 77.

FIG. 78. SUPPORT ON NEAR FORE (3RD TIME). FIG. 79.

CANTER OF HEAVY HORSE.

FIG. 80.—SUPPORT ON OFF HIND (1ST TIME).
CANTER OF HEAVY HORSE (*continued*).

The Canter.—The typical canter is a pace of three time, in which the supports are, for instance: (1) off hind (*see* Fig. 74), (2) off fore and near hind (*see* Fig. 76), and (3) near fore (*see* Fig. 78), which may or may not be followed by a period of suspension before the horse again brings down his off hind (*see* Fig. 80). In the canter of the cart horse which is shown in Figs. 74 to 80, there is no period of suspension.

In the canter, the fore leg which does not belong to the diagonal support is called the *leading fore leg*. If the near fore, as in Figs. 74 to 80, be the leading one, the movement is said to be a *canter to the left;* if the off fore, it is called a *canter to the right;* the reason being that at this pace, or at the gallop, the horse should lead with the leg of the side to which he is being turned or circled. If when leading with the off fore, for instance, he be turned to the left, he will be liable to cross his legs and fall. I may remark that in the gallop or canter, a horse can cross his fore legs only with the leading leg. We may observe that the hind leg which, in due rotation, alone supports the weight of the body, is on the side opposite to the leading fore leg. I may point out that this typical canter is rather an up-and-down move-

FIG. 81.

FIG. 82.

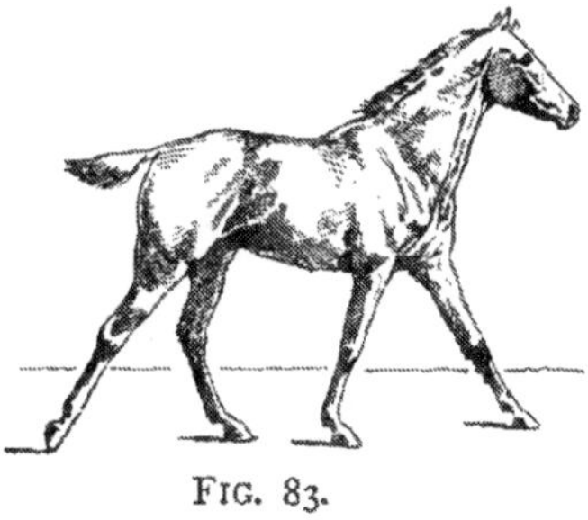

FIG. 83.

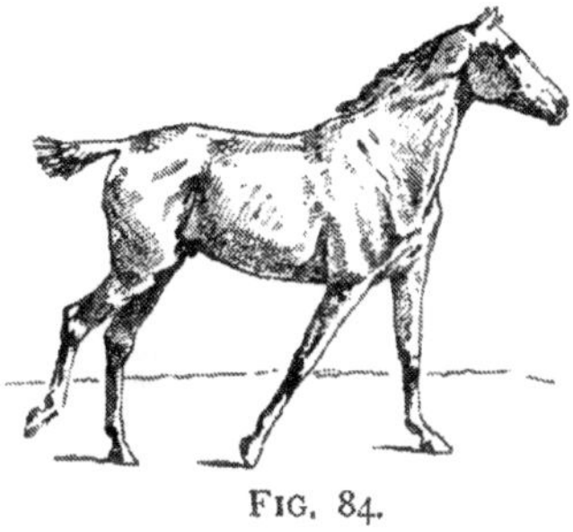

FIG. 84.

FIG. 85.

FIG. 86.

CANTER OR "HAND GALLOP" OF LIGHT SADDLE HORSE.

FIG. 87.

FIG. 88.

FIG. 89.

CANTER OR "HAND GALLOP" OF LIGHT SADDLE HORSE (*continued*).

ment, and is not as easy to the rider as the form of canter portrayed in Figs. 81 to 89, in which the diagonal support (off fore and near hind in this case; *see* Figs. 82, 83 and 84) does not at any time act unaided (as in the other form of canter; *see* Fig. 76); but is assisted by the other hind leg and the other fore leg in turn. This smooth style of canter, which approximates somewhat to the gallop, might be termed (to use a popular expression) a *hand gallop.* We may note that when there is a period of suspension in the canter, and also in the gallop, it is obtained by the forehand being raised by the straightening of the leading fore leg (and especially by that of its fetlock joint), as it quits the ground (*see* Figs. 85 to 87).

The movement shown in Figs. 81 to 89, being a canter, is one of three time, which, however, is irregular; for the interval during which the suspension takes place, between the coming down of the near fore and off hind, is longer than either of the other two intervals. Supposing that the speed be the same, and that there be the same interval of suspension in an irregular canter of this kind and in a typical canter, the former would be less distressing to the horse than the latter; for the weight is better distributed in it. Thus, the off hind is on the ground when the right diagonals come down (take the case shown in Figs. 81 to 89), and they are supporting the body when the near fore reaches the ground (*see* Fig. 83).

We see that, in the canter, the leading fore has more work to do than the non-leading fore leg. Hence, if this pace be long continued, the rider should, if possible, make the horse change the leading fore leg.

The Gallop.—This is a pace of four time, in which the feet follow one another in succession, with an interval of suspension between the coming down of the leading fore foot and that of the opposite hind foot (*see* Figs. 90 to 105). If we compare that series with Figs. 74 to 80, and with Figs. 81 to 89, we shall see that, in the canter, the fore leg of the diagonal support comes to the ground at the same moment (*see* Fig. 75) as, or slightly before (*see* Fig. 82), its hind fellow; but, in the gallop, at a well-marked interval after it (*see* Figs. 92 to 94). We may note that this interval, in which

FIG. 90.

FIG. 91.

FIG. 92.

FIG. 93.

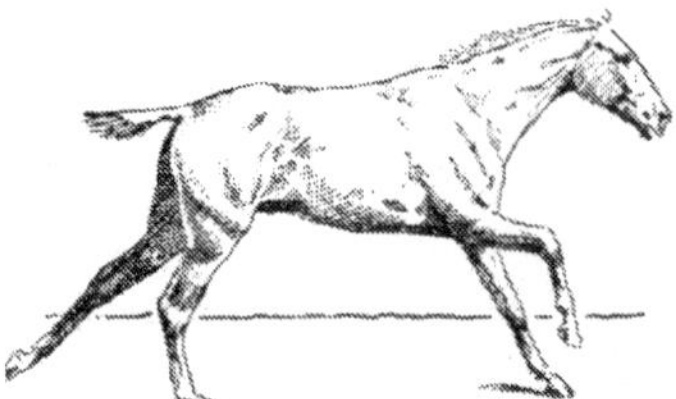

FIG. 94.

FIG. 95.

FAST GALLOP.

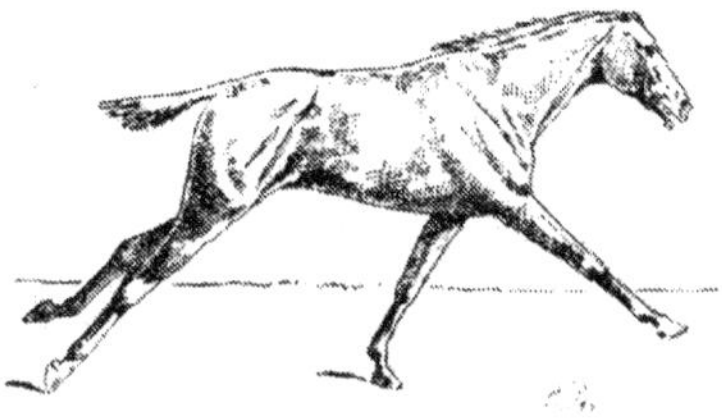

FIG. 96.

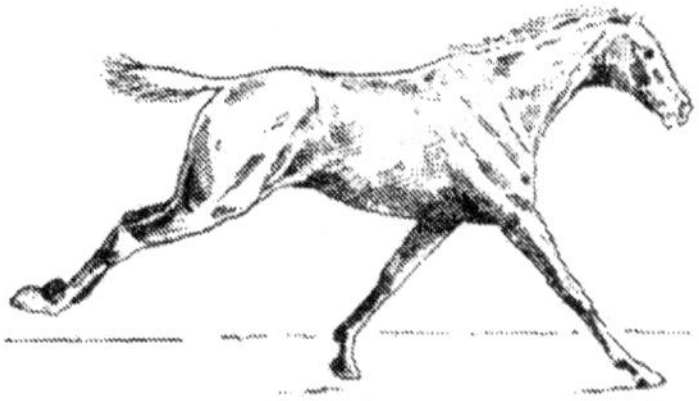

FIG. 97.

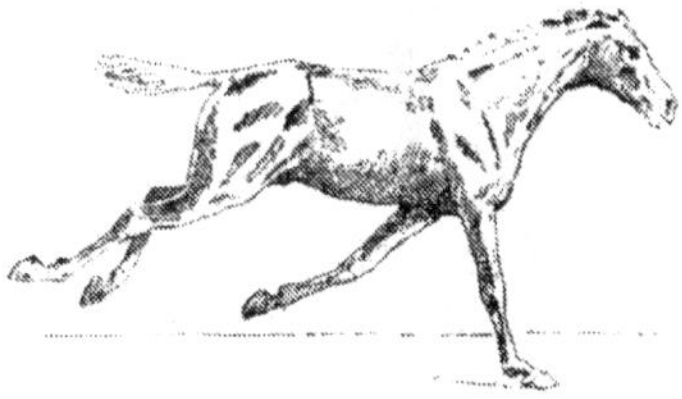

FIG. 98.

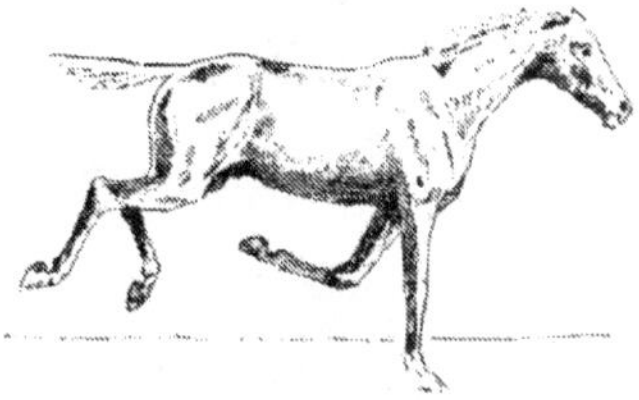

FIG. 99.

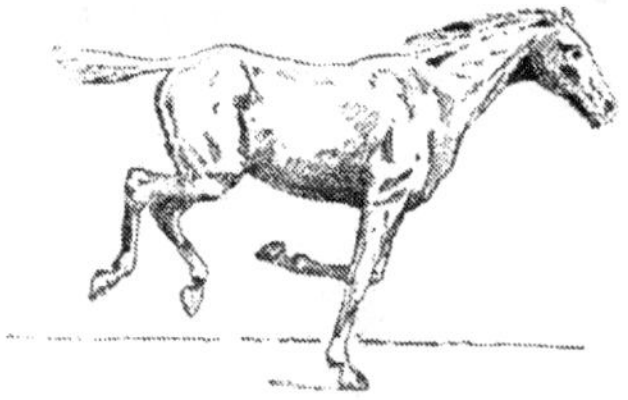

FIG. 100.

FIG. 101.

FAST GALLOP (*continued*).

FIG. 102.

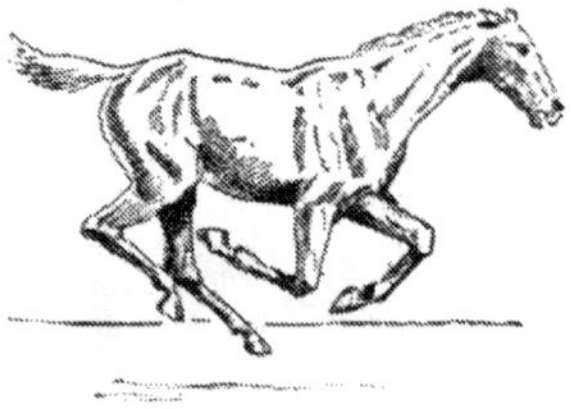

FIG. 103.

FIG. 104.

FIG. 105.

FAST GALLOP (*continued*).

consists the difference between the canter and gallop, is dependent on the extent of the forward reach of the non-leading fore leg. Hence we see that the canter merges imperceptibly into the gallop, and that the difference in these paces, in the same animal, is simply one of forward reach of fore leg—that is, of speed. I may mention that the intervals of time between each of these positions represented by Figs. 90 to 105 are all equal. We may see, starting with Fig. 90, that the near hind, off hind, near fore, and off fore (the leading fore leg) remain for nearly the same time on the ground. The leading fore, however, has to perform a longer period of support than any of the other three. It is also more extended when it touches the ground than is the non-leading fore leg, as we shall note if we compare Fig. 97 with Fig. 94. Hence it is more liable than the other limb to suffer from sprains of the suspensory ligament and check ligament (*inferior carpal*), both of which structures aid in supporting the fetlock joint. As regards the injurious effect of concussion, it would appear that the non-leading fore leg (*see* Figs. 93 and 94), by reason of its coming to the ground at a moment when it is wholly unsupported by the other fore limb, would suffer more from concussion than the leading fore. Consequently, I venture to submit that when the ligaments of the leading fore leg get sprained during the fast gallop, the cause is over-extension, rather than the popular one of concussion, or even of sudden jerk. We may also see from Figs. 100, 101 and 102, how it happens that the back tendons (especially the *flexor perforans*) of the leading fore, during a fast gallop in "heavy" ground, are far more apt to become sprained than those of the non-leading fore leg; for these tendons, immediately before the period of suspension, have (on the contraction of their muscles) not only to help in raising the forehand by the straightening of the fetlock (*see* Fig. 101), but have also to overcome the resistance which the soil offers to the withdrawal of the foot from its surface.

A horse galloping at full speed sometimes brings the toe of the advanced forefoot in front of the end of the nose, as we may see in Mr. Muybridge's admirable book *Animal Locomotion*, vol. ix. Also, at this pace, the angle which the face, when viewed in profile, makes with the horizontal plane more often exceeds than is less than 45°. I may say that, unless in very exceptional cases, it is never less than 40°.

We have on rare occasions, in jumping, extreme extension of the neck.

Passage.—Having no more suitable term to express the artificial pace under consideration, I am forced to employ the French word, *passage*, that signifies a short and very high trot in which each fore limb, in its turn, when it is raised to its highest point, is poised in the air for an instant, and is

FIG. 106.—THE PASSAGE.

bent at the knee and fetlock. It may be called the prelude to the *piaffer* (*see* p. 94), and is an *air de manège* (high school pace). The "passage" of the English military riding school is a movement (*à deux pistes*) by which ground can be taken to the right or left without the rider being obliged to turn his horse. In Fig. 106, which shows the *passage*, the rider's bridle hand is held high, so as to bring the animal's neck in a more or less vertical direction. When it is held in this position, the muscles of the neck will be in the best position for raising the fore limbs, alternately, high off the ground (*see* p. 82).

The Spanish Walk and Spanish Trot.—These high school paces are, respectively, similar to the ordinary walk and trot, except that when each fore leg is advanced in its turn, it is poised for a moment, and is kept more or less

FIG. 107.—THE SPANISH TROT.

straight out, and about as high as the elbow. Fig. 107 gives a representation of the Spanish trot. With respect to the position of the rider's bridle hand, see preceding paragraph.

The Rein Back.—The movement to the rear called the rein back may be executed at the walk, trot or canter. The first and second are natural paces, the third is artificial. The rein back at the walk is performed in a reversed, though exactly similar, manner to the walk to the front (*see* p. 102), except that it is always a "short stepping walk." The trot, which is simply the trot to the front reversed, is also a short trot

I wish to draw my readers' particular attention to the two different methods of backward propulsion adopted by the horse, when he makes this movement to the rear (1) When he is at liberty, or when he reins back "collectedly" with a capable rider in the saddle, he lowers his head so as to put weight on the forehand, and pushes himself back by the alternate straightening out of his fore legs; while the hind legs, being comparatively free of weight, are raised higher and with greater freedom than the front ones. It is evident that this high and light action of the hind limbs is as conducive to the safety of the rein back, as would be the same style of movement of the fore legs in paces of forward progression. (2) When the horse in harness tries to push a heavy weight to the rear, or when he "plants" his hind legs on the ground owing to unwillingness to rein back or to unskilful handling by his rider or driver, he will make his effort or his "defence," as the case may be, by throwing the weight on his hind quarters. In the event of the centre of gravity of the horse (and of the rider) falling to the rear of the base of support (*see* p. 57) formed by his four feet, he will, if in saddle, have to make a hurried and consequently a low step to the rear with one hind foot, which may be followed by the other feet in a more or less disorganised and insecure manner.

If the hind feet fail to come quickly enough to the support of the centre of gravity, a fall will be the inevitable result. Besides the danger of this rein, or rather run, back, the fact of the hind limbs (which are far less suited to bearing weight than the fore ones) being surcharged with weight, will render them liable to become injured, and will make this movement to the rear far more fatiguing to the animal than if it were executed in the manner first described. It behoves us, therefore, if we wish to rein back a horse which we are riding, to adopt the safer and less tiring method. With this object in view, when we wish to make a horse which we are riding, rein back, we should keep our hands "down," so as to allow him, or, if needed, to induce him, to lower his head and put weight on his forehand. We should avoid the practice usually taught in riding schools, of taking an equal pull on both reins; for, if we do so, we shall adopt the best means to induce the animal to throw his centre of gravity to the rear, and to adopt the second method of the rein back, which is objectionable in all cases, except in heavy draught. Instead of this "even feeling" on both reins, we may effect our purpose by, for instance, taking a stronger pull on the near rein, so as to bend the horse's head and neck more or less to the left, draw back the right leg, and touch him with it on the side. The weight, then, on account of the head being turned to the left, will be placed more on the near limbs than on the off ones. Consequently, when the off flank is touched by the drawn-back right foot, the animal will, as a rule, readily lift up the off hind foot from the ground, and, feeling the backward pull of the near rein, his natural impulse will be to take a step to the rear with his off hind, and, in order to preserve the previous distribution of weight, he will follow it with his near fore. When the rider has obtained this diagonal step (with the near fore and off hind) to the rear, he can get the other diagonal step (with the off fore and near hind) by slackening the near rein, taking a pull with the off rein, drawing back the left foot, and touching the horse's left side with it; and so on. I need hardly say that, as each step is obtained, the drawn-back leg should be brought forward. I may also remark that a straight direction to the rear is maintained by the pressure of the drawn-back leg, whichever it may be at the time. We may see that the tendency of the well-broken horse, when reined back in this way, will be to adopt the diagonal movement (or trot) to the rear. Of all unhorsemanlike proceedings, the practice of "chucking" the animal in the mouth with the reins, to obtain the rein back, is one of the worst; for it will tend to make him, in his endeavour to escape the painful pressure of the bit (curb or snaffle), throw his weight to the rear, and run back according to the dangerous second method. Although the well "collected" rein back may be done at the walk or the trot; the rein back by the second method is never executed at the trot, for the weight is too unequally distributed to admit of the simultaneous action of an off fore and a near hind, and of a near fore and an off hind. I need hardly say that the rein back in light harness may be similar to the rein back in saddle. When the object of the rein back is to push a great weight to the rear, as in heavy draught, the horse will have to exert his powers in bringing his centre of gravity as far back as possible. Consequently, he ought to have his head well raised, and ought to get his hind feet under him as far as he can without slipping. In this he will be greatly assisted by having calkins on his hind shoes. Continental *écuyers* have not alone taught their horses, when in the saddle, to rein back at the canter, but even at the canter on three legs, as we may see on referring to M. Fillis's *Principes de Dressage.*

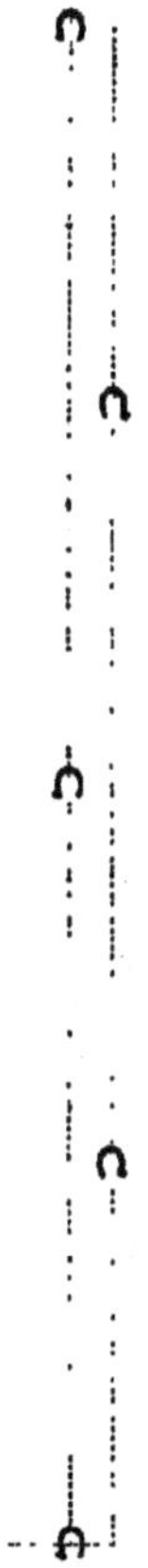

FIG. 108.
ORDINARY WALK.

FIG. 109.
LONG STRIDING WALK.

FIG. 110.
SHORT TROT.

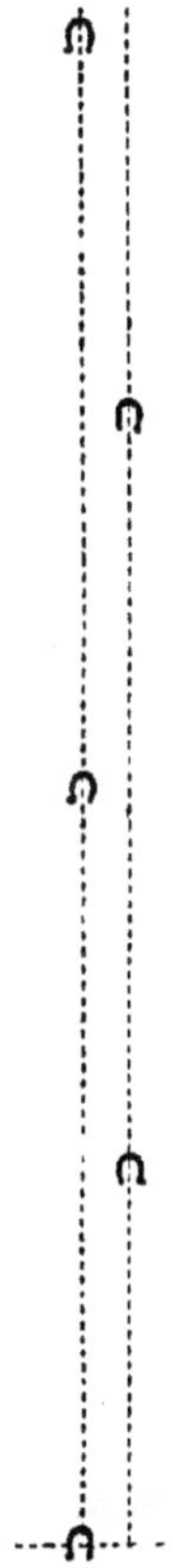

FIG. 111.
SLOW TROT.

FIG. 112.
FAST TROT.

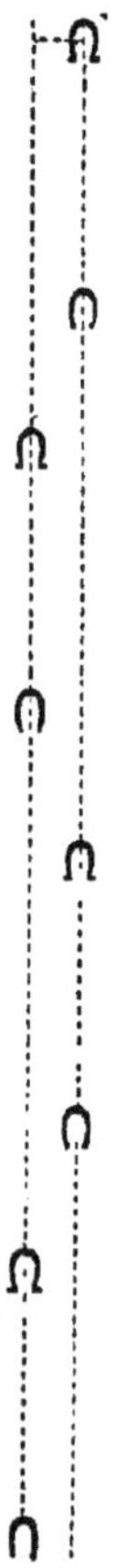

FIG. 113.
SLOW AMBLE.

FIG. 114.
SLOW CANTER.

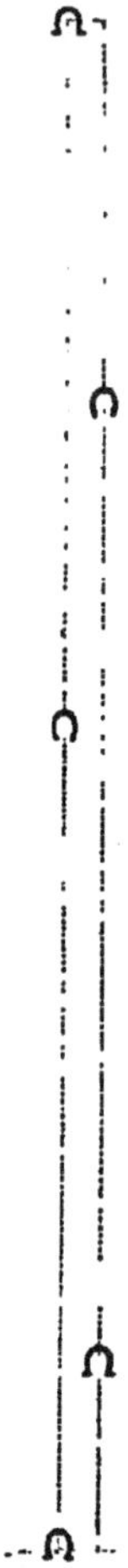

FIG. 115.
FAST GALLOP.

Foot-prints of the Horse during various Paces.—In the study of the foot-prints of the horse we are struck with two notable facts : (1) The faster the pace, the greater tendency has the hind foot to be placed beyond the fore foot of the same side. Here we have the influence of instability of equilibrium in increasing the speed (*see* p. 67). (2) The faster the pace, the nearer do the foot-prints of all four feet tend to come into the line of direction in which locomotion takes place. As Lenoble du Teil expresses it, the foot-prints of the race-horse at full speed resemble the marks that would be made by the spokes of a wheel which had no felloes. This fact proves the undesirability, from a speed point of view, of any undue width between either the fore or hind legs (*see* p. 65). In Figs. 108 to 115, for which I am indebted to MM. Barrier and Lenoble du Teil, the left hand dotted line of each diagram represents the direction of the prints of the near feet; and the right one, those of the off feet. In Figs. 108 and 111 the prints of both fore feet are covered by those of the hind feet. In Figs. 114 the prints of the near fore foot are covered by those of the near hind foot. In these figures, only the succession of the foot-prints has been noted. No attempt has been made to mark the lateral distances between the respective lines of direction of the near and off feet.

The length of stride in the canter is about 12 feet; that of the full speed gallop of the race-horse, about 24 feet.

CHAPTER XIII.

LEAPING.

Definition of the Leap—Varieties of the Leap—Manner in which the Horse takes off in the Running Leap—Difference between the Horse's Leap and the Suspension of his Body during the Canter or Gallop—Period of Stride at which the Take Off is effected—Effect of Pace and Speed on the Leap—Taking off and clearing a Fence—Landing over a Jump—Influence of Blood in Jumping—The Standing Leap.

Definition of the Leap.—The ordinary leap or jump is the projection of the body off the ground by means of the hind limbs, after the forehand has been raised.

Varieties of the Leap.—We may divide the leap into the *running jump* and the *standing jump*; and each of them into the *high leap* and *long leap*.

Manner in which the Horse takes off in the Running Leap.—The animal makes his preparation when he supports his body on his leading fore leg (*see* Figs. 116 and 139), by straightening which (and especially its fetlock joint) he raises his forehand. At the same time, he brings one hind leg down (generally that on the same side as the leading fore), followed by the other hind (*see* Figs. 117 and 118, and Figs. 140 and 141), and, by straightening them out, projects the body upward and forward (*see* Figs.

142, 143 and 144). We may note that there is, practically, no period of suspension (*see* Figs. 116 and 117, and 139 and 140) between the removal from the ground of the fore leg

FIG. 116.

FIG. 117.

FIG. 118.

"TAKE OFF" OF LEAP, WITH HIND FEET NOT BROUGHT WELL UNDER THE HORSE.

that supported the weight, and the putting down of the hind leg which first comes on the ground.

Difference between the Horse's Leap and the Suspension of his Body during the Canter or Gallop.—In the leap, the period of suspension takes place when the hind legs quit the ground; in the canter or gallop, when the leading fore leg is raised (compare Figs. 143 and 144 with Figs. 85, 86, and 87, and also with Figs. 100, 101, and 102). It is instructive to note that a definition founded on this difference is not of general application to other animals. In the gallop of the greyhound, there is a period of suspension (*see* Figs. 122 and 123) similar to that of the horse's leap, as

FIG. 119.

FIG. 120.

FIG. 121.

FIG. 122.

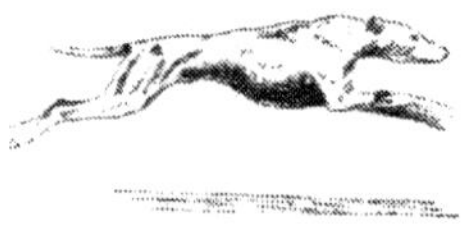

FIG. 123.

FIG. 124.

FIG. 125.

GALLOP OF THE GREYHOUND, SHOWING TWO PERIODS OF SUSPENSION.

well as one (*see* Figs. 119 and 120) like that in the horse's gallop. It seems that the former is longer than the latter in the full speed gallop of the greyhound. It appears that if this dog begins his stride on one fore leg, the right for instance (*see* Fig. 119), he will after his two periods of suspension (*see* Figs. 120 and 123) "take-off" from the opposite fore leg, the left (*see* Fig. 125) in this case. If this be true, his stride (counting it as the interval between the supports of the same leading fore leg) will include four periods of suspension. In

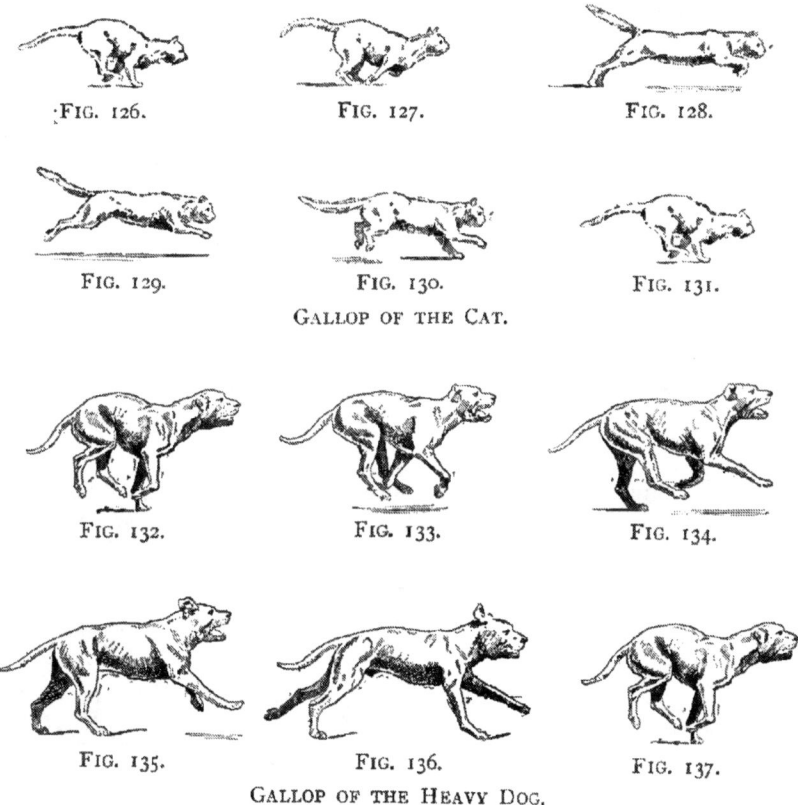

FIG. 126.

FIG. 127.

FIG. 128.

FIG. 129.

FIG. 130.

FIG. 131.

GALLOP OF THE CAT.

FIG. 132.

FIG. 133.

FIG. 134.

FIG. 135.

FIG. 136.

FIG. 137.

GALLOP OF THE HEAVY DOG.

the gallop of the cat (*see* Figs. 126 to 131), and also in that of the tiger, panther, and cheetah, the leaping form of suspension appears to be the only one present. I may mention that I

FIG. 138.

FIG. 139.

FIG. 140.

FIG. 141.

FIG. 142.

FIG. 143.

THE HORSE'S LEAP.

FIG. 144.

FIG. 145.

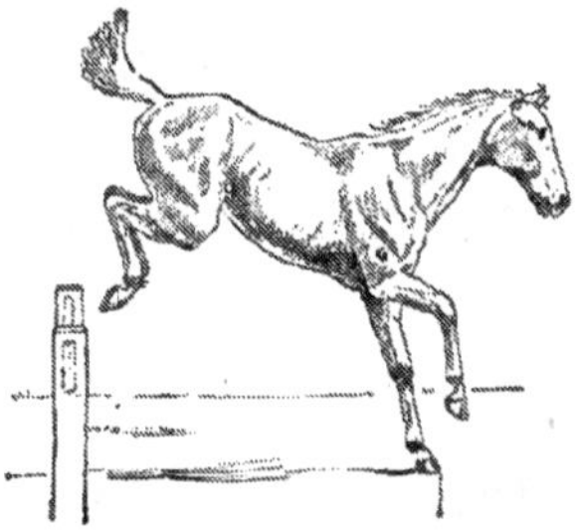

FIG. 146.

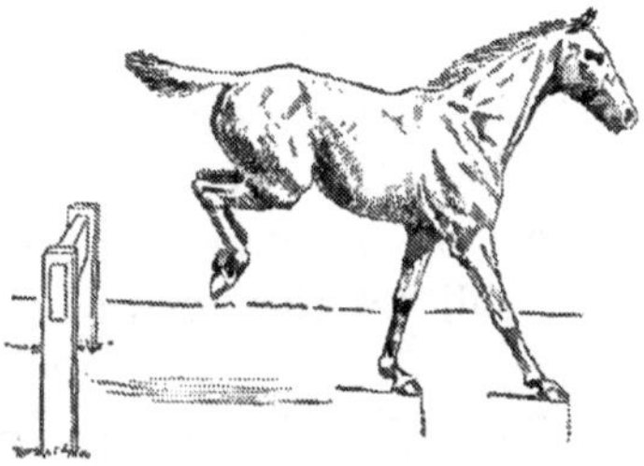

FIG. 147.

FIG. 148.

FIG. 149.

THE HORSE'S LEAP—(*continued*).

FIG. 150. THE HORSE'S LEAP—(*continued*). FIG. 151.

have not had an opportunity of observing the paces of other large felines. The Indian black buck and the South African springbok, which are two remarkably fast kinds of antelope, generally begin their gallop by a series of leaps, when suddenly startled. The gallop of the mastiff (which is a comparatively slow dog), depicted by Figs. 132 to 137, resembles that of the horse. I may remark that the longer the period of suspension, the faster and more fatiguing, as a rule, will be the gallop.

Period of Stride at which the Take Off is Effected.—In the running leap from the canter or gallop, we may regard the putting down of the leading fore leg (*see* Fig. 138) as the commencement of the take off; for, at that period, the character of the pace is changed, and the "take off" by the hind legs is made close to the foot-print of that leg. We therefore see that during the stride of, say, from four to seven yards in length, there is only one moment at which the "take off" can be executed. Hence, if a horse does not regulate the length of his stride when coming up to a fence, he may easily make a mistake. Let us suppose that, while taking a stride of five yards, he brings down his leading fore leg three yards short of the proper spot at which he ought to take off; he will then have to jump three yards "bigger," or chance an accident by taking off two yards too near. The longer the stride, the greater will be the tendency to this error. Consequently, other things being equal, a short striding horse will be safer over a "cramped" country than a long striding one. Also, we may say that no horse merits the title of "a safe conveyance," unless, when coming up to a jump, he is careful to regulate the length of his stride, so as to take off correctly.

Effect of Pace and Speed on the Leap.—The running jump is usually executed at the canter or gallop. A few horses can leap (especially height) cleverly from the trot, which is a useful accomplishment in the hunter; for it may enable him when in a difficult position (as when jumping out of a lane) to utilise a "run" which would be too short for the longer stride of the canter or gallop. Besides, at these paces there is only one period of the stride at which the animal can take off (see preceding paragraph), but in the trot there are two such periods, namely, when the respective diagonals come to the ground. A horse, however, cannot jump so freely and "big" from the trot as from the canter or gallop, in each stride of which, the hind legs are brought nearly together under the horse's body (*see* Figs. 86 and 100), ready, if need be, to change the pace into the leap (*see* Fig. 116). In the trot, each hind limb moves harmoniously with its diagonal fore leg; but in the opposite direction to its hind fellow.

In examining the various kinds of leap of the horse, we must remember that he has a long distance (that from his hocks or buttocks to his muzzle) of body to carry over a fence, independently of raising it to a sufficient height ; hence his high jump partakes much more of the long jump than the high jump of a man, whose body is carried more vertically, than horizontally. For this reason, it is more essential for a horse than for a man, to "get up" a certain degree of speed in order to jump height well.

The speed at which a horse goes at a jump (supposing that it does not prevent him from "collecting" himself properly), influences the width he can clear ; because (as we have seen on p. 61) the force by which he is projected forward into the air is equal to the force of propulsion derived from his limbs, plus the impetus due to the speed at which he is going. The greater this impetus, the lower will be the "angle of elevation" at which the centre of gravity of the body is propelled forward.

We may, with approximate accuracy, define the "angle of elevation" as the angle which a line passing through the centre of gravity and a point midway between the prints of the two hind feet, makes with the horizontal plane, at the moment when the body leaves the ground.

Looking at the subject from a hasty point of view, those of us who have not had practical experience, might come to the conclusion that a horse would jump height as well when going fast as when going slow, and that the only difference is that, in the former case, the animal would be obliged to take off further from the fence than in the latter. This supposition, however, does not hold good ; for the faster the pace, the more weight is thrown on the forehand, and the greater difficulty will the leading fore leg have in raising the forehand off the ground. Hence, even without the valuable experience of the hunting field and steeplechase course, we may accept the truth of the old saying that one should ride slow at "timber." Also, I am inclined to think that a horse will not clear as great a width when taking a water jump if he is sent at his topmost speed at it, as he would do were his rate of going slightly moderated, so as to enable him to raise his forehand sufficiently off the ground in order to obtain the angle of elevation which will enable him to cover the maximum distance.

Taking off and clearing a Fence.—It is evident that the more a horse, in the leap, brings his hind feet forward as compared to the position of the prints of the fore feet, the greater will be the angle at which he can, at the speed he is going, project his body upward. Also, the more he raises his head, the more will he, by bringing back the centre of gravity, increase its angle of elevation. Besides, as the forward and upward movements of the fore limbs depend on the action of the muscles of the neck, the direction in which the fore legs will be raised, will naturally depend on that of the neck. A horse, therefore, when approaching a fence which will tax his powers to clear, should regulate his speed, so that the impetus obtained from it may be in due proportion to the propulsion derived from the limbs; should bring his hind feet well under his body; and should hold his head high. I am here supposing that the animal takes off at the correct distance from the obstacle. These actions constitute, as regards the horse, what is popularly and somewhat vaguely called "collecting" himself.

We may note that although, when preparing to leap, the

hind legs are brought down on the ground in a straightened out position (*see* the off hind in Figs. 117 and 141), and leave it in the same attitude (*see* Fig. 143), they are somewhat bent at the hocks and stifles (*see* Fig. 142) at a time intermediate to these two moments. Hence, we see from these drawings that the propulsion from the hind legs in the leap is due to their being suddenly straightened out, in which action, the fetlock joint also plays an important part.

As the ability to clear height depends greatly on the power of raising the forehand; the rider should refrain from leaning forward when the horse is rising at an obstacle. He should, on the contrary, if anything, lean back at this moment, so as not tc put any unavoidable weight on the forehand.

In almost all cases of the well executed high jump, the fore legs are bent up together and the hind ones fully straightened out at the moment of taking off (*see* Fig. 143). The fore legs will be kept more or less in this position till the fence be cleared. If the obstacle be "stiff" and the horse hit it with his knee or forearm, he will probably fall; but if any part of the leg below the knee strike it, he will generally get over all right, or with a "peck" at most. Hence, a clever horse will try to avoid an accident by raising his knees well out of harm's way. Another danger consists in the horse catching the fence with his hind legs, which he will best avoid by bending them as much as possible at the stifles and hocks (*see* Fig. 145). Consequently, the clever jumper, the moment his hind legs quit the ground when taking off, will tuck them under him as if they were on springs suddenly let go, after having been drawn out. The slovenly fencer, on the contrary, will drag his hind legs after him, at the imminent risk of catching them in the fence and falling.

In the high jump, the animal should keep his hind legs well bent until he is clear of the obstacle (*see* Pl. 69), so that, if need be, as might occur in the case of an unexpected wide drain being met with at the landing side, he may strike the fence with his hind legs, and thus give himself a fresh forward impulse.

When a horse is suspended in the air during a leap, he may move his limbs or retain them in one position, according to what he feels to be most conducive to his safety.

Landing over a Jump.—The prettiest style, and probably safest manner, of landing in the leap, is for the two fore legs to be kept straightened out and comparatively close together (*see* Figs. 152 and 153) until they are near the ground,

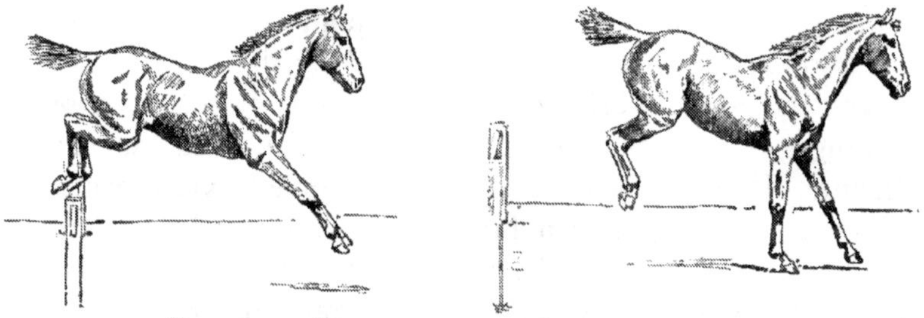

FIG. 152. LANDING OVER A JUMP. FIG. 153.

when one of them comes down, and is followed by the other, which is placed a little distance in front of it. This neat method of landing gives the impression to the observer that the horse comes down on both fore feet at the same time. If we compare Fig. 153 and Pl. 69 with Fig. 146, we shall feel convinced that the plan of landing with one fore leg bent, as in the latter style, is not so safe as in the former; for in the event of any falter being made by the supporting fore leg, the other fore leg will be better prepared to save the horse from a fall, if at that moment it be straightened out, and not bent.

It is evident that, for safety, the knee of the leg upon which the animal lands, should be as straight as possible; for if the knee "gives," the horse will almost certainly fall. Hence, we may regard the condition of being "over at the knees" (*see* p. 217) as a grave defect in the jumper, especially if he be required to go fast.

As a rule, when landing over a jump, the hind foot which first comes down, has been made way for by the fore foot of the same side, somewhat beyond the print of which it is placed. The other hind foot and the other fore foot act in a similar manner. We may see from Figs. 147 to 151, that a horse "gets quickly away from a jump" by the raising of the forehand, which is accomplished by the straightening out of the fore limbs. The rider should, therefore, avoid throwing any undue weight on the forehand at this moment. It sometimes happens that a horse "over-reaches" (strikes a fore leg with a hind foot) when landing over a jump, on account of the rider being jerked on to the animal's neck; the injured fore leg having been prevented from getting out of the way of its hind fellow by the surcharge of the forehand.

A horse should not land with his head and neck bent, as might be caused by the action of a severe bit which he is afraid to "face"; for when the neck is bent, the muscles *

* The chief of these muscles is the *levator humeri*, which is attached to the top of the head and to the upper third of the humerus. The nearer its points of attachment are brought together, the less power has it to draw the limb forward.

which draw the fore legs forward and enable them to reach well to the front, will be more or less thrown out of action. Hence, the rider ought to give the horse plenty of rein on landing, and should try to avoid bringing his weight forward. As an interesting point in the action of a severe bit in leaping, I may mention that if we observe a horse that is being ridden up to a high jump in a bit which he is afraid to "face," he will land, in the event of his clearing the obstacle, more or less on all four legs at the same time, in his endeavour to save his mouth from any sudden "job," by keeping the weight as much as he can off his forehand. He may act in the same way, even with a snaffle, if too short a martingale be used. I may remark that the two "defences" which a horse generally uses against a severe bit, are to poke his nose up in the air, and to draw his chin in towards his chest, and thereby arch his neck. Many persons, against the evidence of photography, assert that a clever jumper will generally land first on his hind legs, and will then (so they say) be in the best position to "get away" quickly. They quite forget (or perhaps do not know) that the hind limbs of the horse are altogether unfitted to stand the violent shock which would be transmitted through them, if they had to bear the weight of the body on landing. Such poor weight-bearers are they, that they have great difficulty, as a rule, in enabling a horse to walk a few yards on his hind legs. Almost all circus horses which have to perform this trick, throw out, after a short time, curbs, spavins and thorough-pins of amazing size. What, I wonder, would be the state of the hocks of a hunter or chaser, had he always to land first on his hind legs! The fore limbs, on the contrary, being attached to the body only by muscles, are singularly well adapted to support shock, like that of landing over a fence. Besides, if a horse, which, like all other animals, is obliged to "take off" from his hind legs, were, also, to land on them, he would lose all the advantage which the forward reach of his fore legs gives him.

In the well executed leap, the fact of the horse landing on one fore leg and then on the other, lengthens the base of support, and thus increases the stability. The hind legs coming down in the same manner enables the horse to at once take up the gallop, which is in four periods, without loss of time (*see* Fig. 151). The safest way for a man, on the contrary, to alight is on both feet kept together, with the knees somewhat flexed (*see* Fig. 26), in order to break the shock of concussion; for his body is placed vertically, and not horizontally, as is the case with the horse. In drawing any comparison of this kind, we must remember that our legs are attached to the trunk by bony union, at our hip joints, and not, as in the fore legs of the horse, by muscles which act as springs in nullifying any injurious effect from the force of impact with the ground. Again, in the horse, although the knees must be kept straight, on landing, in order to insure stability; the fetlock, elbow and shoulder joints act as springs. As man is a plantigrade animal (one that walks on his hocks; *see* p. 32), he must utilise the "play" of the knee-joints, with which to break the force of concussion, when he lands on the ground with any great force. If, in such a case, the knees be kept straight, the shock will fall in its entirety on the pelvis, at the hip joints, and may be transmitted with very serious effect to the spinal cord. Men who practise hurdle-racing on foot, alight on one foot, and then bound off on to the other; as their great object is to lose no time in getting away from their fences, which, being comparatively low, do not greatly affect the athlete's stability.

We may see from the foregoing considerations, that for safety and quickness in "getting away" after a leap, it is essential for the fore legs to be removed out of the way of the hind feet, and for the forehand, which was previously depressed by the weight of the body falling on it (as in Fig. 146), to be raised by the straightening of the fore legs (*see* Figs. 147 to 151). These two actions, I need hardly say, have to be performed with speed and precision. Hence, it is necessary for the horse to see where he is going to place his feet on landing; so that he may be prepared for the required movements of the limbs. If he be prevented from seeing when his feet will come down on the ground, there will be loss of time in calling the muscles of the limbs into action, and the probability of an accident will be greatly increased. A common way some riders have of making a horse, when jumping, fall or overreach in this manner, is to "throw up their hands," and thus cause the animal to unduly raise and extend his head, which he does with the object of "saving" his mouth; the result being that the horse cannot accurately see where he is going to put his feet. The rider, on the contrary, should keep his hands low and should give his mount plenty of rein, so as not to interfere with the animal's movements when landing.

Influence of Blood in Jumping.—Seeing the manner in which the rate of speed influences the extent of the long jump, we may reasonably conclude that a fast galloper, other things being equal, would jump a greater width than a slow horse. The possession of great galloping speed, however, would not,

PHOTO. BY M. H. HAYES

PLATE 16—HURDLE RACER "TAKING OFF"

PHOTO. BY M. H. HAYES

TO FACE PAGE 140

PLATE 17—THE INDIAN LYNX.

of itself, materially assist the high jumper. I regret to say that I have no exact data to go on; but my own experience leads me to conclude that the majority of big water jumpers will be found among well-bred horses. As the height or distance over which the body is propelled by the limbs depends on the speed at which they are straightened out; we shall find that a horse which is quick in his movements, other things being equal, will jump higher and broader than another which is slower. For this reason, the thorough-bred, properly selected and trained, will make the best of all jumpers, over height as well as over length.

The Standing Leap consists of a rear by which the fore legs are raised off the ground, and of the forward projection of the body by the straightening out of the hind legs, as in the running jump. To make the fact that this rearing action always takes place in the leap, no matter how fast is the pace at which the animal is going, still more graphic, I give in Pl. 16 a photograph of a mare "taking off," at racing speed, in front of the last obstacle of a hurdle-race of which she was the winner.

CHAPTER XIV.

NOTATION OF THE PACES OF THE HORSE.

THAT distinguished French savant, M. Marey, published in 1878 his researches on the paces of the horse. He prosecuted them by means of a registering apparatus somewhat similar to the one, the sphygmograph, used by doctors for recording the movements of the pulse. The machine consisted of a cylinder which was made to revolve round by clockwork. Attached to it were four pointed levers that were arranged so as, when pressed upon, to trace lines on a piece of blackened paper. Each of these levers was provided with an India-rubber tube, which communicated with a rubber ball filled with air and fixed on the ground surface of one of the animal's feet. These levers and their connections were made so that, when the horse during movement put a foot on the ground, the rubber ball attached to that particular foot would be compressed, and the air rushing into the tube would raise the lever and bring its point against the sheet of blackened paper. When the animal lifted its foot from the ground, the air would go back into the ball, and allow the point of the lever to be taken off the surface of the paper. As, while this was being done, the cylinder revolved round at a uniform rate of speed, it follows that the line traced by each lever point would be a record of the duration of the contact of the foot with the ground, and that the intervals between two such contacts would be a measure of the time the foot was suspended in the air. By this means, M. Marey investigated the nature of the paces of the horse. He also devised a very ingenious method of representing them on paper, which I shall now try to explain to my readers.

If we wish to express on paper the running pace of a man, we may do so by making a scale with rectangles, which, for convenience sake, we may use instead of M. Marey's lines. Thus, if the time of contact be about equal to that of suspension, Fig. 154 will express the nature of the pace. To render

FIG. 154.—RUN OF MAN (*see* Figs. 15, 16 and 17).

FIG. 155.—RUN OF MAN (*see* Figs. 15, 16 and 17).

FIG. 156.—WALK OF MAN (*see* Figs. 1C, 11 and 12).

FIG. 157.—TYPICAL SLOW TROT.

FIG. 158.—ORDINARY SLOW TROT (*see* Figs. 39 to 42).

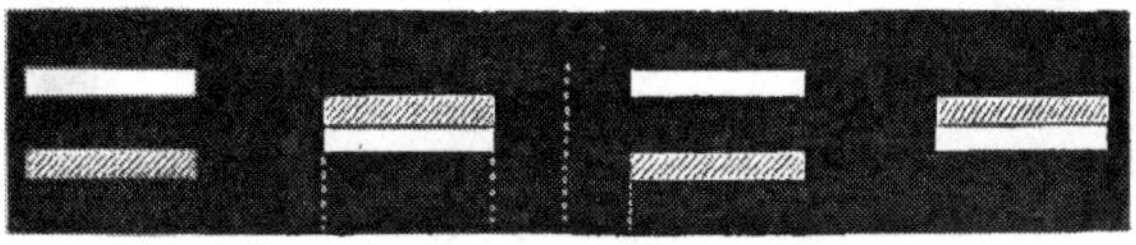

FIG. 159.—FAST TROT (*see* Figs. 43 to 47).

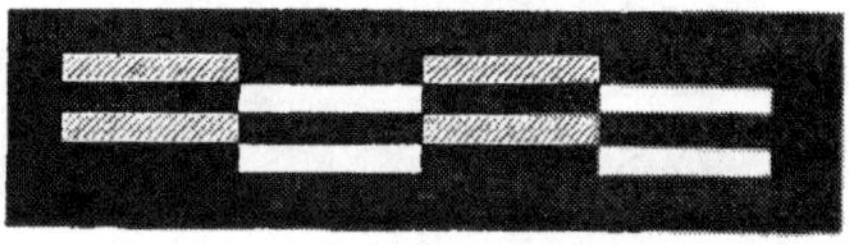

FIG. 160.—TYPICAL SLOW AMBLE.

FIG. 161.—FLYING AMBLE (*see* Figs. 48 to 52).

FIG. 162.—TYPICAL WALK.

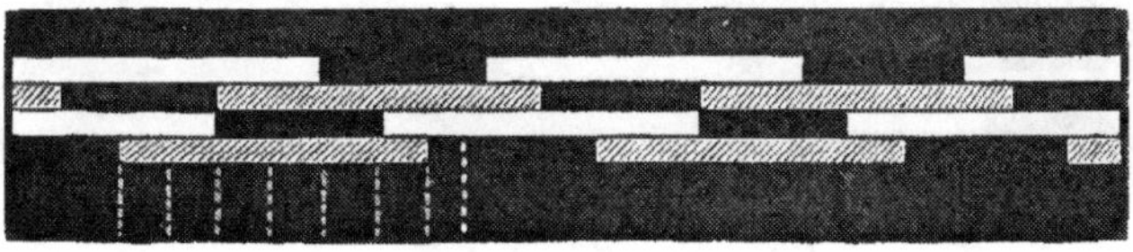

FIG. 163.—ORDINARY WALK (*see* Figs. 53 to 60).

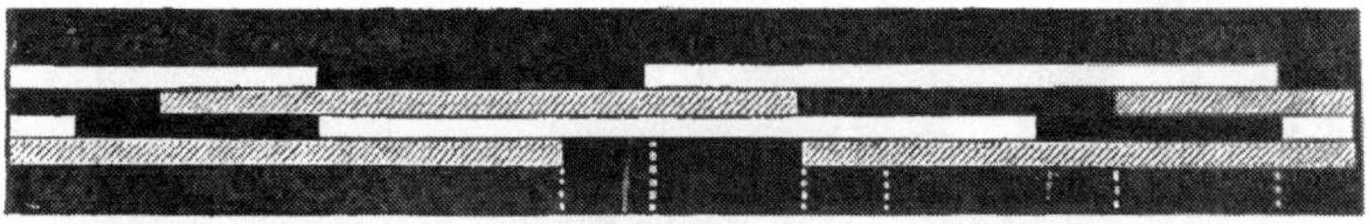

FIG. 164.—SLOW WALK IN DRAUGHT (*see* Figs. 67 to 73).

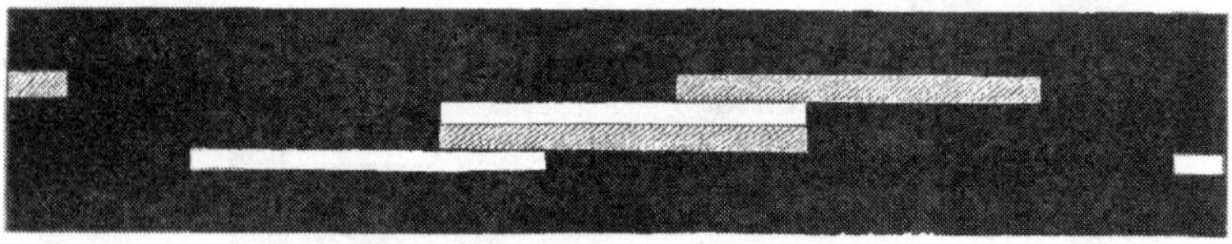

FIG. 165.—TYPICAL CANTER.

FIG. 166.—CANTER OF HEAVY HORSE (*see* Figs. 74 to 80).

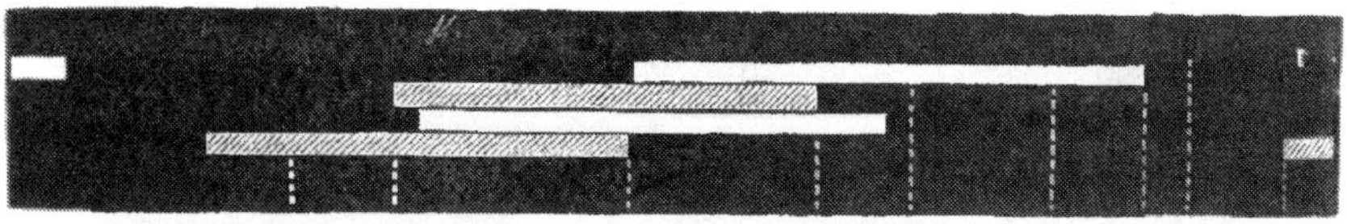

FIG. 167.—CANTER OF FAST HORSE (*see* Figs. 81 to 89).

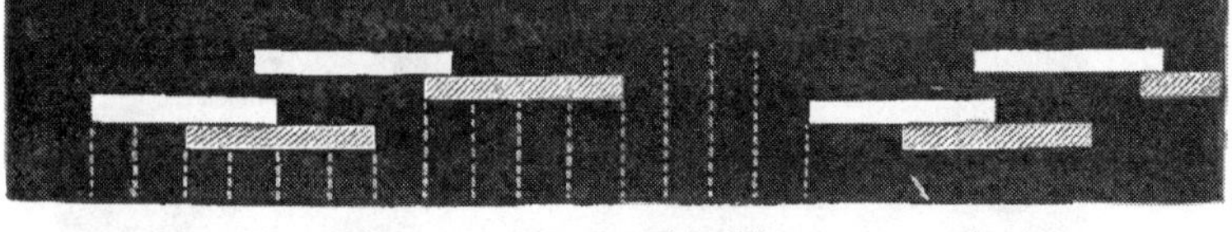

FIG. 168.—THE GALLOP (*see* Figs. 90 to 105).

FIG. 169.—THE LEAP (*see* Figs. 138 to 151).

this figure more graphic, I have used plain rectangles to mark the supports of the left foot, and shaded ones, those of the right foot. If we desire to represent the ordinary walk of a man in the same manner, we shall be confronted with the difficulty that, as both feet are on the ground at certain periods of this pace, the rectangles would naturally have to overlap each other. We may, however, get over it by placing the diagrammatic prints of, say, the left foot on a line above those of the right foot. In this manner, in order to represent the run, we would place these prints as they are shown in Fig. 155; not as in Fig. 154. We may indicate the walk by Fig. 156, in which I have assumed that both feet are on the ground for one-sixth of the period of support of each foot.

We must remember that these scales or notations give us only the order of succession of the feet, and their respective and proportionate periods of support and suspension; but they do not furnish us with a clue to the speed of any particular pace, except, that when there is a period of suspension; the longer it is, the greater, as a rule, will be the speed.

To construct the respective notation of the various paces of the horse, we may employ the rectangles of Fig. 154 for the fore legs, and may use similar ones, placed underneath them, for the hind legs. Thus, Fig. 158 will give us the scale of the trot as shown by Figs. 39 to 42.

My readers will notice that the dotted lines on Fig. 159 mark the respective moments at which the horse assumed the positions depicted in Figs. 43, 45, 46, and 47. In the remaining notations in this chapter I have similarly marked the connections between these scales and the corresponding figures in Chapters XII. and XIII.

CHAPTER XV.

COMPARATIVE SHAPE OF HORSES.

General Remarks—Limit of Height—Length of Limb—Length and Depth of Body—Thickness of Limb—Comparative Length of Fore and Hind Limbs—Length of Neck—Length of Head—Width between the Legs—Comparative Weight of Body—Comparative Length of the Bones of the Limbs—Differences of Conformation between the two Sexes.

General Remarks.—In order to simplify comparison and to prevent tedious repetition, I shall confine myself in the present chapter chiefly to the consideration of the principal differences of proportion between the race-horse and the heavy cart animal, which are, respectively, the extreme types of horses of speed and horses of strength.

The method of working from the whole to a part should be followed as rigorously in judging a horse, as in painting or land surveying. If we desire to obtain correctness in these arts, we must, as a rule, first get our general outline, and then fill in the details. If, in our preliminary examination, we allow our eyes to be caught by some isolated beauty or defect, we would be—to use an oft-applied simile—like a painter who begins a full-length portrait of a person by drawing the nose, and then hangs the remainder of the body to it. I cannot too strongly insist on the fact that the degree of adaptability of an animal for any special kind of useful work, depends more on his general shape, than on the possession or absence of any particular "point."

I may mention that, in making comparisons, we should not be disconcerted by the fact that some of the proportions of the horse may vary a little according to the position in which he stands, and the nature of his bodily condition. Some allowance has to be made for the fact, in my illustrations, that the majority of the gallopers were taken when they were in hard training, and some of the heavier horses when they were in a "lusty" state. It would have been more satisfactory, had I been able to have had their photographs taken at a time when they were all in the same condition; but that, obviously, was out of my power to do. The method I shall indicate will, however, give results sufficiently uniform for our purpose. We must also remember that the respective proportions of animals of the same class and of equal merit are not always the same; for a defect in one point may be compensated by increased excellence in another point.

Limit of Height.—In all species of animals there appears to be a limit of height which the respective members cannot, as a rule, exceed, and at the same time retain strength, activity and symmetry of form. We see this law well exemplified in dogs, which can rarely surpass, say, thirty-four inches in height, without becoming weak in the loins and clumsy in their movements. For cart-horses, I shall put this limit at, say, seventeen hands two inches; and for race-horses, at, say, sixteen hands three inches. Besides this maximum, there is a certain height which it is no benefit for a horse, from a useful point of view, to exceed. Although, to employ an old saying, "a good big one will beat a good little one;" it is no advantage for a racer, chaser, hunter, hack or light trapper to be more than fifteen hands three inches, or a heavy cart-horse to be higher than sixteen hands three inches. It is an interesting fact that this standard of useful height varies considerably in different breeds. I would put it approximately as follows :—English, North American, Australian and New Zealand thoroughbred and half-bred horses, fifteen hands three inches; ordinary South African horses, fifteen hands; Arabs, fourteen hands two inches; East Indians (country-bred without admixture of English blood), and Basuto ponies, fourteen hands; Mongolian, Yarkundi, Spiti and Bhootiah ponies, thirteen hands two inches; Baluchi, Herati and Cabuli horses, fourteen hands two inches; Burma and Deli ponies, thirteen hands; Manipuri ponies, twelve hands. On Indian race-courses, it has been proved, times out of number, that an Arab of fourteen hands two inches is as good as any other son of the desert, no matter how much he may exceed that height. In fact, there have not been many Arabs which have gone to India, that were better than the gallant little Chieftain, who was only fourteen hands high, and who was the best of his time. The records of the Shanghai and Hongkong races prove that a good Mongolian of thirteen hands two inches (like Teen Kwang, see Fig. 180, who was the Eclipse of the Celestial Empire) can hold his own with any of his class, even at level weights. In China an allowance of only three pounds for an inch in height is given, and yet the best ones are found at about thirteen hands two inches. In India, on the contrary, an allowance of twelve pounds an inch is given; but, with very rare exceptions, a thirteen hands one inch or a thirteen hands two inch English, Australian, Arab or "country-bred" has no chance with a fourteen-hander of its own class. These striking differences in the standard of useful heights are no doubt chiefly due to the effects of climate; for if foreign blood be introduced into any country, it will, in a very few generations, assume the characteristics of the local type of horse or pony.

Careful selection in breeding, good feeding, and healthy conditions of life have a great influence in tending to increase the size, not only of individuals, but also of breeds; in which case, the standard of useful height, will, naturally, become raised. Thus the average English horse is, at the present day, probably six inches taller than he was 200 years ago. From my own observation, I am inclined to think that horses in England have increased about an inch in height during the last thirty years. We should remember, that when we refer to certain breeds of ponies, we allude to horses that have, for generations, been kept small by privation, inclemency of climate, or other influences which have retarded their growth. Were they placed under conditions favourable to their development, their descendants would soon become full-sized horses, even in the case of ten-hand Shetland (Pl. 61) or Corean ponies. It is impossible, therefore, to maintain a race of ponies which are well-fed and well-cared for.

Length of Limb.—We have seen in Chapter I. that the fundamental difference between animals of speed and those of strength, is that the former have comparatively long legs, and that the latter have comparatively short ones. We have in the camel a well-marked exception to this rule. The Ship of the Desert, as we may see in Fig. 170, has very long legs in comparison to his length of body, and yet he is extremely slow for his size. The cause of his lack of speed is chiefly owing to the weakness of his "rearing muscles" (*see* p. 64), and to the straightness of the column of bones of his fore-limb (*see* p. 63). Hence, when he tries to go quickly, he is unable to raise his forehand sufficiently to obtain a well-regulated period of suspension, like that of the horse (*see* Figs. 46, 88 and 102). His gallop, which he attempts

FIG. 170.—CAMEL.

only on rare occasions, has so much up and down motion in it, that he can continue it but for a very short time. His usual fast pace is a kind of amble which has no period of suspension. Many "weedy" horses (*see* p. 267) which have long legs, are deficient in speed from causes similar to those that render the camel slow. The law as to length of limb can be amply verified, other things being equal, in the case of the horse, by the hard logic of statistics. I accordingly give the following table of measurements in inches, taking Ormonde (Frontispiece) and St. Simon (Pls. 7 and 18) as examples of the fleet of foot, and the Shire horse, Cheadle Jumbo, and the Shire mare, Chance (Pl. 19), as illustrations of strength.

	Ormonde.	St. Simon.	Cheadle Jumbo.	Chance.
Height at withers . . .	$64\frac{1}{2}$ *	$63\frac{1}{4}$ *	67 *	67 *
Length of body	$61\frac{1}{2}$	$59\frac{1}{2}$	76	76
Depth from withers to brisket.	29	$27\frac{1}{4}$	$35\frac{1}{2}$	34
Distance of "girth place" from ground	$35\frac{1}{2}$	$36\frac{1}{4}$	$31\frac{1}{2}$	33
Length of head	$24\frac{1}{2}$	24	29	28

* Without shoes.

I took the measurements of Ormonde on the 20th July, 1887, when he was a four-year-old; and those of St. Simon in September, 1884, when he was a three-year-old. I may mention that the photographs of Ormonde and St. Simon are particularly valuable, as these animals were probably the two best race-horses that have ever lived, and as their photographs were taken when they were in racing condition. I may mention that the outlines of Pl. 18, have been taken from a photograph which was too much "fogged" to bear reproduction. The shadows, however, have been added by an artist, Mr. Oswald Brown.

We see from the foregoing table, that some three and four year-old race-horses of the best class are 3 or 4 inches higher at the withers (and at the croup) than they are long in the body; and that the Shire horse, which is the most

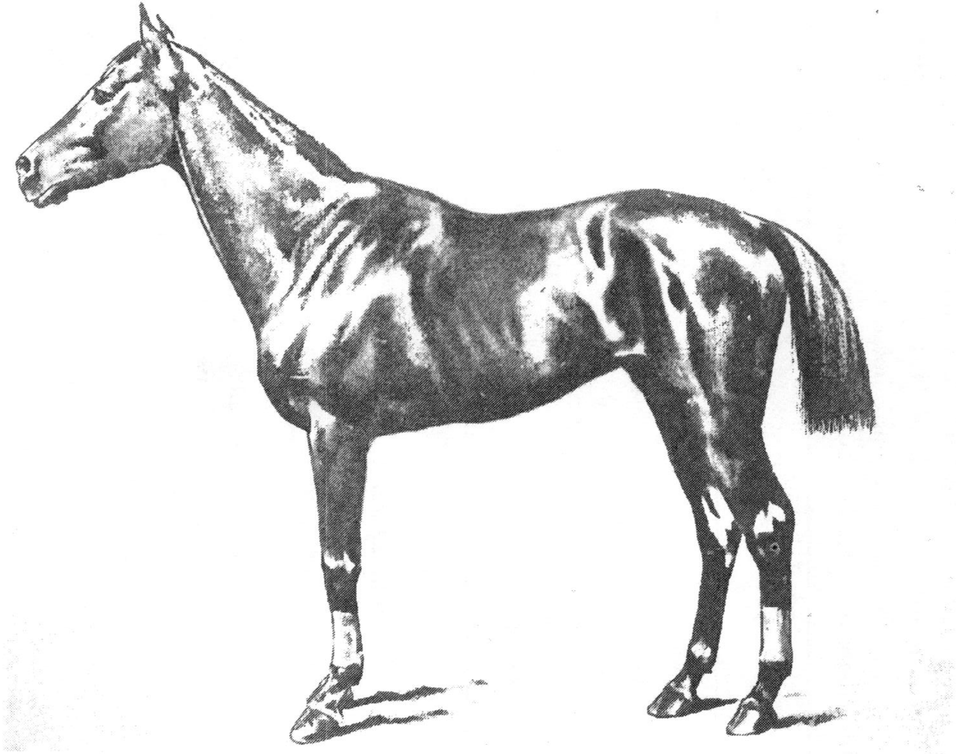

powerful of all horses, is about 9 inches longer than he is high. The difference between the two types with respect to their length of leg, as compared to their depth of chest, is equally well marked. The intermediate classes, in this respect, partake, as a rule, of the characteristics of the respective types to which they are most nearly allied. Thus, if we take Ormonde (Frontispiece) as the highest type of the race-horse, we shall find that the distance from the top of his withers to his brisket, if applied down his fore leg, will reach from his brisket only to the bottom of his fetlock. In the light-weight hunter (*see* Pl. 15) it will come down to the middle of the pastern; in the middle-weight hunter, to the coronet; in the heavy-weight trooper or light cart-horse, to the ground; and in a Cheadle Jumbo, it will be four inches more in length. Hence we may conclude that the term, "short on the leg," is one to denote the possession of strength rather than of speed. The reckless manner in which it is used with respect to race-horses is as incorrect as it is ridiculous. I may add, that with age, good feeding and want of exercise, a horse usually lengthens, deepens, and thickens somewhat as regards his height. Mr. W. F. Shaw, F.R.C.V.S., who has charge of the horses belonging to the London Streets Tramway Company, tells me that he has frequently observed that comparatively light, well-bred horses, when put to tramway work at about five years of age, thicken and get coarse after a few months, to a far greater extent than if they had been used at fast paces. I need hardly say that labour between the rails is slow; and the feeding (eighteen pounds of corn and twelve pounds of hay) ample for these not very large animals. We may accept the fact that both muscles and bones accommodate themselves in time to the nature of the work to which they are put. The difference here is one of thickness, and not of length. I have often noticed among thoroughbred Australian and New Zealand stock, that they became coarse and lost their appearance of blood if kept under rough conditions and used for ordinary hack work.

I may mention that St. Gatien, the celebrated son of The Rover and St. Editha, who ran a dead heat with Harvester for the Derby of 1884, won the gold cup at Ascot and the Cesarewitch (carrying the unprecedented weight of eight stone ten pounds for a colt of his age) in the same year, was a very deep-chested horse, as his depth from his withers to his brisket (just behind the elbow) was an inch more than from his brisket to the bottom of his fetlock. He was thus an inch deeper than Ormonde, who was one and three-quarter inches deeper than St. Simon. St. Gatien, I need hardly say, was particularly distinguished by his ability to stay a distance.

Length and Depth of Body.—We may advance a step further in our search after the true principles of horse conformation; for if we compare the proportions of the body of the racer with those of the heavy draught animal, we shall find that they are essentially the same, and that the only real difference which exists between these two classes is in the length of their legs Were those of Ormonde, as he is in the Frontispiece, cut down nine or ten inches and proportionately thickened, and were he swelled out by "bulky" food, he would pass fairly well as a cart-horse! The statement which I have just made concerning the comparative proportions of the two extreme types of horses, may not appear so outrageous as it might do at first glance, if we consider that the

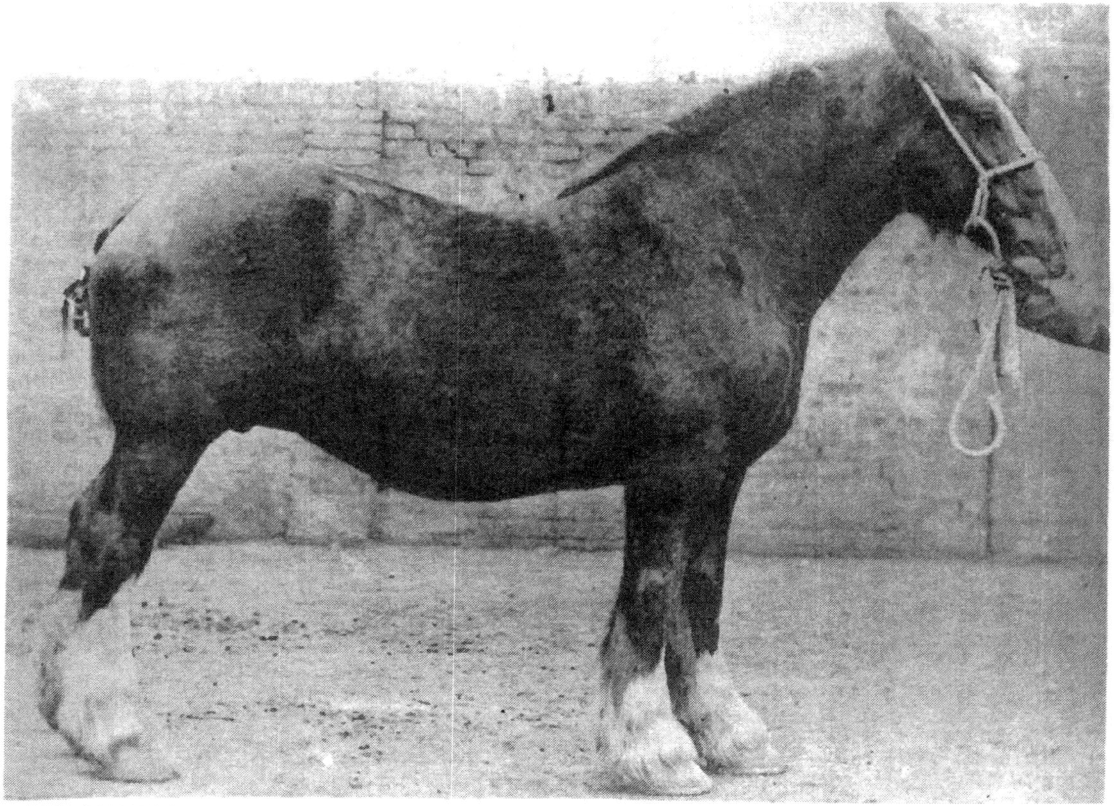

PHOTO. BY DIXON & SONS

TO FACE PAGE 154

PLATE 19—MR. E. COLE'S CHAMPION SHIRE MARE, CHANCE.

difference of work between them is one of limbs and not of body. The galloper needs the highest possible development of speed, with a sufficiency of strength; the cart-horse, a maximum of strength with a very moderate amount of speed; both the strength and speed being derived from the muscles of the limbs. The two classes, however, are in their work equally dependent on the organs (those of breathing, circulation, digestion, excretion, etc.) which are contained in the body. The lungs of the draught animal, when facing a stiff hill with a heavy load behind him, have to be in as good order as those of a racer who is finishing in front of the Grand Stand at Epsom or Newmarket. His stomach, bowels, liver, spleen, kidneys, etc., will also require to be as healthy as those of the other. Hence, we need not expect to find, nor shall we meet with, any material difference in the proportions of the respective bodies of these two animals. If we take from the table given on page 152, the depths (from withers to brisket) of the four representative horses, and divide them respectively into the lengths of these animals, we shall find the ratio for Ormonde, St. Simon and Cheadle Jumbo to be 1 to 2·1, and for Chance, 1 to 2·2; while the ratio of their depths at the lowest point of their backs to their lengths will be, in all four cases, 1 to 2½ (nearly). This is sufficient to prove the close identity of proportions between the depth and length of body both in racers and heavy cart-horses, and *a fortiori* with those of the intermediate classes, such as hunters, troopers, and light harness horses.

It may be objected to the foregoing remarks that, in the heavy draught animal, the shoulders are thicker, and the breast, broader in proportion to the length of the body, than in the case of the galloper. To this I may reply that the difference is due, not to the shape of the body, but to the size of the muscles which attach the limbs to the body, and which consequently partake of the massive character of the legs. We must also remember that the pelvis is a portion of the hind limb (*see* p. 31).

Thickness of Limb.—Continuing the argument begun in Chapter I., we find that the muscles of the limbs of gallopers are comparatively long and slender. Hence, the bones, being dependent on the muscles for their shape, must partake of the same character. It is advantageous for another reason that they should be slight; for, were the bones of the legs of the galloper massive, there would be entailed a large amount of friction in the working of their joints, with consequent loss of speed, which would be of little importance in the heavy draught animal, in which the opposite kind of conformation should be sought for.

Comparative Length of Fore and Hind Limbs.—The conditions under which the limbs play their part in locomotion, are so complex and varied, that I can lay down rules on this subject only in very general terms. We must also bear in mind that there is a certain limit of height (largely influenced by breed) which the horse should not exceed, and which has been discussed on page 148 *et seq.* I may state the present question as follows: at any given height, is it advantageous for the horse to be higher at the withers than he is over the top of the croup, or *vice versâ*, when he is intended for galloping, or for heavy draught; and to what extent may such difference, if any, amount to? It is evident that the longer the hind leg, the greater—other things being equal—will be the speed of propulsion. Excess of height at the croup will, however, be accompanied by two serious drawbacks, namely, it will entail proportionately increased work, during fast paces, on the fore limb (*see* p. 63) and on the muscles of the back and loins (*see* p. 64) in raising the forehand at each stride; and, by surcharging the fore legs (*see* p. 49), it will naturally tend to render these limbs more liable to the injurious effects of work than they would be, were the weight more equally distributed between the fore and hind extremities. Under the former, we would have increased speed purchased by loss of staying power, which is as dependent on the free action of the fore limbs and loins, as it is on that of the hind limbs. Under the latter, the gain in the rate of progression would be obtained at the risk of impaired soundness. Those speedy animals, the cheetah, the Indian black buck, and the grey-hound, are a little longer in the hind limb than they are in front. As a rule, race-horses of the highest class are about the same height at withers and croup. This difference between the racer and the other gallopers may be accounted for by the fact, that the proportion of weight which the fore limbs of the race-horse have to carry, is still more increased by the presence of a jockey on his back. Among the fleet of foot, I purposely omitted mentioning the hare, which is, for its size, the fastest animal of the lot. Its speed, however, can be maintained, as we might have inferred, only for a short distance on level ground; though it is particularly hard to catch up a hill, the difficulty of ascending which is directly lessened by the fact of the fore limbs being shorter than the hind ones. Any disadvantage, in progression, arising from undue shortness of fore legs is, more or less, compensated for, in the hare, by great development of the muscles of the loins ("rearing muscles," *see* p. 64). The lynx (Pl. 17), which is very high behind, has an extraordinary turn of speed; but only for a short distance. Its gallop, like that of other cats, is a series of leaps (*see* p. 128). From practical observations, I do not think that it is an advantage for a race-horse to be higher over the croup than at the withers. With regard to this point, we may study the Frontispiece (Ormonde), and Pl. 55 (Favonius). Could a horse be reserved for races up-hill, like on the old Cambridgeshire course, which finished at "the top of the town," increased height at the withers might be an advantage; but such a policy would hardly be practicable. We may conclude from the foregoing remarks, that if a race-horse be higher over the croup than at the withers, he will require, all the more, to have sloping shoulders, oblique pasterns and powerful loins, and to be "light in front."

We have now to consider the very practical question—which, no doubt, every man who goes in for pony racing has asked himself—is it an advantage for a pony which has to pass the standard at a certain height, to be considerably higher over the croup than at the withers? The results of my experience make me reply "no" to this query. The statement, which I have often heard urged, that a pony which measures, say, 14·3 over the croup, and which can pass the standard at fourteen hands, must have a "pull" over others of its own class which are as high at their withers as over their croup, is not borne out in practice. The best racing ponies I have seen, had no great difference between these two measurements—certainly not more than two inches. Among this list I may mention: the English ponies, Lord Clyde, Water-lily, Dorothy (Pl. 39), Maythorne, Mike (Pl. 38), St. Helena, Skittles (Fig. 171), Rex, Selena, and

FIG. 171.—CAPTAIN MOWBRAY'S PONY MARE, SKITTLES.
(Drawn from a photograph.)

Sylvia; the New Zealanders, Little Wonder, and Parekaretu; the Australians, Mayflower, Achievement, Chester, Bob, and Jeannette; the Arabs, Caliph, Little Hercules, Blitz (Fig. 179), Sweet William, and Magistrate (Pl. 28); the Barb, Kangaroo; the Indian country-breds, Ruby, Bonnie Doo, and Daphne;

and the South African, Coachman. As an extreme case of a pony being high behind, I give the photograph of a pony mare (*see* Pl. 20) who, though she passed the standard at 13·3, measured nearly fifteen hands over the croup. Even allowing for a certain amount of "fakement," there was about four inches difference between her height at the withers and at the croup. As she was also rather heavy in the shoulders, it is almost needless to say that she did not stand training. I may remark that instability of equilibrium (*see* p. 67), which is increased according as the weight on the fore legs exceeds that on the hind ones, should be obtained, in the galloper, more by the body being short and the legs and neck long, than by the difference of height between the withers and the croup.

The lower a horse is in front, the rougher will be his paces; hence an animal of this kind of conformation will not, as a rule, make a pleasant hack; nor would he, in most cases, do well as a hunter; for the excess of weight in front would proportionately militate against his safety when landing over a fence, and against the soundness of his fore legs.

The heavy cart-horse, viewed from a purely draught point of view, ought to be higher in front than behind (*see* p. 74).

Length of Neck.—As the muscles which draw the fore leg forward (namely, those of the neck) are muscles of locomotion, they should be proportionate in length to those of the fore limb. Hence, if a horse has long fore legs, like the race-horse, he ought to have a long neck; and *vice versâ*.

PHOTO. BY M. H. HAYES

TO FACE PAGE 160

PLATE 20—PONY MARE, VERY LOW IN FRONT.

Length of Head.—As the head is a part of the spinal column (*see* p. 30), their respective lengths should be proportionate to each other; but the head can bear no fixed ratio to the length of the limbs, which varies according to the kind of work to which the particular horse is best suited. Thus, we find that although the length of the head has the same proportion (about 1 to $2\frac{1}{2}$) to the length of the body in both the racer and cart-horse, the comparison does not hold good with regard to the height, which is naturally influenced by the length of the fore legs.

Width between the Legs.—In the heavy draught horse, the fore legs are kept apart by the massive pectoral muscles (*see* p. 38) which draw the fore limbs back. The hip joints have also to be widely asunder to permit of great width of the pelvis for the attachment of extremely large muscles. In the galloper it is different. For remarks on this subject, *see* p. 65.

Comparative Weight of Body.—The body of the race-horse should be as light as is compatible with the due performance of his work. The heavy cart-horse, on the contrary, requires a deep, massive body for the attachment of his powerful muscles, and, also, to give him the necessary weight to throw into the collar. This subject has been discussed in Chapter IX. (*see* p. 73).

Comparative Length of the Bones of the Limbs.—If we "pick up" in succession the fore feet of a number of differently shaped horses, and bend the limbs at the knees as far as they will "go," we shall find that in almost all cases, the heel will touch the elbow at about the same place. As the proportion between the length of the fore-arm and cannon bone evidently varies in different horses, a comparatively long or short forearm must be accompanied by a similar condition of the bones below the fetlock. Lecoq remarks: "The length of the fore-arm varies inversely as that of the cannon bone." I think I may venture to extend this principle somewhat further, in stating the following inverse proportions:—Shoulder blade, long; humerus (from point of shoulder to elbow), short; fore-arm, long; cannon-bone, short, pastern, long. In other words, a long shoulder blade is accompanied by a long fore-arm and long pastern, and by a short humerus and a short cannon-bone. The converse of this holds equally good. Taking the shoulder blade as the base to start from, we may infer that the difference between these alternate proportions should be best marked in animals, like the hunter or steeple-chaser, which specially require to have this bone of considerable length (*see* p. 210). It may be objected that the greyhound, which is possessed of extraordinary speed and marvellous jumping powers, has, comparatively speaking, a short shoulder blade and long humerus. Although the length of the latter, which is detached from the body, gives him great forward "reach;" the shortness of the former makes him too bad a weight-carrier (*see* p. 207) for him to be accepted as a model for our purpose. I think we may assume that a similar series of inverse proportions should exist in the hind limb. Thus: pelvis, long; thigh, short; tibia (from stifle to hock), long; cannon-bone, short; pastern, long. As the muscles which give length to the tibia are far more concerned in the extension of the hind limb of the jumper and galloper than in the cart-horse; we should look for greater length from stifle to hock, in the first two, than in the last named. I would also expect in them a shorter thigh and a shorter cannon-bone. I may mention that I am confirmed in this opinion by the practical experience of Mr. Tom Jennings, junr., the well-known trainer, who once remarked to me that he always regarded as a good point in a race-horse, the fact of its stifle being set high up in its flank—*i.e.*, its having a short thigh bone, and consequently being long from its stifle to its hock.

In the remainder of the body we might, possibly, also find a series of inverse proportions as follows:—Head, short; neck, long; back and loins, short; croup, long; bones of the tail, short.

Although I am well aware that the proportions of the skeleton do not rigidly follow any strict mathematical rule; still I am strongly of opinion, from close study of the horse, that in the large majority of cases the foregoing deductions will be found to be correct.

Differences of Conformation between the Two Sexes.—As a rule, the mare, as compared to the horse, has a lighter neck, a broader pelvis, and is higher behind and slacker in the loins than he is.

CHAPTER XVI.

HEAD AND NECK.

Size of Head—Leanness of Head—Profile of Face—Front view of Face—Size of Brain—Top of the Head—Ears—Eyes—Hollows above the Eyes—Nostrils—Lips—Lower Jaw—Setting-on of the Head—Neck—Throat

Size of Head.—We have seen on page 161 that as the head is a portion of the spinal column, it should correspond in size to the bones of the back, loins, croup, and ribs, and not to those of the limbs. Agreeably to the axiom that "the function makes the organ," we find, in the majority of cases, that a horse's breathing capacity is proportionate to the size of his air passages, of which the cavities that lead from the nostrils towards the windpipe and lungs cannot be large, unless the bones which form them are of a fair size. We must remember that a horse breathes, normally, through his nostrils and not through his mouth. Besides, as the tube (*larynx*) through which air enters the lungs from the nasal cavities, lies between the two branches of the lower jaw; it follows, speaking generally, that the broader and more open the nostrils are, the greater will be the calibre of this tube, and the more perfect the breathing power. Although it is impossible to draw any hard and fast rule on this subject, we may infer that a comparatively small head is not a desirable "point" in horses whose success depends on their power of breathing. I venture to think that men of experience will agree with me in saying that unusually neat and trim heads are far more common among "the five furlong division," than among genuine stayers. Again, the head should be of sufficient size to afford a broad surface for the attachment of the muscles of mastication, for those that extend, flex, rotate and move the head from one side to the other, and for muscles which draw the limb forward, and which are, consequently, important agents of movement. The connection between the size of the head and the amount of intelligence possessed by an animal is, as with ourselves, too ill-defined to admit of any practical deductions being made from it. As the usefulness of a horse is generally limited by the amount of work his legs will stand, the possession of a large head by an animal which is "light of bone" in his extremities, is a serious defect; for it not alone shows that his frame is wanting in symmetry, but it also tends to indicate that the bones of his body, and, probably, the muscles and other tissues, are too heavy for his legs. If, however, he showed great substance and good quality of bone, tendon and ligament, we might very well "put up" with some "plainness" about his head. Any useless weight of that part, acting at the end of the lever formed by the neck, will naturally be objectionable. Agreeably to the facts mentioned on page 161, we may judge the length of the head by that of the body, the usual proportion being about 1 to 2½. Probably, a more practical rule is to compare the length of the head with the depth of the body at the lowest point of the back. In a well-shaped horse which is not in gross condition, these two measurements are very nearly equal; although the head, from its isolated position, looks much less long, at first glance, than the body is deep Besides this, the fact of the body being round, while the side of the horse's head, as seen in profile, is flat, will cause the depth of the former to appear to measure more than the length of the latter. We may prove the approximate correctness of the ratio of 1 to $2\frac{1}{2}$, by reference to the table given on p. 152. From it we see that in Ormonde the proportion is 1 to 2·5; in St. Simon, 1 to 2·48; in Cheadle Jumbo, 1 to 2·6, and in Chance 1 to 2·7. Here, possibly to our surprise, we perceive that the cart-horses have comparatively smaller heads than the racers—a difference which, no doubt, is due to their grosser "condition;" as the fat on their chests and quarters must add slightly to their length of body. Bourgelat, followed by all, or nearly all, the French writers on equine conformation, adopted the length of a horse's head as a measure of its height, in the proportion of 1 to $2\frac{1}{2}$. This eminent Frenchman based his calculations on a type of horse (such as the ordinary saddle nag) which was about as high at the withers as it was long in the body, and did not take into consideration the great differences between the respective heights and lengths of animals of various classes, ranging from the racer to the Shire horse. From my own observations, I would put the length of a horse at about $2\frac{1}{2}$ to $2\frac{2}{3}$ times the length of his head.

The fact that the size of the head of the horse is proportionate to his length of body, and not to his height at the withers, accounts for the cart-horse appearing to have a comparatively larger head than the thoroughbred.

Leanness of Head.—In the lighter classes of horses, the head should present a general appearance of "leanness," that is to say, the skin which covers it should be fine; its bony prominences sharply marked; and the muscles, blood-vessels, and nerves which are immediately under the skin, clearly defined.

The absence, thus indicated, of an excess of loose underlying tissue will suggest the possession of strength of muscle and bone (*see* p. 15). When the head is large and "fleshy," we may generally assume that the animal is "soft" and wanting in "blood." The presence on the head of well-developed muscles, of which those of mastication are the most powerful, will naturally suggest to the observer that the horse has a good constitution. As pointed out by MM. Goubaux and Barrier, we must not mistake for "leanness" an emaciated or wasted appearance of the muscles, due to old age or debility.

The Bombay Arab dealers (such as that fine judge, Ali bin Abdullah, and that prince of Bedouins, the late Shaikh Esa bin Curtas) regard thinness of the lower jaw at its angles as a sure sign of pure desert blood.

Profile of Face.—The line of the forehead and nose, when viewed in profile, will, as a rule, be straight, concave or convex. The first two forms of contour are more or less characteristic of the thorough-bred and Arab; although it is only correct to say that many horses of aristocratic English blood have Roman noses, especially those bred in the Colonies. I have never seen a high caste Arab have such a conformation. For straight profiles we may point to Pls. 35 and 39. Pl. 31 shows a concave profile. The true concave face is obtained, not by a prominent forehead, as in Pl. 21; but by a dip in the nose between the eyes and nostrils. Ormonde's face (*see* Frontispiece) tends to concavity. For a convex profile (Roman nose) *see* Pls. 19 and 23. This shape might be objected to on account of its liability to render the air passages of the head curved, instead of straight, in which case there might be some slight interference with the ready ingress and egress of respired air. I have, however, never met with a case in which a Roman nose was the cause of impaired breathing power; although I have known a horse become a roarer from alteration in the shape of the nasal cavities from a disease of the bones called *osteo porosis*, or "big head." I may mention that many heavy cart-horses have Roman noses.

Colonel John Anderson, late Inspecting Veterinary Surgeon, Bombay Army (than whom no better judge of a horse exists), remarked to me many years ago, that a prominent forehead (*see* Pl. 21), or a rise between the eyes, is an indication of a bad, or at least of a wayward, temper in a horse. I have no theory to advance in support of this idea, the truth of which, however, I have seen verified in many instances. The original of Pl. 21 was a rascal of the deepest dye. Tristan (*see* Fig. 172), had this fatal bump between his eyes, and he was a "thief," as well as a bit of a "savage." His name will recall to many old race-goers the memorable struggle for the Cambridgeshire of 1881, when, ridden by poor George Fordham, he finished third to Foxhall and Lucy Glitters. It is but just to the chestnut son of Hermit and Thrift to say that his trainer, Mr. Tom Jennings, junr., tells me that Tristan's temper had been spoiled by bad usage when he was a yearling.

Front view of Face.—Good width of forehead between

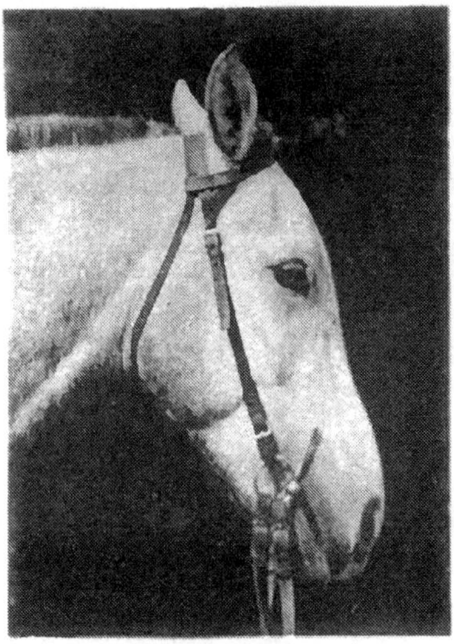

PL. 21—PROMINENT FOREHEAD.

PL. 22—BROAD FOREHEAD.

PHOTO. BY M. H. HAYES

TO FACE PAGE 168

PL. 23 UNDER BRED HEAD

the eyes (*see* Pl. 22) indicates, as a rule, free breathing power and strong muscles of mastication; for the bones of that part (*frontal bones*) form a portion of the roof of the cavities

FIG. 172.—MR. LEFÈVRE'S TRISTAN.
(*Drawn from a photograph.*)

through which air enters on its way to the lungs, and gives attachment to a powerful muscle which aids in closing the jaws, and which is fixed in the large depression that is just above the eye. Good width between the eyes is generally regarded as a sign of intelligence and of a generous disposition; and it may indicate large capacity of brain, by reason of the frontal bone forming a portion of the covering of that organ. I shall refer, under the next heading, to the subject of the desirability, or otherwise, of a large brain in the horse.

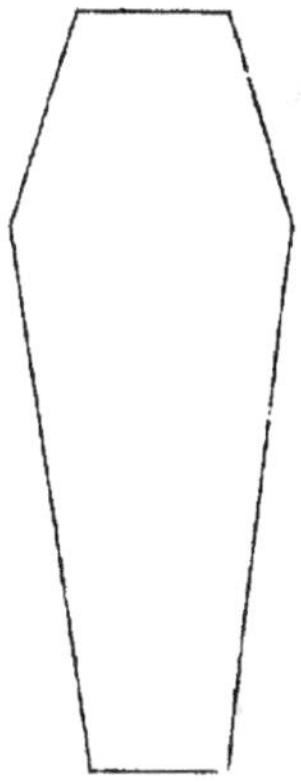

FIG. 173.—COFFIN SHAPE OF HEAD.

As seen from the front, the bones at each side of the head, from the outside corner of the eyes to the hollow above the eyes, should run nearly parallel to the long axis of the head, and should then narrow inwards. This desirable shape is well shown in Pl. 24. If the reader will compare this photograph with Pl. 25 he will see my meaning, for in the latter, the line from the outside corner of the eye to the base of the ear is nearly straight. This peculiarity and a certain fulness of nose (which is very different to the fine modelling of the nose in Pl. 24) gives a coffin shape (*see* Fig. 173) to

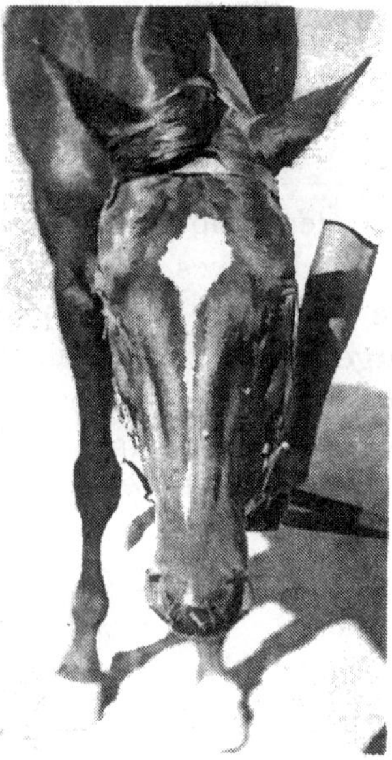

PL. 24—WELL BRED HEAD.

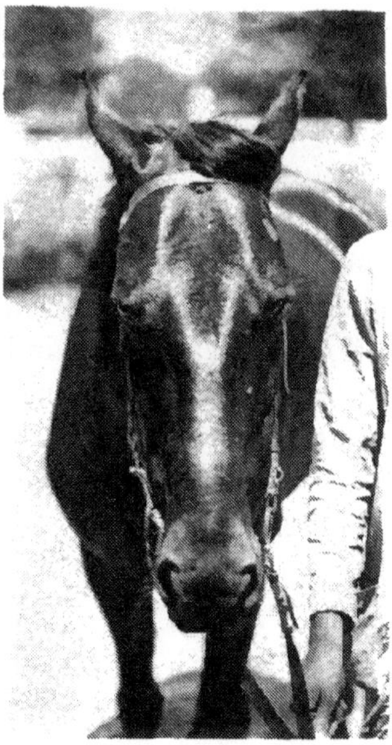

PL. 25—UNDER BRED HEAD.

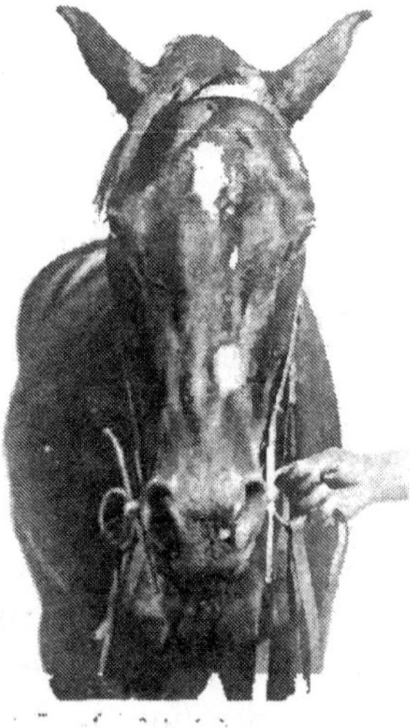

PL. 26 HIGH OCCIPITAL CREST.

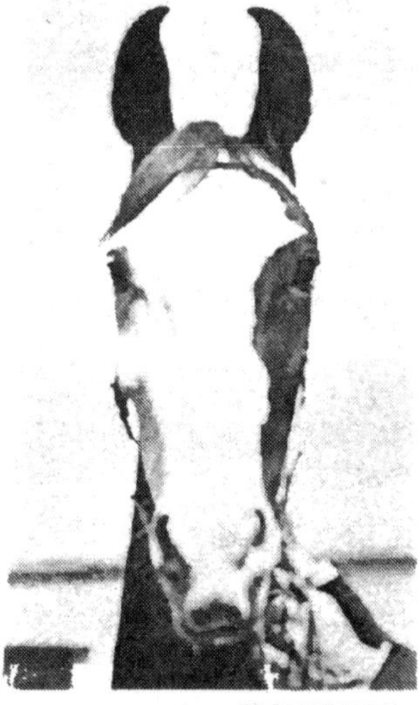

FACE PAGE 170

PL. 27 TURNED-IN EARS.

the head in Pl. 25 I may mention that this head is slightly foreshortened, and consequently does not appear as narrow as it ought to be. I need hardly say that I am aware that the stable term, "coffin-shaped," as applied to a horse's head, has reference to its appearance in profile, and not to its front view.

Experience tells us that the forehead should be prominent immediately below the brow band, and should be marked on each side by a well-developed lump of muscle which is shown fairly well in Pl. 24. This formation is usually accompanied by the possession of pluck and "cleverness." Its good or poor development is, I regret to say, as difficult to clearly explain in words as it is to show in a photograph; although its recognition in actual practice is an easy matter. Prominence of that part may possibly have some connection with a good development of the *cerebellum* (*see* p. 43).

It is regarded as a beauty for the eyes to be *set high* up in the head. As far as I can see, their position varies but little in the horse. In the zebra (Pl. 29) they are set rather low down.

The bones on the sides of the nose are prominent in youth, but gradually "fall in" with age, on account of the fangs of the back teeth, which are lodged in them, descending lower and lower as the animal grows older.

This change in the form of the nose will serve to indicate, to some extent, the age of the horse.

Size of Brain.—Without entering into any physiological argument, we may assume that, as a rule, size of brain is an indication of brain power. According to the classic idea entertained by writers on equine conformation, a large development of brain is a desirable "point" in the horse. Thus we read in *Achat du Cheval,* by M. Gayot, that: "The more voluminous is the brain, the larger is the spinal cord, proportionate to the size of which are the nerves that issue from it. It is thus that a large forehead, denoting a high degree of intelligence, is the index of a good nervous system —that is to say, of high mental and physical qualities." As regards this, I would suggest a doubt respecting the connection claimed between "high mental and physical qualities." It did not exist among the ancient gladiators, nor does it in the case of our modern prize-fighters and pedestrians. Although the bull-dog is stronger and the greyhound faster for their size than the poodle and collie, they are certainly not more intelligent. A long and intimate acquaintance with horses—especially that acquired during my professional horse-breaking tours—convinces me that a comparatively high degree of mental (*i.e.* reasoning) power is not desirable in a horse; because it is apt to make him impatient of control by man. A jibber in harness, or a refuser in the hunting field, when the vice has not been induced by pain or infirmity, such as galled shoulders or weak hocks, usually "baulks," because "he knows too much," or at least he knows more than the animal that will pull at the traces or follow the hounds till he drops. So far from a horse taking delight, as he is supposed by novelists to do, in obeying the wishes of man, he very seldom yields to his would-be master without a struggle. If this takes place in the hoped-for manner, when the horse is quite young, the victory on the part of the man is generally easy, and a few repetitions of it quickly confirm the habit of obedience. If, however, the attempted subjugation be delayed till the animal is "aged"—when he will be able to think for himself without the promptings and influence of man—it will be found that his breaking will be ten, if not a hundred, times more difficult than if it had been undertaken in his early youth. This theory of the undesirability of a horse knowing too much, which I have applied to refractory animals, appears to hold equally good in greyhounds that run "cunning." In these remarks on the intelligence of horses, it must be clearly understood that I refer to reasoning power and not to power of memory, which is independent of the capacity to draw a conclusion from given premises. It is evident, without the necessity of writing a treatise on the subject, that the useful (to man) intelligence of the horse lies in his power of memory and to the quickness with which his muscles act in response to the impressions received by his senses. In other words, his useful intelligence depends on the high development of his instinct, and not of his reason. We demand of the horse ready obedience; but not obedience matured by reflection, like what the shepherd would expect his dog to display when getting his flock home on a stormy night, or when driving them through a crowded thoroughfare. We do not ask him to take the initiative from the deep affection which he does not bestow on us, nor to reason out problems; we only want him to remember that if he does certain things, we shall "make much of him"; that if he does other things, we shall punish him.

We know that reflex action, prompted by stimuli from outside the body, acts best when it has but little connection with the brain (*see* p. 42). In fact, the smaller is the comparative size of the brain, the quicker and more accurately are instinctive movements performed. Thus we see animals with, comparatively a very small brain, or with none at all, get out of danger, or seize their prey, with an amount of speed and precision which it would be hopeless for any man to attempt to rival; simply because the action of his instinct is impeded by the influence of a large brain We see this demonstrated in ourselves, in the case of movements, as in fencing, boxing and dancing, for instance, which could be executed only slowly and clumsily at first, when they needed the exercise of thought, become capable of being performed with the speed and correctness of a machine, as soon as practice had made them almost automatic.

The prominent forehead (*see* Pl. 21), to which I have alluded on p. 168, indicates a large size of the intellectual portion (*cerebrum, see* p. 43) of the brain, which at that part of the forehead is covered by only a thin plate of bone. Without wishing to import any of the jargon of phrenology into a discussion on this subject, I may hazard the suggestion that the portion of the brain which is consecrated to the functions of memory and perceptive power, as well as the *cerebellum* (the organ of "muscular sense," *see* p. 43), lies underneath the upper part of the forehead, where prominence and convexity of the part is a marked beauty, as I have mentioned on p. 171.

For the foregoing reasons, I do not look upon the possession of a large brain as a desirable "point" in a horse. Hence, apart from the practical experience I have had, I do not like, as I have just said, a bulging-out condition of the lower part of the forehead, nor a long distance between the eyes and the top of the head (*see* p. 171), both of which peculiarities of conformation point to large brain capacity.

Top of the Head.—The bone (the *occipital crest*) at the top of the head should be prominent and well developed (*see* Pl. 26); as it affords attachment for the powerful suspensory ligament of the head and neck (*see* p. 33), and for several important muscles. Large development of the occipital crest is considered by some authorities to indicate corresponding size of the cerebellum.

Ears.—Personally, I cannot say much as regards the indications afforded by the ears. In common, probably, with most observers, I have remarked that animals which move their ears in a quick decisive manner, evidently with the same intent as they use their eyes to see what kind of ground they are going over, are, generally, of the "clever" sort which do not know how "to put a foot wrong." Their method of employing their ears is quite different to the restless, "listening" (if I may use the word) style adopted by horses that have defective sight. The former have their attention chiefly directed to the ground in front of them; the latter distribute it on all sides. It looks well for the skin and hair which covers the ears, to be fine; and the ears themselves, thin and lean. Whether in horse or man, I dislike to see ears set up high on the head, and think that the part of the skull which is between them should be moderately broad, as in Pl. 22. At the same time, I must say that I have seen many clever horses, especially among those bred in India, that had their ears close together and set up high on the head, as in Pl. 27. This photograph gives us an idea of the peculiar manner in which the points of the ears of some Indian breeds (Kathiawars and Wuzeerees, for instance) are directed inwards when the ears are pricked forward. To show what diverse opinions exist as to the ears of the horse, I give from different works on conformation the two following extracts, which are far from being in accord with each other. The reader, however, can decide from his own practical experience as to their respective correctness. "There can be no greater ornament than long, fine, active-looking, upright, tolerably close-set ears, with the points a little inclined towards each other. I never saw a soft constitutioned horse with ears of this description" (*Dr. Carson*). MM. Goubaux and Barrier state: "It is a fact worthy of notice that horses which have short ears are always energetic and plucky. There seems to be a certain relation between their length and the timidity of their bearers. At least, this is the conclusion we may draw from a comparison made among different kinds of animals, of which the most timid and inoffensive have them greatly developed. Carnivorous animals, on the contrary, have them small. Short ears render the head lighter, and the expression of the face brighter, more expressive and more pleasing to the eye. In this respect, the Arab horse greatly excels English and continental animals. It is considered a beauty for a horse to have his ears well directed to the front at an angle of about 45° with the axis of the head. Quick and energetic animals carry their ears in this manner. To sum up, the ear is beautiful when it is short, directed to the front, well placed, lean, fine, and covered with thin skin, which should be adherent, and comparatively free from hair in the interior of the ear." With respect to the ears being "well directed to the front at an angle of about 45° with the axis of the head," I may remark that such a carriage of the ears, being produced by voluntary muscular effort, can be sustained only for a comparatively brief space of time Almost all horses which are not prevented therefrom by disease, malformation or accident, have the ability to direct their ears forward in the manner mentioned, but do so only when their attention is attracted to something in front of them. The same may be said of donkeys, mules and zebras (*see* Pls. 29 and 37). It is true that some horses "prick their ears" more frequently than others; but, for all that, such carriage of the ears can be regarded as but a momentary lighting-up of the face, and not as an intrinsic beauty. I may add that if a horse habitually carries his ears more or less directed behind him, we might suspect him to be wanting in courage and good temper. This is by no means an invariable rule; for I have met with some notable exceptions.

M. Richard remarks that deaf horses carry their ears steadily pointed in the direction the horse is looking, without side "play." Such animals are generally docile and attentive to the indications received from the rein and leg.

A horse is said to have lop-ears when they are set on in a loose and somewhat pendulous manner. I have not observed that lop-eared horses are less clever than those whose ears are carried more uprightly.

Eyes.—The eye should be clear and free from tears, the pupil black, and the eyelids thin and comparatively free from wrinkles. A small eye (*see* Pl. 23) in the horse is called a "pig-eye," and is generally considered to denote a disposition that is either sulky or wanting in courage. In this photograph, the straight shoulder, ewe neck, Roman nose, and pig-eye point to the plebeian origin of the animal whose portrait it is. The prominent "buck-eye" is generally regarded as an unfailing sign of short sight. Horses which show a good deal of white in their eyes, as the term is, are, with much justice, usually suspected of being vicious; for kickers, as a rule, uncover a portion of the white of the eye (on the side to which the head is turned), when they look back, ready to "let fly." This justifiable suspicion is naturally heightened, if, at the same time that the danger signal in the eye is displayed, the ears are pressed back close on the neck, the front teeth are exposed by the drawing back of the lips, and a hind foot is kept raised off the ground. I may mention that, under ordinary conditions, the human eye always shows a good deal of white; but that the horse's eye, as a rule, does not do so, except when its glance is directed to the rear, or inwards. Some game, honest horses (like St. Gatien, for instance) show, without looking in a backward direction, a certain amount of white of the eye, which, when it is of a constant reddish tinge, is thought by some to mark hardiness of constitution and staying power.

Hollows above the Eyes.—The existence of deep hollows above the eyes is objectionable; for it denotes that the animal is old and more or less worn out, or that either its sire or dam was well advanced in years when it was bred, and, consequently, that it is somewhat wanting in vigour.

Nostrils.—The nostrils should be thin, flexible and of large capacity, so as to suggest the possession of large air passages. During rest, they should be more or less closed. If they are kept constantly dilated when the breathing ought to be tranquil, we may infer that the animal has something wrong with his "wind."

Lips.—The lips should be lean and comparatively thin; should possess considerable power of movement; and, as a rule, should be kept closed, for the sake of appearance. We may generally consider that a pendant condition of the lower lip indicates want of vigour; for it is much more frequently observed among old horses than among young ones. M. Richard considers that it is often inherited. "We have," says he, "ridden horses full of energy, which had a pendant lower lip. Delphine, formerly a brood mare at the stud at Pin, daughter of Massoud and of a Selim mare, dam of Eylau, had a drooping lower lip, and all her foals took after her in this respect. She, however, possessed energy and blood which have left their mark." Some horses have great length of upper lip, which undoubtedly looks ugly. Both this conformation and the possession of a thick tuft of hair or moustache on the upper lip, are indicative of coarse blood.

Lower Jaw.—The branches of the lower jaw should be broad, as viewed from the side, and should be wide apart at their angles, so as to give plenty of room for the tube (the *larynx*) which lies between them, and which opens into the wind-pipe. The space between the jaws should not alone be broad, but should also be hollowed out, a condition which will show that the parts are of firm texture and free from excess of loose connective tissue (*see* p. 14). The old practical rule of finding whether a horse is wide enough between the jaws, is to see if the clenched fist can be placed within the hollow. I venture to think that few horses could successfully pass this test, if it were applied with an ordinary sized man's hand. When this space is broad and well hollowed out, the horse will naturally be able to bend his head more freely than when it is narrow, and he will, consequently, be pleasanter to ride and drive.

Setting on of the Head.—The part where the head is set on to the neck should be lean and muscular, and should show a slight depression behind the ears and lower jaw, and also above the wind-pipe. This will indicate absence of an excess of loose connective tissue and ability on the part of the horse to bend his head freely. The beautiful manner in which the neck "runs into" the head of some horses, is due to the arrangement of the bones of the neck and to the lean and well-developed condition of the muscles. The profile of this junction will, then, form a curve, which will be a fitting commencement of the graceful, undulating line that sweeps over the neck, slightly dips in front of the withers, over which it curves, and now, rising a little along the back, swells boldly over the loins and quarters, dips again at the root of the dock, and, finally, ends in the flowing lines of the tail. The setting on of the head and the curves alluded to were beautifully exemplified in St. Simon, whose photograph (Pl. 7) is not nearly as good as I could have wished. These points also come out well in the Arab pony, Magistrate (Pl. 28), and in the Australian gelding, Romance (Pl. 35). In the Arab pony, The Brat (Fig 31), the curved line is perfect from the head to the croup, but, on account of the way he is standing, it descends too abruptly from the top of the croup to the tail. In Ormonde (Frontispiece) the head is set on to the neck in a coarse, stiff manner. I may mention that the ideal contour

which I have described, is an affair of beauty rather than of usefulness.

Neck.—As the length of the neck indicates the length of the muscles which draw the shoulder forward (*see* p. 37); the more we seek for speed in an animal, the longer should be his neck, its thickness being limited by the amount of strength the muscles have to put forth. The race-horse, therefore, should have a long and comparatively thin neck, and the other classes should have their necks proportionately shorter and thicker according as they recede from the galloping type and approach that of the heavy draught animal. The operation of this rule should be restricted only so far as to allow sufficient length of neck for grazing purposes. Some heavy cart-horses have such short necks that they cannot feed off level ground with comfort to themselves. When the art of breeding is pushed to such an extreme as this, I cannot help thinking that there must be some defect in its practical working. I may mention that the combination of a large head and a thin neck is not alone unpleasing to the eye, but is almost always a sign of general weakness.

The all-essential power which men possess to guide and regulate the movements of a horse, largely depends on the flexibility of the animal's neck. Were we unable to make him bend it, and to oblige him to turn his head to one side or the other in obedience to the "feeling" of the hands on the reins, he would be all but useless to us in saddle and for ordinary harness work. With reference to this subject, I may mention that I once undertook to saddle and get ridden an old entire zebra (*equus zebra*, *see* Pl. 29), whose feet were becoming gradually deformed; as it would not allow its owner, a dealer in wild animals, or his assistants to handle it. In less than an hour after I had turned it into the ring of Frank Fillis's circus, which was then in Calcutta, I had its feet rasped down to a proper level, and had it saddled and bridled for the first time in its life. It was then ridden by Steve Margarett (a brilliant Australian rough-rider) and by my wife. Although I was able to quickly teach it to carry its unwonted burden quietly, I made far less progress in giving it a "mouth," during the two days I had it in hand, than I would have done in half an hour with any wild Colonial horse caught for the first time on a "run;" the reason being that the zebra's neck was so stiff and strong, that I was unable to bend it in any direction. I soon taught it to do what I wanted in the circus; but when I rode it outside, it took me wherever it liked. In fact, I had not the slightest power to either stop or guide it. Pl. 29 will show what a "bull-necked" specimen it was. Some horses, like this striped ass, though not to the same extent, are very stiff in the neck, a fact which may be owing to an obstinate temper, bad breaking-in, or to a thick and rigid condition of the muscles and joints of the part. This natural want of flexibility may be overcome to a great extent by judicious "bending." As it militates against the ready turning and easy regulation of the paces of an animal, it should be regarded as a grave defect of conformation in the saddle-horse and light trapper. It may, however, be overlooked in the heavy cart-horse, whose normal pace being a walk, will not require to be as "supple" (to use a riding school term) as an animal that has to go at a faster pace, and whose line of progression, instead of being along a more or less straight road, may be across

PHOTO. BY M. H. HAYES

TO FACE PAGE 182

an intricate country, or in conformance with the word of command in a riding school or on parade. Besides this, to have the necessary power in his fore limbs, the heavy draught animal will need massive neck muscles (*see* p 37) to draw them forward. When "cleverness" is essential to a horse, he should have a flexible neck, and should be able to bend and extend it with the utmost facility, so as to use his head and neck as a balancing pole for preserving the equilibrium of his body.

Some extra weight in the neck, apart from that required for the due development of the neck muscles, will probably be no detriment to the usefulness of a powerful cart-horse; for it will aid him in "throwing weight into the collar." In the saddle-horse, on the contrary, it would be of the greatest disadvantage. Firstly, it would make him heavy on his fore-hand; and, secondly, it would directly tend to wear out his fore legs and feet. In this connection, I may mention that entires, who, as a rule, have much heavier necks than geldings, do not, when they are employed at fast paces, stand as much work, retain their "form" as long, nor get into galloping condition as quickly as those which have been "added to the list." We see this rule well proved in steeplechasing and racing, as witness the long careers of those geldings, Liberator, Regal, and Reindeer. If I do not greatly mistake, the fact of the unsexed Knight of Burghley winning the Lincolnshire Handicap in 1883 was chiefly due to his requiring but little work to get him fit. I would therefore strongly advise owners of race-horses to have the operation performed on all their colts which did not give promise sufficient to warrant their being kept for stud purposes; especially if there was any doubt as to their standing work. Several experienced trainers with whom I have discussed this subject—Mr. Tom Brown and Mr. Edwin Martin, among others—have expressed to me their belief in the practical utility of this proceeding. The lesson to be learned, from a conformation point of view, from the foregoing remarks, is that the faster a horse is required to go, the lighter should be his neck.

As regards the contour of the neck, I may state that, according to its shape, it is designated high-crested (or convex, *see* Pls. 30 and 31), straight (*see* Pls. 28 and 35), or ewe-necked, concave (*see* Pl. 23). The contour varies a good deal according to the manner the animal holds his head, and should be judged by the form it assumes when the horse stands in an ordinary manner at attention, with the line of its face at an angle of about 45° to the ground. Pl. 30 shows us a horse with, for a saddle nag and for the substance of his fore legs, a very over-loaded neck. If we compare that photograph with Pl. 31, we shall see that the convexity of the latter is not, as in the former, obtained at the cost of undue weight in the neck. We may also note the difference, as regards beauty, in the respective curves of the line of the neck in these photographs. The height of the crest in Pl. 30 is due chiefly to an excessive amount of fat in the crest above the suspensory ligament of the head and neck. The only objection I see to a high crest in a galloper, is the possibility of its putting extra weight on the fore legs.

The fact of a horse being ewe-necked seems to be of no detriment to his speed. It might, however, affect his handiness, on account of depriving, to some extent, his rider or driver, as the case may be, of command over him; and by causing his head to be brought into a direction which might prevent him seeing clearly where he was going. On page 80

PHOTO. BY M. H. HAYES

TO FACE PAGE 164

PLATE 30—HEAVY-CRESTED ARAB.

et seq., I have discussed at some length the subject of the carriage of a horse's head and neck.

In saddle-horses, the place where the neck comes out of the chest should be marked, above, by a slight depression in front of the withers; below, by another depression at the point where the jugular groove meets the chest; and at each side, it should be nearly flat with neck and shoulder. In cart-horses, the large muscles of the shoulder stand out in prominent relief from the neck, and the dip in front of the withers is either absent or but faintly indicated. Owing to the comparative lightness of neck in mares and geldings, the union of the neck with the head and trunk is better marked in them, than in entires. The jugular groove, in which the jugular vein lies, may be seen on the lower part of the side of the neck, and is well shown in Pls. 20, 23, and 35.

Throat.—The wind-pipe should be large and well detached from the neck; as it will then indicate good breathing power. This shape is seen in the justly admired "game cock throttle," which is also associated with a good forward carriage of the head. I have noticed that roaring often accompanies a wasted appearance of the tissues which cover the larynx. I am of course aware that the typical form of roaring is caused by paralysis of one or both of the muscles which open the larynx; but their size is too small to account for the peculiarly emaciated condition to which I have alluded.

CHAPTER XVII.

THE TRUNK.

General View of the Trunk—Chest and Ribs—Abdomen—Withers—Breast—Back and Loins—Points of the Hips—Flank—Croup—Anus—Tail.

General View of the Trunk.—We have seen on p. 155, that, as the work which the organs (heart, lungs, liver, spleen, stomach, intestines, kidneys, etc.) contained in the trunk have to do, is the same, whatever may be the kind of horse; the shape of the trunk will not be affected by class distinctions. In this particular, the conformation which will, for instance, be most suitable for a Derby winner, will be that which is best for a cart-horse. In laying down this general rule, I must make an exception of the withers, which (*see* p 194) are concerned in locomotion, and not in the performance of any vital function. Although the shape of the horse's body remains constant—without, of course, taking into consideration individual peculiarities—the bones which make up the entire structure should agree as to thickness with those of the legs; for several of the muscles that are attached to them, are also attached to the limbs. I may mention that the strength of a muscle regulates the thickness of the bone to which it is fixed.

In all cases, the body should be as short as possible compared to its depth; or, in other words, as deep as pos-

PHOTO. BY M. H. HAYES

TO FACE PAGE 126

PLATE 31—COLONEL ANDERSON'S ARAB PONY, THE BRAT.

sible, compared to its length. The longer it is, the further removed will the fore and hind limbs be from each other, and the less able will the animal be to carry weight. On p. 65 we have seen that a short body is a desirable point in the race-horse and jumper. In draught, also, any undue length of body is a disadvantage; for the farther the fore and hind legs are apart, the less rigid will be the connection between them, and the less efficiently will they work together. When speaking of the depth of a horse's body, I refer to its depth at the lowest point of its back (*see* Fig. 2). If an animal shows a good measurement at this part, he is almost certain to possess fair substance of body. The measurement from withers to brisket is very fallacious; for it is not alone affected by the height of the withers themselves, but it also affords hardly any indication of the nature of the "centre-piece" of the body. Many horses, which are very light in their loins and back ribs, have good depth from withers to brisket, as in Pl. 56. In Pls. 32, 33, and 34, the length of the body is, respectively, about 2.44, 2.5, and 2.8 times its depth.

Chest and Ribs.—Although the heart, as well as the lungs, is contained in the chest, I shall not consider it here; for I can offer no clue as to its action from the consideration of the conformation of the chest, which is influenced chiefly by the shape, size, and setting-on of the ribs. The points which we should seek for in the ribs of the horse, in order to obtain the best possible breathing power, are:—

1. Convexity or roundness of ribs ("barrel") behind the shoulder.
2. Good length of ribs.
3. Ribs well inclined to the rear.

I may explain that the convexity of a curve may be measured by the proportion which its height (*c d* Fig. 174 or Fig. 175) bears to the length of its cord, *a b*. Thus, if *c d*

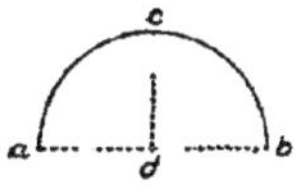

FIG. 174.

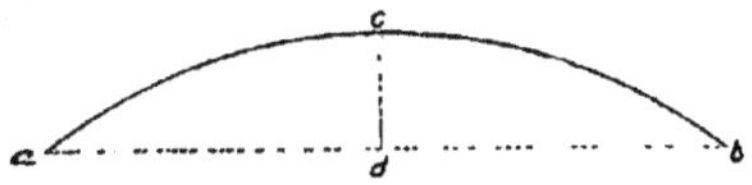

FIG. 175.

is equal to $\frac{1}{2}$ *a b* in Fig. 174, and equal to $\frac{1}{6}$ *a b* in Fig. 175, the curve *a c b* will be three times as convex in the former, as in the latter.

Among the higher animals, we find that chest capacity is obtained either by convexity or by length. Hence, those species which have short chests, have round ones; and those that have long ones, have them flat-sided; the capacity being increased by roundness of the ribs, and decreased by flatness of these bones. We have already seen that undue length of body is detrimental to speed, weight-carrying power, and strength in draught. Consequently, we should seek for roundness of chest in order to obtain good breathing power. Youatt, in his book on *The Horse*, appears to have originated a fallacy concerning the conformation of the ribs, which has been repeated by many English writers. He says that "the circular chest could not expand, but every change of form would be a diminution of capacity." This statement seems to be based on the supposition that the chest expands and contracts, by the ribs opening and closing in a direction at right angles to the length of the body. Instead of this being the case, the difference in capacity of the chest is due to the fact of the ribs, which are inclined to the rear, turning round towards the front on their upper and lower ends, as on pivots,

PHOTO. BY M. H HAYES

TO FACE PAGE 199

PLATE 32—BURMA PONY.

when air is drawn into the lungs; and then revolving back again, when the air is expelled from them. I may explain that the (tidal) air is expelled from the lungs by the elastic recoil of the ribs, which takes place the moment the muscles which drew the ribs forward, become relaxed. Youatt's statement is altogether incorrect; for the rounder the ribs are, other things being equal, the greater will be the difference of chest capacity when the lungs are full, to what it would be when they are comparatively empty.

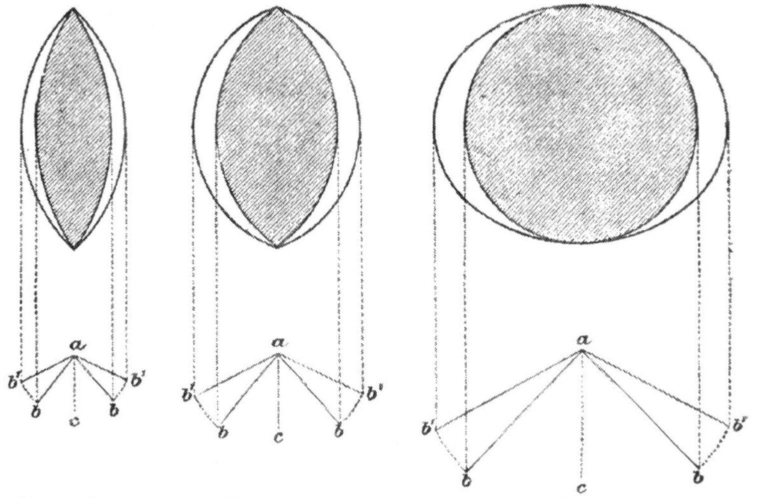

FIG. 176. FIG. 177. FIG. 178.
DIAGRAMS SHOWING DIFFERENT DEGREES OF EXPANSION OF CHEST.

We may prove the foregoing remarks as follows: Let the shaded oval in Figs. 176, 177 and 178, diagrammatically represent the space respectively enclosed between pairs of ribs of different degrees of convexity, but of the same depth, viewed from behind, at the end of an expiration. Let $a\ b$ ($= a\ b^1$) be, respectively, the distance of the centre of each rib from its vertical axis; $b\ a\ c$ the angle at which the ribs in all three figures are inclined to the rear; and $b^1 a b$ the angle through which they, respectively, turn during an inspiration. We shall then see that the difference of capacity—shown by the difference of area between the shaded oval and the one which circumscribes it—is greatly in favour of the round barrel. If it were possible to have a chest perfectly circular (as in Fig. 178) at the end of an expiration; the transverse axis of the chest, when the lungs were fully inflated, would exceed in length the vertical axis.

The second desirable condition—namely, good length of ribs—should, as we have seen, be obtained rather by rotundity than by the distance which the ends of the ribs, respectively, are from each other. Given ribs sufficiently round, we need not trouble ourselves much as to their length, except as regards the farthest back ones, which should be as long and as much directed outwards as possible, so as to afford a broad attachment to the diaphragm (*see* p. 46). It would be easy to prove that the more inclined the ribs are to the rear, the greater will be the difference in capacity of the chest when empty, to what it would be when full of air, and consequently the better the breathing power; but I do not think that it is possible to estimate this inclination with sufficient accuracy to make it a practical guide. My experience leads me to conclude that all useful purposes, in this respect, will be served by satisfying ourselves whether or not the horse under examination is "well-ribbed up." If the last rib be short, flat, and but little inclined to the rear, the animal will be "slack in the loins," and will most certainly not have as good breathing power as he would have had, if that rib had been long, "springing" well out from the side, and inclined so much to the rear that there would be space only for the ends of two or three fingers between it and the point of the hip. Such a desirable shape would give the utmost width of base to the diaphragm, which is a very important muscle of

PHOTO. BY M. H. HAYES

TO FACE PAGE 190

PLATE 33—ENGLISH COB PONY.

breathing. Although I mention in this connection only the last ribs, I take for granted that its neighbouring ribs would conform, more or less, to its length, shape and inclination to the rear. From the foregoing considerations, I would regard roundness of barrel behind the girths; depth of body (as compared to length of body) in the centre of the back; and being well ribbed up, as the great signs, in conformation, of a horse having good breathing power. As "the middle false ribs are those which have the greatest power of being drawn forwards and outwards" (*see* p. 35), they, in comparison to the length of the body, should be as long, as well as convex, as possible. On account of their lower ends being difficult to trace in the living animal, we may conveniently judge of their approximate lengths, by the depth of the body at the centre of the back, making due allowance for the "condition" of the animal. If we examine the Frontispiece and Pls. 35 and 56, which show three horses in training for racing, we shall notice that the back ribs of both Ormonde and Romance were of good length, thus indicating fine breathing power; and that those of the "weed" were unusually short. As might have been expected, this mare, though fast, was a very poor stayer. I need hardly say that the shape of the body should be judged by the body itself, and without reference to the length or substance of the legs. The fact, as often occurs, of the body being too heavy for the legs, in no way affects the proportion which its length, depth and thickness bear to each other. The popular term, "slack in the loins," which I have used, is applied to the objectionable condition of the last rib being short and at a considerable distance from the point of the hip. As this kind of conformation usually accompanies a more or less weak state of the muscles of the loins, the expression is not altogether inappropriate. Some persons ignorantly think that it is an advantage for a horse, as regards speed, to be a bit "slack in the loins;" because (so they say) such a shape allows the animal more freedom in bringing his hind legs forward, than if he were well ribbed up. I need hardly point out that the form of a horse's back ribs cannot in any way affect the action of his hind legs. This absurd notion was, no doubt, started by some person who supposed that the hip joints were at the points of the hips! Owing to sexual causes, mares, as a rule, are not so well ribbed up as horses. Hence, some slight slackness in the hollow of the flank is not such a grave fault in them as in entires and geldings. The fact, however, remains, that for all purposes of work, a horse or mare cannot be too well ribbed up.

M. Merche remarks that: "Among common horses, the last rib is less arched and less carried back than among blood horses; and the flank consequently appears longer."

St. Simon, among many other great race-horses, was an instance of a fine stayer, who possessed singularly little depth at the withers, but had great roundness of chest behind the girth, and also fair depth of body at the lowest point of his back. It is essential for the race-horse to obtain good breathing power by roundness of ribs, so that his body may have its powers of breathing fully developed without its length being unduly increased.

The great advantage of depth in the front portion of the chest is to allow of good length of shoulder blade, which is indispensable to the weight-carrier and jumper.

Abdomen.—We have seen on p. 45 that the centre

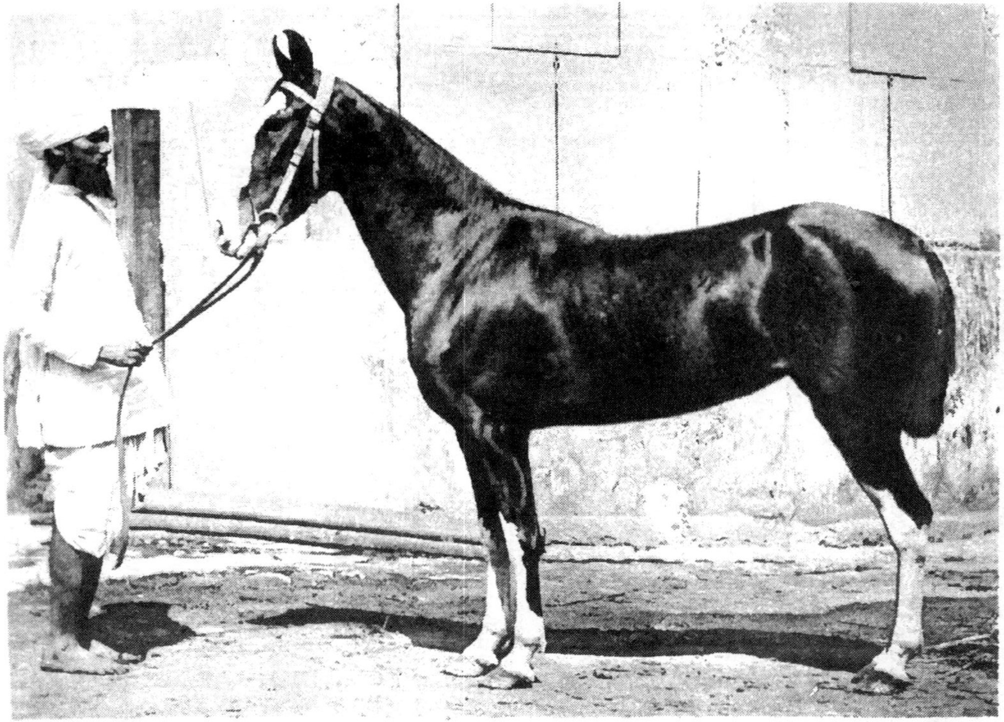

PHOTO. BY M. H. HAYES

TO FACE PAGE 192

PLATE 34—KATHIAWAR MARE.

piece of the body is divided by the diaphragm into two portions, the chest and abdomen; the former containing the lungs and heart; the latter, the stomach, liver, intestines, bladder and other organs. The ribs form the walls of the chest. The contents of the belly (consisting mostly of the intestines) are kept in their place chiefly by powerful ligaments, the principal one of which is the *abdominal tunic* (*see* p. 34), and by muscles. These structures are respectively attached to the margin of the front part of the pelvis, to the rear part of the breast bone, rearmost edge of the ribs, and to the sides of the loin vertebræ, thus bridging over the vacant space. We may, then, fairly assume that the abdomen should follow the general contour of the chest. As the straight muscle of the abdomen which covers the lower portion of this cavity, is the chief muscle that bends the back, the horse cannot be thoroughly "fit" for work, if this muscle is unduly pressed down by the intestines. We may also conclude that, when a horse has a naturally pendulous belly, he will be wanting in quickness and stamina, which cannot be possessed without the ability to freely move the spine. This and the other muscles of the abdomen aid in the process of breathing, which will be more or less interfered with, if these muscles have to constantly strive against undue pressure from the cavity they cover. Besides this, if the intestinal mass is greater than it ought to be, it will hamper the action of the lungs by forcing the diaphragm too far into the chest; it will add to the weight to be carried; and will militate against speed by tending to bring the centre of gravity to the rear (*see* p. 51). Although the subject of feeding is not within the province of this book, it may not be out of place if I mention that the practice of giving horses large quantities of soft food. (boiled turnips, for instance), which they can quickly consume, exerts, among other evils, a most injurious effect on the muscles of the stomach, intestines and abdomen; for, being deprived of the rest which is necessary to their repair and development, by the continued pressure resulting from the presence of the bulky food, these muscles soon become ill-fitted to perform their work. On the other hand, we should guard against a "tucked up" condition of belly, which will indicate illness, over-work, too excitable a temperament, or improper management of some kind. If we consider that these abdominal muscles act by tending to become straight between their points of attachment, and that when in a passive state they are longer than when they contract, we shall see that, when in a condition of rest, they should be gently rounded, and should be neither drawn straight nor bulged out. In Chapter XXII., I shall consider the special development of these muscles.

Withers.—The chief object which the withers fulfil, is to afford attachment for the suspensory ligament of the head and neck; for muscles which extend the head and neck; for muscles that draw the shoulder blade forward; for the powerful muscle that runs along the top of the back and extends the vertebræ; and for a muscle which aids inspiration by bringing the ribs forward. If we look at the skeleton (*see* Fig. 3), we shall readily see that the fact of the withers rising, as they do, above the line of the back, greatly assists the action of the elastic ligament that supports the head and neck, and of the muscles which extend these parts. It also increases the power of the muscle which extends the back and loins. Besides, it tends to give length to the muscle which is at-

PHOTO. BY M. H. HAYES

TO FACE PAGE 194

PLATE 35—MR. VANSITTART'S AUSTRALIAN HORSE, ROMANCE.

tached to the withers and which helps to draw the shoulder forward, and by affording increased space for the top of the shoulder blade, it favours length of this important bone. The further back the withers extend, the more do they, by giving a big surface for attachment, indicate large development of the muscle which extends the back and loins, and the more room do they afford for the backward slope of the shoulder blade. Hence, withers which are high and which extend far back, are generally associated with a good carriage of the head and neck; free movement of the shoulder; long and sloping shoulder blades; and strength in the back and loins. Such a conformation is desirable in every kind of horse, and especially in the race-horse, hunter, and steeplechaser. Low withers, on the contrary, are usually accompanied by heavy, short and upright shoulders. Lecoq observes that "in the mule, and especially in the ass, the withers are always low; a conformation which is in accordance with the small development of the paces of these animals." Dealers and others, when "showing off" a horse which has high withers, not unfrequently endeavour to direct attention to this fact, as a proof of the length and obliquity of the shoulders. I need hardly point out, even to the inexperienced horseman, that any particular part should be judged, if possible, on its own merits, and not by those of another part, however much excellence in the latter may indicate its possession by the former.

The Height of the Withers is, strictly speaking, that of the spines of the vertebræ of the part and the soft tissues which cover their summits. Their apparent height is the distance they project above the top of the shoulder blades; although I must confess that it is often difficult to tell how high they are in horses which have very thick withers. Animals that are comparatively high over the croup, appear to have lower withers than those which are high in front, even when we make allowance for any difference that may exist in the length of the spines themselves. The reason for this seems to be that, as elevation of the croup causes the weight of the body to be shifted forward, such a conformation tends to depress the body between the shoulder blades, and consequently reduces the distance between them and the top of the withers.

"*Leanness of the Withers*" depends on their apparent height, the actual thickness of the spines and their cartilages; the size of the muscles of the part; and the amount of loose tissue about it. Although we cannot expect leanness of withers in the cart-horse, the presence of whose massive muscles that lie between the trunk and shoulder blades, separates the ends of the latter widely asunder; still it is a very desirable point in the saddle-horse, as it indicates absence of an excess of connective tissue (*see* p. 14), lightness of forehand, and height of the withers themselves. Very thin, high withers are objectionable; for they are liable to become hurt by a saddle, especially by a side-saddle. We are all aware that when the part is of this shape, it is difficult to keep the "gullet-plate" of the saddle from touching it, however high this iron arch may be, the reason being, as far as I can see, that such a condition is usually associated, as might be expected, with emaciation of the neighbouring muscles; among the rest, those which give rise to the prominence behind the shoulder blade, and against which the "points" of the tree of the saddle should rest. When the part is thus unduly flat, the saddle is naturally liable to slip forward. With horses which have thick withers it is also difficult to keep the saddle in its place; for the presence of large shoulder muscles and abundance of connective tissue conceals the outline of the shoulder blades and renders the part, upon which the points of the tree rest, smooth and round.

"Age and sex have an equal influence on the leanness of withers, which, badly defined in the colt, come well out only towards five or six years old, at the time when the bones have attained their full length, and the body its definite size. The withers are less high in the mare than in the gelding or entire. As a set off, the last mentioned, whose forehand acquires a considerable development, has this part thicker, especially in the case of a heavy draught animal" (*Goubaux and Barrier*).

Breast.—*Width of breast*, or *width of chest*, as the distance between the fore legs is usually called, "is generally looked upon as a measure of the size of the chest, or, rather, of its rotundity. This is an error which we have cleared away by more than fifty observations made on the living animal, and afterwards completed on the dead subject. We have never been able to ascertain, with respect to this point, any practical difference among animals of the same height, whatever might have been their width of breast; for the simple reason that it is not in its front part that the chest varies much, but rather in its middle and back portions. To what cause, then, other than bulging out of the anterior ribs, is width between the fore legs due? We must attribute it to the greater or less thickness of the pectoral muscles which form its base. We may see the truth of this from the fact that this part may become narrow in animals which have large chests. It is merely necessary to place them under bad sanitary conditions as regards work and feeding, to convince one that their state of emaciation brings on the loss of width of which we speak" (*Goubaux and Barrier*). If we take the trouble to compare the width between the fore legs of badly-shaped cart-horses which happen to be "flat-sided" and wanting in girth, with that of thoroughbreds having large capacity of chest, we shall note that the width in question bears no relation to the size of chest. Again, it is no rare occurrence to see horses that have been once broad-chested, become narrow in front when they are old and worn out. The pectoral muscles, to which the eminent French professors alluded in the foregoing extract, lie between the humerus and chest. The fact that horses which are broad between the fore legs are very rarely good stayers at a gallop, has been used as an argument that roundness of rib is inconsistent with good breathing power. We may, however, I venture to think, account for it more correctly by saying that the failure in "staying" is owing to the undue weight of the forehand consequent on the large muscular development of the part, and to the tendency to lateral displacement of the centre of gravity (*see* p. 65). I may add that we rarely see a horse wide in front which is not at the same time thick in the withers, a condition which is also caused by the largeness of the muscles that lie between the chest and the fore limb, as well as by the thickness of the bones themselves. When a horse is narrow between the fore legs by reason of the emaciated condition of his pectoral muscles, "the keel of his breast bone becomes prominent, the points of the shoulder are pushed forward to the front, and allow to be seen, between them and the breast, two deep depressions in which the jugular grooves terminate below" (*Goubaux and Barrier*). These writers point to the fact that narrowness in front may therefore be either natural or acquired. In the cart-horse, width of breast is a desirable point; for he requires to have massive muscles. Although the race-horse, cross-country animal, and hack should be light in front, and should consequently not be broad between the fore legs; still undue narrowness of that part (*see* Pl. 10), indicating, as it would do, want of proper muscular development, would in all cases be a defect. As "width" and "narrowness" of breast are comparative terms which are practically impossible to define with accuracy, I have given in Pl. 9 a front view of a well-shaped hack which was nearly thoroughbred.

Back and Loins.—The upper line of these parts should, it is generally considered, run in a straight line, or with the slightest possible rise, to the croup (*see* Pls. 7, 31, 33 and 62). When the animal has a "roach-back" (*see* Pl. 36)—that is, when this line is decidedly convex—the muscle which runs along the top of the back, and which has a powerful action on all the paces of the horse, will be found wanting in development; and the chest will, as a rule, be flat-sided. This condition of back, from the fact of its assuming, to some extent, the form of an arch, is generally supposed to be advantageous for carrying heavy burdens, as in the case of baggage animals. I am not, however, able to furnish any actual proof that such is the case. A "hollow-backed" or "saddle-backed" horse, on the contrary, is one which has this line concave on account of the arrangement of the vertebræ of the part. It is frequently the result of relaxation of the ligaments which bind the vertebræ together, owing to the effects of hard work and debility. Thus, we may often see a horse which in his youth had a straight back, become hollow-backed in his old age. From the different position assumed by man when moving, the opposite to this occurs to ourselves. An appearance of hollow back may be given by unusually large development of that part (*posterior iliac spine, see* Fig. 3) of the pelvis which forms the highest point of the croup. I have also observed, especially among Arab ponies, the same kind of conformation arise from the pelvis being set up particularly high in animals which were low in front. No exception can be taken to an apparently hollow back produced by the putting-on of the pelvis.

Without any exception, the top of the back and loins should be as flat and broad as possible; for this condition indicates the presence of powerful rearing muscles (*see* p. 64), and rotundity of the back ribs (*see* p. 191). In many draught animals, the upper muscles of the loins and back stand out as distinct ridges of muscle on each side of the backbone. This beauty in the coarser breeds is not confined to them, but may sometimes be seen in well-bred horses, as was the case with Mr. Kelly Maitland's Kingcraft, which was one of the best race-horses that has ever been in India. This Australian was a singularly muscular, short-backed animal, to whom distance and weight made comparatively but little difference. This "double-backed" condition may come on or disappear according to the amount of "flesh" which the animal carries. A false appearance of flatness and strength of back and loins may be temporarily given by excessive fat.

Shortness of Loins and Back.—The appearance of comparative shortness or length which the back and loins (or

PHOTO. BY M. H. HAYES

TO FACE PAGE 200

PLATE 36—UNDER-BRED HORSE.

back, if we include the loins in this term, *see* p. 24) may present, is due, I would submit, chiefly to the following causes :—

1. The manner in which the croup runs into the loins. For instance, the back and loins will appear short and the croup (or "quarters") long, if the pelvis be more or less horizontal; the contour of the croup free from angularity; the muscles over the loins largely developed; and the flanks well ribbed up. I regret that I have omitted to give among the equine portraits in this book, one of a good specimen of a long-backed horse. My meaning will, however, be understood if my readers will compare the line of the croup and loins in the Frontispiece and Pls. 19, 33, 35 and 55, with that in Pls. 15, 34, 39 and 56.

2. The distance to which the withers run back. I may point out that the extreme lowness of the withers in the Burchell's zebra (Pl. 37), the kiang (Pl. 67), and the onager (Pl. 66), gives the backs of these animals a false appearance of undue length. The angularity of the contour of Mike's croup (*see* Pl. 38) might lead one to form the wrong opinion that he was long in the back and loins, if his withers did not extend so far to the rear as to counteract that impression. The same may be said of Dorothy (Pl. 39).

3. The degree of slope of the shoulder and pelvis. It is evident that the greater the angle formed by the respective directions of the shoulder blade and pelvis produced (the more oblique the shoulder and the more horizontal the croup), the shorter will the back and loins appear to be; and *vice versâ.*

4. Length of neck. I need hardly say that a long neck (or a "long rein," if we include the withers) will give an air of shortness to the back and loins, and *vice versâ.*

5. Depth of back ribs. To see this we need only to contrast the Frontispiece, or Pl. 32 with Pl. 56.

Without indulging in any tedious repetition, I think we may safely assume that, in all cases, a horse's back and loins should have the appearance of being as short as possible.

Points of the Hips.—When these parts are very prominent, the horse is said to have "ragged hips." Such a condition gives the animal an angular appearance, and is consequently displeasing to the eye. A horse thus formed is more likely to hurt his hips by "catching" them against door-posts, or by lying on a hard surface when he is not supplied with a sufficiency of bedding, than one of different conformation. The fact of a horse having flat or ragged hips does not appear to influence his usefulness in any way. Among thoroughbreds, certain strains of blood have them prominent Although it would be more correct to consider the points of the hips along with the hind limb; I have placed them, for convenience sake, under the present heading.

Flank.—The only thing to remark about this part is that the "hollow of the flank," which is included between the loins, point of the hip and end of the last back rib, should be well filled up and should be as small as possible. If it is hollowed out, it will indicate that the animal is in bad health, out of condition, or of weak constitution. If the extent of the hollow of the flank be small, the animal will be well ribbed up, a form of conformation which I have discussed on p. 190 *et seq* It is more essential for race-horses to be well ribbed up than for any other class; as they can ill afford to make up, by increased length and depth of chest, for any deficiency in this point. Increased depth or increased length of chest, besides

PHOTO. BY M. H. HAYES

TO FACE PAGE 202

PLATE 37—BURCHELL'S ZEBRA.

adding to the weight to be carried, would militate against the possession of speed, on account of its tending to lower or bring back the centre of gravity, and thus to increase the stability of the equilibrium (*see* p. 67).

Croup.—The upper line of the croup, from the loins to the root of the tail, should remain convex, even when a fairly heavy weight is carried. This convexity, more or less regular, is caused by the prominence of the inner angle of the pelvis; by the action of the muscles which flex the back; and by the strength of the ligaments which preserve the stability of this arch. We may note how relaxation of these muscles will affect this state of convexity if we pinch the loins of a horse, so as to make him crouch, which he does by the contraction of the muscles that lie on the top of the loins. When he crouches in this manner, the upper line of the croup will tend to become straight. Hence we may accept the conclusion, which is fully borne out in practice, that undue straightness of the upper line of the croup indicates weakness of the part. Not being able, at present, to get a living animal from which to obtain a photographic illustration of this bad point, I may refer my readers to the horse of the statue which stands in the centre of Holborn Circus. I may also mention that when a horse is affected by paralysis of the muscles of the loins, the croup will usually assume an abnormally flat appearance, especially when weight is put on the back, which, in this disease, can badly support it. The slope of the croup (whether it is "goose rumped" or horizontal) will be considered on pp. 232 and 233.

Anus.—The anus should be prominent, and the tissues around it should be well filled out. It should be firm in appearance and closed when at rest. A hollow, flabby and open condition of the part indicates illness or general debility.

Tail.—The tail should be muscular at its root, and naturally short as regards its solid portion (dock). Strength of tail, as may be tested by endeavouring to lift it up with the hand under the root, usually shows vigour of body A naturally long dock is, to a certain extent, a sign of inferior breeding.

The tail should, in all cases, be set on "high" (*see* Frontispiece and Pl. 58); as this form points to a more or less horizontal position of the sacrum. If this part be bent downwards, as in Pls. 32 and 36, so as to form a decided angle with the vertebræ of the loins and back, the backbone will not be as well adapted to purposes of locomotion as it would be if it were comparatively horizontal.

The tail should be carried well away from the quarters; for this will indicate that its muscles are in good order. Some horses, especially those of high spirit and good blood, when going fast, carry the tail "like a flag," having the dock raised and more or less concave. It looks very bad if the tail, when carried low down, say, at the walk, has a concave bend in it, particularly if there be an abrupt turn or "kink" in the tail near its end. Such a carriage of tail is usually supposed to be associated with an "ungenerous" disposition; although this is not always the case. In coming to a decision on this subject, we should not fail to take into consideration the indications afforded by the eyes and ears. Thus, if the horse, although carrying his tail "meanly," had a "kind," fearless look about the eyes, and kept his ears well to the front, and worked them in a quick

PHOTO. BY M. H. HAYES

TO FACE PAGE 204

PLATE 38—COLONEL SIMPSON'S ENGLISH PONY, MIKE.

decided manner, we might reasonably conclude that the defective carriage of the tail was due to faulty conformation, and not to a sulky disposition, which would be the greater of the two evils. In making these remarks, I am, of course, alluding to horses that have not been docked.

Any unnecessary whisking of the tail when the animal is in motion is objectionable; as it is often a sign of "jadiness" and bad temper. We may not unfrequently remark that the fact of an animal being beaten in a race or steeplechase is often first made manifest by its tail beginning to go round and round. The swishing of the tail may here, however, be due rather to the application of the spurs or whip, than to any "unkind" running on the part of the horse. On the other hand, we may observe instances of thoroughly game race-horses, when "finishing," being so engaged in the keen struggle for victory, that they will keep the tail without movement, even under severe "punishment." Mares, as a rule, undoubtedly whisk their tails about more than horses and geldings Some of them, which are in a state of continual irritation from sexual causes, do so to an extent that is very unpleasant to their riders or drivers. Such animals are, generally, of but little use. Almost all Arab horses, and certain horses in all countries, keep the tail rigidly fixed to one particular side, near or off, when walking, unless, indeed, to use it when occasion demands. English thoroughbreds, however, at the same pace, generally swing it from side to side in an easy, free manner, somewhat similar to that in which a fast and fair walker uses his arms when going along at, say, the rate of six miles an hour. The difference, here, seems to be due to the thoroughbred's longer stride and greater freedom of action.

CHAPTER XVIII.

THE FORE LIMB.

General View of the Fore Limb—Chief Duties of the Fore Limb—The Shoulder — Humerus — Elbow—Fore-arm—Knee—Cannon—Fetlock—Pastern—Hoof.

General View of the Fore Limb.—The term "fore limb" or "fore leg" is applied to the column of bones from the shoulder blade to the coffin bone (inclusive), and the attendant soft parts. As the chief muscles of the neck are concerned in the movement of the fore limb, we must take into consideration the conformation of the former part while studying that of the latter. The shape of the muscles which lie between the upper portion of the limb (above the elbow joint) and the chest must not be neglected; for they, respectively, connect the limb to the trunk, and draw it upwards and backwards. As the action of the neck muscles, as regards the fore limb, has been considered in Chapters X. and XVI. (*see* pp. 82 and 181), and that of the other muscles in Chapter IV. (*see* pp. 37 and 38), they need not be specially noticed here. I shall now examine the nature of the work which the fore limb has got to do, with the object of drawing conclusions as to the conformation most suitable to it in particular cases. As its various parts

PHOTO BY DIXON & SONS

TO FACE PAGE 208

PLATE 39—MR. W. H. WALKER'S ENGLISH PONY, DOROTHY.

should move in harmony together, it will at first be more profitable to study them collectively than particularly.

Chief Duties of the Fore Limb are—(1) to support weight; (2) to resist the injurious effects of "work" on its own structures; (3) to preserve the stability of the body; (4) to propel the body forward or backward; and (5) to raise the forehand.

To support weight, the horse requires bones and muscles strong in proportion to the nature and amount of work to be done, a more or less straight condition of the bones, and a shoulder blade sufficiently large for the muscles which attach it to the trunk, and whose size is a measure of their strength. The comparative straightness of the column of bones will be largely affected by considerations of propulsion and of the effect of work on the legs. In all cases, the bones at the knee should be straight.

To resist the injurious effect of "work" on its structures, the bones of the shoulder and pastern (at each respective end of the limb) should be placed obliquely, if the ground be hard, so as to diminish the injurious effects of concussion, which are seen in, for instance, navicular disease, laminitis, ringbone, wind-galls, sore shins and splints. The obliquity, however, will be obtained at the expense of mechanical advantage. Hence, the softer the ground and the slower the pace, the less sloping need the shoulder and pastern be, as regards injury to the parts from work.

To preserve the stability of the body, we require sloping shoulders and oblique pasterns. With the former, the leg can be raised readily and freely to the front. With the latter, the danger of catching the ground with the toe is minimised; for the more oblique the pastern, the easier will it be for the horse to bring his heel first on the ground at each step.

To propel the body forward to the best advantage, we require a humerus not much removed from a horizontal position; for the pushing force derived from the fore limb takes place through that bone. Also, in propulsion, the muscles which bend the fetlock joint will act best, the more upright is the pastern (*see* p. 69). I need not say anything here about backward propulsion, as it has but little bearing on conformation. I have made some remarks on reining back in Chapter XII. (*see* p. 119).

To raise the forehand effectively, we require obliquity of shoulder blade and pastern, so as to favour the straightening of the limb (*see* p. 63).

From the foregoing observations we may see that the conformation most suitable to one function of the fore limb may differ essentially from that best adapted to other offices performed by it. Consequently, the conformation to be sought for in the fore limb of a horse will be the best possible combination of somewhat conflicting elements.

The Shoulder.—*The degree of slope of the shoulder* is difficult for inexperienced persons to determine, especially when the part is covered by fat or by thick muscles. French writers give rules for measuring with a kind of clinometer the obliquity of the shoulder blade, which is an operation, I must confess, that I have not been able to perform satisfactorily. I have studied the subject for many years, and find that I can rely fairly well on the instruction my eyes have received during that time. The horse with the most oblique shoulders

I have ever seen was St. Simon (*see* Pl. 7), whose photograph, I regret to say, does not show this point properly, as it is a little foreshortened. The lines of his shoulder are correctly shown in Pl. 18, which is a reproduction of a painting made from a photograph that was too badly done to bear reproduction. As this illustration gives his exact outline taken in strict profile, it is valuable for comparison; although much of the detail which would have been given in a good photograph is, naturally, wanting. The Arab pony, The Brat (*see* Pl. 31), had singularly good, sloping shoulders. The horses depicted in Pls. 15, 38 and 39 had also the wished-for obliquity in this part. As instances of straight shoulders, I may give Pls. 23, 36 and 48. Taking into consideration everything I have written in the present book on this point, I think we may accept the conclusion that obliquity of shoulder is a desirable point in every kind of horse, except perhaps in heavy draught animals which are not required to go out of a walk. If they have at times to exceed this pace, as dray horses have to do in London, they should undoubtedly have sloping shoulders, so that their legs may be preserved as much as possible from the injurious effects of concussion.

The thickness of the muscles about the shoulders should be proportionate to the amount of strength which the animal may be called upon to display. We may judge it by the thickness of the withers, by the width between the fore legs, by the degree of definition of the muscles which cover the shoulder-blade, and by the amount of depression there is immediately in front of the shoulder-blade where it joins the neck. This dip is well shown in Pls. 23 and 36, and would have come out in Pl. 19, had the light fallen on the part so as to emphasise the presence of the depression. This difference of level between the neck and shoulder will be best observed when the former is thin and the latter thick. I need hardly say that such a combination is objectionable; for the degree of muscularity of the one ought to agree with that of the other. At the same time, a properly shaped, heavy draught-horse will always have prominent shoulders, which in him are desirable, so as to give a broad surface for pressure against the collar.

Length of shoulder-blade is a valuable "point" in all classes of horses. In the racer, considerable length of the muscles which open and close the angle made by the shoulder-blade and humerus, is conducive to speed. As the size of a bone is, as a rule, proportionate to the strength of the muscles which are attached to it; the length of the shoulder-blade may generally be taken as a measure of the strength of the muscles which connect it with the trunk, and upon which the weight-bearing powers of the animal are mainly dependent. Hence, a large shoulder-blade is not alone advantageous to the weight carrier and heavy cart-horse; but it is also essential to the jumper, in order to enable him to bear the shock of landing over a fence with a man on his back. The dog, which has a short shoulder-blade, as compared to the horse and ass, is, as we might expect, a very bad weight carrier. We may prove this practically by testing the respective strength of back of a mastiff weighing, say, ten stone, and a very small donkey, who, although he might not have as great draught power as a dog, would be able to carry far more weight.

The shoulders of the race-horse, as I have already indicated, should be long, oblique, and as light as is compatible with their work. As far as mere speed goes, great obliquity of shoulder appears to be no advantage. As the weight is brought more forward by the shoulders being upright, than if they were sloping, the former condition, by increasing the instability of the equilibrium (*see* p. 67), is equally, or even perhaps more conducive to speed than the latter. It also, by tending to bring the humerus into a more horizontal position, places that bone in a more advantageous direction for forward propulsion than it would have with an oblique shoulder; because the impetus given to the forehand in progression to the front, takes place through that bone. Those particularly speedy animals, antelope and deer, have, I may mention, comparatively straight shoulders. Many of our fastest race-horses have been built in this way. It is not, however, sufficient for a horse to have the great gift of speed in order to shine on the turf; but he must also be able to "stand training," which will more or less severely test the durability of the bones, ligaments and tendons of his legs, and especially of his fore ones. Both in training and in racing, the animal has to carry a rider, whose weight will add materially to the "wear" of the fore legs, the jar on which will be far less when the shoulders are oblique, than when they are comparatively upright.

Important as obliquity of the shoulders is in the race-horse, it is not nearly so much so as lightness of that part; for heaviness of the forehand not alone throws increased strain on the fore legs, but also detracts from speed. A simple and practical guide by which we may judge of the lightness or heaviness of the forehand is afforded us by the manner in which the neck runs into the shoulders. If we observe that at their point of union there exists a marked depression (*see*

p. 209), we may with reason conclude that Nature, having furnished the animal with a good surface for the collar, intended him for draught rather than for speed. Here we must not be led astray by the appearance of any undue thickness of the neck muscles which might fill up this dip; for the fact of their being heavy would be even more prejudicial to the galloping pretensions of the horse than if the shoulders were somewhat "loaded." I may here mention that, as the neck projects beyond the fore legs, weight in it, by its increased leverage, will interfere with the action of the fore limb to a proportionately greater degree than weight in the shoulders, which will be placed more or less above this bony and muscular spring, to which I have alluded in Chapter VIII.

I would wish to draw special attention to the fact that obliquity and lightness of shoulders, by tending to render the animal's action perfect, are indispensable requisites for enabling him to "stay" over a distance of ground. I have seen many "sprinters" which have had upright and loaded shoulders; but I have never known a genuine stayer—like what Ormonde, St. Gatien, or Robert the Devil was—who had that kind of conformation.

In the *shoulders of the draught-horse* we should have plenty of power and a broad bearing surface for the collar, into which the animal should be able to put all his weight. It is evident that he cannot do this, if his shoulder-blades be very oblique, which is a form aimed at by the majority of exhibitors. Any such "show" question does not concern us at present; for I am regarding the horse entirely from a useful point of view. I find that the deductions I have made in this chapter are, generally, in accordance with the experience of practical men like Mr. G. M. Sexton, Secretary of the English Cart-horse Society. He admires "the shoulder well let down into the chest, and with a moderate slope; it is not necessary to be too oblique, as with a hunter or a race-horse, but just sufficient to ensure free action of the fore legs, encased with plenty of muscle, which will enable him to lean into the collar . . . . It is essential that he should be a free, fast walker . . . . Action means power, time and money." Mr. F. Street, in *The History of the Shire Horse*, advocates, "Shoulders well thrown back." Mr. Thomas Dykes, late Secretary of the Clydesdale Horse Society, remarks in the Stud Book of that breed, that "the shoulder should be more oblique than in the English draught-horse. This, indeed, is one of the distinctive features of the Clydesdale, as to his formation of shoulder is largely owing his long, quick step, for which he is so justly admired. The upright shoulder of the English cart-horse may certainly give greater power in the collar, but if shortness and slowness of step be considered, this cannot be called an advantage. The English horse, besides, is more accustomed to sheer dragging and to working in chains, while his Scottish rival is chiefly employed in the two-wheeled cart, which occasions a considerable amount of weight being balanced on the animal's back. A medium slanted shoulder gives a horse, in such circumstances, an advantage; and doubtless those who carted the minerals of Lanarkshire in ante-railroad days, found this formation well adapted for their purpose. Even yet no one will affirm that it is unsuited to the traffic of the day, if he will only take the opportunity offered for forming an opinion by the sight of the Clydesdale horses yoked to cart or lorry in the streets of Glasgow." Mr. Reynolds, M.R.C.V.S., in his *Essay on the Breeding and Management of Draught-horses*, while recommending that the shoulders should be massive and well thrown outwards to afford ample space for the collar, cautions his readers, as follows, against extreme views as to oblique shoulders:—"Many good judges insist that a cart-horse should possess very sloping shoulders. Whilst admitting the necessity of such a conformation for good saddle and light harness horses, and appreciating its beauty in heavy animals, I am decidedly opposed to the opinion, on the ground that such a form is almost invariably associated with thin withers and shoulder blades closely applied to the front ribs, affording an insufficient and insecure seat for the collar, and, consequently, one very defective for the purposes of heavy draught."

Horses—like the heavy draught animals of Edinburgh, Liverpool and Manchester—that have toe-pieces on their shoes, and consequently make full use of their fore legs as propellers, should, for this object, have fairly upright shoulders, and should have no bearing-reins, which would impede them in advancing and lowering their heads. Dray-horses, like those in London which have flat shoes in front, should have sloping shoulders. I may, therefore, venture to settle this question by saying that heavy cart-horses which are not required to go out of a walk, and which, in order to perform their work to the best possible advantage, ought to have toe-pieces, should have upright shoulders; and that those which have to trot as well as to walk, should have sloping ones. If the ground, such as wood pavement or asphalte, be unsuitable to the use of toe-pieces, the animals, even if they have not to go out of a walk, should have oblique shoulders, because in this case the fore legs will be concerned more in maintaining the stability of the body than in propelling it. We may also infer that horses which have toe-pieces on their fore-shoes, will do their work best when their shoulders are upright.

The *shoulders of the hack and light harness horse* ought to be oblique and light in order to obtain sure-footedness, good forward reach, and sufficient knee action. Although the *match trotter* should be built more or less like a race-horse, it is even more necessary for his shoulders to be sloping than for those of the galloper; because, unless they are so, he cannot have free knee action. I may mention that the fast trotter requires to be able to bend his knees a good deal more than the race-horse.

The *shoulder-blades of the jumper*, as I have before noticed, should be long and particularly oblique, so as to enable him, in the best possible manner, to resist the shock of landing over a fence. On account of having this special kind of work to do, his shoulders should be more muscular than those of the race-horse. The fact of his shoulders being sloping, will enable him to "take off" more cleverly at any obstacle than he could do, were they upright.

The Humerus.—The position and form of this bone, which lies between the shoulder joint and elbow, are so hidden by the muscles about it, that it is difficult to form a correct opinion as to its conformation. Even if it were exposed to view as much as is the fore-arm, I cannot see how the fact of its being so, would greatly help us. We know that forward propulsion given by the fore limb must take place through it; but I cannot say exactly what is its best direction for purposes of progression. We are aware that the different paces of the horse require, in varying proportions, the propulsion to be partly upward and partly forward; but we cannot tell what these proportions should be. It is evident that the heavy cart-horse which requires the aid of his fore limbs to propel him forward, should not have an upright humerus. It appears probable that the angle which the shoulder-blade makes with the humerus, varies but little in different horses; in which case, the more oblique the shoulder-blade, the more upright the humerus, and *vice versâ;* and consequently, from observing the slope of the former, we might estimate that of the latter.

Elbow.—The point of the elbow should be capable of being drawn well away from the side. It will then have plenty of freedom, and will not be tied down to the chest.

Fore-arm.—This part in all horses should be muscular; as its muscles have to do all the work of the limb below the elbow. On p. 162, I have alluded to its comparative length. In Pls. 15, 35, 39, 40, 55, and 57, are shown well-shaped fore-arms; in Pls. 46 and 48, mean ones. Although a race-horse might have a somewhat light fore-arm without much detriment, it is imperative for the jumper to be strong in this part; for in leaping, great strain falls on the muscles at the back of the fore-arm in straightening the fetlock, by which action the forehand is raised. It goes almost without saying that the heavy cart-horse should have a powerful fore-arm.

Castors or chesnuts.—On the fore-arm, generally, but not always, nearer the knee than the elbow, there is a horny growth, called a castor or chesnut. It is more or less in the form of an oval, the greater diameter of which is about two inches in length. MM. Goubaux and Barrier state, as an extremely rare occurrence, that absence of castors from the fore legs has been observed in horses. There are, in almost all cases, similar, though somewhat smaller, castors on the inside of the hind limbs, just below the hock and near the back of the leg. M. Huzard and MM. Goubaux and Barrier remark that they have seen instances of the hind castors being absent in the horse. They are larger and of a more horny texture in coarse-bred horses than in blood animals. Nothing is known of the origin of castors (*see* p. 303).

Knee.—Looking at the knee in profile, while the horse bears weight on the leg, we should find that the cannon-bone and radius are nearly in a straight line. In reality they are not quite so in perfect specimens; but are united by a slightly undulating line of great beauty, the contour of which I am unable to lay down with mathematical accuracy. Pls. 39, 41 and 55 furnish us with admirable illustrations of well-set-on knees. Pls. 35 and 40 are also good. Pls. 34 and 45 are examples of the condition known as "calf-knees," to which there is a slight tendency in Pls. 36 and 47. The opposite formation ("being over at the knees") is shown in Pl. 46, to which there is an inclination in Pl. 59. This condition is generally due to hard work.

The fact of a horse being "*calf-kneed*" renders the back tendons and check ligaments (not the suspensory ligaments, the attachments of which are below the knee) more liable to sprain by violent descent of the fetlock than if the knee were straight. It tends, however, to make the animal more sure-footed, by bringing the weight back from the toe. In all cases this condition adds to the tension to which the back tendons are put when they are flexing the foot. Although it is in no way an advantage, it is much less a detriment to the cart-horse which has rarely to go out of a walk or slow trot, than to the saddle-horse or fast trapper. Many heavy cart-horses are "back at the knees" (*see* Pl. 19), which is a shape of the fore limbs that is not uncommon among Arab and East Indian horses.

We know from experience that the more nearly parallel the back tendons are to the cannon-bone—other things being equal—the better able will the limb be to stand work. Why this should be the case I cannot say with certainty. I may, however, hazard the conjecture that, as this "tying-in" below the knee is due to the smallness of the bones which form the groove through which the back tendons pass, this condition may point to want of size in these tendons; for "the function makes the organ." It appears that the calibre of this groove (or rather canal), which, to a great extent, is formed by the trapezium, is, as a rule, ample for the working of these tendons; for when such "tied-in" tendons happen to become damaged by work, the seat of injury is very rarely behind the knee. Hence I think we may conclude that when this groove—which is dependent for its size on that of the bones behind the knee—is comparatively small, the tendons are also proportionately wanting in substance, and consequently unduly weak. I have always remarked that, in legs of about the same size of cannon-bone, when the back tendons approached a direction parallel to the cannon-bone, as in Pls. 35, 40, 41 and 43; they were naturally larger and consequently stronger than those which were tied-in, as in Pls. 44 and 47. We should, I may observe, regard a large degree of backward projection in the trapezium

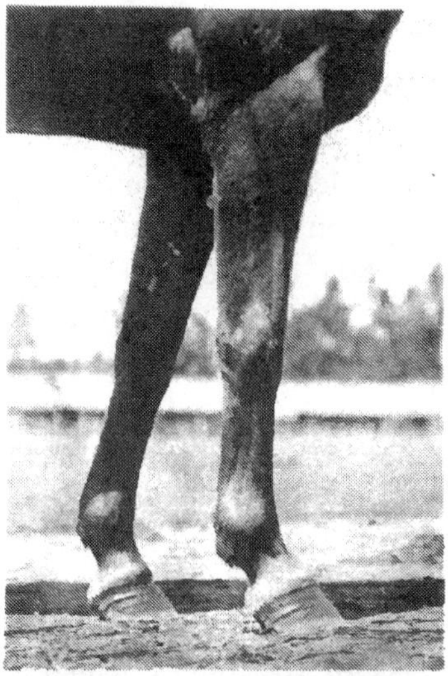

PL. 40—GOOD FORE LEGS.

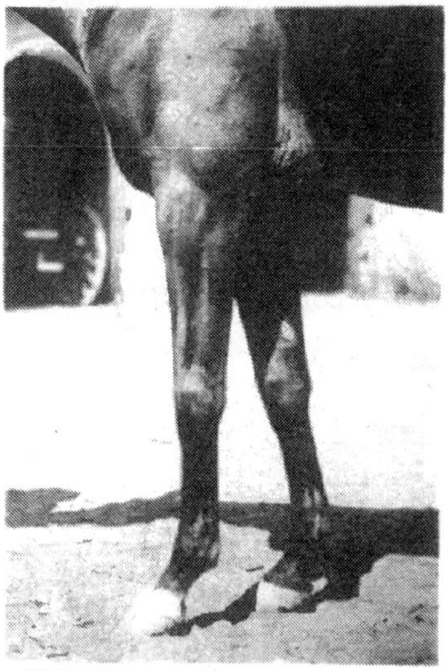

PHOTO. BY M.

PL. 41—GOOD FORE LEGS.

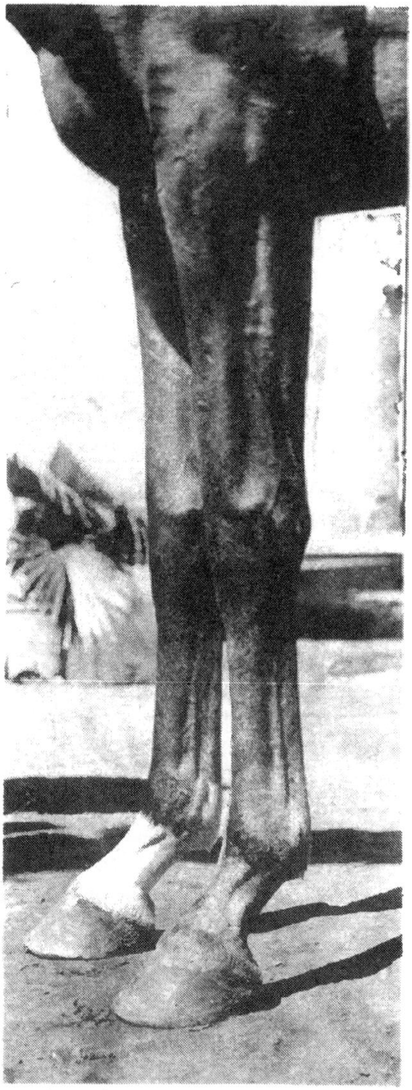

TO FACE PAGE 218

PL. 42—CLEAN FORE LEGS.

as a desirable "point"; not merely as indicating the size of the bone itself, but also that of the other bones of the knee.

The objectionable tying-in of the knee, which we may see in Pls. 44 and 47, is, I believe, due in almost all cases to an admixture of more or less cart blood. Although individuals of other breeds may be light below the knee, I have never seen in them this fault emphasised by undue width of pastern (from front to rear), in the same manner as it is in the draught animal of Western Europe. Experience tells us that a leg which shows the form of tying-in below the knee to which I allude, is altogether unfit for fast work, or for jumping, and is unobjectionable only for labour which does not require the animal to go quicker than an ordinary trot. The reason for this is, as far as I can see, that a large fetlock is characteristic of cart blood, and consequently indicates that the bones of the part are unfitted for work at fast paces. As bones are subordinate to muscles, we may take for granted that, if the former be weak in structure, the latter, as well as the tendons and ligaments, will also be wanting in strength. Eastern horses, and those of Oriental blood, are often very light below the knee; but they hardly ever possess undue width of fetlock. A thoroughly sound rule, which is borne out in practice as well as by theory, is to judge (as regards this particular point) the wear-resisting powers of a fore leg by the direction which the back tendons make with the cannon-bone, and not by its measurement below the knee, which is absolutely worthless, unless that round the fetlock is also taken into consideration. It is important to note the difference between a leg which is light below the knee, and one which is tied-in below the knee.

The latter is always objectionable ; the former, only when the body is too heavy for the legs, as in Pl. 30.

The knee should be broad in front for the attachment and passage of the extensor tendons.

With respect to knees being "well let down," *see* p. 237.

Cannon.—Under this heading I shall include the cannon-bone, back tendons, and suspensory ligaments.

This bone should be of good substance, as in Frontispiece and Pls. 35, 40, 43, and 55. It should feel hard to the touch and free from any excess of soft tissue between it and the skin, or from enlargement from the effects of work or disease —any one of which conditions would give it an appearance of undue roundness. The back tendons, as I have just pointed out, should be as nearly as possible parallel with the cannon-bone. They should be straight, and hard as if they were made of catgut ; and in well-bred horses with fine skins, the division between the two tendons should be visible on close inspection. Any deviation out of the straight line, or any fulness or softness, will indicate the presence or previous existence in them of injury or disease. If the leg be free from an excess of hair, the suspensory ligament should stand out in bold relief (*see* Pl. 42) between the cannon-bone and back tendons, and it should feel as tense and hard as a fiddle-string. If there be any difficulty in tracing its course with the fingers, or if it feels soft or rounded, we may rest assured that it has suffered from injury, which fact will probably prevent it from standing much work. I may mention that in "clean" legs (*see* Pl. 42), we should be able to trace the course of the suspensory ligament for some distance on each side, as it proceeds obliquely down the pastern.

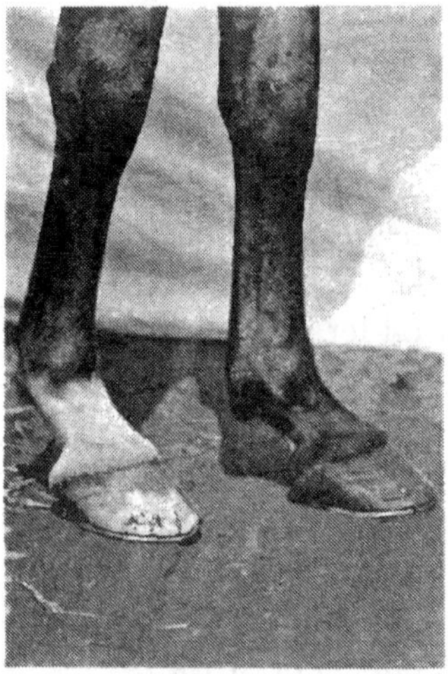

PL. 43—SLOPING PASTERNS.

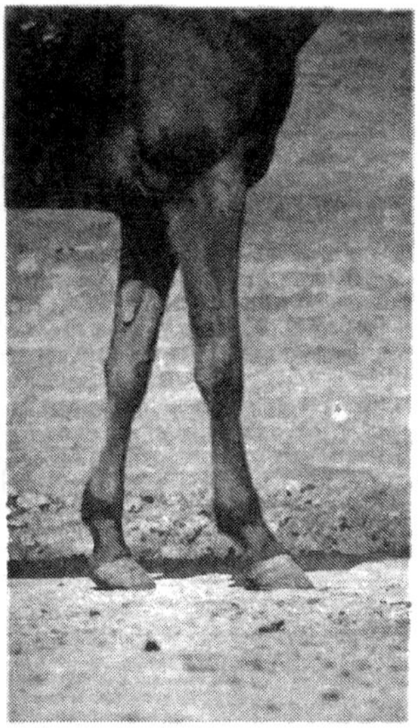

PL. 44—TIED-IN BELOW KNEE.

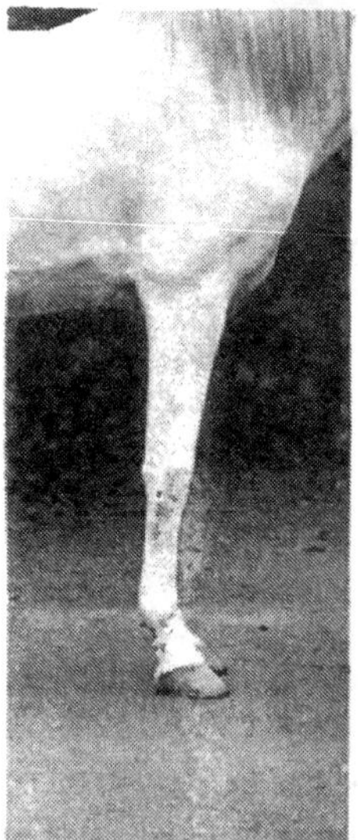

PHOTO. BY M. H. HAYES

PL. 45—CA[illegible]

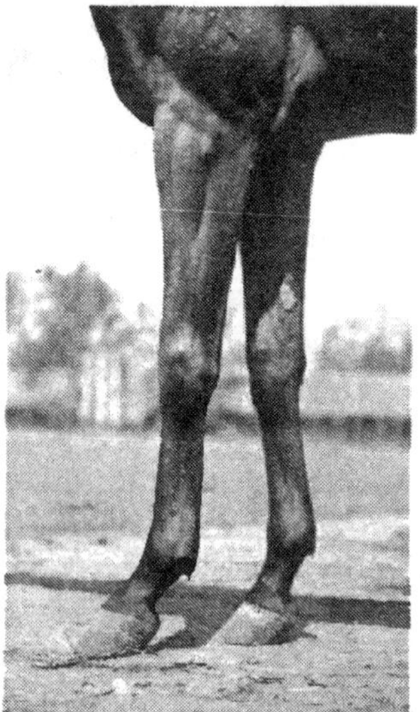

PL. 46—OVER AT KNEES.

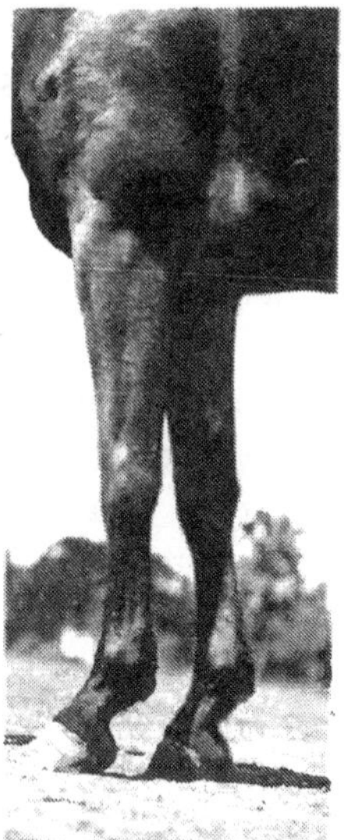

TO FACE PAGE 220

[illegible] LOW KNEE.

Fetlock.—The chief points about this joint are: that it should be flat from side to side, and that, viewing the leg in profile, it should not (as I have previously remarked) be broad as compared to the width of the leg just below the knee (*see* Pl. 47). Any roundness of the fetlock, which will be caused by undue thickness from side to side of this part, will betoken the effects of "work," or of injury. The peculiar roundness of fetlock, caused by sprain of the suspensory ligament at its attachment to the sesamoid bones, will be readily noticed by the practised observer.

At the back of the fetlock there is a lock of hair which gives its name ("feet-lock") to that joint, and which is particularly abundant in cart-horses. This tuft of hair covers a fatty mass (the fetlock pad), and has in its centre a horny growth, called the *ergot.*

Pastern.—By the working of the fetlock and pastern joints, the injurious effects, on the limbs, of concussion are more or less obviated, and assistance is given in the straightening of the limb, to raise the forehand. As the horse will have no difficulty, under ordinary conditions of soundness and labour, in bringing his pastern into the same straight line as his cannon-bone; the amount of "play" which the fetlock will have, will depend on the distance through which the fetlock can descend, or, in other words, on the acuteness of the angle which the pastern can make with the ground, when weight is thrown on the part. Although we cannot, by mere inspection of the animal, determine the efficient limit of this angle, we may assume that horses which have, when standing, what are called sloping pasterns (*see* Pl. 43), will have more play in these joints than those that have upright pasterns.

On the other hand, their back tendons and suspensory ligaments will work at a greater mechanical disadvantage. As the expressions "oblique (or sloping) pasterns," and "upright pasterns," are more comparative than absolute, it is impossible to define them with precision. Pls. 43 and 13 may be taken as good examples of these respective forms of conformation. I need hardly say that pasterns which would be far too upright for fast work, especially on hard ground, might do admirably for slow draught. We may accept, as an axiom, the statement that the harder the ground and the faster the work, the more sloping should the pasterns be, in order to save the legs from the injurious effects of concussion (*see* p. 69). Providing that the pastern bones are strong, they can hardly be too oblique (supposing, of course, that this condition has not been brought on by injury), if the horse be required to gallop over hard ground. I may point to Pl. 43 as an extreme case of sloping pasterns in an Arab horse that had remarkably sound legs. I may mention that such instances are in no way uncommon among the sons of the Desert; and that, as a rule, they are animals which like to "hear their feet rattle." As a case in point, I may instance Mr. Covey's famous Arab, Marquis, who won all over India, at all weights and all distances (in his own class, of course). After doing as much work as would break down a dozen ordinary horses, his legs were as clean as when he was foaled; although, even when only walking, his fetlocks came nearly down to the ground at each step—so oblique were his pasterns. Their bones, though long and sloping, were, however, of good substance. My experience among horses in many lands leads me to the conclusion that the drier the country in which they are bred and reared, the more sloping are their pasterns. I advance no theory in support of this instance of the "survival of the fittest," which I give merely for what it is worth. Australian horses, I may mention, have their pasterns more oblique than English horses (though practically of the same blood), and are consequently better fitted for work on hard ground. As the shoulder-blade and pastern are at the opposite ends of the spring made by the bones of the fore limb, we may infer that they should be more or less at the same slope. Hence, if it be desirable that a horse should have oblique shoulders, he should also have well sloped pasterns. I may point out that in good, elastic pasterns, the joint (which is just below the coronet at the front part of the foot) between the coffin-bone and short pastern bone, should have particularly free play. I would direct attention to Pl. 35 as the portrait of a horse that had pasterns of a nice slope for fast saddle work of an average kind. In fact, he is a well-shaped horse "all round."

The two curses which remain on English thoroughbreds, are upright pasterns and roaring. The former condition is such a common defect that it generally passes without notice, and is accepted by the ignorant as the proper kind of conformation. Of the two, I certainly think that undue straightness of pastern is the cause of the turf career of more English horses being cut short than is roaring. Pl. 13 gives a good example of this fatal shape in the thoroughbred.

As I have already said, the defect of uprightness of pastern in the fore limb, not alone militates against the speed of a horse by causing him to suffer to an undue extent from the injurious effects of concussion; but also tends to decrease his power of raising his forehand by the straightening of the fore limb, as we see done in Figs. 97, 98, 99, 100, and 101. It is evident that with pasterns like those in Pl. 13, there could be but slight descent of the fetlock joint, and consequently their "play" could affect but little the length of the limb. I may here repeat (*see* p. 58) that propulsion is accomplished by the straightening out of the limb, to effectually do which, the joints in question must possess the ability to be freely extended. Every experienced trainer will have noticed that as a race-horse's fore pasterns become more and more upright from work, the more will he lose his speed and his "level" style of galloping. This will also occur to a horse whose pasterns have become abnormally oblique on account of sprain of the suspensory ligament, in which case the defect will lie in the inability to straighten the joint freely when weight is thrown on the limb. It is evident that the longer the pastern, the greater will be the play of the fetlock joint. Hence, length, as well as obliquity, of pastern is an indication of speed.

Lecoq remarks that: "The direction of the pastern is almost always influenced by its length. The shorter the pastern, the more upright is it; and the longer it is, the more is it sloped." This rule may hold good in horses of the same class; but not, at least to the same extent, among animals of different breeds. This French writer also adds with justice that: "There are, however, horses—and especially mules and asses—in which the pastern, although very short, is well sloped." As the evil effects of concussion fall much more severely on the fore limb than on the hind leg, its pastern is, normally, more sloping.

Referring to Clydesdales, Mr. Dykes writes: "No doubt the upright pastern suits well the upright shoulder and slow action of the English draught-horse, a conformation which can scarcely be called the best for any purpose; but it will not do in the Clydesdale, which requires a pastern to suit the formation of the shoulder, and to confer the necessary elasticity to counteract the concussion caused by his quick firm step. Short upright pasterns always get worse with age and feeding, and the action in due course of time becomes impeded. A horse with an upright pastern has little or no command of his foot, and literally walks as on a crutch; and if he has no power of his foot, he cannot have much in his shoulder. The streets of Glasgow are very trying to horses which have to scramble for a footing in the furrows between the hard, smooth paving-stones; and horses with upright pasterns are sometimes almost powerless to move, where those with pasterns moderately sloped, and of medium length, can walk with comparative ease. Farmers around Glasgow are alive to this, and will not readily use a stallion which has this defect, however strong and shapely." I need hardly say that the comparisons which Mr. Dykes draws between the Clydesdale and the Shire horse in no way concern us here.

The Hoof.—The hoof serves as a horny boot in which to enclose the bones and soft structures of the foot. The horn of the wall, sole, and frog should be thick, hard and tough, so as to resist in an efficient manner the effects of wear. Moisture has a well-marked softening and weakening influence on the horn, and it consequently affects the form of the foot. We shall find that the drier the climate; the stronger is the horn of horses reared in it; the more upright are the feet; and the more concave are the soles. I may explain that when the horn of the wall and sole is weak, it will not be able to efficiently support the weight thrown on the leg, and the foot will have a tendency to become flat. The feet of, for instance, horses bred in Australia are far stronger than those produced in England, owing to the climate being drier; although both are practically of the same blood. The fact that water mechanically softens horn, does not explain why the hoofs of horses in damp climates should be produced thinner than those of animals in dry climates. We know from experience, however, that moisture has a great influence in quickening the growth of horn, as we may see in horses turned out on marshy ground. Also, in those parts of India where the yearly rain-fall, though large in quantity, is practically confined to about four consecutive months, it is found that the growth of the horses' feet during the "monsoons" is much greater than it is in the dry weather. Hence, we may reasonably conclude that this stimulation in growth is one of length of horn, and not one of increased horny material. The case, I submit, is somewhat analogous to that of plants, which, under the influence of an excess of moisture, spring up quickly, with tissues full of water, but with little solid matter. The great trouble with heavy cart-horses in England is from the weakness of their hoofs, the horn of which, as a rule, is neither thicker nor stronger than that of well-bred horses, although the strain which falls on it is much greater than that which tries the tenacity of the horn of the feet of saddle horses. Considering the greater size of the muscles and bones of the draught animal, we should expect that the horn of his hoofs would be proportionately stronger than that of the half-bred. The fact that it is not stronger, is a proof that English cart-horses are deficient in one of the most important points of usefulness. Veterinary surgeons in practice in England and Scotland could tell us that the large majority (I would say about nine-tenths) of cart-horses which come to them for treatment, are foot cases. The ideal hoof for a cart-horse should in no way differ from that which is most suitable to a light trapper, hunter, or race-horse, except that it should be larger and consequently stronger. Therefore, we should regard with disfavour the weak feet, with their low, spread-out heels and flat soles, which, from their frequent occurrence, have become too generally accepted as characteristic of cart-horses. Small contracted feet are equally bad.

The inner quarter of the foot is more upright than the outer quarter, and its ground surface is straighter; conditions which provide for the fact of more weight falling on the inner than on the outer part of the foot. The horn has its maximum amount of thickness at the toe (at which part there is the greatest amount of wear from friction with the ground), and gradually gets thinner as it approaches the heels. As the fore feet are intended to support more weight than the hind feet, their ground surface is broader, their frogs are larger, and their heels are lower.

From many careful measurements of well-formed feet, both in a natural state and when subjected to the influence of shoeing, I have come to the conclusion that the slope of the fore foot, at the toe, should be about 50°, with a variation, one way or the other, of, say, not more than 3°. The slope of the hoof will conform somewhat to that of the pastern. The outside surface of the hoof should be naturally smooth, and should be straight from the coronet to the ground; for undue roughness, bulging-out, or concavity of surface will probably indicate the presence or previous existence of disease.

The heels should be strong and the "bars" well developed, so that the proper slope of the foot may be maintained, and that the liability to "corns," or to contraction of the heels, may be lessened. I may point out that one effect of shoeing in the ordinary manner is to cause the heels to be subjected to more wear than the toes; for, at the latter part, the position of the iron with regard to the wall is fixed; but at the former there is a certain amount of "play" between the shoe and the horn. Consequently, the tendency of the shod foot will be to acquire a less slope than it ought to have at the toe. This difficulty in preserving the proper shape of the hoof is a troublesome one to every careful and competent shoeing smith. Some horses have such weak heels, that if they wear ordinary shoes, it is impossible to keep the feet at a proper slope, or to prevent them getting corns. The fact of the feet being at a less slope than natural, will cause an undue amount of strain to be thrown on the back tendons (*see* p. 69). I may mention that if the bars be weak in proportion to the wall, or if they be cut away, the heels of the shod foot will have a tendency to contract. Unusual width between the heels is generally associated with weakness of those parts. At the same time they should have no tendency to contraction, which will not be present if the frog, as it ought to be, is well developed. I may remark that an abnormal size of frog, especially if the sole be convex, or even flat, will, as a rule, point to the effects of laminitis (fever of the feet). If, however, the frog is in a healthy state, and if the sole, as it should be, is concave in form, the observer need not fear that the frog is too big. Horses which have never been shod, have their frogs much larger, their heels further apart, and the ground surface of their feet of greater area, than those which habitually stand on iron. The cleft of the frog in a healthy foot is merely a slight depression in the centre of the frog, and does not communicate with the sensitive structures immediately above the frog. If the wall be strong and the sole be concave, we may rest assured that the horn which covers the sole is of sufficient substance, provided, of course, that it has not been pared away by the shoeing-smith. Some horses have an excess of soft tissue at the back of the foot, which then makes the distance between the coronet and heels abnormally long. This condition is known as "boxy" or "fleshy heels," and is objectionable in that it cramps the action of the foot, and renders it weaker, and consequently more liable to injury, than if the foot were in a normal state.

An undesirable kind of conformation which is sometimes seen, usually in horses that have an admixture of cart and thoroughbred blood, is that which gives the hoof the appearance of being too big for the bones which it covers, without being in any way deformed by disease, or by an overgrowth of horn. This condition is due to the pastern bones being slight in comparison to the size of the pedal bone, which, in health, regulates that of the hoof. In such cases, the leg is not alone abnormally weak, but the fact that its bones are not symmetrical, points to the probability that there are, in other parts of the framework, other instances of lack of harmonious conformation.

CHAPTER XIX.

THE HIND LIMB.

General View of the Hind Limb—The Pelvis—Thigh and Stifle—Tibia—Hock—Cannon and Fetlock—Pastern and Hoof.

As many points of resemblance exist between the fore and hind limb, I shall assume, in order to avoid needless repetition, that my readers, before arriving at this chapter, have studied the preceding one; and also Chapter VIII., in which I have tried to explain the action of both pairs of legs.

General view of the Hind Limb.—As the pelvis, which is analogous to the shoulder-blade of the fore leg, is essentially a portion of the hind quarters, I have reserved its consideration for this chapter, instead of the one (Chapter XVII.) in which I have attempted to treat of the trunk. Although the chief function of the hind limb is that of propulsion, it has, like the fore extremity, to bear weight; but to a lesser extent, and is also less exposed to the effects of concussion. Thus we see that while the shoulder-blade is connected to the body by muscles which work like a spring, and which admit of extended reach in order to preserve stability; the pelvis is firmly united to the spine, so that the force of propulsion may be transmitted to the body with but little mechanical loss. The pastern and hoof of the hind quarters are naturally more upright than those of the forehand, and, consequently the muscles which bend them, act to greater mechanical advantage.

We have seen in Chapter VIII., that for the attainment of high speed, the horse should possess the fullest ability to bend and extend the hind limb. Hence the beauty, in the race-horse, of a "straight dropped" hind leg. As this power chiefly depends on the action of the hock, I shall defer its further consideration, until I come to that joint.

On page 162, I have remarked that the desirable proportions for the bones of the limb are: pelvis, long; thigh, short; tibia (from stifle to hock), long; cannon, short; and pastern, long.

The sets of muscles which move the joints of the hind limb, appear to complete their respective actions, in succession, from above downwards, namely: the hip-joint first; then the stifle; and, finally, the hock and fetlock; the former being extended by the muscle that bends the latter. We may infer that to be effective in the production of speed, these actions must increase in rapidity in the same order. As the muscles that "start" the weight at each step, are those which extend the hip-joint, we must look for, in the cart-horse, special muscular development of the croup and thigh. In the race-horse, however, length and power of the muscles of the gaskin, which cause acceleration of speed at the end of the "stroke," should be particularly sought for. These deductions, I may remark, are in accordance with the nature of the conformation, respectively exhibited by horses that are the representative types of the two classes.

The Pelvis.—For speed we require the pelvis to be as long as possible; for strength, as broad as it can be.

The consideration of the best slope for the pelvis is a much more difficult question than that of the most suitable angle for the shoulder-blade, which, for most purposes, cannot be too oblique.

If we examine Fig. 72, and refer to Chapter IX., we shall see that the push, in draught, by the hind leg, is in an irregular line from the toe, through the bones of the hind limb, the pelvis, and the body, to the centre of pressure of the collar on the shoulder. In Fig. 96, the line of propulsion is similar to that in heavy draught, except that it passes through the centre of gravity, instead of the centre of pressure on the shoulder by the collar. It is evident that the straighter, or less convex this irregular line is, the more effective will be the propulsion. In draught, therefore, shortness of the hind limbs, as compared to the forehand, will be an advantage (as I have also pointed out on p. 74), in that it will tend to render the line of bones through which propulsion takes place, straight. As good length of hind limb is a necessity in the galloper; any reduction in the convexity of this line will have to be obtained by the opening out of its angles, and not by curtailing the length of the hind limb. Thus, the hind leg will be stretched out as much as possible to the rear (compare Figs. 72 and 96), and the direction of the pelvis (as a point of conformation) will be more horizontal than in the draught animal. The so-called horizontal croup is not alone a great beauty in the saddle horse, but it is also a decided mark of speed. If the pelvis or croup (which in this case is practically the same thing) be too level (*see* p. 203), we may suspect that the back is weak.

I need hardly point out that the pelvis is more upright when the animal is standing still, than when he is in movement; and when he has no burden on his back, than when he is mounted. Although I am aware that horses with drooping quarters are not looked upon with disfavour in Irish hunting fields; I cannot help regarding this kind of conformation as a serious defect in every class of horse which is required to go faster than a slow trot. Its existence implies that the backward sweep of the hind leg is proportionately curtailed, and consequently the compass of the stride is more or less cramped. Also, on account of the point of the buttock being depressed, the muscles (the *ischio tibial*) which are attached to it and to the head of the tibia, and which aid in the extension of the hip-joint, will be unduly shortened in length. This condition, by bringing the hip-joint too far forward, is apt to throw too much weight on the hocks and will thus be liable to lead to injury of these joints. Pl. 36 shows that the hind legs of the horse represented in it, bear an abnormal amount of weight, as compared to the forehand. To have the point of the buttock placed high and projecting well to the rear, is a great beauty, which may be seen in some thoroughbreds and high-caste Arabs. I may state that this kind of conformation is found in a high state of perfection in the hare, in which animal the pelvis is not alone more or less horizontally placed; but the portion of it (the *ischium*) that is behind the cavity in which the head of the hip-bone works, is much longer in proportion to the remainder of the pelvis, than it is in the horse.

A horse with unusually drooping quarters, as in Pl. 36, is said to be "goose rumped."

The prominence which some horses show in the middle of

the croup (*see* Pl. 38), is due to the large development of the inner angle of the pelvis (at each side), and points to the presence, in the part, of strong muscles. St. Gatien, I may mention, had this prominence well marked.

Thigh and Stifle.—The muscles of the thigh should be well developed, so that, when viewed from the rear, they should leave no unsightly cavity between the legs. For speed, the thighs should be comparatively short (*see* p. 162), and will then give the stifle the appearance of being placed high up on the flank (*see* p. 163). The stifle should be directed well outwards, so that it will have no difficulty in clearing the abdomen, which the peculiar construction of the hock joint that is explained on p. 70, enables it to do. It seems probable that the fact of some "cow-hocked" (hocks turned in, *see* p. 235) horses being able to show an unexpected turn of speed, is frequently due to this kind of conformation conferring on them increased ability to bring their hind feet well forward.

Tibia.—Under this term, I wish to include the muscles and tendons between the stifle and point of the hock, with their coverings, as well as the tibia (*see* Fig. 3), which, I may repeat, is the bone that lies between the stifle and hock joint. For speed, the tibia should have a maximum of length (*see* p. 162). This is particularly the case in the hare.

The *Gaskin* is one of the most important points by which we may judge of the suitability of a horse for fast work; for I venture to assert after a long and careful study of the subject, that it is impossible for a horse to have a really fine turn of speed, unless he has broad gaskins. I may point

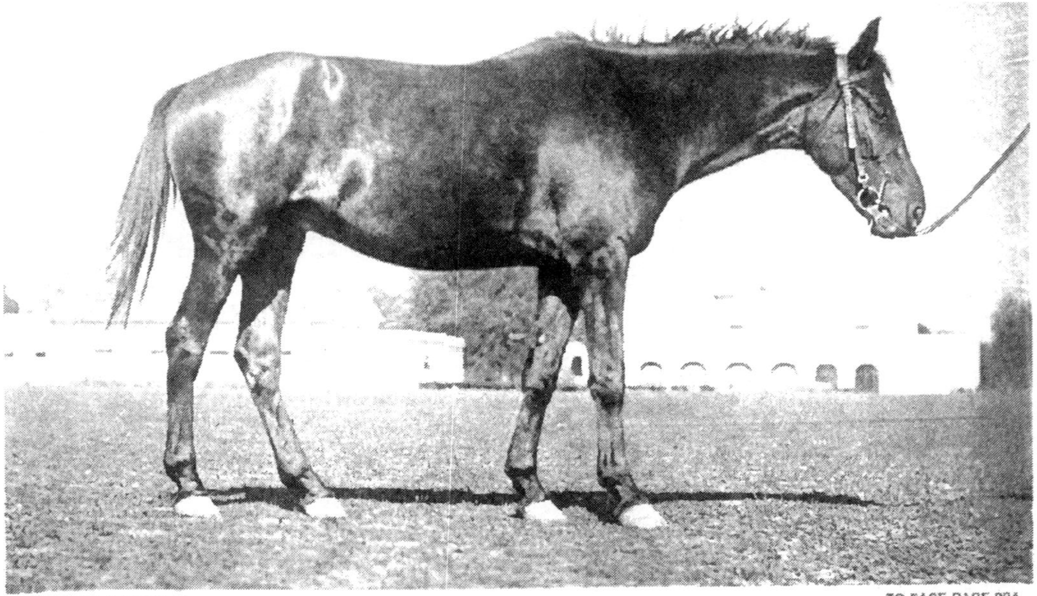

PHOTO. BY M. H. HAYES

TO FACE PAGE 234

PLATE 48—PONY WITH WEAK GASKINS AND UPRIGHT SHOULDERS.

out that width of gaskin is conferred by length of *os calcis* (*see* p. 32). We may see from p. 70 that the longer the *os calcis*, the greater is the mechanical advantage at which the muscles that are attached to the point of the hock, work. I may add, that these muscles agree in length with the tibia, and that the longer they are, the quicker will be the action of the hock in propulsion. The gaskin should not alone be broad, for purposes of speed; but in all cases its muscles should be well developed. In Pl. 48, the gaskin is poor.

The Hock.—On page 77, I have indicated the direction which the hock should have, as viewed from behind. We have seen on page 70, that by a special arrangement of the bones of the hock, the stifle is enabled to clear the abdomen, without altering the direction of the hind foot, when the hind leg is brought forward during movement. This action is facilitated by the fact that, in a normally shaped leg, the hock is directed slightly outwards as well as forwards (*see* Pl. 12). When the points of the hocks are turned in to excess (*see* Pl. 14), the effect to the eye is bad; but the mechanical loss is small, unless, indeed, the defect be much exaggerated. If, on the contrary, the points of the hocks be naturally turned outwards, the forward reach of the hind legs will be impeded by the abdomen. Also, if we observe, from behind, a horse which has this kind of conformation, and which is walking, we shall as a rule find that each hock instead of moving steadily in a straight line, receives a peculiar twist (which must be accompanied by loss of power) while it is propelling the body forward. Experience certainly teaches us that of the two faults, it is better for a horse to have his hocks turned in than to have them turned out.

For purposes of speed, the hock should possess the power of being fully extended (*see* p. 63); hence, the beauty of a "straight dropped" hind leg (*see* Pl. 51). In all great gallopers (*see* Pls. 18 and 55), we may see this kind of conformation; although it is true that some fairly speedy horses (but not of the highest class) have had their hocks more bent than the types I have given. This ability to straighten the hock is not required to any great degree, in animals that are used at slow paces. "Sickle-hocks" (*see* Pl. 49), as those are termed which remain bent to a marked degree, when the joint is extended as much as possible, are, however, objectionable in any kind of horse.

While recognising the desirability of straight hocks for speed, we must not forget that this kind of conformation, to be effective, must be accompanied by good length of hind limb from hip-joint to foot, in order to obtain adequate flexion as well as extension. If the hind leg be comparatively short and the hock straight, as in Pl. 36, it is evident that there will be but little straightening out of the limb, when the "shove-off" is being given.

The width of the leg, immediately below the hock (looking at the limb in profile), should be as great as possible compared to the width of the fetlock. This desirable shape (which has its analogy in the fore limb, *see* p. 219) is well shown in Pls. 51, 52 and 53. I may remark that the hock shown in Pl. 52, which is that of a half-bred saddle nag, is not a particularly straight one, although it is otherwise well shaped. Pl. 50, is a capital illustration of the defect known as "tied-in" below the hock.

We are all agreed that a horse should have large hocks, an expression which—granting that the other points of the

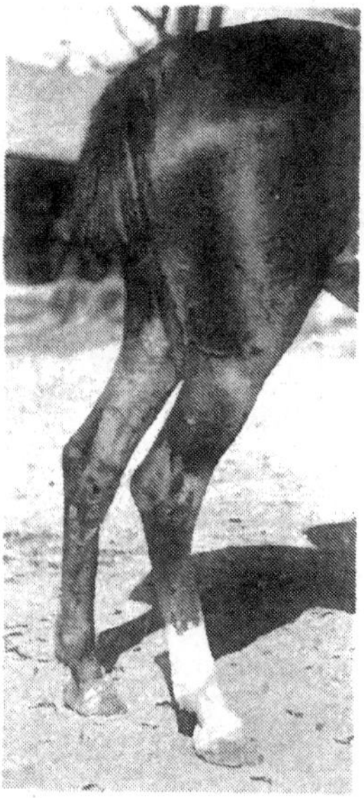

PL. 49—SICKLE HOCKS.

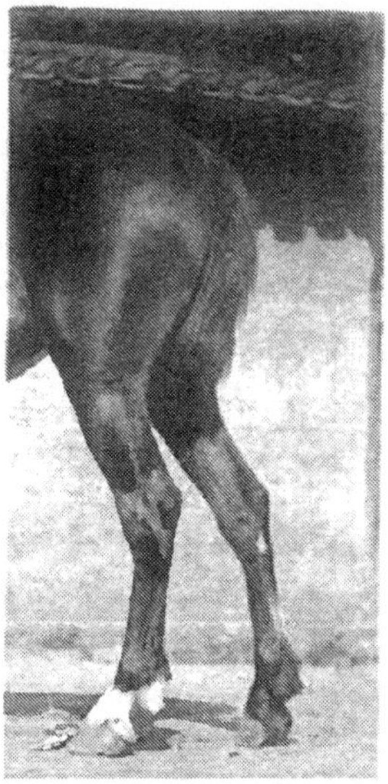

PL. 50—TIED-IN BELOW HOCK.

PHOTO. BY M.

PL. 51—STRAIGHT AND GOOD HOCKS.

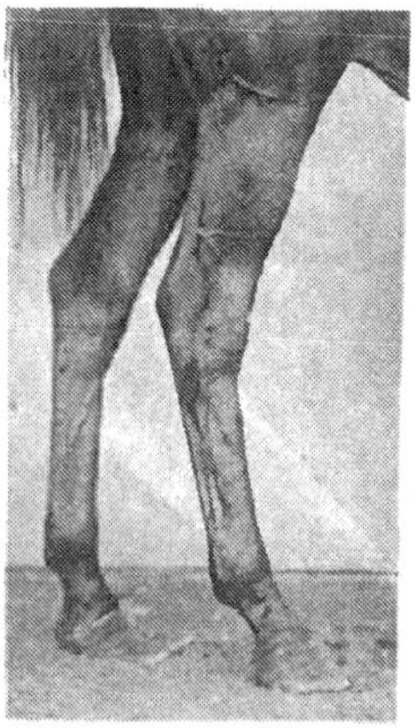

PL. 52—GOOD HOCKS.

FACE PAGE 286

PL. 53—GOOD HOCKS.

part are good—is synonymous with "strong hocks." If we find that a horse is not "tied-in" below the hock, and that his gaskins are broad (*i.e.* his *os calcis* long), we may rest assured that his hocks are of good size.

As the diseases and injuries of the hock belong to the domain of equine surgery, and as I have investigated them in *Veterinary Notes for Horse-owners*, I shall not allude further to them here. The desirable absence of synovial enlargements and of an undue amount of cellular tissue will be indicated by the bones, tendons, and ligaments, and by the hollows and eminences formed by them, being clearly defined underneath the skin.

The horse has on the inside of each hind limb, and a little below the hock joint, a *castor* or *chesnut* somewhat similar to that found in the fore leg (*see* p. 216).

Hocks and Knees well let down.—There is no point in the conformation of the horse, upon which more stress is usually laid, than that which may be described in horsey language as "hocks and knees well let down," or "hocks and knees close to the ground." The cheetah (*see* Pl. 2) has this point well marked. The black buck, another speedy animal, is, on the contrary, much longer from his hocks and knees. From an examination of the comparative length of the bones of the limbs (*see* pp. 161 and 162), we know that the proportion of the length of the column of bones below the knee and hock to that of the radius and tibia, respectively, remains more or less constant. How then comes it, we may well ask, that the idea of the hocks and knees of some horses being better "let down," than those of other horses, has gained currency? As regards the fore limb, the answer is easy; for the knee of a leg which has a comparatively short cannon-bone and a sloping pastern, would, naturally, be somewhat closer to the ground, than it would be, were the cannon-bone long and the pastern upright. Besides this, the appearance of a comparatively long cannon may, I venture to think, give the impression of greater length below the knee and hock, than would be the case, were the cannon short in comparison to the pastern. As regards the opinion that the length from hock to toe, as compared to that from hock to stifle—irrespective of the slope of the pastern—being less in some horses than in others, I must say that I think it is founded on an optical delusion. If we examine Pl. 51, we shall see a hock which certainly gives us the idea that it is "well let down"; but a look at Pl. 49 will convey to our minds the opposite kind of impression. And yet if we take a pair of dividers and describe a circle, with the point of the hock as a centre, and its distance from the toe as a radius, we shall find that in the case of both Pl. 51 and Pl. 49, the circumference will cut the curved fold of skin near the groin at the same point! For convenience sake, I have taken these measurements, which are sufficiently accurate for the purpose in question; although it would have been more correct to have made them from the hock joint to the toe, and to the stifle joint, respectively. From whence arises, then, this difference of appearance between these two hind limbs, as regards the height of the hock off the ground? To this I would reply that the fact of the hock in Pl. 51 being "straight" (*see* p. 236), gives the impression to the observer that it is better "let down," than the "bent" hock in Pl. 49; for, as the eye runs down the limb, it would not be so abruptly arrested by the former, as by the latter kind of conformation. Also, the broader the bone is immediately below the hock (contrast

Pl. 53 with Pl. 50), as compared to the width of the hind fetlock; the easier will the eye of the observer run down the hind leg.

Cannon and Fetlock.—Concerning these parts, I have nothing to add to what I have already written in this chapter and in the preceding one, beyond saying that if the leg is of good width immediately below the hock, its shape will be all right down to the fetlock.

Pastern and Hoof.—As the hind limb is concerned more in propulsion than in resisting the evil effects of concussion; its pastern should be more upright, than what would be required in that of the fore leg. The hoof should more nearly approach the perpendicular, than the fore one; its slope, when viewed in profile, being, in unshod horses, about 60°. It is, as compared to its length, narrower; the ground surfaces of its quarters are straighter; and their respective curvatures differ less from each other, than those of the fore extremity. The horn at the toe is not so thick; the sole is more concave; the frog is narrower and less developed; and the heels are higher and closer together.

CHAPTER XX.

SKIN, HAIR, AND COLOUR.

Skin—Colour—Colour in relation to Heat and Cold—Hair—Hair on the Legs of Cart-horses—Markings.

Skin.—The chief functions of the horse's skin, as far as we are at present concerned, are: (1) to regulate the temperature of the system, (2) to aid in removing waste matters from the blood; and (3) to protect the body. As the first and second duties are intimately connected with each other, we may consider them conjointly.

The internal temperature being maintained by the changes which take place in the tissues; exercise, by promoting these changes, increases the production of heat But as it also determines blood to the surface of the body, and thereby stimulates the sweat glands; the surplus heat is removed by an increased amount of evaporation from the skin, which performs this work, and also that of radiating heat, best when it is thin. Although the subject of health is outside the scope of this book, I may remark in passing, that a soft and pliable condition of the skin is due to the fact of the oil glands which are imbedded in it, being in good order. Granting the employment of clothing when necessary, we may assume that the skin of hard-worked horses, especially those which are engaged at fast paces, should, within reasonable limits, be as thin as possible, consistent with its being able to stand the friction and pressure of harness and saddle-gear.

Colour.—The colour of a horse's coat, as a rule, does not seem to be of much importance, as far as his useful qualities are concerned, although we cannot help being favourably impressed with those of rich and decided shades. Personally, I admire most a dark chestnut, or a dark brown with a tinge of rich claret-colour through it, as may be met with on rare occasions. Dark, bright bays are also very pleasing to the eye Generally speaking, a horse looks best when his legs below the knees and hocks, mane and tail are darker than the rest of his coat. Bright chestnuts, with white stockings and blaze, like many of the Blair Athol blood, form, perhaps, an exception to this. I cannot help sharing the general dislike to "mealy" chestnuts, and to bays and browns which are lighter on the insides of the limbs and on the lower part of the belly than on other portions of the body. The existence of this partial deficiency of colouring matter in the skin seems to infer want of nervous power; for we must remember that the distribution of pigment is greatly influenced by the nervous system. The common belief that if one fore leg is dark and the other white, the latter will be more apt to go wrong than the former, holds good, I think, only as far as the skin and hoof are concerned. Many persons consider black a "soft" colour, except, indeed, in the case of cart-horses, which are much admired when of that hue. The prejudice to which I have just alluded is, probably, due to the fact of many animals of this shade being "foreigners." Grey is, undoubtedly, an unpopular colour. Apart from any feeling as regards the colour itself, it is true that it gets fainter as the horse gets older, and then unmistakably and perhaps unpleasantly proclaims the fact that the animal has passed his first youth. Besides this, a grey coat is difficult to keep clean, and is liable to contract stains which are hard to remove. The extra trouble thus entailed predisposes grooms to dislike grey horses, a fact which may account for the small number of grey horses in England, compared with those met with in the East, where stable duties are not so onerous as in this country. I may mention that grey horses appear to be more liable to *melanosis* than animals of other colours. Shire horse fanciers do not like greys ; for the majority of foreign buyers object to them. Some of their best horses, as What's Wanted and Rokeby Fuchsia, for instance, were of this hue. For my own part, I am very fond of dark iron or dappled grey with dark mane and tail. Among the cleverest jumpers I have seen, I must say that a comparatively large proportion of them have been greys, a fact for which I can offer no explanation. Blue and red roans, and dun with black points, are supposed to be "hardy" colours The most showy colours for harness work, are bright chestnut and red roan with more chestnut than grey hairs, and free from white patches. When there is a large admixture of white with the red, the colour may be called strawberry roan, which is an ugly hue, particularly if the animal that wears it has a blaze and white stockings. Both piebald and skewbald are suggestive of the circus. The colours found among high-caste Arab horses are practically limited to bay, brown, chestnut, and grey. The same remark applies to our own thoroughbred stock, except that we have a few roans, and a very small proportion of greys, chiefly through Chanticleer. I may mention that chestnuts are generally thought to be more impetuous than horses of other colours. I do not think that this idea is worthy of much weight.

The colour of the skin itself is either black, pink (free from pigment), or it may be partly black and partly pink in patches. Although the large majority of grey and white horses have black skins ; pink skin will have invariably white hair, and will secrete (at the coronets) white hoofs. Black skin will form dark-coloured horn, even when the coat is white. Although, as I have just said, white horses may have black skins ; we shall find that the skin of white markings (stars, blazes, reaches, snips, stockings, etc.) on dark-coloured horses is, as a rule, white. In fact, I venture to say that the skin of white stockings is always pink, and consequently the hoofs of these legs will be white ; provided, of course, that the white hair is continued down to the coronet. In the East we may not unfrequently see pink-skinned horses, which, of course, are white, and which, according to my experience, are much "softer" in constitution than animals with dark skins. This fact is, I think, chiefly owing to the greater effect the rays of the sun have on skins which are free from pigment, than on dark-coloured skins. Besides, as human albinos are generally inferior, intellectually and physically, to their fellows, we may suppose that the same rule holds good with respect to these equine albinos. Experiments show that dark-coloured hair is capable of sustaining greater tension than blonde hair Hence we have reason to assume that the protective cuticle and horn (both of which, like hair, consist of epithelium), secreted by dark-coloured skin, are stronger than those formed by pink skin.

English stable-men who make a practice of washing horses' feet, rightly consider that the animals under their charge which have white pasterns, are more liable to get cracked heels than those which have dark ones. The supposed idiosyncracy in this case is no doubt chiefly due to the extra amount of washing which the white pasterns receive, so as to give them a clean appearance.

Colour in relation to Heat and Cold—Experience in tropical climates teaches us that the darker a horse's coat is, the better will he stand the effects of the sun. I may explain that dark surfaces radiate out heat and also absorb it faster than those of a lighter hue, as we may prove by the two following experiments If we fill with boiling water two crockery teapots of the same form—one being white, the other black—we shall find that, if they are both placed in a cool spot, the latter will lose its heat quicker than the former. If, however, they are filled with icy cold water, and are then exposed under similar conditions to the effect of the sun on a hot day, the black one will get warm in a shorter time than its fellow. We are also aware that the skin of natives of tropical climates is darker than that of inhabitants of temperate or cold countries; and that in the Arctic regions, the coats of various animals turn white on the approach of winter. The working of this natural law is most beneficent; for, as the temperature of the body of the polar bear, for instance, is much higher than that of the atmosphere in which he lives, he can lose nothing on account of his white coat being a bad absorber of heat; while the fact of its parting with (radiating) heat slowly, helps the body to maintain its normal degree of warmth The skin of the negro, for example, although it absorbs heat quickly, radiates it still faster; for the vapour given off by the skin cools the surface, and also, by the mechanical protection it affords, tends to prevent the absorption of heat from the atmosphere. At first glance, we might, possibly, imagine that if the surrounding air was warmer than the internal temperature (about 100·5° Fahrenheit for the horse), no cooling effect could be produced by radiation. When, however, the skin is in healthy and untrammelled action, its temperature, on account of the free evaporation of perspiration, is considerably under that of the deeper structures, even when the thermometer stands, say, 115° Fahrenheit in the shade. If, under such circumstances, clothing be worn, the garments will soon become almost, if not quite, as hot as the surrounding air, evaporation will be checked, except from the exposed parts, the temperature of the skin will rise, and the cooling process of radiation will be more or less stopped. In this case, any gain which may be obtained in lessening the absorption of heat, as persons do in hot countries, by wearing white will be a direct gain. During the summer months in tropical latitudes, the hair on a horse's body will, usually, be so short and thin, that its presence will offer no impediment to the action of the skin. Agreeably to the foregoing observations, we find that black and brown horses stand heat best; and that white—especially if they have pink skins—and grey animals sustain it comparatively badly. I have frequently observed on hot days in tropical climates that, other things being equal, horses of light hues sweated far more readily and profusely than those of darker shades.

Hair.—The possession of a fine glossy coat will naturally indicate that the skin is in active working order, and consequently in good condition for removing the surplus heat generated in the body by hard labour. The Desert Arabs, who have no objection to a thick mane, consider that unless a horse has a thin tail, he cannot be of high caste. The same idea seems to have given rise to the saying that one never sees a bad rat-tailed horse. As remarked by "Stonehenge," waviness in the hair of the tail is a sign of want of breeding.

Hair on the Legs of Cart-horses.—It is a common belief that cart-horses with a good supply of hair on the legs have better bone than the cleaner limbed animals. Mr. G. M. Sexton, secretary to the English Cart-horse Society, in his essay on cart-horses, writes as follows: "One of the characteristics of the Shire horse is to have hair on the legs. The hair should be long and thin, finer in quality on the mare than the stallion; it should grow from the fetlock above the knee, and the same behind the hock. By many this is thought to be a useless appendage, and that this abundance of hair is a cause of grease; but it is not so by any means. Hair is an indication of bone and size." Mr. Frederick Street, in his *History of the Shire Horse*, gives "plenty of long silky hair on the legs" as one of the desirable points in the Shire horse. Mr. James Howard, M.P, in his *Notes on Cart-horses* (Royal Agricultural Journal, 1884), remarks that: "A grave doubt, however, arises whether the profusion of hair and 'feather' insisted upon in show-yards and among the leading breeders of Shire horses is really so essential to strength and constitution as is generally asserted and believed. As a farmer of heavy clay land—much of it hilly—which requires very powerful horses in tillage and in carting, I have long entertained doubts as to the policy of the present tendency to such a profusion of hair. Breeders not only contend for hair on the rear of the legs, but many have also come to insist upon a mass of hair in front from the knee downward, doubtless a characteristic of many of the old Shire horses bred in Derbyshire early in the present century. Of course, no one contends that all this hairy covering is desirable in itself; it is advocated as being essential to hardiness of constitution and size of bone. This contention merely means that the desired constitution and sufficient bone have not hitherto been obtained without an abundance of hair" This gentleman cites cases in which, for railway work, clean-legged horses are preferred to those with a plentiful supply of hair, on account of the latter being pre-disposed to grease and other forms of inflammation of the skin of these parts. We may readily see that legs which have a large amount of coarse hair on them would be pre-disposed to grease and other allied ailments; for, as both hair and scurf skin are secreted by the true skin, we may infer that if the former is thick and coarse, the latter will be strong and harsh, and, consequently, the oil which is secreted to keep the surface soft and supple, will not be able to perform its duty as efficiently as it would do, were the scurf skin thin. When the scurf skin gets hard and cracks from the effects of the climate and from its being insufficiently supplied by this oil, the highly sensitive true skin becomes inflamed from irritation due to exposure. The fact of cart-horses being peculiarly liable to "sallenders," if they are blistered for "bog spavins," taken in connection with the coarseness of their hair, as compared to that of lighter breeds, would seem to support the opinion that the coarser the hair, the more liable is the animal to suffer from inflammation of the skin, of which grease is a form that is very difficult to entirely allay. We may safely conclude that if hair on the legs be desired, it should be soft and silky in its nature. I may mention that Prince William, who, as a two-year-old, was the champion of all classes in the Shire Horse Society's show for 1885, had the best hair I have ever seen on a cart-horse. Mr. Thomas Dykes, in his essay on *The Clydesdale Horse*, states that "the back part from the knee down should possess a nice flowing fringe of silken hair, which should spring from the very edge of the bone. This hair should be of what a judge of a Skye terrier would style a 'pily' nature; and good judges will not have a horse at all, the feather of which has a coarse matted appearance. The high value set upon nice silky hair is on account of its being an indication of strong, healthy bone, and as hair of a short coarse matted kind suggests a tendency to grease."

Markings.—When a dark-coloured horse has a small patch of white, more or less in the centre of his forehead, it is called a "star." If the white spreads over the forehead, it is termed a "blaze." If it runs down his nose in the form of a line of no great width, it is known as a "reach." A white or pink patch on either lip, is called a "snip." White, reaching down to the coronet, on the leg of a dark-coloured horse is, as we all know, termed a "white stocking," an expression that might be reserved for one that comes up as high as the knee or hock; while that of a "white sock" might be used to signify the marking when it is shorter.

CHAPTER XXI.

ACTION, HANDINESS AND CLEVERNESS.

Action.—*General Remarks on Action.*—The three chief requisites of action, from a useful point of view, are: sure-footedness, effectiveness, and lightness, so that the limbs may not unduly suffer from the effects of concussion. As remarked many years ago by Dr. Carson, the safety of a horse's action depends on the way he puts his feet down, rather than on the manner in which he picks them up. We should, therefore, from this point of view, attach no value to high action, beyond what is sufficient to enable the animal to avoid striking his toes against any inequalities which may be on the surface over which he is going. The stability of the fore limb, when the foot comes on the ground, depends, to a great extent, on the knee being kept straight, which is mechanically done, without the expenditure of muscular force, if a line drawn from the heel to the centre of the elbow joint, falls at that moment, in front of the centre of the knee joint. The more upright the pastern, the further will this line be drawn back as regards the position of the knee. As the shoulder-blade and pastern are at opposite ends of the column of bones of the fore limb, and as they both slope in the same direction; it follows that the degree of slope of the shoulder will influence that of the pastern. Hence, for safe action, we should seek for oblique shoulders, sloping and long pasterns, knees in which there is no tendency to "stand over," and lightness of forehand.

For effectiveness, the action should be the happy medium between a cramped style of going, and one in which command over the limbs is, to a certain extent, lost by the stride being too long.

By the term lightness of action, I wish to specify well-balanced movements of the limbs, by which undue weight is thrown on none of them, and particularly not on the forehand. The action from a "level" point of view, is influenced by the conformation of the body, and by the carriage of the head and neck. To be perfect at fast paces, we require the animal to be light in front, to have oblique shoulders and sloping pasterns, so as to have full power to raise the forehand, and to have good loin muscles. In Chapter X., I have treated of the carriage of the head and neck. In heavy draught we do not require lightness of action, which is the direct opposite of throwing weight into the collar.

The Walk.—At this pace, like at all others, the shoulders should work with the utmost freedom, and the fore foot should be thrown well to the front and only high enough to clear and cover the ground. We may see this beautiful play of the shoulders to perfection in young thoroughbreds. The hind legs should be swung freely to the front, so that they will considerably overstride the imprints made by the fore feet. Viewed from behind, as well as from the front, the near and off pairs of legs should respectively move in the same line, so that there may be no "dishing" or crossing of the legs. The hocks should have no in-and-out movement, as may be sometimes seen, and had better work rather close together than wide. Any tendency to stumble or knuckle over behind, is a serious fault, unless it be solely due to bad shoeing. If the horse be given a long rein, he should carry his head rather low and well advanced, and should be able to walk at the rate of about five miles an hour.

The Trot.—At the fast trot, the fore leg should be brought to the front with a straight knee, the foot appearing as if suspended for a brief moment before being placed down. The knee should not be raised higher than what would be sufficient to make the fore-arm horizontal, or not quite so much. The hind legs should be carried well forward, and should work in perfect unison with the fore limbs. Nothing looks worse than to see a horse trotting high in front, and dragging his hind legs along the ground. As I have already remarked, with reference to the walk, there should be no "dishing" or crossing of the legs, so that, when viewed from behind, a clear space will be preserved between the near pair and the off pair of legs. I may explain that a horse "dishes" with a fore leg when he throws the foot outwards as he raises it off the ground In fast trotting, mobility of the shoulder (which largely depends on the possession of a long neck, *see* p. 181) is a point of the utmost consequence. Hence American breeders employ, as much as circumstances will allow, thoroughbreds for the production of their matchless trotters. In the trot, the head should be carried much higher than in the walk; as the limb has to be raised to a greater extent.

The Gallop.—In order that the animal may utilise to the utmost his forward reach in the gallop, his knees should be kept as straight as possible when his fore legs are being extended to the front. In fact, the straighter they are at that moment, the more perfect will be the front action on level ground. A race-horse should, like a ballet dancer, move as if he had no knees. I may, however, qualify my praise of low action by remarking that a horse who bends his knees a little, is better suited for going up a hill, than a "daisy cutter"; as his "round" style of going will aid him in climbing the ascent. Heavy shoes on the feet have a marked influence in making horses go "high" in all their paces, a fact which has been largely utilised by American trainers in regulating the action of their trotters. As this tendency is detrimental to the speed of race-horses, light tips of sufficient substance to stand wear, should, as pointed out to me by Mr. Tom Jennings, the well known trainer, be much more extensively employed, than they are at present. In India, where but very little rain falls during the racing season, I have trained and run many of the horses I have had in my stable, without shoes of any kind. I have mentioned on p. 83, that curb bits are objectionable for use with race-horses, on account of their tendency to make horses gallop "round," or to "fight" in their action In the former case, the animal will carry his head low and bring his chin into his chest with the object of transferring the pressure, as much as possible, to his poll, over which the head-piece of his bridle passes, and will consequently bend his knees too much. In the latter case, the animal will keep his head stuck up in the air, probably, in the vain attempt to get his jaw away from the painful contact of the curb chain.

If we observe a "true" galloper, we may note that he holds his head and neck in a more or less uniform position (*see* pp. 84 and 85), so as to enable the muscles of the neck to work in a machine-like manner.

The hind legs, at the gallop, should be brought well forward under the body, with particularly quick recovery after having been straightened out. Their action, like that of the forehand, should be characterised by the machine-like regularity of their forward and backward sweep. The limbs should move in such perfect accord one with the other, that there should be the least possible rise and fall of the forehand; for if the weight be depressed at one moment, it will have to be raised during the next, by an expenditure of force which will be wasted as far as progression is concerned.

Leaping.—In Chapter XIII. we have seen that the "take-off," in the leap consists in the raising of the forehand and in the propulsion of the body. Hence, at that moment, the animal should have his head raised and somewhat drawn back, so as to "lighten" the forehand, for which object, and in order to be able to fully bend the hind legs, he should have them well under him. To obtain the maximum effect of propulsion, the horse should straighten his hind legs to their utmost extent; and to clear the object, if it be one that is likely to tax his powers to "negotiate," he should raise his knees well and should bend them as much as he can. The instant the hind feet quit the ground, they should be drawn up as quick as possible and close to the body, so that, in high jumping, they may not catch in the fence, but be ready to save the animal from a fall in the event of an accident, and to enable him to land in safety. On clearing the obstacle, the fore feet should be brought well to the front, and as they respectively come to the ground, their knees should be quite straight. The head should be somewhat raised and the muzzle drawn in a little, so as to bring the weight back, and to enable the horse to see where he is going to place his feet.

Handiness and Cleverness.—The "handiness" or "cleverness" of a horse depends on his conformation, disposition, and training, with which we are not at present concerned. It goes almost without saying, that a placid-tempered animal would be easier to stop or turn, than an excitable one, and would be consequently handier; but I cannot say that he would be cleverer. I have known several terribly hard-pulling steeple-chasers that were as "clever as cats," and always had a "spare leg" for every difficulty, provided their rider did not interfere with their mouth; and I have seen other equally stiff-necked, cross-country horses, whose sole delight, no matter how lightly they were handled, seemed to be punching a hole in every fence they met. Some temperate ones are just as "chancy," apparently, from pure laziness; though many quiet animals are incapable of making a mistake.

The points of conformation which conduce to handiness and cleverness are:—

1. Well set on head and neck, so that the horse may be able to bend readily to the rein.

2. Light in front (head, neck, and shoulders), and having well-sloped shoulders and front pasterns, in order that he may be able to raise his forehand with ease, and bring his weight back.

3. Strong loins. We must remember that the upper loin muscles are "rearing muscles" (see page 64), and that the lower ones assist to bring the hind legs under the horse.

4. Strong hocks and broad gaskins.

CHAPTER XXII.

CONDITION, AND GOOD LOOKS.

Condition.—I use this term here to signify the bodily state in which a horse can, in the best possible manner, do work that will test the power of his lungs and muscles to the utmost. I shall make no reference to "dealers' condition," which is a subject that does not come within the scope of either conformation, or of horsemanship.

A horse to be in condition should be healthy and sound; should have his breathing apparatus in the best possible working order; his muscles developed to the highest degree of perfection, with regard to the nature of the task they have got to perform; and the amount of fat in his system should be reduced to a minimum consistent with health.

I shall now glance at the chief signs of condition in the horse.

1. *Health and Soundness.*—The latter, apart from the former, need not be considered here; for it belongs to the domain of veterinary science. The ordinary indications of health are: coat, bright; skin, cool (except when heated by exercise, or by the sun), soft and loose over the muscles; eyes, bright and soft in expression; visible mucous membranes (of the eyes and nostrils), healthy looking; mouth,

sweet smelling, internal temperature (in health about 100·5° F.), pulse (from about 35 per minute for heavy cart-horses, to about 45 for small ponies), and rate of breathing (10 to 12 per minute, when at rest), normal. The dung should be fairly well formed, free from mucus, and from any offensive smell The appetite as a rule should be good; although horses may become a bit "dainty" in their feeding, when they have been wound up in their training to "full concert pitch."

2. *Development and Leanness of Muscles.*—The muscles of the croup (those over the quarters) should present a rounded surface, and those over the loins and back, at each side of the backbone, should stand out in bold relief. The line (sometimes known as the "water-mark") down the thigh (*see* Pl. 55) should be clearly apparent. The muscles just above the fore-arm should form a rounded mass, and those of the shoulders should be well defined There should be over the ribs a thick sheet of muscle, which should show well above the level of the part of the flank in rear of it. This muscular covering of the ribs terminates abruptly in an irregular line which goes downwards and backwards in the direction of the groin, and which can be seen plainly only when there is no excess of fat about the part. I may explain that in forced respiration (*see* p 47), the muscles which cover the ribs are brought into active play, and they consequently, become largely developed by the process that brings the galloper, or fast trotter, into condition. Hence, if there be in a horse a marked difference of level between the surface in front of the line in question, and that in the rear of it (*see* Pl. 54); we may reasonably conclude that he has done a good deal of that kind of work which brings his lungs into

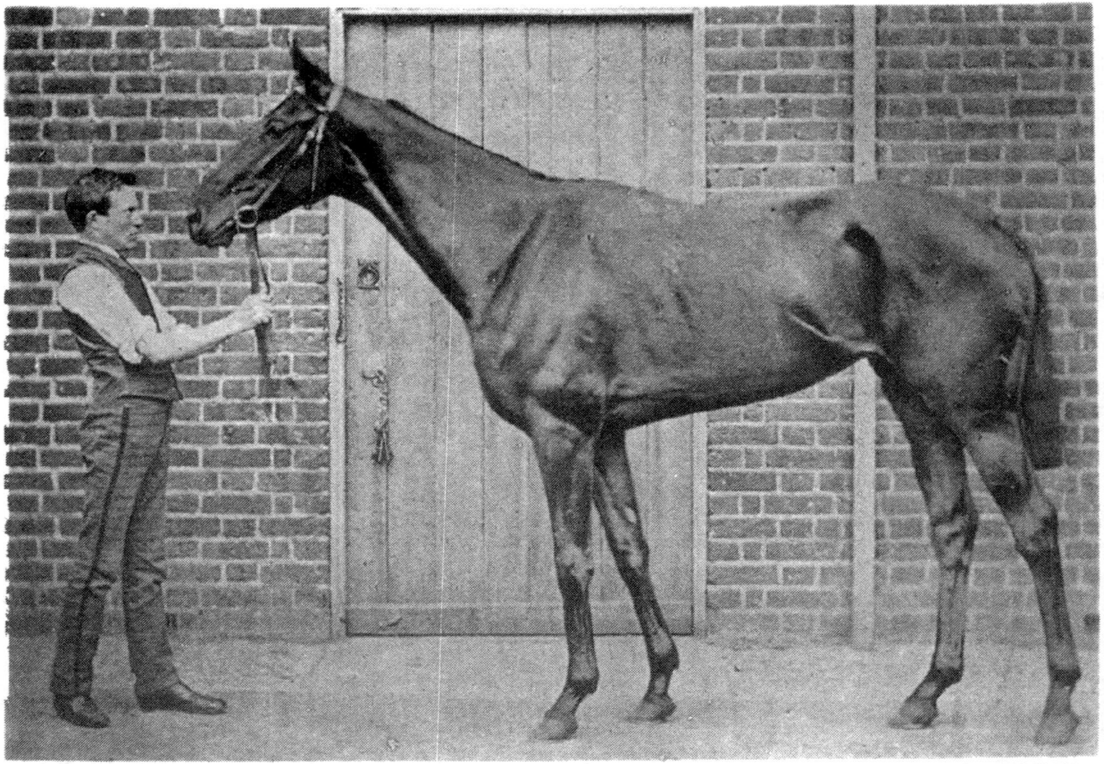

PHOTO. BY FRANK HAES

TO FACE PAGE 256

PLATE 54—BARON ROTHSCHILD'S HANNAH.

rapid action, and that his system is not overloaded with fat. The fact of the "water-mark" being clearly indicated is also dependent on the absence of fat about the part.

The line which marks the termination of the sheet of muscle to which I have alluded, corresponds to the posterior border of the fleshy portion of the *panniculus*, and indicates the commencement of the aponeurotic portion. The "water-mark," or "quarter-mark," to which I have also drawn attention, is the line of separation between the *rotator tibialis* and the *abductor femoris*.

The most time-honoured method of ascertaining whether or not a horse is in condition is to feel his crest with the hand, so as to find out if it be hard or soft. This plan has its merits; for the crest is a part on which many "gross" horses (like the one represented in Pl. 30) have a tendency to deposit fat. I need hardly say that a thick layer of fat would feel softer to the touch than a mass of ligament, muscle, and tendon.

The diagonal line on the flank, the appearance of the ribs through a thick layer of muscle, and the lean though muscular condition of the shoulders of a race-horse in training, are well shown in the Frontispiece.

3. *Signs of condition afforded by the state of the breathing.*—Although a practical trial would give an experienced observer the best possible idea of the state of an animal's organs of breathing; the question depends so much on individual merits and defects, that it is very difficult to lay down any fixed rules for guidance in making such a test. Supposing that the horse had done his work in what we considered a satisfactory style, we might prove the correctness of our judgment, by observing the manner in which he would recover from the effects of his exertion. If after a sharp

"rough-up," his lungs resumed a tranquil form of breathing, when he had rested or (better still) had been walked about for a few minutes, and if he did not show any appearance of being distressed by the severity of the work, we might fairly conclude that his "pipes" were in good order. Trainers generally think that the fact of a horse "blowing his nose" (as a kind of sneeze which these animals sometimes make after a quick "spin," is called) is a sign of his wind being all right. I may also point out that if a horse's wind is not "clear," he will be unable to quickly "come again," if he gets out of breath during a run, even if he be "eased off" for a little, with the object of letting him "catch his second wind." If a strong gallop has the effect of making a horse unusually thirsty, we may doubt that his lungs are in good order. To test whether or not a horse is a roarer, we had best, immediately after the animal has done some fast or severe work, apply the ear close to one of his nostrils.

I may remark that large calibre and thinness of the walls of the nostrils, which condition predisposes a horse to "high blowing" (*see Veterinary Notes for Horse-owners*), is a sign that the animal's organs of breathing are naturally good.

4. *Signs of condition manifested by the state of the sweat.*—The fatter a horse is, the thicker and more greasy will be his sweat. When a horse is in condition, his sweat will come off like water, will have lost the saline taste it previously had, and, unless the animal is in a state of excitement, it will dry on the skin with extreme quickness, as soon as the work which had opened the pores, has been stopped. If a horse which has no excess of fat in his system, shows a tendency to sweat on very slight provocation of work or "closeness" of atmosphere, and if the perspiration thus induced, takes a

long time to dry on the surface of the body, we may reasonably conclude that general weakness is the cause of this excessive action of the pores of the skin. I may explain that when a horse sweats from excitement (as on a race-course), the surface of the body thus moistened, will not dry quickly; for as long as the excitement lasts, the outpouring of the fluid will more or less continue.

Good Looks.—Beauty in the horse is dependent:—

1. On the uniformity of type which the various parts of the body bear to each other. Thus, a Shire horse with his Roman nose, loaded shoulders, and short legs, may be quite as handsome as a good-looking English thoroughbred, or a showy, high-caste Arab.

2. On the artistic arrangement of the lines of his body. We may see the importance of this from a beauty point of view, if, for example, we contrast a photograph of a horse having the ears pricked forward, with another one of the same animal, taken a moment afterwards, but having the ears in a normal position. The former may look handsome, and the latter plain; although the two may be absolutely identical in every particular, except in that of the ears. The "line of beauty" (alternate convexity and concavity, or *vice versâ*) is well exemplified from the tip of the off ear to the top of the croup, in Pl. 31; in which there is, however, a too sudden depression of the quarter. The curves from tip of ear to end of tail, are also good in Pl. 35. except that the line of the crest and that of the croup would be improved if they were slightly more convex. For very beautiful curves of the upper line of the body, from tip of nose to tail, *see* Pl. 55. One reason (which possibly might escape

the notice of a casual observer) why the grey horse in Pl. 35 looks so well, is that the curves of the under part of his body—from muzzle, lower lip (assisted by the rein), along lower jaw, under throat, down neck, in front of chest, along the belly, under groin, and carried in front of both hind legs—are very graceful. In all cases, oblique shoulders, sloping pasterns, long and well-arched back ribs, muscular loins, more or less horizontal pelvis, tail set high up, straight-dropped hind leg (contrast Pl. 51 with Pl. 49), will be beauties.

As heavy cart-horses are often somewhat "back at the knees" (*see* p. 218), the presence of a good supply of fine hair behind the back tendons, increasing in amount from the knee to the fetlock, will balance this concavity. I do not think that docking, except when it is done to remove an unsightly "kink," ever improves the appearance of a horse, from an artistic point of view. The removal of the forelock, when hogging the mane, is always an eyesore. Whenever good looks are sought to be studied, the mane should not be hogged, if the animal has a light neck. As a horse is looked at more frequently from the near than from the off-side, his mane, as a rule, should fall to the off-side.

As regards colour, *see* Chapter XX. With it we may include a bright, healthy-looking coat.

Under this heading we must also put good carriage of the head and tail, and true and showy action. For carriage of the head and neck, *see* p. 80, *et seq.* The tail during movement should be held well out, with the hairs falling from it in graceful curves. To look well, the limbs should work in lines parallel to the direction in which the horse is going; for any crossing or dishing of the legs will detract from the

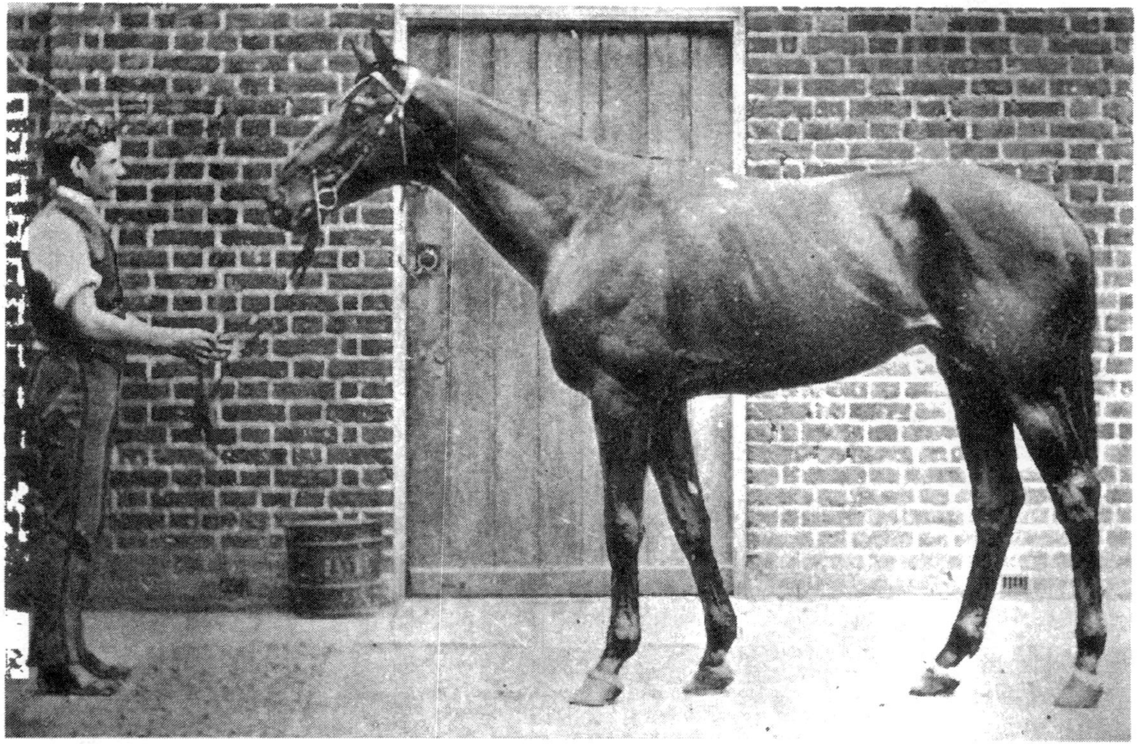

PHOTO. BY FRANK HAES

TO FACE PAGE 250

PLATE 55—BARON ROTHSCHILD'S FAVONIUS.

grace of their movement. Somewhat lofty, "cadenced," action in the walk or trot of the hack or charger will be pleasing to the eye, as it will suggest the possession of force and speed held well in reserve.

I need hardly say that a bright, intelligent expression of face, which is greatly assisted by the movements of the ears, adds greatly to the beauty of the horse.

CHAPTER XXIII.

WEIGHT-CARRYING AND STAYING POWER.

Weight-carrying Power.—The special points for weight-carrying power, are :—

1. Length and obliquity of shoulder-blade (*see* p. 207).

One might be inclined to think that very oblique shoulders are not an advantage from a weight-carrying point of view ; for they necessitate the saddle being put farther back on the horse, than would be the case with shoulders of only a moderate slope. At the same time, we must remember that with horses of the same depth of body at the withers, the more oblique the shoulder-blades, the longer they will be.

2. Strong loin muscles.

3. Good substance and fine quality of bone.

Ormonde (Frontispiece), "the horse of the century," and St. Gatien, the dead-heater for the Derby and winner of the Cesarewitch, were horses of great bone, and were marvellous weight carriers.

4. Pasterns not too sloping.

5. Absence of undue weight of body beyond that which would be necessary for the movements of the limbs, and for the performance of the various vital functions.

The foregoing rules would apply to all classes of horses.

For absolute weight-carrying power, the animal should have short legs (a fact which would be incompatible with the possession of speed), and should have his pelvis somewhat drooping.

Staying Power.—The ability to "stay a distance," granting the possession of health and condition, depends (1) on the breathing power being good; (2) on the muscles working to advantage, and on the conformation being of the required kind; and (3) on the action.

With respect to the first condition, we require the barrel to be deep and rounded behind the girths (*see* p. 191), and the flanks to be well ribbed up.

The second condition will be best fulfilled, from the point of view of speed, when the muscles over the loins are powerful, and when the forehand is light; that is to say, when the shoulders and pasterns are oblique, and the head, neck and shoulders light, in which case the fore legs will not be wide apart (*see* p. 197). As thick muscles are unsuited to bear the strain of continued quick work, we usually find that genuine stayers at fast paces are not heavily built horses. Any excess of height over the croup, as compared to that at the withers, will add to the weight on the forehand (*see* p. 49). The fact of the neck (*see* p. 181) being abnormally short in comparison to the limbs, will naturally detract from the staying power. The same remark applies to the possession of "sickle-hocks" (*see* p. 63). In heavy draught, the mechanical advantage will be on the side of a heavy forehand.

I may remark that there is an important difference between staying-power (using the term in its racing sense), and ability to endure fatigue. For instance, East Indian ponies, though often very fast for a short distance, are notoriously bad stayers; and yet they are wonderfully good animals on a long journey. Thus, many of them which are incapable of "getting" beyond three furlongs in a race, would, if harnessed to an *ecka* (*see* Pl. 8) do, comfortably, 70 or 80 miles from sunrise to sunset, with the thermometer at noon up to 110° F. or more, in the shade. Here the lack of staying-power would be due to the organs of breathing being unable to continue work under high pressure. As might be expected, these "country-bred" ponies (*see* Pl. 34) are, as a rule, light behind the girth, flat-sided, and badly ribbed up. With thin necks and light shoulders, their good legs and feet have but little weight to carry, and as the quality of their tissues is of the best, and their spirit undeniable, they can go marvellously long distances without getting knocked up—provided always that they are not over-paced or over-weighted. I need hardly say that a genuine stayer will also be capable of appearing to advantage in a "go-as-you-please" task; for he will possess all the good points of the other, with better organs of breathing. The small amount of extra weight (on account of increased length of rib) which he will have to carry, will be more than compensated by the larger space allowed for his digestive organs. As a rule, in proportion to their respective sizes, small horses will stay better, and will be capable of enduring more fatigue, than big horses. The reason for this appears to be that the former have more vitality than the latter, on account of the rate of the circulation of their blood being quicker.

I need not point out the advantages of good action in the present connection.

CHAPTER XXIV.

BLOOD, SYMMETRY, AND COMPENSATIONS.

Blood.—The relation of "blood" to conformation is its only one which need be considered here

The term "blood" usually signifies more or less pure descent from animals mentioned in the English Stud Book, or from high-caste Arabs. In our Colonies, the initials T. B. have a more elastic application than in the Mother-country. English thoroughbred horses having been bred almost entirely with the object of their utilisation on the Turf; their conformation more or less resembles that of the galloper. Were I to be asked to particularise the "point" or "points" most characteristic of the English "blood" horse, I would answer: "The legs below the knees and hocks." Their special peculiarities, in this respect, are: lightness of bone, thinness of skin, fineness and shortness of hair, small amount of underlying connective tissue, near approach to parallelism of back tendons to cannon-bones, with consequent smallness of fetlock joints (*see* p. 218), good length of pasterns, and small hoofs with well-arched soles. These hard-looking, though light-shaped legs, are evidently an inheritance from the East; for although we rarely, if ever, see them in pure Western stock, we may find them in profusion among Arab, Barb, Persian, East Indian, and South African horses, all of which have been bred in a hot, dry climate. The speed of the thoroughbred is the result of careful selection in breeding, by which, not only has the best form of conformation been obtained, but also the most suitable kind of nervous organisation. The effect of heredity is specially shown in the working of the nerves, which regulate the exhibition of all muscular force. Although they can in no way increase the actual strength of a muscle, its failure or success in putting forth its full power, and also its speed of contraction are dependent on them. Hence, two horses of identically the same "make and shape" (if such a thing were possible) might differ widely in pulling power, handiness, or speed, on account of a want of similarity in their nervous systems. We see this fact well marked among men, in whom uncommon quickness and great dexterity of muscular movement is often inherited. The speed, then, obtained from "blood," independent of conformation, may be regarded as an outcome of heredity. In judging, therefore, by a horse's conformation, of his suitability to any particular kind of work, we should take into careful consideration all the "blood" points which he may possess. I may mention that the fact of a horse having Arab blood in his veins, is, in itself, no reason for our inferring that he has a good "turn of speed;" for Arabs, though charming hacks and admirable light cavalry troopers, are not race-horses.

It is noteworthy that thoroughbred stock which are allowed (as they often are in the Colonies) to run wild, say, up to four or five years old, before they are taken up, and which are then put to ordinary labour, lose in a great measure the blood-like appearance they might have possessed, had they been handled early and put into training in the usual way.

Symmetry is the conformance, as regards size, shape and arrangement, of the various parts of the body to some particular type of useful horse.

In violation of this condition, we may have united in the same animal, the long legs and light body of the race-horse, and the heavy head, loaded neck, and thick shoulders of the cart-horse; or the contours of the race-horse, with the exception of the loins being weak, and the hind legs short with drooping croup. Even with the ordinary saddle-nag, to say nothing of the hunter and officer's charger, we have too frequently the massive shoulders of the draught-horse. A coarse, heavy head, which reveals but too plainly a cart-strain, is a terrible eyesore to an animal whose neck and shoulders are light, and which might otherwise figure as a high-class hack.

We may see short-legged, deep-bodied cart-horses, with great power of limbs and shoulders, having weak loins. I may also mention that a horse which has oblique shoulders should also have sloping pasterns and a horizontal croup. We must here remember that the effect of "work" is often to render the pasterns abnormally upright. We may witness many instances of want of symmetry in the "tying-in" of the legs under the knees, short pasterns, and large, flat feet of long and slender-limbed horses. I need hardly say that a mean carriage of the tail will contrast most unfavourably with a showy and graceful bearing of the head and neck.

The generic term "weed" is applied, usually, to long-legged animals which are weak in the loins, and are light in the back ribs. As a rule, the cause of their comparative worthlessness is wrongly attributed to the length of their limbs, rather than to their defects of loin and rib. If we compare Pl. 56 (which represents a typical weed) with the Frontispiece, we shall see that the mare in the former was actually "longer" and "lower" (taking the proportion between her height at the withers, and her length of body), than the deep-ribbed and strongly "coupled" Ormonde. It is evident that no amount of shortening of her legs could improve her conformation.

Compensations.—The points which I shall consider under this heading have special reference to the saddle-horse and light trapper :—

"*Plainness*" *of head* will be best "carried off" by a "kind," intelligent expression of face; quick play of the ears, which will do well to be small; good carriage of the head; and graceful setting-on of the head with the neck. The size of the latter should conform to that of the former.

Undue lightness of neck.—Full mane; light head, small ears, sloping and flat shoulders.

Heavy neck and loaded shoulders may be corrected to some extent, from a beauty point of view, by a good-looking, intelligent head, nice crest, and light mane. From considerations of utility, we should have the shoulders and pasterns sloping; the bones, muscles, tendons, and ligaments of the fore limb below the shoulder strong; feet good; and loins and hind quarters powerful.

Fore legs below the elbows too light; Pasterns too upright, or too oblique.—Legs otherwise well-shaped; light forehand; sloping shoulders; and good loins.

"*Calf knees,*" *or* "*over at the knees.*"—Strength of leg below the elbow; parallelism of back tendons with cannon-bones (*see* p. 218); sloping shoulders; light forehand; strong loins.

PHOTO. BY M. H. HAYES

TO FACE PAGE 298

PLATE 56—THOROUGHBRED WEED.

Ribs "flat-sided."—Good depth of body at lowest point of back; flanks well ribbed-up.

Too hollow in the back.—Light forehand, sloping shoulders, and in all cases, broad, powerful loins, which is the special kind of compensation in this instance.

Loins too light, and flanks badly ribbed-up.—Light forehand; shoulders and pasterns oblique; light abdomen; well rounded barrel; strong hind quarters; good gaskins; "straight-dropped" hind legs.

Hind quarters too light.—Light forehand; shoulders and pasterns oblique; light, but well rounded barrel; muscular loins; good gaskins; "straight dropped" hind legs.

"*Sickle-hocks.*"—With this defect in a saddle horse which would be required for fast work, it would be well for him to have good length of hind legs, the possession of which will presuppose that of a horizontal pelvis; and the compensations mentioned in the preceding paragraph, with the exception of "straight dropped" hind legs, which is the opposite kind of conformation to that which we are considering

CHAPTER XXV.

SPECIAL POINTS OF VARIOUS CLASSES OF HORSES.

The Race-horse—The Racing Pony—The Jumper—The Heavy Cart-horse—The Harness-horse—The Hack—The Lady's Horse—The Cavalry Trooper—The Officer's Charger—The Artillery Horse—The Polo Pony.

The Race Horse.—1. The height of the galloper at the withers, and also over the croup, should be at least equal to his length of body (*see* p. 152 *et seq.*).

2. The depth at the withers should be considerably less than half his height (*see* p. 153).

3. The loins behind the cantle of the saddle should be flat on account of the presence of largely developed muscles (*see* pp. 64 and 200).

4. The gaskins should be broad (*see* p. 234).

5. The neck should be long (*see* p. 181).

6. The forehand should be light (*see* p. 211). Consequently, the neck should be free from "lumber;" the distance between the fore legs should be short (*see* p. 65); the shoulders flat and without any "place for the collar" (*see* p. 212); and the horse should not be thick between the upper ends of the shoulder-blades (*see* p. 196)

7. The withers should be high, and should run far back.

8. The hind legs should be long.

9. The hocks should possess the ability of being freely straightened out, as well as bent.

The Racing Pony should possess all the points of the race-horse which have been described under the preceding heading, but modified where necessary, by conditions suitable to superior ability for carrying weight ; for ponies, in comparison to their height, have almost always to bear much heavier burdens than horses which are used for racing.

The Jumper.—1. The forehand should be light.

2. The jumper, as a rule, should have no tendency to be higher at the croup than at the withers ; for he requires to be light in front (*see* p. 49), and to have the bones of his fore limbs comparatively long, so as to be able to efficiently raise his forehand, both when taking off and landing.

3. The shoulder-blades and pasterns should be long and sloping.

4. The muscles which lie along the front portion of the shoulder-blade, and the lump of muscle above the fore-arm should be well-developed (*see* Pl. 57) ; as the former straighten the shoulder joint, and the latter straighten the elbow joint ; two actions which help to prevent the horse from falling when he lands over a jump.

5. The muscles over the loins, behind the saddle, should be particularly strong (*see* p. 64).

6. The hocks should be large ; and their straightening power (the gaskins) broad.

The *steeple-chaser* may be regarded as a combination, in fairly equal proportions, of the race-horse and jumper. The *hurdle-racer*, as a rule, will have more of the former than of the latter in him. The *hunter* should be essentially a jumper.

In a "flying" country, he may be more or less of a steeple-chaser. In all cases, he should be a thorough stayer. His galloping and weight-carrying powers (*see* Chapter XXIII.) should of course vary according to the nature of the work he will be called upon to perform. In a "flying" country, a tall horse, other things being equal, will tire less than a smaller one, from jumping big fences. In a "cramped" country, the difference may be all the other way. As the ordinary hunter has to carry a fair weight, and as he may have to raise it frequently over fences, besides having at times to go through heavy ground; he will require to be much stronger than the mere galloper, and his legs should consequently be shorter in comparison to his length of body.

The Heavy Cart-Horse.—1. The legs should be as short and massive as possible: consequently the animal will be considerably longer in the body than he is high at the withers or at the croup, and he will be deeper from the withers to the brisket, than from the withers to the ground.

2. He should be of great width of body when viewed from behind; and across the chest in front.

3. His muscles, bones, tendons, and ligaments should be as thick and strong as possible.

4. The shoulders should be sloping in cart-horses which do not use their fore legs, to any marked degree, as propellers; and somewhat upright in those which utilise them in that manner (*see* p. 212).

5. The height over the croup may be less than that at the withers (*see* p. 74).

The Harness Horse.—For convenience sake, I use the expression "harness-horse" to signify all horses which go in

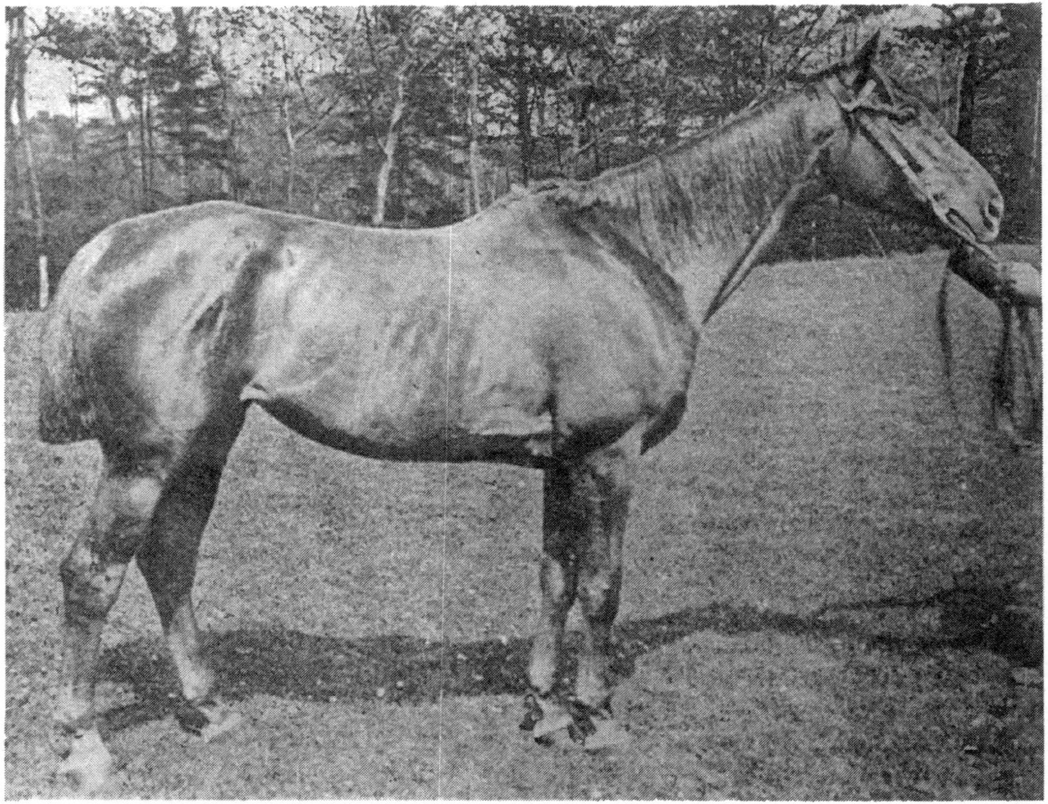

TO FACE PAGE 272

PLATE 57—MR. MUIR'S BLUE RIBBON.

draught, except the heavy cart-horse. Taking the limits as the racer and Shire horse, I may say that the conformation of the animal should approach that of the former, or of the latter, according as his work is fast or slow. The only difference which I can discover between the respective shape of the race-horse and match trotter (or match pacer), is that powerful loin muscles and shortness of body, in comparison to height, are not so essential to the latter as to the former. The reason for this difference, as far as I can see, is that in galloping, more muscular effort has to be spent in raising the forehand, than when trotting or pacing. The ordinary trapper should be thicker in the shoulders than the saddle nag, and, if he has strong hind quarters and fair action, he may be pardoned if he be long in the back, slack in the loins, and somewhat flat-sided. For fashionable town work, the harness horse will, as a rule, require to be either one of the smart small sort, or of the imposing brougham type. The former should have all the good looks and "quality" of a well-bred, middle weight hack. The latter should measure high at the withers; should have sloping shoulders, so as to have free action in front; and should carry his head high. Owing to the manner in which he is bitted and "checked," his hind action is not taken much into consideration. Between these two kinds of horses, there is as much difference, as between a clever bull-terrier and an overgrown, weak-loined mastiff. Being a professional breaker, I can vouch for the fact that fashionable trotting action is the result of training and not of conformation. For pairs and teams, horses should match in height, colour, general character, action, manners, and mouth.

The Hack.—The chief points about the hack are that he

should be "light in front," have sloping shoulders, and sound legs and feet, so that he may be sure-footed and able to stand work; and he should be rather high in front (*see* p. 160). The conformation of his head and neck should be such as to allow him to bend readily to the rein. The action of the hack should be somewhat "high," and should be "true," so that, when viewed from behind, the near pair of limbs, in the walk, trot and canter, should move in a line parallel to that of the off pair. Action, good looks, and a showy carriage of the head and tail are essentials in the high-priced hack. "Mouth" and "manners" are two other indispensable requisites which do not come within the province of this book.

The Lady's Horse.—A lady's horse should be a good-looking hunter or smart hack, according to the work for which he is intended. He should carry his head and neck particularly well; because his rider, owing to the nature of her seat, cannot keep her hands low down. His forehand should be inclined to be high, so that his paces may be easy. His withers should not be high and thin; for if they are, they will be liable to be galled on the off side by the saddle.

The Cavalry Trooper.—The chief requirements as regards conformation, which the cavalry trooper should possess are:—

1. That he should be up to the weight he has got to carry. But he should on no account be too heavily topped for his legs, or for the work he will be called upon to do. His loins, therefore, should be strong, his shoulder-blades long, and his legs should be as short as is compatible with the possession of sufficient speed for military purposes.

PHOTO. BY FRANK HAES

TO FACE PAGE 274

PLATE 58—LORD STAMFORD'S DIOPHANTUS.

2. His legs and feet should be particularly sound and well able to stand work. As he will be called upon at times to go fast and to leap; his back tendons should be more or less parallel with the cannon-bone, and he should have no tendency to undue width of fetlock (*see* pp. 218 and 219).

3. His forehand should be light, so that his legs and feet may continue sound, and that he may be able to do his school work properly.

4. He should have a good carriage of the head and neck, so that he may be obedient to the rein.

5. He should be a "good doer," and have a strong constitution, which will usually be the case with a horse that has a bright eye; soft, cool skin; deep rounded barrel; full flank; firm, prominent anus; and is well-ribbed up.

The Officer's Charger.—A cavalry officer's first charger, with all the useful points of the cavalry trooper, should have undeniably good looks, and a showy carriage of the head and tail, which should not be docked. As he will have to carry less, and will cost considerably more than an animal in the ranks, he should be well bred, and, with a rider of ordinary weight, he should approach the type of a handsome chaser, or well-bred hunter. A second charger should have all the useful points of a first charger; but need not be so good-looking. The colour will, as a rule, depend on regimental regulations. Speaking generally, he should not be less than 15.3. A man at the head of a regiment of cavalry, or of a battery of horse artillery, looks best on a tall horse.

The Artillery Horse.—Artillery horses are divided into those for the horse artillery and those for field batteries. As the teams of the former have to manœuvre with cavalry, and also drag their guns, they require to be exceptionally strong, smart horses. The latter, as they are supposed not to go faster than a trot, are stronger and slower horses than those of light cavalry. The wheelers are active, light-draught cart-horses. For their work, they need to be somewhat thick in the shoulders, short on the leg, and of considerable weight to stop the gun when the order to halt is given. For this, their hind-quarters, loins, and hocks should be particularly strong. The riding horses of the No. 1 and markers of field batteries should be of the light cavalry type.

The Polo Pony.—Handiness and speed, with sufficient staying and weight-carrying power, are the two chief requirements of the polo pony. Consequently, he should be light in front, should carry his head and neck well, have sloping shoulders and particularly strong hocks. The fact of his being slightly "goose rumped," will be no detriment. English ponies, nearly, if not quite thoroughbred, are the best for the game. In India, country-bred ponies are generally found to be better for polo than Arabs ; for they are "quicker on their legs," probably on account of the sons of the Desert having their croup very horizontal. To sum up, the polo pony should be a remarkably handy sprinter.

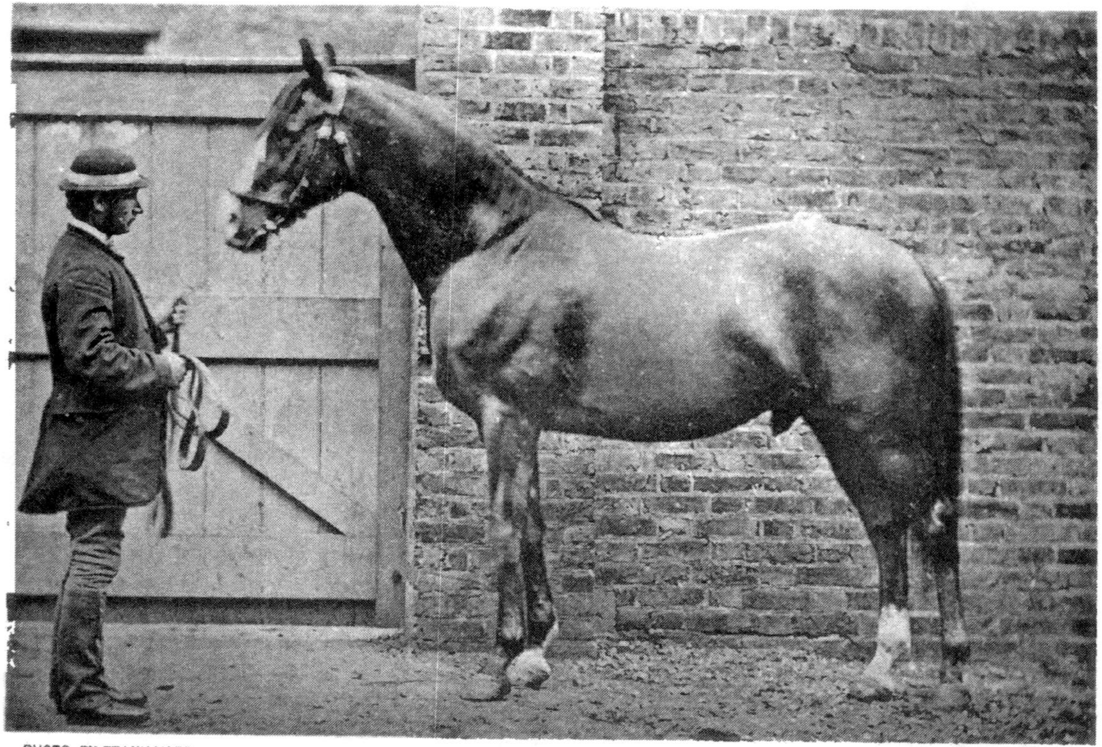

PHOTO. BY FRANK HAES

TO FACE PAGE 278

PLATE 59—MR. SNEWING'S CARACTACUS.

CHAPTER XXVI.

REMARKS ON VARIOUS BREEDS OF HORSES.

English and Irish Horses—Australasian Horses—South-African Horses—South-American Horses—Arab Horses—East Indian Horses—Burma and Manipuri Ponies—Sumatra and Java Ponies—Mongolian Ponies—Corean Ponies—Japanese Ponies.

In this chapter, I shall confine my observations on conformation to those breeds of horses with which I have had some personal experience.

English and Irish Horses.—The great beauty about English and Irish half-bred and cart-horses is that they are generally "well topped;" their chief defect, that they are inclined to be poor below the knees and hocks. Lack of substance in the bone of the legs, and undue uprightness of pasterns is but too apparent. "Weediness" is probably the greatest fault of our thoroughbreds. Good carriage of head and neck, well rounded and well ribbed up barrel, powerful loins, more or less horizontal croup, and muscular thighs are certainly characteristics of the horses of these islands, and are the products, to a certain extent, of good feeding and careful management. The large majority of our hunters and saddle hacks are disfigured by cart blood, and consequently have too thick shoulders. The Shire horse is a model of gigantic strength, but he often fails in his hocks and feet. The Shire and the Clydesdale seem equally inclined to contract foot troubles, such as laminitis (fever in the feet) and side bones. The chestnut Suffolk horses are a beautiful breed of compact, smart cart animals, which are admirably fitted for agricultural work. The Cleveland Bay and Yorkshire carriage horse are grand types for harness work. The Norfolk trotter and other roadsters have at present great attention paid to their breeding. The English racing pony, thoroughbred or nearly so, like Lord Clyde, Predominant, Sylvia, Dorothy (Pl. 39), Water Lily, Maythorne, and Mike (Pl. 38), is by far the best of its class in the world. Among the best known native breeds of ponies, are the Welsh, Exmoor, Kerry, and Shetland (*see* Pl. 61), which averages not much more than ten hands in height. England does not seem to lend itself well to the production of very large race-horses. I think that in comparison, say, with Australasia, thoroughbreds under fifteen hands, in England, would be found to be better than those over that height If this be the case, the fact that big horses are more liable than small ones to contract roaring in countries where, like in this country, that disease is rife, would no doubt have an important bearing on this point.

Though somewhat foreign to the present subject, I cannot resist saying that much of the judging at English horse-shows, seems to me to be conducted on an entirely wrong principle. Thus, prizes are awarded to "hunters" which have never been over a fence in their lives; and ribbons are given to decorate the heads of heavy cart-horses for their action in trotting, and their general appearance, instead of for their style of work between the shafts with a ponderous load

PHOTO. BY FRANK HAES

PLATE 60—ICELAND PONY.

PHOTO. BY FRANK HAES

TO FACE PAGE 278

[illegible]

behind them. The cruel and senseless system of overfeeding horses which are intended to be "shown," is a fruitful cause of laminitis and other ills.

Australasian Horses.—The special good points of Australian, Tasmanian, and New Zealand horses, from a saddle point of view, are their excellent flat shoulders, light necks, well-shaped legs, and sound feet. Their loins, barrel, and croup are not, as a rule, as good as those of English horses; but they are able to stand more work. Animals that are brought up on extensive "runs" till they are, say, four years old, develop better shoulders and sounder legs and feet than those which are "taken up" early; although, other conditions being equal, they may, perhaps, not be as neatly "topped." Their light forehands and good shoulders make the Australasian horses clever jumpers. The Colonial animals, taking them all round, have more thoroughbred blood in them than their English cousins.

The Antipodes, as far as I can judge, are far more favourable for the production of thoroughbreds with large bone and substance, than is England. Hence we find, in these colonies, a comparatively large number of animals of the weight-carrying hunter and charger type which have little or no stain in their pedigrees. On the other hand, although thoroughbreds in England have a greater tendency to "run light" than in Australasia, they certainly show more "quality" than those of any other country. Without wishing in any way to dogmatise, I would venture to say that the Colonies are capable of producing more useful saddle-nags and cavalry troopers than Europe; but not as high-class "sprinters." As an exception to their general utility for

Army purposes, I think that better field artillery horses, and especially field artillery wheelers, which require a strong admixture of cart blood, can be obtained in England, than in Australia. As a proof of deterioration in racing "quality," I may mention that up to the present, the produce of imported sires has, as a rule, been more successful on the Australian turf than that of Colonial-bred sires, of which the best has been Yattendon, whose two most distinguished sons at the stud were Grand Flaneur and Chester, both out of imported mares. The best Australasian sires have been imported horses, such as Panic, Musket, Fisherman and St. Albans. The same rule appears to hold good in America, if we may judge by what the *Spirit of the Times* says in the following extract: "The success of imported English sires within the past twenty years, beginning with Leamington, has certainly impressed many breeders with a belief in their superiority. Glenelg, Australian, Bullet, King Ban, The Ill-used, Great Tom, King Ernest, Bonnie Scotland, Rayon d'Or, Prince Charlie, Phaeton, Eclipse, St. Blaise, etc., have well-nigh driven the native stallions into exile. Virgil may be said to have been the only stallion who was native bred on both sides of his pedigree, and who has held his own against the imported horses. Longfellow, Spendthrift, Enquirer, Eolus, King Alfonso, and other successful native sires, were the sons of imported horses. The English mares have also succeeded in a great degree."

As long as Australia and America have to obtain fresh infusions of blood from England, to keep up the excellence of their respective breeds of race-horses; so long should no jealousy, as regards horses, exist between the mother-country and her offspring, who should regard their state of dependency on her, as one of her strongest claims on their affection and support.

Australasian race-horses at long distances are probably as good as any horses in the world. The performance of Carbine (a New Zealand son of Musket) winning the Melbourne Cup, two miles, with 10 st. 5 lbs. up, can compare favourably with anything done by Ormonde, Isonomy, or St. Gatien. Pl 62 is a photograph of Bravo, who won the Melbourne Cup in 1889, beating Carbine, from whom he was receiving 21 lbs. In the Colonies there are many smart racing ponies, like Glengary II., Little Wonder (New Zealand), Mayflower and Jeannette; but they are not, as I have already remarked, as good as the best in England and Ireland.

South-African Horses.—The ordinary horses of the Cape Colony, Transvaal, Orange Free State, and Natal, show a fair amount of "blood," with a dash of the Arab, and have very good legs and feet. They are, however, for the most part "weedy." Although they are admirable "slaves" with a light weight, or with but little to draw, they are quite unsuited for military purposes. Those which are up to the weight of a trooper, or fit to take their place in an artillery team, would, at an average price of £35 or £40, be too slow for cavalry or horse artillery work. The weight-carrying hunter type of horse is practically unknown in South Africa. The success on the turf of locally bred horses, like Prosecutor, proves that the country is capable of producing good race-horses. The freedom in which stock are raised there, undoubtedly accounts for the excellence of their limbs. The chief native breed, the Basuto pony, is a remarkably hardy animal, with capital legs and feet; but as he is rather short on the leg, he is deficient in pace. Indeed, South-African horses, except those that are thoroughbred, are, as a rule, very slow; a fact which is no doubt due, in many instances, to their loins being weak, their gaskins poor, and their hocks being too much bent. South-African breeders are much handicapped by outbreaks of "horse sickness" and by want of water. With the exception of these drawbacks, the country, especially in the Colesberg district and Orange Free State, is admirably suited to the production of good horses. South Africa is singularly wanting in smart ponies, such as those fit for polo. In this respect it forms a marked contrast with England, Australasia, India, and Arabia.

South-American Horses.—In the Argentine Republic many good thoroughbreds are raised by Mr. Kemmis and other breeders. I have no means of "drawing a line" between them and English or Australasian horses, except the fact that Camilla, the aged daughter of Phénix, with 32 lbs. the best of the weights, beat the Australian plater, The Wild Oat, and five others at Calcutta in December 1890. Neither Camilla nor the Wild Oat, at the time, were good representatives of their respective classes; so the result of the race is no criterion to go by. The common Argentine horses, if somewhat wanting in blood, are of the sturdy and useful sort The country seems well suited to the production of excellent stock

Arab Horses.—My friend, the late Shaikh Esa bin Curtas, always maintained that the best Arabs did not, as a rule, exceed 14.1½ or 14 2 in height. Ali bin Abdoolah, another Arab friend of mine, and of nearly as great experience

PHOTO. BY M. H. HAYES

TO FACE PAGE 282

PLATE 62—MR. A. A. APCAR'S AUSTRALIAN HORSE, BRAVO.

as the late Shaikh, likes them bigger. From a galloping point of view, judging by the Indian records of the last half century, there is not much to choose either way; the balance of weight being probably with the big Arabs, like Child of the Islands, Raby, Lucifer, Marquis, Sherwood, Euphrates, and Euclid. Yet with such good fourteen handers as Anarchy, Chieftain, Shere Ali, and Turkish Flag, who, in their time, were second to none in their own class; the fact remains, that for the attainment of galloping excellence, an Arab need not exceed 14.1. My own impression is that among the Arabs sent to India for racing are to be found many of the best and highest caste horses bred in the Desert. This opinion is in accordance with that often expressed to me by experienced Arab dealers whose friendship I have enjoyed. Also, poor Colonel Valentine Baker, whom I knew in Cairo, and who had an intimate acquaintance with Eastern horses, told me that the best Arabs were sent to Bombay, where new importations, if of really high character, readily fetch from £200 to £300 a-piece. We may infer from the foregoing remarks, that the Arab horse is, according to our Western acceptation of the term, a pony. Even restricting him to this class, I feel confident that the best Arab that ever lived, no matter what his height, was inferior, from a racing point of view, to a first-class English or Australian pony of fourteen hands. The English fourteen hand pony mare, Skittles (*see* Fig. 171), the property of Captain Mowbray of the Black Watch, beat in a two-mile match, at Cairo in 1886-7, the Arab Haddeed, in a common canter when giving him 7 lbs. He was looked upon in Egypt as an extraordinary good Arab. Mr. Kelly Maitland's Australian 13.2 mare, Fleur de Lys, several times proved herself as fast as any Arab in India for $\frac{3}{4}$ mile. Taking the time test, which has been applied with great precision to the running of Arabs, we find that their performances in India have been much inferior to those accomplished by the English ponies, Lord Clyde (formerly belonging to Mr. John Watson), Predominant, and Labby (by Wisdom), and by the Australian pony mare Achievement, none of whom exceeded fourteen hands in height. Although Arabs are not race-horses, they are excellent hacks, and particularly excel as light cavalry troopers. In these respects the small Arab, not exceeding 14.2, is, as a rule, undoubtedly better than the bigger Arab. A son of the Desert of the best type has a handsome and intelligent head, with broad forehead, large, "kind" eyes, straight or concave line of the face, large nostrils, well carried ears, lean and wide jaw. His neck, if somewhat coarse, is well set on to his head, has a good crest, is carried bravely, and is fairly long. His shoulders are well sloped, although they often err, from a galloping or jumping point of view, on the side of thickness, and his breast is tolerably broad. He has capital legs and feet. His withers are often somewhat low and thick. His loins are flat, broad, and powerful. For roundness of barrel and length of back ribs, for levelness of croup, and for beautiful carriage of the tail, he is certainly without equal among horses. He is not unfrequently higher over the croup than at the withers, which, in that case, will have a consequent tendency to be unduly low and thick. I do not think that his hocks and gaskins are as good as those of well-bred English or Australasian animals. In justice to the Arab, I must point out that the heaviness of his forehand, as compared to that of the English thoroughbred, is due to the large size of the muscles which attach his shoulders to his chest, and which draw the fore limbs forward and backward. The comparatively large development of the muscles of his forehand and loins makes him a good weight carrier for his size. The common statement, that Arabs have bad shoulders, has evidently been made by persons who do not know that the kind of shoulders which might be very good in

FIG. 179.—CAPTAIN BEDDY'S ARAB PONY, BLITZ.
(*Drawn from a photograph.*)

one class of riding horse, might be equally bad in another kind of saddle animal. The grandly shaped barrel of the Arab plainly indicates that he has clear wind, strong constitution, and that he is a good "doer." Fig. 179 is a drawing from a photograph of Blitz, who was the best 13.1 Arab pony that has ever run in India.

The more an Arab exceeds, say, 14.2 in height, the more inclined is he to be long in the leg, light in the loins and flanks, and flat sided.

East-Indian Horses.—The native horses of India are of the smart, wiry sort. As a rule they are best when they do not exceed 14.1 or 14.2; for the more they overtop this height, the "weedier" do they become. Having light forehands and well-sloped shoulders, they are clever and jump well. They have excellent feet. Their legs, though capable of standing a great deal of work on hard ground, are often, from errors of breeding and bringing up, misshapen; so that turned-out toes, calf-knees, cow-hocks, and sickle-hocks are of frequent occurrence among them. Generally, they are flat-sided and light in the loin. Consequently, they are poor weight carriers, and bad stayers at fast paces; but are marvellously good at enduring fatigue and privation. The best of them make capital light cavalry horses up to, say, 13 st. 7 lbs. Although they are not as strong or as good looking as Arabs, they are probably hardier and better suited to endure hunger and thirst. Many of them, especially if they have a dash of English or Arab blood, have a fair turn of speed, and consequently make good pig-stickers and polo ponies. Indian racing ponies, which have a strong infusion of English blood, are, speaking generally, about 14 lbs. worse than Arabs of the same height, and particularly so over long distances. At fourteen hands it would be difficult to "bring them together" with English ponies in a race for, say, a mile. Without the constant importation of fresh blood from England, it is impossible in India to breed horses fit for racing, or for the

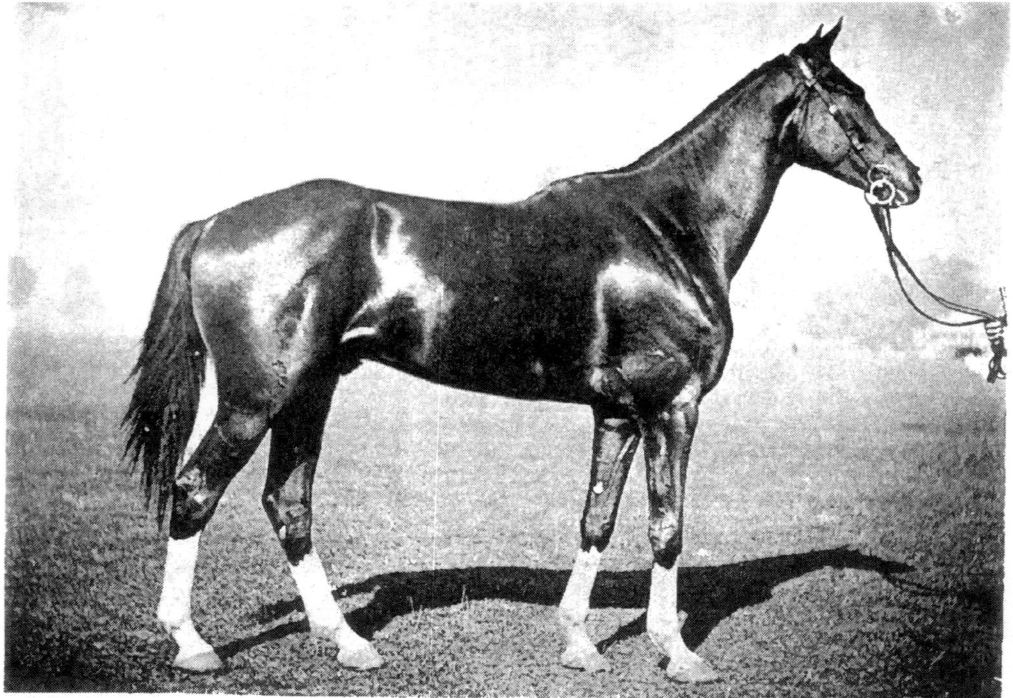

PHOTO. BY M. H. HAYES

TO FACE PAGE 286

PLATE 63—CAPTAIN WOOLMER'S EAST INDIAN HORSE, MINDEN.

requirements of English cavalry and artillery: even then, the results are very poor. Good as Tangri, Minden (*see* Pl. 63), Engadine, and others of General "Ben" Parrott's breeding have been in their own class and against Arabs, their form has been but little better than that of fourteen-hand English ponies. Pl. 34 is the portrait of a typical Kathiawar "country-bred" of a useful kind.

Under the present heading we may put Cabuli, Baluchi, and other Trans-Indus horses which are largely used in India, and which, though stouter and shorter on the leg, are neither as smart nor as hardy in hot climates as the "country-bred." We might consider them as intermediate between the East Indian horse and the Mongolian pony.

Burma and Manipuri Ponies.—The so-called Burma pony (*see* Pl. 32) is chiefly bred in the Shan Hills. He rarely exceeds 13.2, and is probably at his best when about thirteen hands high. He is a grand weight-carrier, jumps well, and is very hardy; though slow. The ponies of Manipur, which has been the home of polo for many centuries, are closely akin to those of the Shan States; but are smaller, and smarter for their size. These two kinds of ponies appear to belong to a distinct breed, which seem to have no relationship with those of any other country except, possibly, with those of Sumatra and Java. The Burma pony is sometimes called a Pegu pony. I may say that in the vast extent of country from Rangoon to Mandalay, there are no good native ponies bred.

Sumatra and Java Ponies.—The strongest ponies for their size I have ever seen, are those of Deli (Sumatra).

Their average height is about 12.2. They have handsome heads set on to high-crested necks, are full of spirit, and are simply balls of muscle. The capable and light-hearted way in which one of these grand Lilliputs can trot away with a four-wheeled carriage containing five or six heavy men, is a sight worth going many miles to see. Acheen, which is in the north of Sumatra, has a good breed of ponies. The Java pony, though a relation of, is inferior to, the Deli pony.

Mongolian Ponies.—Under this broad heading I would class a breed of ponies which is found in the highlands between Siberia and the Himalayas; for I can see no distinctive difference between the ponies of Bhootan, Spiti, Yarkund, and Mongolia, with all of which I have had a good deal of acquaintance. I may remark that the so-called China pony is bred in and exported from Manchuria. They have thick-set bodies, short, sound legs, capital feet, fairly good shoulders for a saddle, and are handy and sure-footed. They average about 13.1 and are very slow. In China, Mongolian ponies are used extensively for racing, of course, among themselves, and with excellent results, as far as sport is concerned; for the entries are large, and the pretensions of the candidates pretty even. It has been found that it is no advantage, from a racing point of view, for a Mongolian pony to exceed 13.2. The once matchless Teen Kwang (*see* Fig. 180), who may be regarded as the Ormonde of the Far East, was a little under that height. An English, Australian, or Arab 13.2 racing pony could give, in a mile race, about 150 yards start to a first-class China pony of the same height, at even weights. The pony of the Himalayas, Yarkund, and Chinese Tartary is a splendid weight-carrier, and is matchless for enduring fatigue and privations in a cold and desolate country.

Corean Ponies.—The indigenous pony of Corea is an extremely small animal, often not more than nine hands high. He is very handsome, being built on fine and graceful lines ; in

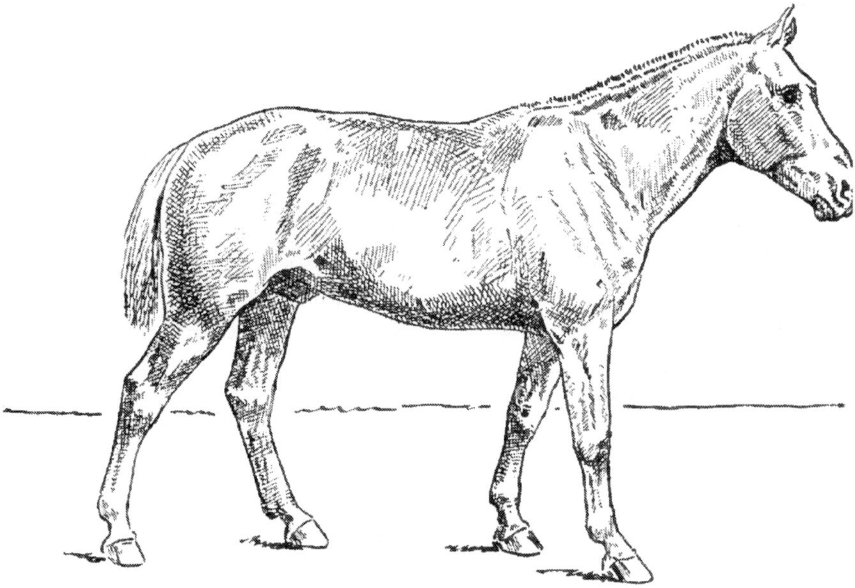

FIG. 180.—THE CHINA PONY, TEEN KWANG.
(Drawn from a photograph.)

fact, he looks like an Arab, or like the Iceland pony in Pl. 60. Despite the smallness of his size, and the slightness of his build, he is capable of doing a good deal of hard work. He seems to be of quite a different breed from the Manchuria pony.

Japanese Ponies are weak-bodied, long-legged animals of about fourteen hands high. In the main island are used a large number of imported Mongolian ponies, which, being thick-set and short on the leg, differ a great deal from the indigenous animals, the best of which come from the province of Namba. There are several half-breds which have been produced by a cross with English or American blood, and which show an advance in height and speed as compared with their local ancestors and with Mongolians. The Nippon Race Club has a very nice course on the Negishi Hill, which is about three miles from Yokohama. In the northern island (Hokkaido or Zezo) there is a distinct breed of ponies, which are weak and weedy.

CHAPTER XXVII.

EXAMINATION OF OUR PHOTOGRAPHS OF HORSES.

In this chapter I intend briefly running over the chief points of the horses whose portraits are given in this book, and shall assume, so as to avoid needless repetition, that my readers have mastered the observations which I have made on the various "points."

Frontispiece.—Ormonde (by Bend Or out of Lily Agnes) was, I need hardly say, the horse of the century. He is a little higher at the withers than he is long in the body; and about as high at the croup as at the withers. His legs, though long, are muscular, and their bones are strong, as we may perceive from the appearance of his fore-arm and gaskin and from the shape of the limbs below the knees and hocks. He has a particularly straight dropped hind leg. Although he was in training when this photograph was taken, he shows great depth of body in the centre of the back: a fact which points to the unusual length of his back ribs, and to the admirable shape of his chest for purposes of breathing. I may point out that his roaring infirmity being a nervous disease of his larynx, had nothing to say to his conformation. As his neck agrees in length with his limbs, and as his withers run far back, he has a very long "rein" His neck, though muscular, is light for a four-year-old entire. He is coarse about the throat, where the head and neck join. The horizontal marks on his legs, on and near his fetlocks, are curls in the hair, due to bandaging. His back view shows that he is narrow behind. The setting-on of the hocks is particularly good. His tail is placed very high on his croup.

Plates 7 and 18.—The former gives us a portrait of the Duke of Portland's St. Simon (by Galopin out of St. Angela) slightly fore-shortened. The latter shows him in strict profile; but as it had to be copied from a photograph which was not good enough to bear reproduction, its details have not come out as well as I would have wished. They were both done in 1884, when St Simon was a three-year-old, and when he was in training. Owing to the death of his first owner, Prince Batthyany, his nominations for the great three-year-old events were rendered void. Despite the fact that he had never met a great race-horse, he won all his contests with such consummate ease that I am inclined to think that as a two-year-old towards the "back end" of the season (1883) and for the first half of his three-year-old career, in other words, as long as he kept sound, he was as fast a horse, with, perhaps, the exception of Ormonde, as ever lived. St. Simon's height at the withers or over the croup, is considerably more than his length of body. Also, his back and loins are remarkably short, and his shoulders are long and extremely oblique. I remember having been greatly struck by the marvellous beauty of his shoulders, and by the shortness of his back and loins, when I saw him for the first time, when he was sold as a two-year-old in 1883, after the death of his owner. He

PHOTO. BY FRANK HAES

TO FACE PAGE 292

PLATE 64—MR. H. SAVILE'S CREMORNE.

had a light head, neck, and quarters, and was narrow when viewed from behind. He was extremely round in the back ribs, and was very well ribbed up.

Plate 15.—Stepaside is a nearly thoroughbred, and very smart, light-weight Irish hunter. She was invincible over hurdles in India, where the class of "timber-toppers" is extremely moderate. She has capital shoulders, light neck, neat head (except for a bump on the nose), powerful hind quarters, and well-rounded ribs. She is a good stayer. As might have been inferred from the fact of her being somewhat longer in the body than she is high at the withers or over the croup, she is no race-horse on the flat.

Plate 19.—The famous champion Shire mare Chance, appears here as a four-year-old. The fact of her being in foal detracts somewhat from her great beauty of conformation. I can find no fault in her as a "show" animal, except that she is a little "back at the knees." For heavy draught purposes, however, her hind legs are, possibly, too long. *Farm, Field and Fireside* says: "Her sire is Lincoln, and dam Brock. This animal has taken twenty-four first and champion prizes, amongst which we may mention that she was twice champion at Islington, and three times at different shows of the 'Royal.' During the whole of her eventful career she was never beaten, and finished in grand style by carrying off the Queen's gold medal at the Jubilee meeting of the 'Royal,' beating Starlight and other famous mares. She was foaled in 1880."

Plate 20.—This pony mare is disproportionately high over the croup, and consequently her weight is put too much on her fore legs. As she is, also, somewhat "back" at the knees ; her fore legs could not be expected to stand a great deal of hard work. As she is much higher behind than she is in front; she could hardly help being rough in her paces.

Plate 28.—Magistrate was a very good 13.2 Arab pony, who shows, in his photograph, the same points of speed (short body, long legs, "straight dropped" hind legs), as the English race-horse.

Plate 30.—This Arab is too heavily "topped" for his legs, which are particularly light below the knees; although they are fairly good below the hocks His neck is very coarse and his shoulders are heavy and upright. He is a useless animal.

Plate 31.—The Brat is a handsome Arab pony which has won a large number of pony races in India. His shoulders and neck are particularly good. He has a nice head; but as he was champing his bit and had his eyes closed when his portrait was being taken, it does not come out well.

Plate 32.—The body of this Burma pony has great depth in comparison to its length. As a hack, he has a nice head and neck, and fair shoulders; but his croup is too drooping. He is much better "topped," than he is below his elbows and stifles His fore-arms and gaskins are poor, and he has "sickle-hocks." As might be expected, Burma ponies, of which this one is rather a good specimen, are strong animals, but slow.

Plate 33.—This is a very handsome cob. He has a neat head (which is somewhat favoured by being slightly turned away), small ears, short back, long "rein," good "middle piece," and capital legs.

Plate 34.—This mare is a "three-cornered" animal; but having been brought up among rough surroundings is capable of enduring much privation and hard work; though necessarily slow on account of her body being much longer than she is high at withers or croup. Her body is also very long compared to its depth. She is "calf-kneed," "sickle-hocked," and slightly "tied-in" below the hocks. As compensations, her shoulders are fairly well shaped; her forearms and gaskins are strong; and her "bone" below the knees is good.

Plate 35.—Romance is a handsome Australian horse of the light or even middle weight hunter or charger type. He has won several races over hurdles and on the flat in Australia and India; but among inferior company. His shortness of leg, as compared to his length of body, precludes the possibility of his being gifted with a fine turn of speed. Though no race-horse, he is perfectly shaped as a fast hunter. He has a short back, long "rein," and particularly strong, well-formed legs. His good shoulders and light head and neck are valuable jumping and galloping "points." His best points of speed are, no doubt, his straight hocks and powerful gaskins.

Plate 36.—This is a picture of an under-bred horse, of the light cart type. His shoulders are very upright; his croup is drooping almost to deformity; he has a slightly roached back; and he is somewhat "calf-kneed." As he has good depth of body and fairly strong legs; it is probable that he would be up to a deal of useful work, if not pushed beyond a moderately quick trot.

Plate 38.—Mike was in a high state of excitement when he was photographed, as we may see by his stiffened tail, erect head, pricked ears, and by the "collected" manner in which he was standing. He has capital shoulders, good legs, and, like St. Simon, has not much to carry. He was one of the best 13.1 ponies that was ever bred in England.

Plate 39.—The thoroughbred racing pony Dorothy (by Exminister out of Rosebud) is a great beauty. Her only weak points, as far as I can see, are that her croup is too drooping and her body too long. The fact of her appearing to be a little "goose-rumped" may be due to the way in which she is standing. Her head, neck, and shoulders are very good. Her muscular fore-arms (as we may judge from the appearance of the off one) are beautifully set on to the portion of the leg which is below the knee. Although the look of the hind legs is somewhat marred by the position in which they are placed, we may note that they are "straight dropped," and that she has strong gaskins.

Plate 48.—This depressed-looking pony is not badly bred; though, on account of his dejected attitude and the rough condition of his mane, he looks worse than he is. He is particularly good behind the girths; his depth of body at the centre of the back, from the great length of the false ribs, is almost as great as it is on the withers. The coarseness of his lower jaw gives a plain look to his head. As the general character of this pony is that of a saddle-nag, or light trapper;

his shoulders are unduly upright. His gaskins are poor. With this exception, his legs are fairly well shaped

Plates 54 and 55.—In 1871 Hannah (by King Tom) won the Oaks and St. Leger; and Favonius (by Parmesan out of Zephyr by King Tom), the Derby of the same year. Both of them and Corisande, who won the Cesarewitch of that season carrying 7 st. 12 lbs., belonged to Baron Rothschild. Lord Suffolk states in the Badminton book on *Racing*, that Favonius was 16 or 18 lbs. better than either of the two mares; but that he became unsound. Accepting this estimation, we must regard him as one of the best horses of the century. We might have inferred the fact of his superiority over Hannah by noting that he was much deeper in the body behind the saddle, than she was, and consequently his chest was better formed for forced breathing than was hers. He looks up to more weight than she does, on account of his fore-arms and gaskins being more muscular, and his bones below the knee being larger. Both animals have equally "straight-dropped" hind legs. Her neck is lighter, and her shoulders appear flatter and more oblique than his. Both have almost exactly the same proportions between the length of body, and the height at the withers; and between the depth from withers to brisket, and the height of the brisket off the ground. As both were in training, and were standing in nearly the same position, we have a capital opportunity of comparing their respective conformation.

Plate 56.—This thoroughbred English mare is a typical "weed," as we may see by her short back ribs, and slack loins. As deficiency in these points is incompatible with staying power, she was unable to "get" beyond half a mile; although she was fast for that distance. Her good length of limb, "straight" hocks and sloping shoulders all point to the possession of speed.

Plate 57.—Blue Ribbon (by New Oswestry out of Miss Honiton) may be taken as a good type of the well-bred middle, if not heavy, weight hunter. Though a fine weight-carrier, she was fast enough to win steeple-chases. I have refrained from calling her thoroughbred; for her sire is not in the Stud-book. Blue Ribbon has capital shoulders for jumping with a heavy-weight in the saddle, as they are oblique and muscular. Her neck is light, her back ribs long, her quarters powerful, and her fore-arms and gaskins good. Her head looks somewhat coarse from the lightness of her neck; but its size is in harmony with that of the body. In the photograph, her fore fetlocks look a bit round, and her fore pasterns a trifle upright—probably from work.

Plates 58 and 59, Lord Stamford's Diophantus (by Orlando out of Equation by Euclid), the winner of the 2,000 guineas in 1861, and Mr. Snewing's Caractacus (by Kingston out of Defenceless), winner of the Derby in 1862, being in stud condition, give us but little idea of their true "make and shape." Diophantus appears very upright on his pasterns; no doubt as a result of work. The fore-arms of Caractacus look weak Both of these horses seem a little "over" at the knees.

Plate 60.—This handsome Iceland pony was only 30 inches high. He looks a miniature race-horse.

Plate 61.—This beautifully "topped" Shetland pony was a great prize-winner at Agricultural shows many years ago. The strength of his legs, though the more important point of the two, is not in proportion to the size of his body. Except that he has a neater head and a better set-on tail, he is much of the same class of animal as the Burma pony shown on Plate 32 (*see* p 294).

Plate 62.—The Australian race-horse, Bravo (by Grand Flaneur out of The Orphan), won the Melbourne Cup in 1889, when in receipt of twenty-one pounds from Carbine (by Musket), who was the best horse that had run in Australasia. When I took his photograph, he was about half-trained, and was consequently somewhat lusty. To judge of him as he was standing for his portrait, he appears to have been a trifle longer in the body, than he was high at the withers, from which fact we might infer that he was not a race-horse of the highest class. He had good shoulders, long neck, short back, and good depth at the centre of his back, and was consequently a fine stayer. His hocks were not as straight as those of Ormonde (Frontispiece), Favonius (Pl. 55), or St. Simon (Pls. 7 and 18).

Plate 63.—Minden was a famous "country-bred" race-horse in India, among his own class, which is not within "measurable distance" of that of English £50 selling platers. Viewed as a smart saddle-nag, I must say that Minden looks a nice-shaped horse. He has capital shoulders and a good "middle-piece." I may mention that he was in training when I took his photograph. The fact of his being longer in the body than he is high at the withers or at the croup, points to deficiency of speed, as the term is understood among racing men.

Plate 64.—Cremorne (by Parmesan out of Rigolboche) won the Derby of 1872 against a bad field, with the exception of the roaring Prince Charlie. He has achieved a great name at the Stud. His produce have been famous for their jumping powers. He is standing so awkwardly in his photograph, that it is difficult to form from it a just idea of his "make and shape." He seems to have had well-sloped muscular shoulders, and a light head and neck, all of which are important jumping points.

CHAPTER XXVIII.

WILD HORSES.

Wild Horses in Australia and America—Tarpans—Prejevalsky's Horse.

Wild Horses in Australia and America.—In Australia, there are many herds of wild horses, which are descended from escaped or "turned out" domesticated animals. Those of America are usually supposed to be of a similar ancestry. This idea is, however, open to doubt; for fossil remains of horses like unto those of the present time, or closely akin to them, are to be found nearly all over North and South America. Considering their former abundance in prehistoric times, and the favourable conditions for equine life which appear since then to have existed in the New World, it seems highly improbable that there were no horses on that continent at the time of the Spanish discovery. This doubt is still more strengthened by the fact that Northern Europe was in communication with North America hundreds of years before Columbus first sighted the Bahama Islands.

Tarpans.—"The nearest approach to truly wild horses existing at present are the so-called Tarpans, which occur in the steppe-country north of the Sea of Azoff, between the river Dnieper and the Caspian. They are described to be of small size, dun colour, with short mane, and rounded, obtuse nose" (*Sir William Flower*). The Russian naturalist, Poliakof, states that they are mouse-coloured, lighter coloured under the belly than elsewhere, and that their legs are black below the knees and hocks.

Prejevalsky's Horse, which has been found in Central Asia near Zaisan and in the desert of Dzungaria, is described by Poliakof (*see* "Annals of Natural History," 1881, p. 16 *et seq.*) as intermediate between the horse and the ass. Like the former it has castors (chesnuts) on its hind legs as well as on its fore extremities; and like the latter it has an erect mane and no forelock. It has no stripe down the back. Its tail is bushy, being furnished, like that of the horse, though not to the same extent, with long hairs from the root of the tail. Poliakof states that it is of a dun colour; has a yellowish tinge on the back; and is lighter coloured under the belly than elsewhere. It is supposed to be indigenous to Central Asia.

I may mention that all kinds of wild horses are smaller and inferior to domesticated animals, in every useful particular, except, perhaps, in the quality of their hoofs, and in the soundness of their constitutions.

CHAPTER XXIX.

ASSES.

Differences between the Ass and Horse—Hybrids between the Horse and Ass—Varieties of Asses—The Domestic and Abyssinian Wild Ass—The Onager—The Kiang—The Mountain Zebra—Burchell's Zebra—Chapman's Zebra—The Grévy or Somaliland Zebra—The Quagga.

Differences between the Ass and Horse.—The following are the chief differences between the two animals :—

1. The ass has castors (*see* p. 216) only on the fore legs.

M. Chauveau is of opinion that the castor is the rudiment of the thumb, or rather first digit. Against this idea, there are the following facts :—

(*a*) The castor has no special connection, bony, ligamentous, or otherwise, with either the bones of the knee, or those of the hock. As, in the evolution of the horse, the wasting away of the digits which have either disappeared or have become rudimentary, began from below ; it is unreasonable to assume that a vestige of the first digit should have remained, after all trace of its metacarpal, or (as the case may be) metatarsal bone had been lost

(*b*.) The second and fourth metacarpal and metatarsal bones still remain strongly in evidence ; yet their digits have entirely vanished.

(*c*.) The castors are situated below the hock and above the knee. In the onager, I have seen them much nearer the elbow than the knee.

I think the foregoing facts are sufficient to prove that the castors are not rudiments of the first digits. I have no theory to offer respecting their origin.

2. The ass has a tufted tail, somewhat like that of a cow; erect mane; and no forelock. The horse has a bushy tail, drooping mane, and a forelock, when they have been allowed to grow. The difference in the mane is due to the length of the hairs of the part. In the horse, the hairs of the tail grow long from the root of the dock. In the ass, they do so only as they approach the end of the tail.

3. Veterinary anatomists state that the ass has five loin vertebræ (*see* p. 30); and the horse, six, unless in some very exceptional cases when he may have five. If we examine the skeleton of the mountain zebra (*see* Pl. 29), which is in the Museum of the R. C. S., Lincoln's Inn Fields, we shall, however, see that it has six loin vertebræ. The skeleton of the famous race-horse Orlando, which is in the same building, has only five loin vertebræ. I have never heard of an instance, in the domestic ass, of the number of these bones exceeding five. I do not know their normal number in zebras.

4. In the horse, the lachrymal duct, which is the canal that conveys tears from the eye, on each respective side, into the nostril, has its opening near the inferior commissure of the nostril and on the line of union between the dark-coloured skin and the pink mucous membrane. In the ass and mule, it is situated at the inner face of the outer wing of the nostril. This orifice is sometimes double.

5 In the ass, the false nostril extends higher up than in the horse.

6. The male ass has two rudimental teats in the form of small tubercles. They are absent in the horse.

7. The ass brays ; the horse neighs.

8. In the ass, the deep depression at the base of the epiglottis is covered by a thin membrane, which is capable of vibrating, and which is wanting in the horse. Its presence may have some influence in causing the voice of the ass to differ from that of the horse. I may mention that the epiglottis is a cartilage that acts as a door to the larynx, which is the organ of voice, and which forms an opening into the windpipe.

9. The ass hardly ever has any irregular markings on its coat, such as a "star," "blaze," "reach," or "stockings," all of which are very frequent among horses. A small star, on one or two occasions, is the only mark of the kind I have ever seen in the ass. At the same time, I must state that I have not had much experience among these animals.

10. I believe I am correct in saying that the colour of the ass is never of a bright bay, chestnut, red or blue roan, or nutmeg grey. I have seen mules of an iron-grey colour ; but have not observed it in the ass. This conservatism in colour and freedom from irregular markings, shown by the ass, is very remarkable ; considering how greatly the coat of the horse varies in this respect, and that the ass has, in all probability, been longer under the influence of domestication than the horse.

11. As regards conformation, I may say that the ass differs from the horse, chiefly, by its greater height over the croup, as compared to that at the withers, and by the narrowness, uprightness, and concavity of its hoofs. The excess of height at the croup tends to make the withers of the ass appear

unduly low (*see* p. 196). The spines of the vertebræ at the withers are only a little shorter in the ass than they are in the horse. As a rule, horses are higher at the withers than they are at the croup.

12. The horse has a thick strong dock to his tail; the ass, a thin, lissom one.

13. The horse, on each side of his croup and covering his pelvis, has, underneath and closely adhering to the skin of the part, a thick and extremely dense layer of connective tissue, which is so close and hard, when the skin has been tanned and dried, that it looks like horn. These two patches of thickened skin, are separated from each other about four or five inches apart, so that there is a strip of skin of ordinary thickness running down the croup towards the tail. These pieces of skin are utilised, chiefly, for the manufacture of long boots for foreign cavalry officers, by curriers, who dress and pare down the "shell," or hardened layer, until it is almost as smooth as glass, and can consequently take the brilliant polish which is greatly esteemed by these *beaux sabreurs.* I need hardly say that the leather which is thus employed, is worn inside out. It is both air and water tight. The "shell" is connected to the skin so closely that the two form one piece; although their respective consistencies are different. If a section be made through the hide, their line of union may be readily seen. In the ass, the "shell" is not confined to the skin that covers the pelvis; but also extends over the ribs, which are consequently not as sensitive to the effects of blows as are those of the horse. I may mention that the tendency which a horse has to turn his rump, as the least sensitive part of his anatomy, towards falling rain, cold currents of wind, etc., appears to be due to the feeling of protection to

that part, which the presence of the "shell" on each side gives him.

Professor Huxley remarks that asses form a distinct species from horses; because "all asses have tufted tails and have callosities only on the inner side of the fore legs. If animals were discovered having the general characters of the horse, but sometimes with callosities only on the fore legs and more or less tufted tails; or animals having the general characters of the ass, but with more or less bushy tails and sometimes with callosities on both pairs of legs, besides being intermediate in other respects, the two species would have to be merged into one. They could no longer be regarded as morphologically distinct species, for they would not be distinctly definable one from the other." When Professor Huxley wrote this, he was evidently unaware that the horse has not invariably callosities on all four legs (*see* p. 217).

Hybrids between the Horse and Ass.—Neither the mule (the produce of the jackass and mare), nor the hinny or jennet (the cross between the horse and the she-ass), is fertile, either among themselves, or with other members of the horse family. Those animals which have been mistaken by superficial observers as fertile mules, have been, I venture to say, in most cases the offspring of mares that have previously bred to donkeys, and have endowed their young with some of the characteristics of their former asinine lovers. Both the mule and the jennet respectively "take after" their dam in size; and their sire, in appearance and disposition.

I know nothing respecting the question of the fertility of the respective crosses between the different kinds of asses, true or striped.

Varieties of Asses.—These animals may be divided into the true or whole coloured asses, including the domestic or Abyssinian ass, the onager, and the kiang; and the striped asses, comprising the mountain zebra, Burchell's zebra, Grévy's zebra, and the quagga.

The Domestic and Abyssinian Wild Ass (*Equus asinus, see* Pl. 65).—The domestic ass or donkey is, with hardly any doubt, identical with the handsome and speedy wild ass which is found in North-eastern Africa, and which is known as the Abyssinian wild ass. The chief characteristics which distinguish it from other asses is the possession of a nearly vertical black stripe running down the shoulders, from the front of the withers, and the narrowness of the stripe down the back. These two stripes, which are, as a rule, only from a half to three-quarters of an inch wide, make the well-known cross. Sir William Flower states that the shoulder stripe is "sometimes double, and not infrequently altogether absent." I believe the stripe down the back is now and then wanting. It is not uncommonly seen among native bred, and especially dun-coloured horses in India. This wild ass is of a light mouse colour except on the muzzle, under part of the body, and inside of the legs, which are more or less white. Its coat, particularly in the case of the domestic ass, may vary from white to a very dark brown, or even black, with tan "points." This animal, both in a wild and tame state, frequently shows dark horizontal stripes on its fore-arms. It resembles the mountain zebra in having very large ears, and a very large head compared to the length of its body. From ancient Egyptian records we learn that this ass was employed for domestic purposes in Egypt many centuries

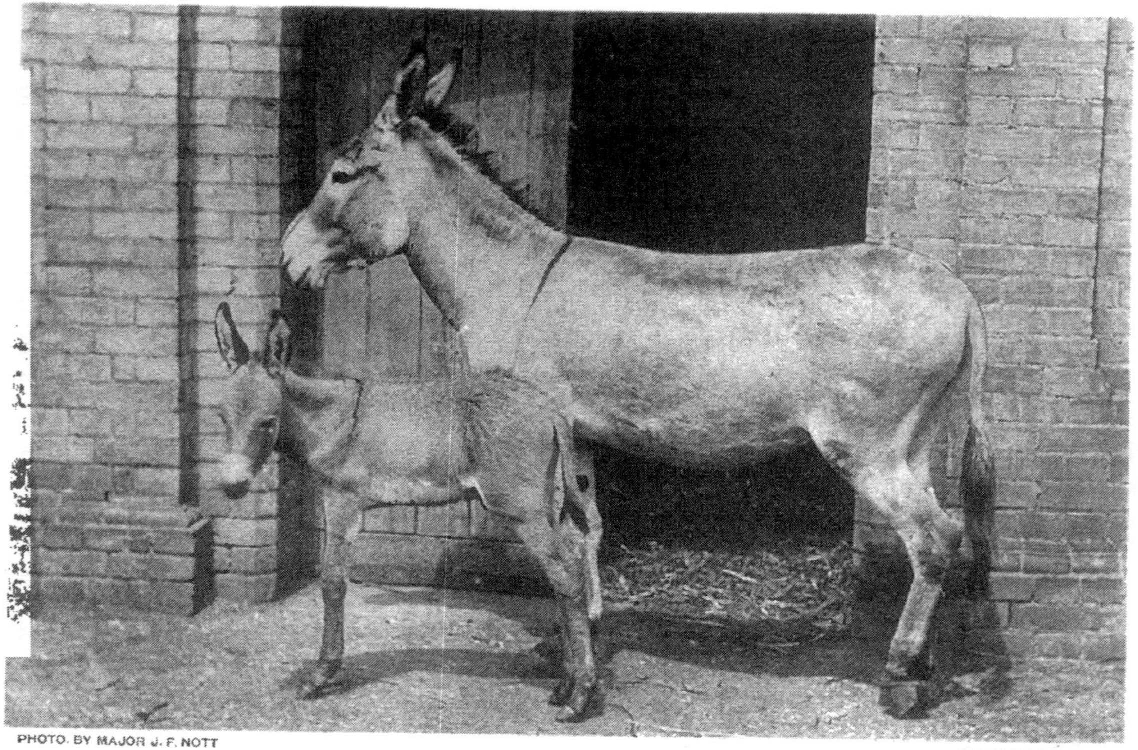

PHOTO. BY MAJOR J. F. NOTT

TO FACE PAGE 308

PLATE 65—THE ABYSSINIAN ASS.

before the horse was known in that country. Its introduction into Europe, however, has been comparatively of recent date. It does not appear to have been known in England before the time of the Saxons, and did not come into general use until the beginning of the seventeenth century. The horse, as we all know, was employed by the ancient Britons, even for purposes of war, at the time (55 B. C.) when Cæsar landed. The donkey, used by native washermen in India, is the smallest and most miserable of its kind. It is often not more than eight hands high, and from overloading at a far too early age, its hocks frequently are so much turned in that they rub against each other at every step, even when the animal is at liberty. In countries like America and Spain, where care has been bestowed on the breeding of this ass, it may be found as big as an ordinary saddle horse, and proportionately strong.

The donkey associates itself to man as readily as does the dog, and, unlike the horse, evinces little or no inclination to return to a wild state of life after it has become domesticated. It is interesting to note that this ass, which is characterised by a stripe (sometimes two stripes), down the shoulder, and frequently by horizontal stripes on the fore-arms, is a native of the country (Africa) in which zebras are indigenous.

The Onager (*Equus onager, see* Pl. 66).—The wild asses which are found in Syria, Arabia, Persia, Baluchistan, Turkistan, Afghanistan, and Kutch (in India), resemble each other so closely that they may be classed under the one heading of "onager," which is the term usually reserved for the Indian and Persian wild ass. It is lighter in colour and longer in the leg, in comparison to its length of body, than the

Abyssinian variety. It is generally of a light mouse or ash colour on the head (with the exception of the muzzle), and on the upper parts of the neck, shoulders, back and quarters; and more or less white on the muzzle and under part of the neck, chest, and belly, and on the legs. Sometimes the colouring is so faint that the animal's coat looks almost of a silver white. It has not, or only to a slight extent in exceptional cases, the cross stripe on the shoulders. There is a broad stripe, about five inches wide at the croup, down the back, nearly similar to that of the Burchell zebra (*see* Fig. 183). Adults are from twelve to thirteen hands high at the withers. Its ears are not quite as long as those of the Abyssinian wild ass. It is handsome, very fast, and extremely difficult of approach.

The Kiang (*Equus hemionus, see* Pl. 67) is the wild ass of Thibet and Tartary. It seems to be identical with the onager, except that it is different in colour, more heavily built, on shorter legs, and that its stripe down the back is narrower. The colour of the kiang is a rather light brown, which is darker and redder than the light mouse colour of the onager. The colour is not red enough to be termed a bay. This ass is about thirteen hands high. It is far less wary than the onager, and consequently falls a ready prey to the cockney sportsmen who invade its domains in the high table-lands of Thibet.

The Mountain Zebra (*Equus zebra, see* Pl. 29) has a more tufted tail, a scantier mane, longer ears, and a larger head for its size than the Burchell zebra. As far as my experience goes, it has a thicker neck, and its legs, especially

PHOTO. BY FRANK HAES

TO FACE PAGE 310

PLATE 66—THE ONAGER.

as regards the back tendons and suspensory ligaments, are not as well suited to civilised requirements as those of the Burchell zebra. The male, at least, appears to have a rudimentary dewlap. Its stripes are black or dark brown, on a white ground. The most distinctive difference between the arrangement of its stripes and those of the Burchell zebra, is the existence of a number of transverse stripes, which run across the top of its croup and across its tail. In some instances, this zebra is white on the underneath part of the body. With this exception, it is distinctly marked all over the body, even down to the coronets, with black and white stripes. It is indigenous to the southern part of Africa. I believe it has not been found north of the Vaal River. At present (1893), it is met with in a wild state, only in a few mountain ranges in the southern part of Cape Colony, where it is preserved. There is a herd of these zebras preserved on a farm near Craddock, which is a small town in the eastern province of Cape Colony. It is much wilder and more intractable to handle than the Burchell zebra. I have been told that on different occasions it has been successfully "inspanned" in South Africa; although I have not heard of its having been put into draught between the shafts. I may point out that the steadiness of an animal is far more severely tested by having to bear weight placed on its back by the shafts, than by merely pulling against breast harness, or even against a collar, in a "span;" and by going in saddle than by any kind of harness work. In the year 1891, at Calcutta, I broke in, after two days' training, an old entire zebra, quiet enough for my wife to ride and to get photographed while on its back. This was certainly the first time a lady has ridden this variety of zebra, which has the reputation all over the world of being unrideable. Although I made many inquiries on the subject while I was in South Africa, I could not obtain a single authenticated case of any one in that country ever having ridden a mountain zebra. With the advantage of the special instruction in horse breaking which I gave during my tour through South Africa in 1892, the residents of that country ought to experience no difficulty in getting any zebras which they may have in captivity, broken to either harness or saddle. The height of the mountain zebra, when full grown, is about twelve hands.

Burchell's Zebra (*Equus burchelli, see* Pl. 37) differs from the mountain zebra in being taller (its full height is about 13 1, or 13.2), having a longer and thicker mane, a more bushy and less tufted tail, smaller ears and a smaller head in comparison to the length of its body; and in the differences of its markings. The dark stripes are more brown than black. The light colour is of a yellowish cream. The stripes are broader and differently arranged (compare Pl. 37 with Pl. 29). A broad stripe runs down the back, and there are no stripes across the top of the croup (*see* Fig. 183). Its legs, below the knees and hocks, from their "flatness," with the back tendons and suspensory ligaments clearly showing, are much more like those of a well-bred horse than are those of the mountain zebra. It further resembles the horse by having a fairly lissom neck and a well-rounded barrel, and in the size of its head and ears. The typical Burchell's zebra has no dark stripes, or only very slight ones, below the elbows and stifles, on the legs. The Orange River has been generally regarded as its southern limit. Mr. F. C.

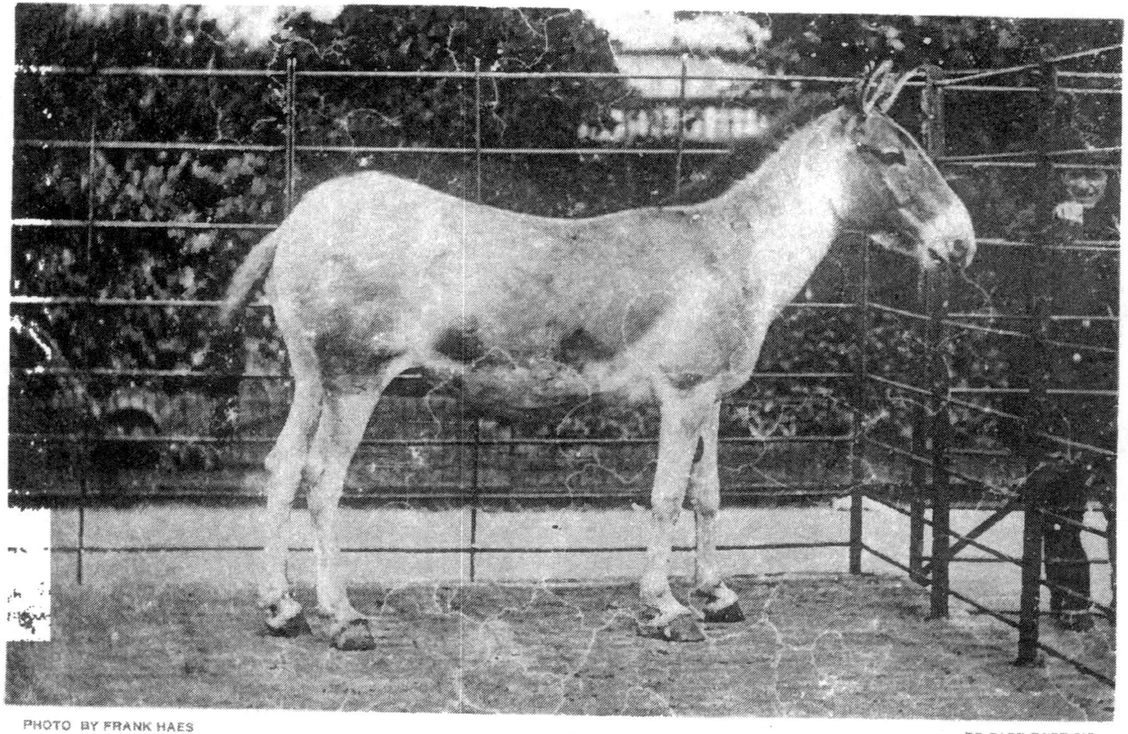

PHOTO BY FRANK HAES

TO FACE PAGE 312

PLATE 67—THE KIANG.

Selous, the celebrated African sportsman and naturalist, tells me that it "was first discovered by Burchell near the Orange River in Southern Bechuanaland. It is still to be met with in Kama's country, and along the northern and eastern borders of the Transvaal. In the neighbourhood of the Pungwe River, it exists in very great numbers, herds of hundreds together being common." It is probably widely distributed throughout Central and Eastern Africa. On account of the fact that this zebra, when in a wild state, possesses immunity from the effects of the bite of the tsetse fly, which is certain death to horses, I strongly advocated, while I was in South Africa, the taming and employment for harness or saddle, of these animals in "fly" infected districts. With respect to this subject, Mr. Selous writes to me that: "although Burchell's zebra, born and brought up in the 'fly' country, does not suffer from its bite, it is my opinion that if a young one was caught and brought up in a locality where there was no 'fly,' and was then taken into a 'fly' infested district, it would die. This, however, is only my opinion.' As the Burchell zebra is comparatively easy to break in, and as it will breed in confinement, there is but little doubt that it will in time become domesticated. If, as is quite possible, it possesses little or no tendency to contract "horse sickness," it will prove a valuable means of conveyance in South Africa. During one of my horse-breaking performances in 1892, at Pretoria, the capital of the Transvaal, I made a young Burchell zebra, after about an hour's handling, quiet to carry a rider. In doing this, I did not throw the animal down, nor did I resort to any of the usual "heroic" horse-taming methods. Throughout South Africa, this variety of zebra is wrongly called a quagga.

Chapman's Zebra (*Equus chapmani*) appears to be identical with Burchell's zebra, except that its legs have stripes continued down to its pasterns. These leg stripes are not so regularly defined as those of the mountain zebra. As we may meet with specimens having all degrees of striping on the legs, I would submit that the presence or absence of

FIG. 181.—THE GRÉVY OR SOMALI-LAND ZEBRA.

stripes on the limbs, is a mere question of individual or local difference, and that the so-called Chapman zebra should not be regarded as a distinct variety.

The Grévy or Somali-land Zebra (*Equus grévyi, see* Fig. 181).—This animal, which is found in Shoa and Somali-land, closely resembles the mountain zebra in being striped

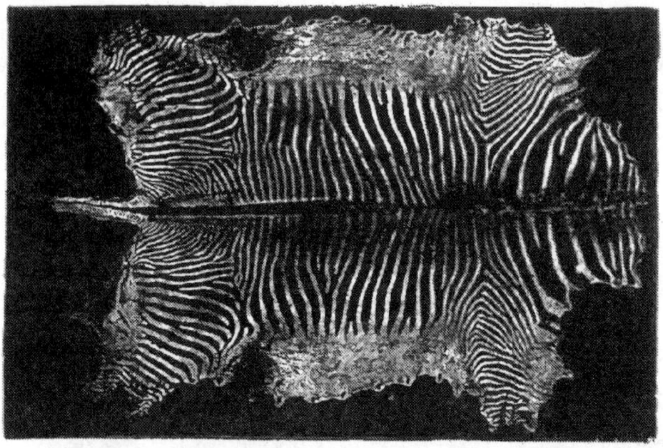

FIG. 182.—SKIN OF THE SOMALI-LAND ZEBRA.

FIG. 183.—SKIN OF BURCHELL'S ZEBRA.

down to the coronets, and in having the hair of its tail

collected as a tuft at the end. It differs, however, in being white underneath the chest and abdomen, and in having white patches on the rear part of the croup at each side of the stripe down the back. Also, there are no transverse stripes on the croup. The stripes are somewhat narrower than those of the mountain zebra, and, in their arrangement, resemble them more nearly than do those of the Burchell zebra, with which it closely agrees in its conformation. The differences in the stripes of these two animals are shown in Figs. 182 and 183.

The Quagga (*Equus quagga, see* Pl. 68), forty years ago, was to be found in immense numbers south of the Vaal river in Southern Africa. I have the authority of Mr. F. C. Selous, for saying that it is extinct in a wild state; although it is possible that there may be a specimen or two in some menagerie or other. During a tour last year throughout South Africa, I failed to obtain any tidings of the quagga. It was a strong, somewhat heavily built animal, slow of pace for a wild ass, and could have been readily broken to harness or saddle. It stood about the height of the Burchell zebra. Its colour on the shoulders and body was brown. The head and neck were marked alternately with white and dark-brown stripes, like those of the mountain zebra. There were on the shoulders and body some faint stripes, which gradually faded away as they went backwards. The colour was more or less white beneath the chest and belly, on the tail, except at the root, and on the legs below the elbows and stifles. It had a broad stripe down the back. It closely resembled Burchell's zebra, with the exception of being differently marked, and being more heavily built.

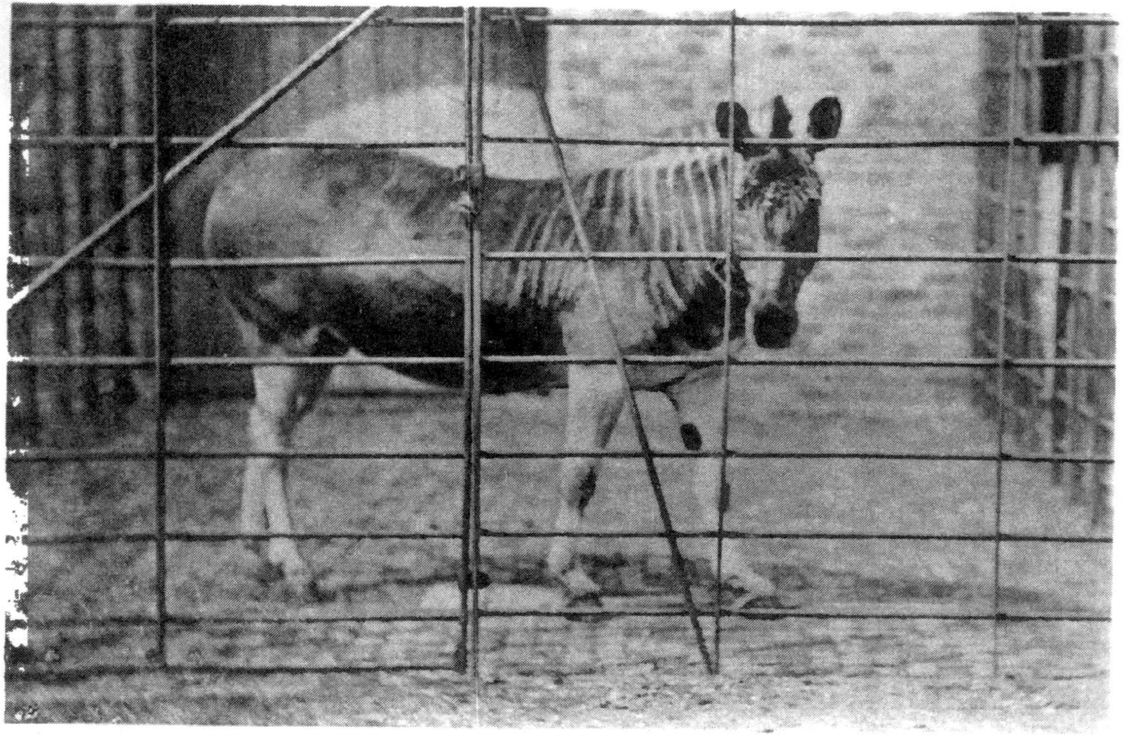

PHOTO. BY FRANK HAES

TO FACE PAGE 318

PLATE 68—THE QUAGGA.

Points of the Ass.—The law which I put forward in Chapters I. and XV., with respect to the influence of comparative length of limb on speed and strength, holds as good in the case of the ass, as it does in that of the horse. From it we may justly infer that the onager is the speediest of its class. From personal deductions, which I cannot support by any precise data, I would think that the onager is faster for its size, and under equal conditions, than any kind of wild horse, or, perhaps, than any horse which has not some English racing blood in its veins. As it is not at all probable that this ass will be bred for racing purposes, I need form no conjectures respecting its future on the turf. On page 305, I have alluded to the fact of the ass being higher over the croup than at the withers, supposing, of course, that it were to stand "at attention" (*see* Fig. 35). In the domestic ass, the gaskins and fore-arms are, as a rule, very poor; but they are not so, at least to anything like the same extent, in the wild ass. Probably, on account of the ass having fewer loin vertebræ (*see* p. 304) than the horse, it has less tendency to be "slack in the loins." Compared to the horse, the ass has a very weak tail, and is consequently unable to "carry its flag" in the style usually affected by a spirited horse during movement.

CHAPTER XXX.*

EVOLUTION OF THE HORSE.

Ancestry of the Horse—Immediate Ancestors of the Horse—Conditions which modified the Form of the Horse—Points of Speed and Strength in the Fossil Horse—The Horse of the Future.

Ancestry of the Horse.—It is my intention here, with special reference to conformation, to write about the descent of the horse in such a manner that my remarks may be easily understood by those who possess no acquaintance with fossils or comparative anatomy. Instead of commencing the history of the horse according to the orthodox method, at a period many millions of years ago, I shall begin with him as he now is, and shall try to trace back his lineage to a time sufficiently remote for our requirements. Although we cannot hope to determine the exact sequence of the footsteps of the animals which, in their march of evolution, became gradually changed into the horse; we shall find on their track marks left by them, or by their near relatives who accompanied them on their journey, that will guide us in the right direction. As science progresses, so will the intervals between these land-marks become filled in from time to time; though it seems impossible

* For fuller information on this subject, *see* Professor A. Gaudry's *Enchaînements du Monde Animal*, and Sir William Flower's *The Horse*.

that the position of every footprint can ever be accurately defined.

We learn from the study of geology that living creatures began to inhabit the earth after its crust, which was once in a liquid state, had cooled down, and the action of physical causes, such as wind and water, had commenced to form sedimentary rocks, in which the bones and other remains of existing animals, became entombed as fossils. Thus, through countless ages, a history of animal and also of vegetable life has been written in stone by the hand of time. The last leaves of this book lie uppermost, while the first ones repose on fused rock, of which granite is a familiar example. This history is divided by scientific men into the Primary, Secondary, and Tertiary periods, of which the last-mentioned is the only one I shall take into account; as, during it, hoofed animals appeared for the first time on the earth. The Tertiary period is divided into the Eocene, Miocene, Pliocene, and Pleistocene periods; the Eocene being the most ancient; and the Pleistocene the one immediately preceding historic times. In searching through the records of the past, an examination of fossil feet is particularly interesting; for we can obtain from it the most direct and the most clearly expressed evidence respecting the capacity of movement possessed by the animals which, during life, walked on the earth.

Before beginning, I may remind my readers that the knee of the horse corresponds to our wrist (*see* p. 32); and his fore fetlock to the row of knuckles nearest to the wrist. Instead of having, as in our hand, five *metacarpal* bones between the knee and fetlock, he has only one entire bone (the cannon-bone), and two rudimentary (or splint) bones. I may remark that in the hind limb, the bones between the hock and hind fetlock are called *metatarsal* bones. Each of our five metacarpal and metatarsal bones is furnished with a *digit*, a synonym for either a toe or a finger; but in the horse the cannon-bone only is provided with a digit. I may mention that the bones of each digit (the *phalanges*) are numbered from above downwards. Thus the long pastern-bone (*see* Fig. 3), is called the first phalanx; the short-pastern-bone, the second phalanx; and the pedal or coffin-bone, the third phalanx.

If we examine the bones of the horse's limbs from, respectively, the knees and hocks downward, we shall notice that although the splint-bones form joints with the knee bones which are immediately above them; their lower ends do not, like that of the cannon-bone, articulate with any other bones. Were a man who knew nothing about the anatomy, working functions, and diseases of any other animal except those of the horse, to criticise the plan according to which the bones below the knees and hocks were constructed; he might justly remark that for purposes of equine labour, it would have been better if the cannon-bone and two splint-bones had been one bone of corresponding size. Such a combination would have rendered the column of bones stronger at that part, and would have obviated the frequent evil effects of sprain to the interosseous ligaments which connect each splint-bone to its cannon-bone. I may here point out that the disease known in veterinary surgery as "splint," is, as a rule, brought on by sprain of this ligament. If we agree in considering the working of the laws of nature to be perfect, we cannot accept the theory of special creation; but must regard the body of the horse, like that of other animals, to be in a transition state; in that it is constantly, though slowly, accommodating itself to the conditions of life in which it finds itself. While indulging in the present train of thought, the first question which the inquirer after knowledge will probably ask, will be: the splint-bones being in a state of transition, what was their previous form and

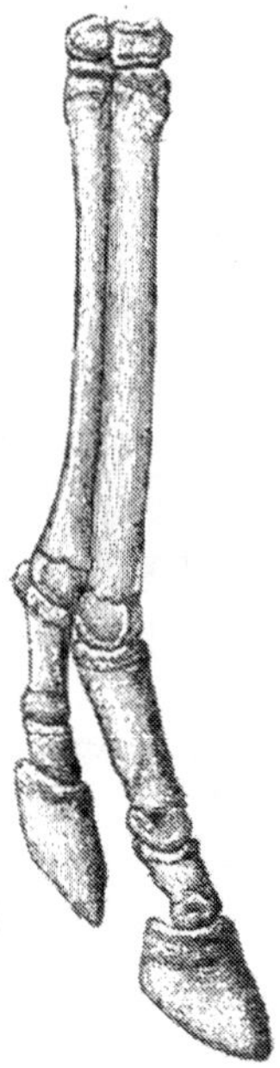

FIG. 184.—(*After Gaudry.*) ABNORMAL LEFT FORE LEG, BELOW THE KNEE, OF HORSE (⅛th real length).

functions, and what conditions have reduced them to their present rudimentary state? I shall now try to suggest answers to these questions.

On rare occasions we find in the horse, that one or more of the splint-bones have the character of the cannon-bone, in that they are provided with a more or less perfect pastern and hoof. From time to time, there have been well authenticated instances of horses which were so completely furnished in this respect on their front feet, that instead of having been shod on only four feet, they carried iron on eight. I need hardly say that the four supplementary shoes were applied merely for exhibition purposes. Such a digit is well shown in Fig. 184, which represents the bones of a colt's near

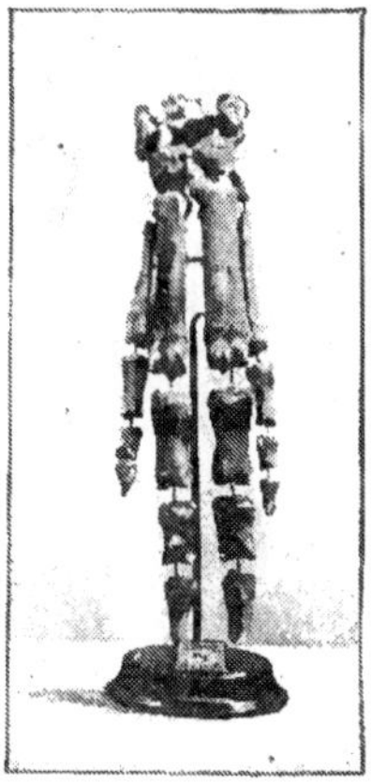

FIG. 185.—FRONT FOOT OF PIG (⅓th real length).

fore leg that was given by Professor Goubaux to the Veterinary College at Alfort. These new digits are no functionless monstrosities, like a sixth finger or toe which sometimes appears on the hand or foot of man; but are the restorations of parts once borne by the horse's ancestors. Here we have a good exemplification of the struggle which is constantly going on in the animal body, between the tendency to preserve the ancestral type, and the effort to adapt itself to its surrounding conditions. If we examine the foot of the pig (*see* Fig. 185), which, like the horse, has hoofs; we shall find that it has two toes upon which it walks, and two supplementary digits which do not touch the ground. As the function makes the organ, we may confidently assert that ancestors of the pig walked on these four toes, two of which, apparently from disuse, have become reduced to their present

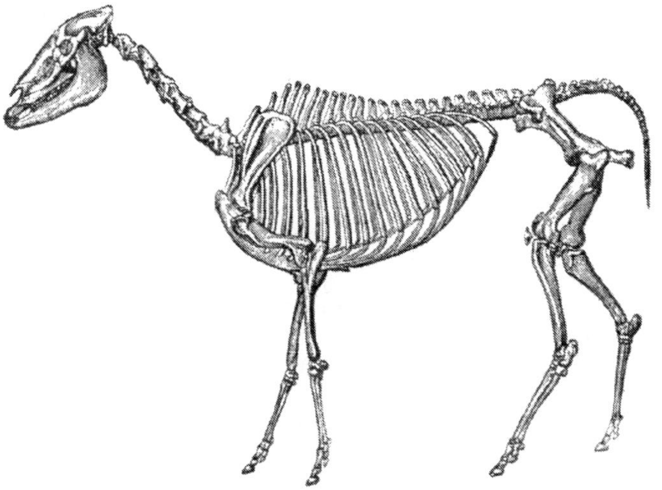

FIG. 186.—(*After Gaudry.*) HIPPARION GRACILE ($\frac{1}{20}$th real height).

insignificant size. We may, with equal certainty, affirm that, if the pig remains under its present conditions of life, which, as we all know, do not demand work from its small side toes, these digits will in process of time disappear, and their metacarpal and metatarsal bones will become as rudimentary as the splint-bones of the horse. Even if it were objected that these facts did not warrant us in assuming that the ancestors of the horse had, on each foot, three toes, two of which were more or less rudimentary; we have the still stronger evidence afforded by fossils of horse-like animals

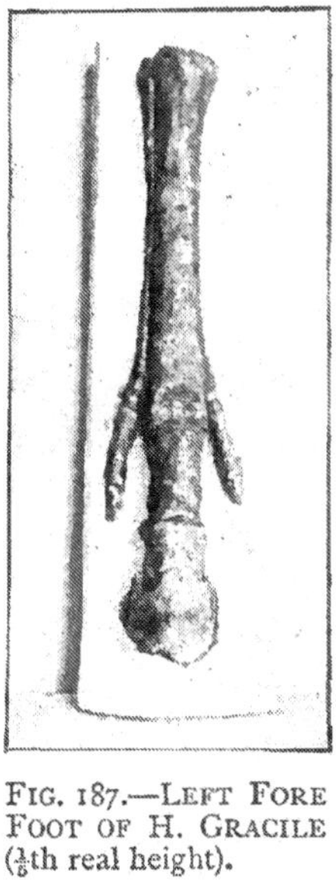

FIG. 187.—LEFT FORE FOOT OF H. GRACILE (⅛th real height).

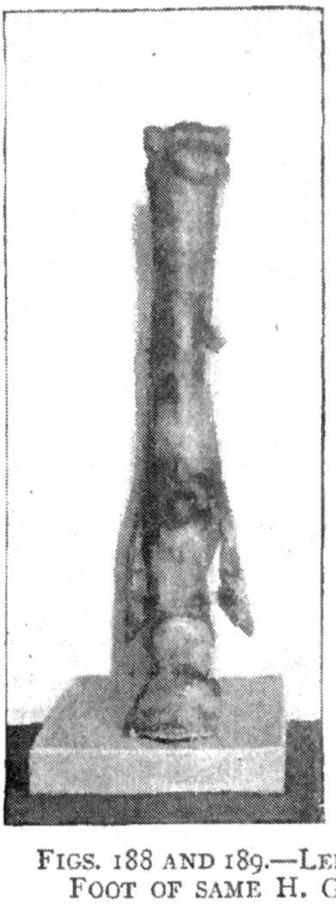

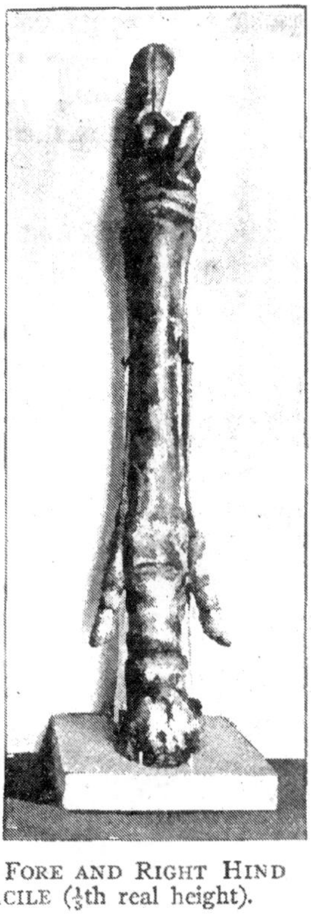

FIGS. 188 AND 189.—LEFT FORE AND RIGHT HIND FOOT OF SAME H. GRACILE (⅓th real height).

(*Hipparion*, *see* Fig. 186), whose feet were in this condition (*see* Figs. 187, 188, 189 and 190). Figs. 191 and 192 give front views of the horse's foot. Sir William Flower points out that the European representative (*Hipparion gracile*) of this fossil family could not have been an ancestor of the horse; for, besides differences in the teeth, it possessed

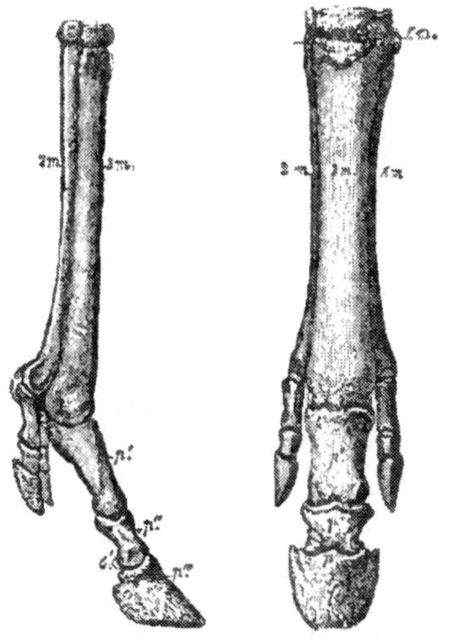

FIG. 190.—(*After Gaudry.*) FRONT AND SIDE VIEWS OF LEFT FORE FOOT OF HIPPARION GRACILE ($\frac{1}{5}$th real length). The lettering is the same as that of Fig. 192.

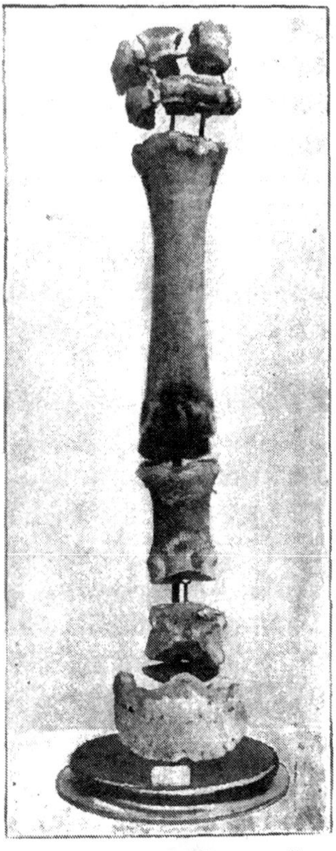

FIG. 191.—FRONT VIEW OF LEFT FORE FOOT OF HORSE ($\frac{1}{5}$th real length).

a deep depression in front of the eye, on each side of the face, in which depression was lodged a large tear or scent gland, similar to that found in several kinds of deer and antelope. Had the *H. gracile* been the ancestor of the horse, this depression would not have entirely disappeared in

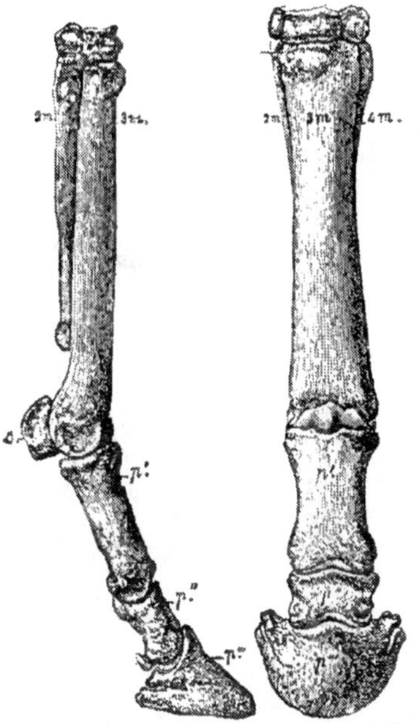

FIG. 192.—(*After Gaudry.*) FRONT AND SIDE VIEW OF LEFT FORE FOOT OF HORSE ($\frac{1}{8}$th real length).

2m, second metacarpal bone (inner splint-bone); *3m*, third metacarpal bone (cannon-bone); *4m*, fourth metacarpal bone (outer splint-bone); *p'*, first phalanx (long pastern bone); *p''*, second phalanx (short pastern bone); *p'''*, third phalanx (pedal bone).

the horse. The *H. gracile* does not appear to have left any descendants. It is probable that the immediate ancestors of the horse of to-day (*Equus caballus*) came, in prehistoric times, from America, in which country are to be found the remains of various kinds of fossil horses which resembled our present ones more nearly than did *H. gracile.* The Hipparion flourished in the upper Miocene and lower Pliocene ages, and was from 13 to 14 hands high.

The Hipparion was preceded in the Miocene period by a somewhat similar, three-toed animal, the Anchitherium, which was about 10 hands high. We may see from Fig. 193 that its side toes were longer than those of its successor. The

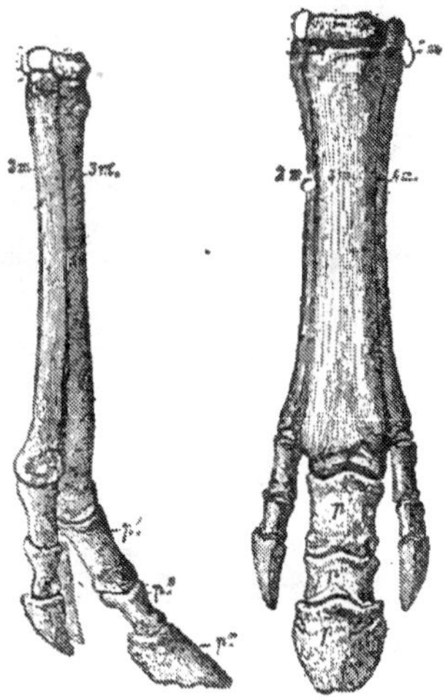

FIG. 193.—(*After Gaudry.*) LEFT FORE FOOT OF ANCHITHERIUM ($\frac{1}{5}$th real length). The lettering is the same as that of Fig. 192.

Russian palæontologist, Kowalevsky, points out that the bones below the fetlock in the Anchitherium, were not so firmly united together, as they were in the Hipparion, and still less so than in the horse; and, consequently, that there must have been a certain amount of lateral play in them. The length, also, of the side digits would lead us to form the opinion that this animal walked on three toes.

The majority of palæontologists, I believe, consider that the Hipparion used only one toe of each foot in progression. Against this opinion I may advance the fact, not very generally known, that some horses, especially high-caste Arabs, have such a naturally large amount of "play" in the fetlock and pastern joints of the fore legs, that during the fast gallop,

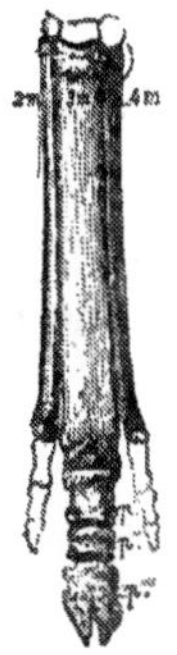

FIG. 194.—(*After Gaudry.*) FORE FOOT OF PALOPLOTHERIUM (⅓rd real length).

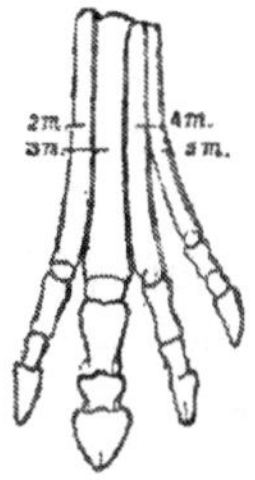

FIG. 195.—(*After Gaudry.*) LEFT FRONT FOOT OF OROHIPPUS AGILIS (full size).

the fetlock pad (*see* p. 221) is liable to come down on the ground and get bruised. The ergot, which is in the centre of this pad, is evidently, as pointed out by Sir William Flower, the rudiment of a structure (like the pad of a dog's or cat's foot) that acted as a buffer to the fetlock at the time when the horse was a digitigrade animal, namely, one which walks *on* its digits, and not as the horse now does in unguligrade fashion, only on their tips. In all horses which have free action, the fetlock descends a good deal in the gallop (*see* Fig. 98). Hence, I am inclined to think, that the Hipparion, whose immediate ancestors were digitigrade animals, used the second and fourth digits, at least of its fore feet, to some extent at fast paces; if not in slow movement.

Still earlier, we find in the middle Eocene age, the Paloplotherium, which resembled the Anchitherium and Hipparion in its feet (*see* Fig. 194); and the horse tribe, generally, in its teeth.* Its principal digit was much weaker than that of its successors. The foot shown in Fig. 194 is that of a small variety of Paloplotherium. Among the Eocene deposits in America is found the *Orohippus agilis* † (Fig. 195), which, as the name given to it by Professor Marsh implies, may be taken as the limit to which we can fairly trace the horse in his character of a one-toed animal. Going further back in the Eocene period, we meet with the Hyracotherium (Fig. 196), which had three toes on its hind feet and four toes on its front feet, and which had hoofs on all of them. It was about 15 inches high, and was closely akin to the tapir, which has maintained its peculiarities of conformation, up to the present day, almost without change, during that vast period of time. Although the Hyracotherium had four toes on its front feet, it may be considered

* The teeth of the Paloplotherium have a plentiful supply of *crusta petrosa* (cement), and thus resemble those of the horse. I may explain that the cement is the outer layer of the teeth. In youth, it forms a thin covering to the enamel on the outside; and a thick one in the depressions which all the teeth, with the exception of the tushes, have on their crowns The cement becomes quickly stained by the action of the food and gives the "mark" in the teeth its characteristic dark appearance. The front teeth of the horse become white with age from the wearing away of the cement.

† Ὅρος, limit; ἵππος, horse.

to have been an odd-toed animal; for one of these digits was off the ground, and was consequently functionless.

The foot of the rhinoceros (*see* Fig. 197) shows a marked tendency to become one-toed. Being three-toed on its fore, as well as on its hind feet, it belongs to a less ancient type than the tapir. The Acerotherium (*see* Fig. 198) was a probable ancestor of the rhinoceros, if not of the horse. The *Brontotherium*, which has been found in the Miocene of

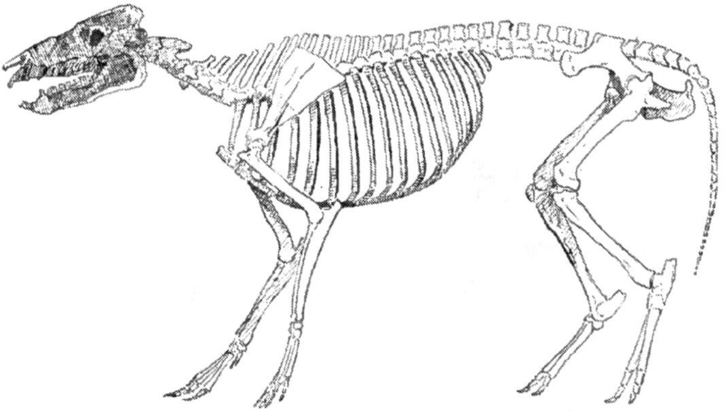

FIG. 196.—HYRACOTHERIUM (1/8th real height).

Colorado, had, similar to the tapir, four digits on its front feet; and three on its hind ones (*see* Figs. 199 and 200).

Proceeding still further down in our search, we find in the early Eocene, the *Phenacodus primævus*, which is supposed to have been the ancestor, or one of the very early ancestors, of all hoofed animals. Fig. 201 shows how it appears in a fossil condition. It was about twenty-one inches high. From the form of the third phalanx of its digits, we may conclude that each of them carried a hoof. We may also see that each of its digits had three phalanges. As I am considering the genealogy only of hoof-bearing animals, I shall not go fur-

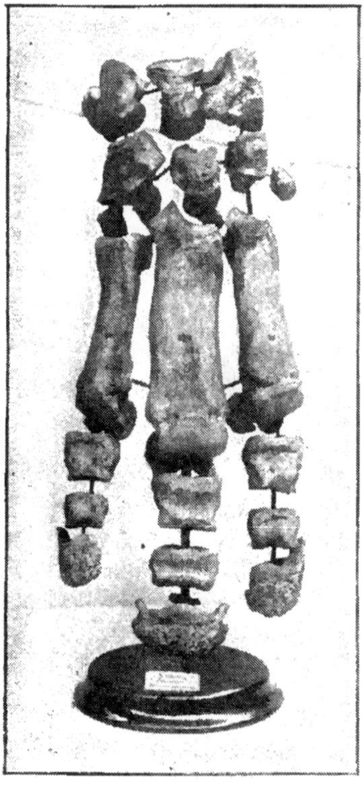

FIG. 197.—FORE FOOT OF RHINOCEROS ($\frac{1}{4}$th real length).

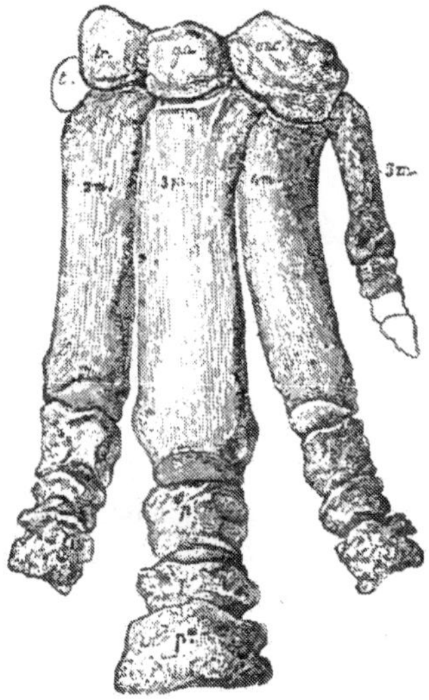

FIG. 198.—(*After Gaudry.*) LEFT FRONT FOOT OF ACEROTHERIUM TETRADACTYLUM ($\frac{1}{4}$th real length).

ther back than the Phenacodus. Having now arrived at an animal with five toes, I may point out that in no case do the digits of any normal mammal (an animal which suckles its young) exceed that number. The digits, I may remark, are numbered from within, outwards. Thus, the thumb on our hand is termed the first digit; the little finger, the fifth digit. Among the ancestors of the horse, the first digit was the first to disappear; and after it, the fifth digit. In the Hyracotherium, the first digit has gone from all four feet. The fifth has vanished from the hind ones, and has begun the process

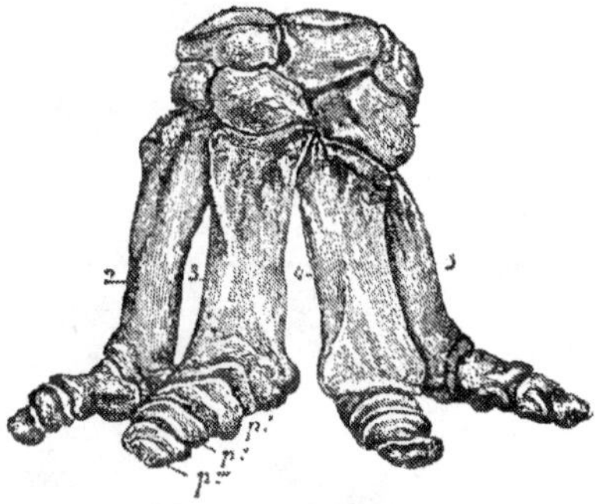

FIG. 199.—(*After Gaudry.*) LEFT FRONT FOOT OF BRONTOTHERIUM ($\frac{1}{7}$th real length).

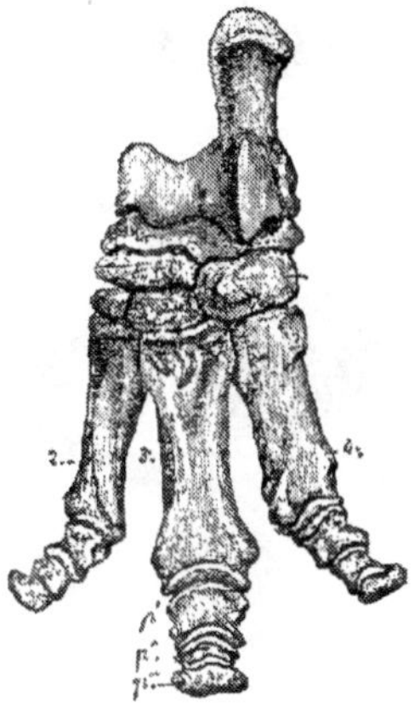

FIG. 200.—(*After Gaudry.*) LEFT HIND FOOT OF BRONTOTHERIUM ($\frac{1}{7}$th real length).

of doing so, in the front feet. The Orohippus has also lost its fifth digit. The Anchitherium (like the rhinoceros) appears as a true three-toed mammal; having lost its first and fifth digits. In the *Hipparion gracile*, the second and fourth digits have begun to disappear; and have done so, completely in the horse of the present day. From the foregoing considerations, its ancestors are classed among odd-toed animals (*Perissodactyla*). We must further observe that, from the Phenacodus to the horse as we now know him, the third digit has remained the principal one of both fore and hind limbs. It is instructive to note that the phalanges and digits of the hind limb have a greater tendency to decrease in number than those of the fore leg. As the fore foot is nearer to the head than the hind foot, its functions are more various,

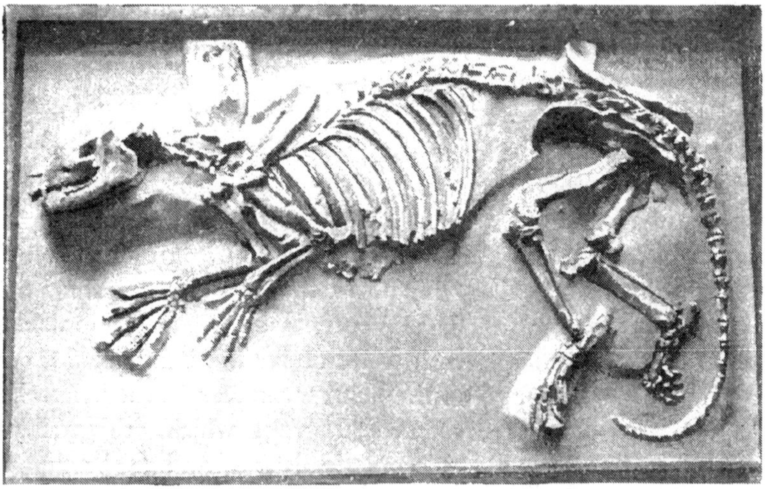

FIG. 201.—PHENACODUS PRIMÆVUS ($\frac{1}{12}$th real length).

and its digits are less liable to become affected by disuse. In man, we find that the toes are smaller than the fingers; and that, in many cases, the little toe has lost its third phalanx; although the little finger still retains that bone. In the case of the reappearance of the second and fourth (as in Fig. 184) digits in the horse, the fore legs are far more frequently supplemented in this way, than the hind ones.

Immediate Ancestors of the Horse.—The type of horse immediately preceding the present one, is a subject which I approach with a great deal of diffidence; as I have not had an opportunity of studying it carefully, much as I would have wished to have done so. Darwin, very justly as it seems to me, points to the probability that all the existing races of horses have descended from "a single dun-coloured, more or less striped primitive stock, to which our horses occasionally revert." This primitive stock, I would conjecture, closely resembled the quagga or Burchell's zebra. The not uncommon appearance in horses of dark stripes on the fore-arms, and a dark stripe along the back and across the shoulders, seems to be cases of reversion to the likeness of an ancestor, especially as these markings, when they do occur, show much clearer in early youth than when the animal grows older. Not alone in this respect does the horse take on the markings of the ass; but his coat not infrequently assumes a near approach to the colour of the ass, with white under the belly, insides of the legs, etc. The ass, on the contrary, never clothes himself in the bays, chestnuts, roans and greys which are greatly affected by the horse; and is practically free from the irregular markings so freely indulged in by his relative. "Stars," "blazes," "reaches," "snips," "stockings," and coats, piebald and skewbald, can hardly be the unbiassed result of domestication; for the ass appears to have been the companion of man even longer than the horse, and he shows little or no tendency to adopt such motley wear. The apparently functionless false nostril of the horse is of lesser depth than that of the ass, and may be expected to disappear in the course of ages. I would therefore infer that the immediate ancestor of the horse, as we know him, was a more or less striped ass. From the drawings made on pieces of bone and horn by the cave men of Southern France, it would seem that the horse of Western Europe, say, ten thousand years ago, was a small, rough, thick-set animal, rather like the Mongolian pony. The instinct this and other horses have of scraping away with their fore feet, snow when it covers the ground, so as to get at the underlying grass, would, as Darwin suggests, point to the probability that our horses originally came from a country in which there were severe winters. It would be interesting to know if this instinct, which no doubt is possessed by the kiang, is retained by the onager, the Abyssinian wild ass, and the eastern horse. The horses of the present day may be divided into two, more or less, distinct types; the one, thick-set and "coarse," like the Mongolian pony; the other of comparatively slight build and smart appearance, like the Arab or Indian pony (*see* Pl. 34). I would refer the aboriginal horses of Western Europe and the various cart strains to the first division. Our saddle horses and trappers are, as we all know, a judicious blend of English and Eastern blood. The differences which exist among the various breeds of horses in the world, are evidently due to the effects of climate, selection, and stable management.

From the remarks made on page 306, with respect to the presence of thickened skin in the horse and ass, we might conclude that these two animals are descended from a thick-skinned ancestor, akin perhaps to the rhinoceros, whose foot (*see* Fig. 197) shows a marked tendency to become one-toed. It is almost needless to say that the rifle of the sportsman will, in the near future, put a summary stop to this process of evolution in the case of this horned pachyderm. The fact of the ass possessing a larger amount of thick skin than the horse, also seems to prove that his type is the more ancient one of the two. Judging by the general conformation, especially as regards the comparative size of head, Burchell's zebra appears to be the nearest akin, among asses, to the horse; and the mountain zebra, the furthest removed. The recent extinct quagga more closely resembled the horse, than does Burchell's zebra.

Conditions which Modified the Form of the Horse.—The conditions which have produced an animal (the horse) with a single toe to each of its feet, from ancestors with five toes, have been, apparently, those of soil, combined with a tendency to place the weight of the limb more on one particular digit than on any other digit. The fact that the feet of the tapir have undergone, practically, no modification for several millions of years, proves that his conditions of life at the present day are nearly the same as they were when the ancestors of the horse, like those of the tapir, had four hoofs on each front foot, and three on each hind one. Feet like these, which, under the influence of pressure, had the faculty of spreading out, were admirably suited for going through soft ground similar to that over which the tapir still roams in a wild state; for the increase of the area of support thus offered by the feet, was a direct help in preventing the animal from sinking too deeply in the mud over which he travelled. It is evident that this lateral play of the digits entailed loss of speed for progression on hard ground, on account of expenditure of muscular power required to restore them to their normal state, and from increased friction. The less lateral play the digits would have, the faster would the animal be able to travel over hard ground. For instance, the wild pig, whose feet (*see* Fig. 185) spread out a good deal more than those of the Steinbok (*see* Fig. 202), is much better through "dirt" (to use a racing and hunting expression) than this speedy South African antelope; but is far inferior to him in a gallop over hard ground. We may, therefore, infer

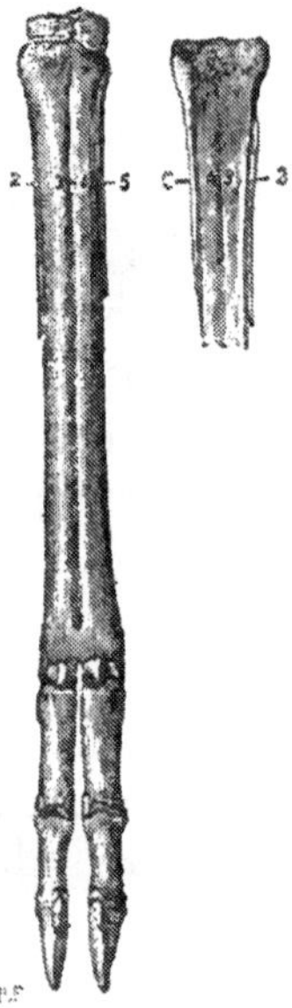

FIG. 202.—(*After Gaudry.*) FOOT OF STEINBOK.

that the decrease in the number of the digits of the horse's foot has been due to residence, during thousands, if not millions, of generations on dry soil. With the loss of lateral play in the foot, there has been a consequent increased of spee, which was necessary for protection against the attacks of carnivorous animals, like the cheetah (Pl. 2), lynx (Pl. 17), and wolf, whose conformation was unsuited for predatory operations in the morasses which had afforded an asylum for ancestors of the horse.

Points of Speed and Strength in the Fossil Horse. —At the outset of this investigation, I am met with the pertinent question: what is a horse? My natural reply to this will be that the horse is an animal which has only one toe to each of its legs. I might also add, for the benefit of those of my readers who are interested in comparative anatomy, that his teeth are plentifully supplied with *crusta petrosa* (*see* p. 329); and that the pulley-like processes on his astragalus are directed forward and outward (*see* p. 70). The fact of unity of digit—a peculiarity which distinguishes the horse from all other mammals—will probably suffice for ordinary inquirers. Taking this test, we cannot with propriety apply the term horse to animals further back in equine descent than the Anchitherium. The Phenacodus resembles a carnivorous animal (a Dandy Dinmont or otter hound) more than he does one of the horse tribe. His great length of humerus must have given him considerable power in raising the forehand by the play of the shoulder and elbow joints, the diminution of which play is compensated for in the horse by the action of the fetlock joint. His hocks and knees, like those of the dog and cat, were "well let down." He might have had a fair "turn of speed" for a short distance; but he was too long in the body to have been a stayer. There is no doubt that the ancestors of the horse were of very slow pace at the time when they were identical with, or nearly akin to the Paloplotherium and the Hyracotherium, animals which were not far removed from the rhinoceros and tapir. With the tendency to the gradual adoption of the one-toed method of progression, there was an evident increase of speed. By examining Figs. 187 to 193, we may see that the length of the bones below the fetlock, compared to that of the cannon-bone, was greater in the Hipparion than in the Anchitherium ; and in the horse, than

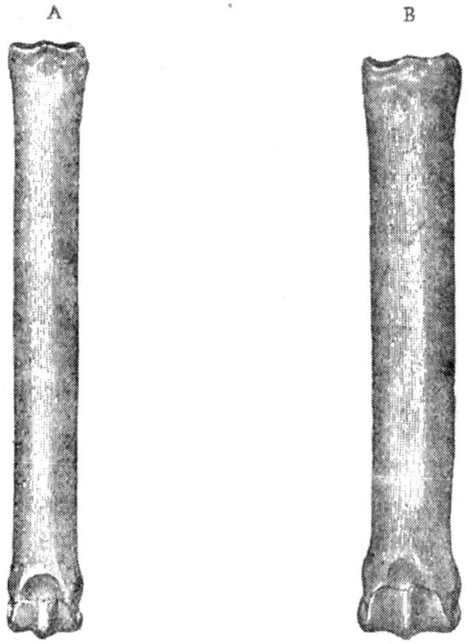

FIG. 203.—(*After Gaudry.*) CANNON-BONES OF TWO DIFFERENT KINDS OF HIPPARION.

in the Hipparion : length of pastern, as we have seen on p. 224, being directly conducive to speed. Taking the converse of this argument, which we may fairly do from our present knowledge of palæontology, we may assume that this increase in the comparative length of the bones below the fetlock, is a sound proof that this kind of conformation is conducive to speed.

Although, as regards the number of toes, the horse's foot is better suited than that of any other animal for the development of a high rate of speed; the fact remains that the four-toed cheetah (*see* Pl. 2), hare, wild dog, and wolf, and the two-toed black buck (*see* Pl. 1) are comparatively, for their size, if not actually, faster than any wild horse or ass. Here we have an instance of the complex nature of physical faculties, which, like speed, are not made up of one component, but of many. In the cat, dog and hare, the muscles of progression are of much greater comparative length than those of the horse; as we may judge by the way the hocks and knees are "let down." Although these joints in the antelope are "high off the ground," the extreme length of his limbs compensates him for this disadvantage, as well as that of having two toes on each foot. In the case of the ancestors of this fleet ruminant, the tendency to place weight both on the third and fourth toe was so evenly distributed on these two digits, that the balance between them has remained practically undisturbed for ages, and under modifying conditions which have nearly doubled the comparative length of the limbs.

Like the horses of the present day, the members of the *Hipparion gracile* tribe differed a good deal among each other as regards conformation, as we may see by the respective cannon-bones shown in A and B of Fig. 203.

The Horse of the Future.—The bones of the limbs, as we have seen, are gradually assuming the character of a single column, and are increasing the rigidity of their connections between the joints necessary for locomotion. We may observe a tendency to bony union between the splint bones and their cannon-bones, and between the lower row of the small bones of the hock and knee, and their respective metatarsal and metacarpal bones. Thus we find that comparatively harmless forms of "simple" splint and "low" spavin are increasingly common among young horses subjected to civilised conditions. They will, as suggested by Mr. H G. Rogers, gradually lose their morbid character, and will become normal processes of development. Agreeably to this we may note that such splints and spavins are less liable to injuriously affect the usefulness of a thoroughbred, than of, for instance, a Mongolian pony or a South American broncho. As ages roll on, the splint bones will disappear, and *pari passu*, the small bones of the knee and hock which rest on them. The increasing prevalence of "side-bones" among heavy cart-horses seems to justify the idea that the Shires and Clydesdales of the near future will have no lateral cartilages. Among other changes, the bones of the sternum will in time become joined together, and anchylosis will take place between the pelvis and sacrum. The racer will become comparatively longer in the legs and neck, stronger in the loins, rounder in the barrel and better ribbed up than he now is; and the draught animal will become shorter in the limbs, and more massive in muscle. Both will increase in height and docility.

CHAPTER XXXI.

PHOTOGRAPHING HORSES.

PHOTOGRAPHY is a very useful aid for the acquisition of a knowledge of conformation; for it enables us to place on record exact results unobtainable by other means. This is a truth which is too evident to need support by argument.

Photographs are taken of a horse with the object of obtaining a picture, a portrait, a combination of the two, or a likeness of the animal by which his "points" may be best seen and compared, with the greatest exactness, to those of other horses. When a picture is the end in view, the pose will have to be subordinated to artistic requirements. If a portrait, the position should be that which will convey to the spectator the best possible idea of the general look of the animal. This will usually be obtained when his body is in profile, and the head and neck carried in the manner most characteristic of the horse in question. The head may, therefore, be turned a little to one side or to the other, as in Pls. 33 or 62. When, however, the photograph is required as a more or less exact record of the horse's "make and shape," he should be in as nearly perfect profile as practicable; just as if he were posed for the inspection of an intending buyer. Owing to the laws of perspective, a photograph is no more an absolutely correct map of the surface in view, than is a carefully drawn picture.

In order to preserve harmony in the graceful curves of the upper line of the body, the horse, to look his best, should have his ears pricked forward, his head carried high, and, if possible, he should not have his tail tucked in between his legs. When standing still, he will look to most advantage when the fore leg of the observer's side is more advanced than the other, and when its hind leg is more drawn back than the other hind leg (*see* Pls. 33 and 35). Unless the background be a specially prepared one, the horse should be well away from it, and it should be out of focus, so that he may stand out in bold relief. (Compare Frontispiece and Plate 62, with Plates 33 and 38.) As a rule, the animal, even when he is a grey or white, should be placed, more or less, against the sky. If possible, the horse should not be put, as is frequently done, close against a building, the lines of which would prevent the eye from following the contours of the animal. I find that horses look more animated and hold themselves better, away from their stables, than near them; and especially when they are in an open plain. My readers can draw their own examples from the photographs given in this book

It is absolutely immaterial whether the camera used is on a fixed stand or is held in the hand, so long as the results are satisfactory. For "taking" horses standing still, it is evident that it would be best, were the plan practicable, to photograph the animal in diffused sunlight, as might be obtained by using a roof of ground glass. The difficulty here would be the attainment of sufficiently long exposure while the animal remained in a suitable position. Although

I generally try to "take" animals with full sunlight coming, if possible, from behind my back; I fully understand that I would do better, were I to wait for the light to become diffused by the intervention, for instance, of a translucent cloud. But being a busy man, I am obliged to utilise the opportunities I get. The distance at which I like to photograph horses standing still, is from 7 to 10 yards; and horses in motion, from 10 to 25 yards. I use a quarter-plate twin-lens hand camera, which can be focussed up to the last moment, and which was devised for me by Messrs. Newman and Guardia. Its full aperture is one inch in diameter; its equivalent focus is about $6\frac{1}{2}$ inches; and it has two shutters: one working at $\frac{1}{500}$ second, placed between the lenses; the other, at from 1 second to $\frac{1}{50}$ second, behind them. I may explain that, up to the present, no shutter has been made which can be regulated with approximate accuracy, between these extreme limits, with the aperture I have mentioned. When time and light permit, I stop the lens down to from $\frac{f}{8}$ to $\frac{f}{12}$ When taking rapidly moving objects, I find it best to direct the lens, by means of the finder, on some point at which I wish to make the exposure, and, while holding the camera as steady as I can, I continue looking at the moving object until I think it is in right position, and I then press the release. In such cases, one has to receive every possible help from light, plate, developer, and, if need be, intensifier. In temperate climates, the best light for very short exposures will usually be obtained about mid-day; in the tropics, some time from eight to ten in the morning, or from two to four in the afternoon, so as to avoid getting the light from too nearly a vertical direction.

CHAPTER XXXII.

PROPORTIONS OF THE HORSE.

BOURGELAT, Merche, Duhousset, Goubaux, Barrier, and other writers on Conformation have laid down certain proportions for an ideal horse, which, unfortunately, does not exist as a distinctive type. Failing to draw sufficient attention to the great difference of shape between horses of speed and those of strength; the comparisons which they have instituted between the dimensions of the limbs and those of the head and body, are wholly arbitrary. I need hardly remind my readers that, speaking generally, although the respective proportions of the head and body are practically the same in all classes of horses, the length of the neck and limbs varies according to the work for which the muscles of these parts are best suited. Hence, the only proportions of the horse, which are fixed within narrow limits, are those of the head and body. We may sum up the most evident ones as follows:—

Proportions Common to all Classes of Horses.

The Measurements here given have Reference to Fig. 204.

(1) Length of body (*a b*) = $2\frac{1}{2}$ to $2\frac{2}{3}$ times length of head (*k l*).
(2) Height at withers (*c d*) = height at croup (*f g*).
(3) Length of head (*k l*) = depth of body at lowest part of back (*h i*).

(4) Length of head = distance of "swell" of muscle at posterior angle of shoulder-blade, to point of hip (*s t*).

(5) Distance (*k p*) of top of head to corner of mouth = distance from point of hip to point of buttock (*t u*).

(6) Width of head (*m n*) = $\frac{1}{2}$ length of head (*k l*).

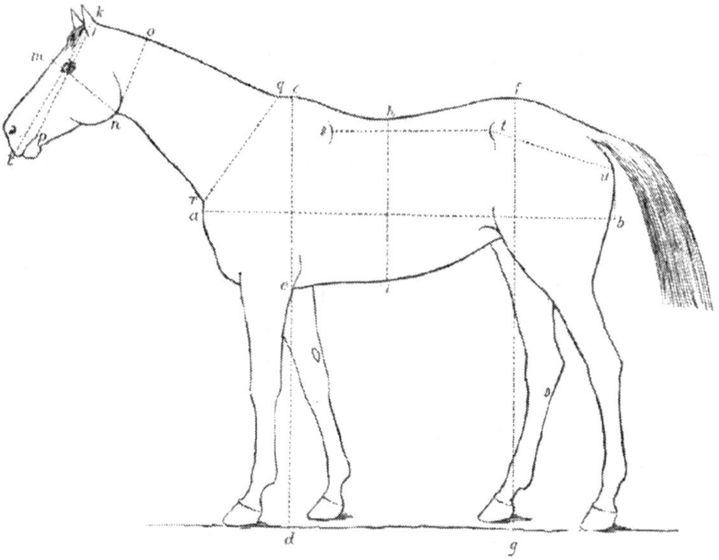

FIG. 204.—PROPORTIONS OF HORSE.
(*Drawn from a photograph.*)

That careful observer, Colonel Duhousset, states that :—

(7) Length of head = distance of point of shoulder to top of withers.

As this proportion must necessarily vary according to the length and position of the shoulder-blade and humerus, I refrain from applying it to all classes.

The following proportions are approximately correct for all horses, except those of the heavy cart type, whose necks are particularly massive (*see* Pl. 19) :—

(8) Width of head (*m n*) = width of upper part of neck (*n o*).
(9) Distance (*k p*) of top of head to corner of mouth = thickness of base of neck (*q r*).

Any attempt—as has frequently been made—to formulate proportions of length between the limbs and body of what might be called an "ordinary horse," would be merely begging the question by constructing an ideal animal to conform to one's own theories ; instead of, as one ought to do, supporting one's hypotheses on the firm basis of fact. As the comparative length of limb varies according to the class of horse ; we find (*see* Chapter XV.), taking the two extreme types, that the legs of the heavy cart-horse are far shorter than those of the racer (compare Pl. 19 with Frontispiece). Thus, the length of the body and its depth at the withers in the former, are, respectively, several inches more than the height, and the distance of the brisket from the ground. The racer, on the contrary, is inclined to be shorter than he is high, and measures much less from the withers to brisket than from brisket to ground.

As the result of my own observations I may add the following proportions for thoroughbreds only :—

(10) Height at withers (*c d*) = length of body (*a b*), or a little (say, up to 4 inches) more.
(11) Depth at withers (*c e*) = distance of "girth place" to lower part of fetlock in a three-year-old, or to centre of pastern in an "aged" horse.

Beyond repeating (*see* p. 160) that the muscles of the neck should be proportionate in length to those of the limbs, I can offer no useful hint as regards the comparative length of the neck; for the only measurement which can be readily taken of it, namely, that from the withers to the top of the head, greatly alters in length, on account of the elasticity of the connecting ligament (*see* p. 34), according to the position in which the head is held. We must here remember that this suspensory ligament of the head and neck is immediately underneath the crest, and that the vertebræ of the neck (*see* FIG. 3) does not follow this line.

CHAPTER XXXIII.

THE PAINTER'S HORSE.

HORSES have been treated by painters, and also by sculptors, in a very unhandsome way, and especially by English so-

FIG. 205.—(*Copied by Duhousset.*) LOUIS XV.

called artists, who continue to perpetuate the conventional or stencil-plate animal in a style long since forsaken by continental draughtsmen. There are, of course, several brilliant exceptions. The most usual faults of conformation to be seen in horse pictures, are absurdly small heads and extravagantly long hind-quarters, from point of hip to point of buttock. We see them well shown in Figs. 205 and 206. The former is a sketch of an equestrian portrait, by the French

FIG. 206.—HORSE BY ALKEN.

artist Parrocel, of Louis XV. in his youth. The latter is from *Beauties and Defects in the Figure of the Horse*, by H. Alken, who published it seventy years ago, and who described the subject of his work as follows: "The animal from which this drawing was made, is accounted one of the finest figures in England." He must have had some misgivings about the dimensions of the head and neck; for he takes care to add that: "A small head and neck in a horse are considered a great beauty; and in the original of this drawing, I think they are the least I ever saw in proportion to the body." All the saddle-horses of some English artists, among whom was that unrivalled caricaturist, Mr. John

FIG. 207.—HORSE AND RIDER IN THE PARTHENON.

Leech, have a remarkably "good place for the collar" (*see* p. 212) on their shoulders. "The old masters" drew horses very incorrectly; and yet we find in the bas-reliefs of the Parthenon done over two thousand years ago, horses depicted with a near approach to truth both in form and action (*see* Fig 207). The greatest of all horse painters, Meissonier, drew horses with marvellous correctness, as we may see in his "Napoléon 1er" (Fig. 208), and in "1814" (Fig. 209).

The stencil-plate man generally represents the walk by the action of the trot. Even the great and careful painter

FIG. 208.—MEISSONIER'S NAPOLÉON 1er.

Géricault sinned in this respect, as we may notice in the mounted horse of the pair shown in Fig. 210. The Arab horse, which forms the second drawing in this figure, is represented at the amble. Géricault evidently meant them to be at the walk, at which corrected pace Colonel Duhousset (*see* his *Le Cheval*) has redrawn these two animals unmounted. He has, however, given somewhat exaggerated action to the near hind leg of his first horse. A well-known English artist drew a picture of Napoleon's charger, Marengo (*see* Fig. 211), balancing himself on a fore and hind leg of the

FIG. 209.—MEISSONIER'S "1814."

same side! Possibly he followed the bad (in this instance) example of Géricault (*see* Fig. 210). Artists of the present time have no excuse for similar lapses into error; for they have the results of the researches of Marey, Muybridge, Anschütz and other photographers to guide them. Figs.

54, 47, 52, 88, Meissonier's "1814," and Pl. 69, prove that the walk, trot, amble, canter, and leap, can be drawn artistically and truthfully at the same time. A combination of these two conditions is harder to find in the canter, than in the other movements just mentioned, and still more so in the gallop. The difficulty, here, lies in the nature of the action rather than in the speed of the pace; for the eye can, for instance, follow the order in which the limbs work, far more easily in the

FIG. 210.—HORSES BY GÉRICAULT CORRECTED BY DUHOUSSET.

fastest trot or amble than in the slowest walk. Here we come to the noteworthy truth that the eye will seldom recognise as true in Art, what it has not actually seen in Nature. The distance at which we usually look at the movements of a horse's legs in the canter or gallop is usually too close to permit us to take in all four together at the same moment. Hence, when critically regarding the action in either of these two paces, we generally content ourselves with studying that of the fore pair, and, subsequently, that of the hind pair; or *vice versa.* In such a case, therefore, whichever pair be focussed sharply on the retinæ of our eyes, the other pair will of necessity be blurred. Consequently, if both pairs of limbs be depicted sharply in the canter or gallop, the chances are that the idea of motion will not be conveyed to the spectator. For this reason, the painter who is trying to give the "feeling" of motion to a horse he is drawing at either of these paces,

FIG. 211.—NAPOLEON'S CHARGER, MARENGO (*After Mr. James Ward, R.A.*).

will do well to blur (by means of dust, snow, etc.) or to hide (by a bush or grass, for instance) one pair, if he desires to make the other pair sharp. I can see no error of technique in giving indistinctness of outline to the limbs themselves. A painter who exhibited, in the Royal Academy or Salon, a picture representing a horse running away with a carriage, would most probably incur no rebuke from the art critics for blurring all the spokes of the wheels, and drawing all the legs and feet of the animal sharp. And yet those of us who know anything of the laws of motion, must be aware that, in such a case, any of the horse's feet which are going forward, must be passing far faster through space, than the more or less perpendicular spokes which are revolving through the lower half of their circle!

At paces in which there is a moment of suspension, the idea of motion, will, as a rule, be best conveyed by drawing the horse with his feet off the ground. On account of violating this principle, old time painters, who represented the horse in the gallop with both hind feet on the ground, failed to give the idea of movement; although, as it happened, the attitude they adopted was not far from true (*see* Fig. 93). The later method of showing the racer at full speed, suspended in the air, with his fore legs stretched out in front and his hind limbs extended to the rear, was absolutely incorrect, as well as utterly impossible; and yet it conveyed the feeling of motion better than that practised by the earlier horse painters. It is manifest that a pictorial attitude which we *know* to be incorrect, will look unnatural to us. Consequently, the more general knowledge becomes, the more difficult will it be for a painter who tries to draw horses in motion, to satisfy the artistic requirements of his public. Hence, pictures of galloping horses appearing to claw the ground, as the fore feet come down with the knees and fetlocks well bent, or committing equally absurd eccentricities, will, to any one who has studied the paces of the horse, look simply ridiculous, no matter how meritorious the painting may be in other respects. M. Barroil (*L'Art Équestre*) justly remarks that the fact that the domain of the painter is what one sees and not what really takes place, is no proof that one sees attitudes which do not exist. "It is, however, by virtue of this theory, set up as an axiom, that many artists represent, in their works, horses in attitudes which they have never assumed, and which they could not assume."

One form of conventional leap appears to have been taken from Alken's drawing (*see* Fig. 212). It is neither

FIG. 212.—HORSE LEAPING, BY ALKEN.

correct nor does it give, at least to a horseman, the idea of what is intended to be represented. A horse which is in the act of landing, is usually represented, by the stencil-plate man, with its fore feet so far to the front, that, when they will come to the ground, it could not possibly raise its forehand,

and a fall would be the inevitable result. The "tail-piece," on this page, gives a correct and far more artistic rendering of the action at this moment. A method of recent date is to give the animal, just before landing, the appearance of being afraid to face his bit (*see* p. 138). Consequently, although the position may be true, it will look constrained and awkward to the eye of a 'cross country expert, which is a rôle that such artists are evidently unqualified to assume. I need hardly say that the more an artist knows, the better will he paint. I venture to think that the requirements of truth and artistic feeling are fairly well fulfilled in Plate 69, which I took at the Dublin Horse Show in 1892, and for permission to do which I have to thank the Committee of the Royal Dublin Society.

(*Photograph by M. H. Hayes.*)
THE WATER JUMP AT SANDOWN PARK.

PHOTO. BY M. H. HAYES

TO FACE LAST PAGE

PLATE 69—WALL-JUMPING AT DUBLIN HORSE SHOW, 1892.

INDEX.

BIBLIOGRAPHY.

The following are the chief books which have been written on the Conformation of the Horse, and on Equine Locomotion :—

Alix, Eugène.—*Le Cheval*, 1886.
Barroil, Étienne.—*L'Art Équestre*, 1st Part, 1887.
Borelli.—*De Motu Animalium*, 1680.
Bourgelat.—*De la Conformation Extérieur du Cheval*, 1808.
Carson, J. C. L.—*The Form of the Horse*, 1859.
Duhousset, Colonel.—*Le Cheval*, 1881.
Fearnley, W.—*Lessons in Horse Judging*, 1879.
Gayot, Eugène.—*Achat du Cheval*, 1862.
Goubaux et Barrier, MM.—*L'Extérieur du Cheval*, 2nd ed., 1890.
Gunther's.—*Beurtheilungslehre des Pferdes*, 1889.
Hofman, L.—*Das Exterieur des Pferdes*, 1887.
Lecoq, F.—*Extérieur du Cheval*, 1843.
Magne, J. H.—*Choix du Cheval*, 1864.
Marey, Professor.—*La Machine Animale*, 1873.
Merche.—*Nouveau traité des formes extérieurs du Cheval*, 1868.
Montigny, Comte de.—*Comment il faut choisir un Cheval*, 1885.
Morris, Général.—*Essai sur l'Extérieur du Cheval.*
Müller.—*Lehre vom Exterieur des Pferdes*, 1884.
Muybridge, E.—*Animal Locomotion*, 1887.
Percivall, W.—*Lectures on the Form and Action of the Horse*, 1850.
Richard, du Cantal.—*Étude du Cheval.*
Roloff.—*Beurtheilungslehre des Pferdes*, 1870.

Besides the books just enumerated, many useful remarks on the form and movements of the horse may be found in the writings of Henri Bouley, "Stonehenge," Youatt, Lupton, Lenoble du Theil, Barroil, Raabe, Colin, and Ellenberger; in chapters on the Exterior of the Horse, in Schwarznecker's *Pferdesucht*, 1879; and in the *Handbuch der Pferdekunde*, by Born and Möller, 3rd ed., 1890.

LONDON:
PRINTED BY WILLIAM CLOWES AND SONS, LIMITED,
STAMFORD STREET AND CHARING CROSS.

No. 56. *May*, 1893.

A Select Catalogue of Works, chiefly Illustrated, published by W. THACKER & CO., 87 Newgate Street, London, and THACKER, SPINK & CO., Calcutta.

TO BE OBTAINED ALSO OF

THACKER & CO., Limited, Bombay.

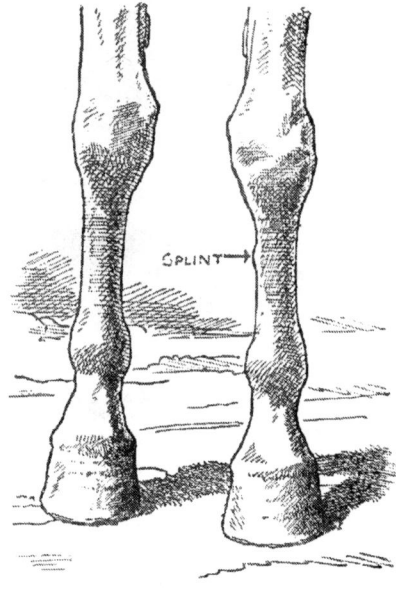

PRESS NOTICES OF CAPT. HAYES'

VETERINARY NOTES FOR HORSE-OWNERS.

Fourth Edition, Crown 8vo. *12s. 6d.*

"Captain Hayes' work is a valuable addition to our stable literature; and the illustrations, tolerably numerous, are excellent beyond the reach of criticism."—*Saturday Review.*

"The description of symptoms and proper methods of treatment in sickness render the book a necessary guide for horseowners, especially those who are far removed from immediate professional assistance."—*The Times.*

"Of the many popular veterinary books which have come under our notice, this is certainly one of the most scientific and reliable. If some painstaking student would give us works of equal merit to this on the diseases of the other domestic animals, we should possess a very complete veterinary library in a very small compass."—*Field.*

"Simplicity is one of the most commendable features in the book. What Captain Hayes has to say he says in plain terms, and the book is a very useful one for everybody who is concerned with horses."—*Illustrated Sporting and Dramatic News.*

"The usefulness of the manual is testified to by its popularity, and each edition has given evidence of increasing care on the part of the author to render it more complete and trustworthy as a book of reference for amateurs."—*The Lancet*

"A volume replete with most interesting information, couched in the simplest terms possible."—*The County Gentleman.*

"The book leaves nothing to be desired on the score of lucidity and comprehensiveness."—*Veterinary Journal.*

Third Edition. Revised and Enlarged. Imperial 16mo. 10s. 6d.

RIDING:

ON THE FLAT AND ACROSS COUNTRY.

A GUIDE TO PRACTICAL HORSEMANSHIP. BY CAPT. M. H. HAYES.

Eighty Illustrations by Oswald Brown, Sturgess and Stanley Berkeley.

PRESS NOTICES OF CAPT. HAYES'

RIDING:

ON THE FLAT AND ACROSS COUNTRY.

(Reduced Size.)

"Captain Hayes' hints and instructions are useful aids, even to experienced riders, while for those less accustomed to the saddle, his instructions are simply invaluable."—*The Times.*

"To possess knowledge and to succeed in imparting it, are two different things; but Captain Hayes is not only a master of his subject, but he knows how to aid others in gaining such a mastery as may be obtained by the study of a book."—*The Standard.*

"We are not in the least surprised that a third edition of this useful and eminently practical book should be called for. On former occasions we were able to speak of it in terms of commendation, and this edition is worthy of equal praise."—*The Field.*

"An eminently practical teacher, whose theories are the outcome of experience, learned not in the study, but on the road, in the hunting field, and on the racecourse."—*Baily's Magazine.*

"We heartily commend it to our readers."—*Sporting Times.*

"The book is one that no man who has ever sat in a saddle can fail to read with interest."—*Illustrated Sporting and Dramatic News.*

"Is as practical as Captain Horace Hayes' 'Veterinary Notes' and 'Guide to Horse Management in India.' Greater praise than this it is impossible to give."—*The Graphic.*

PRESS NOTICES—*Continued.*

"We have seldom come across a brighter book than 'The Horsewoman.'"—*The Athenæum.*

"A more thorough horsewoman than Mrs. Hayes probably does not exist."—*Land and Water.*

"A most useful and practical book in side-saddle riding, which may be read with real interest by all lady riders."—*The Queen.*

"Mrs. Hayes is perhaps the best authority in these countries on everything connected with horsemanship for ladies, and her chapters deal with every possible view of the subject. The style is plain and straightforward without being too technical, and can be readily understood by an intelligent reader. A number of graphic illustrations add considerably to the clearness of the instructions."—*Freeman's Journal* (Dublin).

"The work is the outcome of experiences, aptitudes, and opportunities wholly exceptional."—*Scotsman.*

"J'ai lu ou parcouru bien des traités d'équitation usuelle ou savante; jamais encore je n'avais trouvé un exposé aussi clair, aussi simple, aussi vécu que celui où Mme. Hayes résume les principes dont une pratique assidue lui a permis d'apprécier la valeur. Ce très remarquable manuel d'équitation féminine est bien, comme la désiré son auteur, à la portée de tous et il est à souhaiter qu'il trouve en France l'accueil et le succès qu'il a rencontrés dès sa publication auprès des horsewomen anglaises."—*Le Sport* (Paris).

"With a very strong recommendation of this book as far and away the best guide to side-saddle riding that we have seen."—*Saturday Review.*

BY

CAPT. M. H. HAYES.

ILLUSTRATED HORSE-BREAKING.

Uniform with "Riding," etc. 21s.

ILLUSTRATED HORSE-BREAKING

BY

Capt. M. H. HAYES.

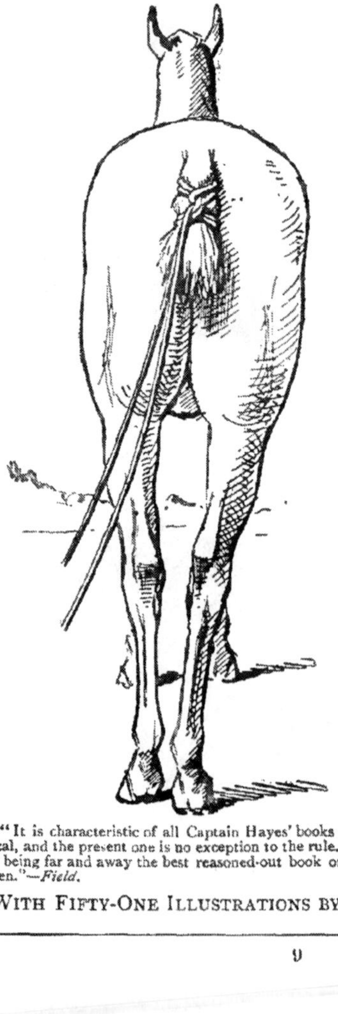

1. Theory of Breaking.
2. Principles of Mounting.
3. Horse Control.
4. Rendering Docile.
5. Giving Good Mouths.
6. Teaching to Jump.
7. Mounting for First Time.
8. Breaking for Ladies' Riding.
9. Breaking to Harness.
10. Faults of Mouth.
11. Nervousness and Impatience of Control.
12. Jibbing.
13. Jumping Faults.
14. Faults in Harness.
15. Aggressiveness.
16. Riding and Driving Newly-broken Horse.
17. Stable Vices.
18. Teaching Circus Tricks.

"The work is eminently practical and readable." — *Veterinary Journal.*

"Clearly explained in simple, practical language, made all the more clear by a set of capital drawings."—*Scotsman.*

"It is characteristic of all Captain Hayes' books on Horses that they are eminently practical, and the present one is no exception to the rule. A work which is entitled to high praise as being far and away the best reasoned-out book on Breaking under a new system we have seen."—*Field.*

WITH FIFTY-ONE ILLUSTRATIONS BY J. H. OSWALD BROWN.

THE POINTS OF THE HORSE.

ORMONDE.

CONTENTS.

Crown 8vo. Uniform with "Veterinary Notes." 8*s.* 6*d.*

SOUNDNESS AND AGE OF HORSES.

WITH ONE HUNDRED AND SEVENTY ILLUSTRATIONS.

A Complete Guide to all those features which require attention when purchasing Horses, distinguishing mere defects from the symptoms of unsoundness; with explicit instructions how to conduct an examination of the various parts.

BY CAPTAIN M. H. HAYES, F.R.C.V.S.

"Captain Hayes is entitled to much credit for the explicit and sensible manner in which he has discussed the many questions—some of them extremely vexed ones—which pertain to soundness and unsoundness in horses."—*Veterinary Journal.*

"Captain Hayes' work is evidently the result of much careful research, and the horseman, as well as the veterinarian, will find in it much that is interesting and instructive."—*Field.*

In Imperial 16mo. 3*s.* 6*d.*

MY LEPER FRIENDS.

AN ACCOUNT OF PERSONAL WORK AMONG LEPERS, AND THEIR DAILY LIFE IN INDIA.

BY MRS. HAYES.

WITH

A CHAPTER ON LEPROSY

BY

Surgeon-Major G. G. MACLAREN, M.D.

ILLUSTRATED BY REPRODUCTIONS OF PHOTOGRAPHS.

"Mrs. Hayes has now published an interesting little book, entitled 'My Leper Friends,' which contains not only an account of her work in Calcutta, but many facts in regard to leprosy in India which deserve to be better known. I feel no hesitation in recommending the book to the attention of my readers."—*Truth.*

"The name of Mrs. Hayes is already familiar to readers of the *Queen.* This lady has been the Miss Marsden of India, for, like the courageous lady who is now traversing the Siberian plains in search of leper hospitals, Mrs. Hayes has devoted her energies with rare unselfishness to the cause of some of the most pitiable sufferers in the world."—*The Queen.*

"This is a book that ought to be widely known."—*Spectator.*

"Mrs. Hayes is a woman of intense and practical sympathy."—*Rock.*

"Mrs. Hayes writes well and vividly, and there is a note of thorough sincerity in all she says that lends an additional charm to the work."—*Home News.*

"Despite the necessarily mournful and repulsive subject of the book, the cheerful and genial spirit in which it is penned, and the native kindliness everywhere visible in its pages, render it refreshing to read."—*Morning Advertiser.*

"An interesting and most heartrending book. To her *Leper Friends* Mrs. Hayes must have been a very angel of light."—*Ladies' Pictorial.*

In Imperial 16mo. Illustrated. 8*s.* 6*d.*

INDIAN RACING REMINISCENCES:

BEING

ENTERTAINING NARRATIVES AND ANECDOTES OF MEN, HORSES, AND SPORT.

Illustrated with Twenty-Two Portraits and a Number of Smaller Engravings.

BY CAPTAIN M. HORACE HAYES.

"The book is full of racy anecdote, and the author writes so kindly of his brother officers and the sporting planters with whom he came into contact, that one cannot help admiring the genial and happy temperament of the author."—*Bell's Life.*

"Captain Hayes shows himself a thorough master of his subject, and has so skilfully interwoven technicalities, history, and anecdote, that the last page comes all too soon."—*Field.*

Fifth Edition. Revised. Crown 8vo. 9*s.*

TRAINING & HORSE MANAGEMENT IN INDIA.

BY CAPTAIN M. HORACE HAYES, F.R.C.V.S.

"No better guide could be placed in the hands of either amateur horseman or veterinary surgeon.'—*The Veterinary Journal.*

"A useful guide in regard to horses anywhere. Concise, practical, and portable." —*Saturday Review.*

In Imperial 16mo. Uniform with "Riding," "Riding for Ladies," "Hindu Mythology." 12*s*. 6*d*.

A NATURAL HISTORY
OF THE
MAMMALIA OF INDIA,
BURMAH AND CEYLON.

BY R. A. STERNDALE, F.R.G.S., F.Z.S., ETC.,

AUTHOR OF "SEONEE," "THE DENIZENS OF THE JUNGLE," "THE AFGHAN KNIFE," ETC.

WITH 170 *ILLUSTRATIONS BY THE AUTHOR AND OTHERS.*

The geographical limits of the present work have been extended to all territories likely to be reached by the sportsman from India. It is copiously illustrated, not only by the author himself, but by careful selections made by him from the works of well-known artists.

"It is the very model of what a popular natural history should be."—*Knowledge.*

"An amusing work with good illustrations."—*Nature.*

"Full of accurate observation, brightly told."—*Saturday Review.*

"The results of a close and sympathetic observation."—*Athenæum.*

"It has the brevity which is the soul of wit, and a delicacy of allusion which charms the literary critic."—*Academy.*

"The notices of each animal are, as a rule, short, though on some of the larger mammals—the lion, tiger, pard, boar, &c.—ample and interesting details are given, including occasional anecdotes of adventure. The book will, no doubt, be specially useful to the sportsman, and, indeed, has been extended so as to include all territories likely to be reached by the sportsman from India. Those who desire to obtain some general information, popularly conveyed, on the subject with which the book deals, will, we believe, find it useful."—*The Times.*

"Has contrived to hit a happy mean between the stiff scientific treatise and the bosh of what may be called anecdotal zoology."—*The Daily News.*

GAME, SHORE, AND WATER BIRDS OF INDIA.

BY

COL. A. LE MESSURIER, R.E.

121

ILLUSTRATIONS.

8vo, 15*s*.

A VADE MECUM FOR THE SPORTSMAN, EMBRACING ALL THE BIRDS AT ALL LIKELY TO BE MET WITH IN A SHOOTING EXCURSION.

"Compact in form, excellent in method and arrangement, and, as far as we have been able to test it, rigidly accurate."—*Knowledge.*

"Will be a source of great delight, as every ornithological detail is given, in conjunction with the most artistic and exquisite drawings."—*Home News.*

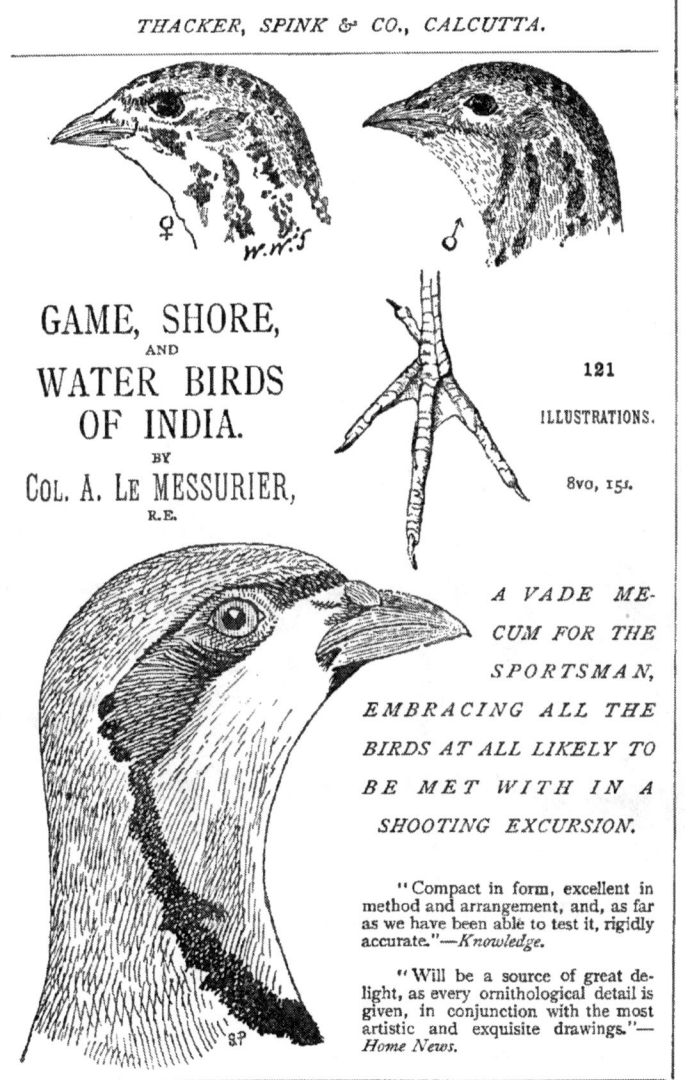

LAYS OF IND. By ALIPH CHEEM.

COMIC, SATIRICAL, AND DESCRIPTIVE

Poems Illustrative of Anglo-Indian Life.

ILLUSTRATED BY THE AUTHOR, LIONEL INGLIS, R. A. STERNDALE, AND OTHERS.

Ninth Edition. Cloth, gilt. 10s. 6d.

"This is a remarkably bright little book. 'Aliph Cheem,' supposed to be the *nom de plume* of an officer in the 18th Hussars, is, after his fashion, an Indian Bon Gaultier. In a few of the poems the jokes, turning on local names and customs, are somewhat esoteric ; but, taken throughout, the verses are characterized by high animal spirits, great cleverness, and most excellent fooling."—*The World.*

"One can readily imagine the merriment created round the camp fire by the recitation of 'The Two Thumpers,' which is irresistibly droll. . . . The edition before us is enlarged, and contains illustrations by the author, in addition to which it is beautifully printed and handsomely got up, all which recommendations are sure to make the name of Aliph Cheem more popular in India than ever."—*Liverpool Mercury.*

"Satire of the most amusing and inoffensive kind, humour the most genuine, and pathos the most touching pervade these 'Lays of Ind.' . . . From Indian friends we have heard of the popularity these 'Lays' have obtained in the land where they were written, and we predict for them a popularity equally great at home."—*Monthly Homœopathic Review.*

Reviews of "Lays of Ind."

"The 'Lays' are not only Anglo-Indian in origin, but out-and-out Anglo-Indian in subject and colour. To one who knows something of life at an Indian 'station' they will be especially amusing. Their exuberant fun at the same time may well attract the attention of the ill-defined individual known as 'the general reader.'"—*Scotsman.*

"To many Anglo-Indians the lively verses of 'Aliph Cheem' must be very well known, while to those who have not yet become acquainted with them we can only say read them on the first opportunity. To those not familiar with Indian life they may be specially commended for the picture which they give of many of its lighter incidents and conditions, and of several of its ordinary personages."—*Bath Chronicle.*

Seventh Edition. In square 32mo. 5s.

DEPARTMENTAL DITTIES AND OTHER VERSES.

Humorous and Character Poems of Anglo-Indian Life.

BY RUDYARD KIPLING.

"They reflect with light gaiety the thoughts and feelings of actual men and women, and are true as well as clever. . . . Mr. Kipling achieves the feat of making Anglo-Indian society flirt and intrigue visibly before our eyes. . . . His book gives hope of a new literary star of no mean magnitude rising in the East." —SIR W. W. HUNTER, *in The Academy.*

"As for that terrible, scathing piece, 'The Story of Uriah,' we know of nothing with which to compare it, and one cannot help the wretched feeling that it is true. . . . 'In Spring Time' is the most pathetic lament of an exile we know in modern poetry."—*Graphic.*

RHYMING LEGENDS OF IND.

By H. K. GRACEY, B.A., C.S. *Crown 8vo, 6s.*

"A series of lively Stories in Verse."—*Times.*

"Are not only amusing but are lively descriptions of scenery and customs in Indian Life . . . Cleverly and humorously told."—*Weekly Times.*

Fourth Edition, Imperial 16mo. 6*s*.

BEHIND THE BUNGALOW.

BY EHA,

AUTHOR OF "TRIBES ON MY FRONTIER."

WITH FIFTY-THREE CLEVER SKETCHES

By the Illustrator of "The Tribes."

As "The Tribes on my Frontier" graphically and humorously described the Animal Surroundings of an Indian Bungalow, the present work describes with much pleasantry the Human Officials thereof, with their peculiarities, idiosyncrasies, and, to the European, strange methods of duty. Each chapter contains Character Sketches by the Illustrator of "The Tribes," and the work is a "Natural History" of the Native Tribes who in India render us service.

"'There is plenty of fun in 'Behind the Bungalow,' and more than fun for those with eyes to see. These sketches may have an educational purpose beyond that of mere amusement; they show through all their fun a keen observation of native character and a just appreciation of it."
—*The World.*

BEHIND THE BUNGALOW.

By the Author of "TRIBES ON MY FRONTIER."

AND ILLUSTRATED BY THE SAME ARTIST.

"'The Tribes On My Frontier' was very good: 'Behind the Bungalow' is even better. Anglo-Indians will see how truthful are these sketches. People who know nothing about India will delight in the clever drawings and the truly humorous descriptions; and, their appetite for fun being gratified, they will not fail to note the undercurrent of sympathy."
—*The Graphic.*

"The native members of an Anglo-Indian household are hit off with great fidelity and humour."—*The Queen.*

Fifth Edition. In Imperial 16mo, uniform with "Lays of Ind," "Riding," "Hindu Mythology," etc. 8*s.* 6*d.*

THE TRIBES ON MY FRONTIER:

An Indian Naturalist's Foreign Policy.

BY EHA.

WITH FIFTY ILLUSTRATIONS BY F. C. MACRAE.

IN this remarkably clever work there are most graphically and humorously described the surroundings of a Mofussil bungalow. The twenty chapters embrace a year's experiences, and provide endless sources of amusement and suggestion. The numerous able illustrations add very greatly to the interest of the volume, which will find a place on every table.

THE CHAPTERS ARE—

I.—A Durbar.
II.—The Rats.
III.—The Mosquitos.
IV.—The Lizards.
V.—The Ants.
VI.—The Crows.
VII.—The Bats.
VIII.—Bees, Wasps, et hoc genus omne.
IX.—The Spiders.
X.—The Butterfly: Hunting Him.
XI.—The Butterfly: Contemplating Him.
XII.—The Frogs.
XIII.—The Bugs.
XIV.—The Birds of the Garden.
XV.—The Birds at the Mango Tope.
XVI.—The Birds at the Tank.
XVII.—The Poultry Yard.
XVIII.—The White Ants.
XIX.—The Hypodermatikosyringophoroi.
XX.—Etcetera.

In Imperial 16mo. Uniform with "Lays of Ind," "Hindu Mythology," etc.
Handsomely bound. 10*s.* 6*d.*

RIDING FOR LADIES.

With Hints on the Stable.

BY MRS. POWER O'DONOGHUE.

AUTHOR OF "LADIES ON HORSEBACK," "A BEGGAR ON HORSEBACK," etc.

With 91 Illustrations drawn expressly for the Work by A. Chantrey Corbould.

THIS able and beautiful volume will form a Standard on the Subject, and is one which no lady can dispense with. The scope of the work will be understood by the following:

CONTENTS.

"When there may arise differences of opinion as to some of the suggestions contained in this volume, the reader, especially if a woman, may feel assured she will not go far astray in accepting what is said by one of her own sex, who has the distinction of three times beating the Empress of Austria in the hunting field, from whom she 'took the brush.' 'Riding for Ladies' is certain to become a classic."
—*New York Sportsman.*

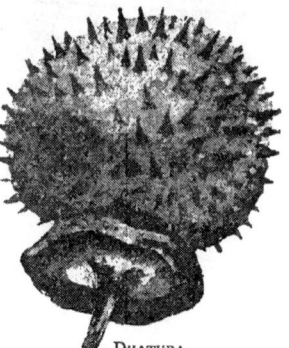

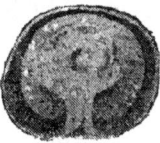

New Edition, Demy 8vo, with all Original Illustrations. *Rs.* 7-8.

THE HIGHLANDS OF CENTRAL INDIA.

NOTES ON THEIR

Forests and Wild Tribes, Natural History and Sport.

BY CAPT. J. FORSYTH, BENGAL STAFF CORPS.

WITH

ILLUSTRATIONS BY R. A. STERNDALE, F.Z.S., F.R.G.S.

In Demy folio, Thirty-nine Plates, Natural Size. 25*s.*

ILLUSTRATIONS OF THE

GRASSES OF THE SOUTHERN PUNJAB.

BEING

Photo-Lithographs of some of the Grasses found at Hissar, with Descriptive Letterpress.

BY WILLIAM COLDSTREAM, B.A., B.C.S.

Uniform with "Lays of Ind," "Riding," etc. 10*s.* 6*d.*

HINDU MYTHOLOGY:

VEDIC AND PURANIC.

BY

REV. W. J. WILKINS,

OF THE LONDON MISSIONARY SOCIETY, CALCUTTA.

Illustrated by One Hundred Engravings chiefly from Drawings by Native Artists.

REVIEWS.

"His aim has been to give a faithful account of the Hindu deities such as an intelligent native would himself give, and he has endeavoured, in order to achieve his purpose, to keep his mind free from prejudice or theological bias. To help to completeness he has included a number of drawings of the principal deities, executed by native artists. The author has attempted a work of no little ambition and has succeeded in his attempt, the volume being one of great interest and usefulness; and not the less so because he has strictly refrained from diluting his facts with comments of his own. It has numerous illustrations."—*Home News.*

"Mr. Wilkins has done his work well, with an honest desire to state facts apart from all theological prepossession, and his volume is likely to be a useful book of reference."—*Guardian.*

"In Mr. Wilkins' book we have an illustrated manual, the study of which will lay a solid foundation for more advanced knowledge, while it will furnish those who may have the desire without having the time or opportunity to go further into the subject, with a really extensive stock of accurate information."—*Indian Daily News.*

THE CULTURE AND MANUFACTURE OF INDIGO:

With Description of a Planter's Life and Resources. *By* W. M. REID. *With Nineteen Illustrations by the Author.* *7s. 6d.*

"A concise and readable manual, not only of everything relating to the industry, but of the whole round of business and recreation that makes up the Planter's life. . . The writer is at once accurate and graphic, and on the strength merely of reading these bright pages one almost feels competent to take full charge of a 'concern.'"—*Englishman.*

W. THACKER & CO., LONDON.

300 Illustrations. Imperial 16mo. 12*s.* 6*d.*

A HANDBOOK OF INDIAN FERNS.

By COLONEL R. H. BEDDOME, F.L.S.,

Late Conservator of Forests, Madras.

AUTHOR OF THE "FERNS OF BRITISH INDIA," "THE FERNS OF SOUTHERN INDIA."

"It is the first special book of portable size and moderate price which has been devoted to Indian Ferns, and is in every way deserving of the extensive circulation it is sure to obtain."—*Nature.*

"I have just seen a new work on Indian Ferns which will prove vastly interesting, not only to the Indian people, but to the botanists of this country."—*Indian Daily News.*

"The 'Ferns of India.' This is a good book, being of a useful and trustworthy character. The species are familiarly described, and most of them illustrated by small figures."—*Gardeners' Chronicle.*

"Those interested in botany will do well to procure a new work on the 'Ferns of British India.' The work will prove a first-class text book."—*Free Press.*

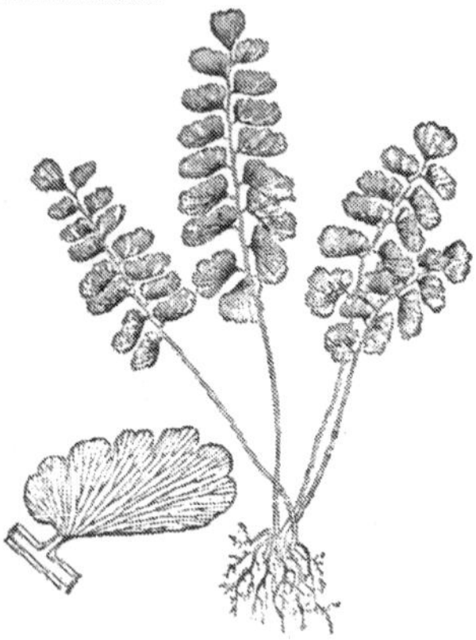

3*s.* 6*d.*

SUPPLEMENT to the FERNS OF BRITISH INDIA, etc.

By COLONEL R. H. BEDDOME.

Containing Ferns which have been discovered since the publication of "The Handbook to the Ferns of British India," etc.

Crown 8vo. 7*s.* 6*d.*

THE INDIGO MANUFACTURER.

A Practical and Theoretical Guide

FROM THE RECEIPT OF THE PLANT TO THE PRODUCTION OF THE CAKE;

With numerous EXPERIMENTS Illustrating the Scientific Principles bearing on each Phase of the Manufacture.

By J. BRIDGES-LEES, M.A., F.C.S., F.Z.S., F.R.A.S. Bengal, etc., etc.

The Reconnoitrer's Guide and Field Book, adapted for India. By Major M. J. KING-HARMAN, B.S.C. Third Edition, Revised and in great part re-written. In roan. *Rs.* 4.

Can be used as an ordinary Pocket Note Book, or as a Field Message Book; the pages are ruled as a Field Book, and in sections, for written description or sketch. "To officers serving in India this guide will be invaluable."—*Broad Arrow.*

Tales from Indian History: being the Annals of India retold in Narratives. By J. TALBOYS WHEELER. Sixth Edition. Crown 8vo, cloth gilt. 3*s.* 6*d.*

Hindustani as it ought to be Spoken. A Manual with Explanations, Vocabularies and Exercises. By J. TWEEDIE, C.S. Second Edition. *Rs.* 2-8.

A Memoir of the late Justice Onoocool Chunder Mookerjee. By M. MOOKERJEE. Third Edition 12mo. *Re.* 1.

A most interesting and amusing illustration of Indian English.

"The reader is earnestly advised to procure the life of this gentleman, written by his nephew, and read it."—*The Tribes on my Frontier.*

The Indian Cookery Book. A Practical Handbook to the Kitchen in India: adapted to the Three Presidencies. By a Thirty-five Years' Resident. *Rs.* 3.

Indian Notes about Dogs: their Diseases and Treatment. By Major C——. Third Edition, Revised. Fcap. 8vo, cloth. *Rs.* 1-8.

Indian Horse Notes: an Epitome of useful Information. By Major C——, Author of "Indian Notes about Dogs." Second Edition, Enlarged. Fcap. 8vo, cloth. *Rs.* 2.

Horse-Breeding and Rearing in India: with Notes on Training for the Flat and Across Country; and on Purchase, Breaking-in, and General Management. By Major J. HUMFREY. Crown 8vo. *Rs.* 3-8.

Hygiene of Water and Water Supplies. By PATRICK HEHIR, M.D., F.R.C.S. Edin.; Lecturer on Hygiene, Hyderabad. Surgeon, Bengal Army. 8vo, limp cloth. *Rs.* 2.

Plain Tales from the Hills: A Collection of Stories by RUDYARD KIPLING. Third Edition. Crown 8vo. *Rs.* 4.

"They sparkle with fun; they are full of life, merriment and humour."—*Allen's Indian Mail.*

Departmental Ditties and other Verses. By RUDYARD KIPLING. Being Humorous Poems of Indian Officialdom. Seventh Edition. 5*s.*

". . . . His book gives hope of a new literary star of no mean magnitude rising in the east."—*Sir W. W. Hunter in "The Academy."*

The Management and Medical Treatment of Children in India. By EDWARD A. BIRCH, M.D., Surg.-Major, Bengal Establishment. Second Edition Revised (Being the Eighth Edition of "Goodeve's Hints"). Crown 8vo. 10*s.* 6*d.*

Our Administration of India. Being a Complete Account of the Revenue and Collectorate Administration in all Departments, with special reference to the Work and Duties of a District Officer in Bengal. By H. A. D. PHILLIPS. 6*s.*

The Indian Medical Service. A Guide for intended Candidates and for the Junior Officers of the Service. By W. W. WEBB, M.B., Bengal Army. Crown 8vo. *Rs.* 4.

Thacker's Indian Directory. Embracing the whole Territories under the Viceroy, with the Native States. Published Annually. 36s.

INDEX.

CPSIA information can be obtained
at www.ICGtesting.com
Printed in the USA
LVHW082138200621
690728LV00002B/25

9 781340 00311